RESERVE
BOOK

D1213815

SOURCES OF INDIAN TRADITION

Volume Two: Modern India and Pakistan

INTRODUCTION TO ORIENTAL CIVILIZATIONS
Wm. Theodore de Bary, General Editor

Sources of Japanese Tradition (1958)
Sources of Chinese Tradition (1960)
Sources of Indian Tradition (1958, revised 1988)

SOURCES OF INDIAN TRADITION

Second Edition

Volume Two: Modern India and Pakistan

Edited and revised by
STEPHEN HAY

WITHDRAWN

First edition edited by Wm. Theodore de Bary
with Stephen Hay *and* J. H. Qureshi

Columbia University Press
New York   1988

Burgess
DS
423
.S64
1988

V. 2

C. 3

Library of Congress Cataloging-in-Publication Data
Sources of Indian tradition.
(Introduction to Oriental civilizations)
Translations from various sources by various
individuals.
First ed. (1958) compiled by William Theodore de
Bary and others.
Includes Bibliographies and index.
Contents: v. 1. From the beginning to 1800—
v. 2. Modern India and Pakistan.
1. India—Civilization. 2. Pakistan—Civilization.
3. India—Religion. I. Embree, Ainslie Thomas.
II. Hay, Stephen N. III. De Bary, William Theodore,
1918– . IV. Series.
DS423.S64 1988 954 87-15607
ISBN 0-231-06650-3 (v. 1)
ISBN 0-231-06651-1 (pbk. : v. 1)
ISBN 0-231-06414-4 (v. 2)
ISBN 0-231-06415-2 (pbk. : v. 2)

Columbia University Press
New York Guildford, Surrey
Copyright © 1988 Columbia University Press
First edition copyright © 1958 Columbia University Press
All rights reserved

Printed in the United States of America

Clothbound editions of Columbia University Press are Smyth-
sewn and printed on permanent and durable acid-free paper

Book design by Ken Venezio

CONTENTS

RSM 71919618

PJ.1989.6.78-1

PREFACE TO THE SECOND EDITION

In this second edition of the *Sources of Indian Tradition* (the first was published in 1958), some of the original selections have been deleted and new
material has been added, but the purpose and general emphasis have not
changed. Now, as then, the intention is to provide source materials that
give an understanding of the intellectual and spiritual traditions of the peoples of South Asia through their long and varied historical experience.

The preface to the first edition, reprinted here, should be read for an
indication of the principles that guided the selection of material. It is essentially a presentation of materials, from within the various Indian traditions,
that illustrate main aspects of the intellectual history of the whole subcontinent of South Asia, not just the modern nation of India. By "South Asia"
is meant the area that throughout the centuries was known as "India," but
which now includes the modern nation-states of India, Pakistan, Bangladesh, Sri Lanka, and Nepal. Generally, then, when "India" is used, it refers
to the whole of the subcontinent before 1947 and, in terms of religious
traditions, includes not only Hinduism but also Islam, Buddhism, Jainism,
Sikhism, and the other varieties of religion found in the area.

In making our revision, we have considered the many suggestions made
by readers of the earlier book and also the comments of reviewers. In the
end, however, choice of material has been determined, as it was in the
original version, by the fact that we are confining ourselves to written texts,
which also explains why, for example, we have made little reference to the
Indus civilization, or to the tribal societies that provide a rich component
to the Indian mosaic. There is also no representation of the great achievements in music, sculpture, and architecture—except for selections on aesthetic theories. Nor is there any sustained representation of the dramatic
and secular poetic traditions of India but, it should be noted, these have a
significant place in the translations of Indian literary classics sponsored by
Columbia's Committee on Oriental Studies.

Comment on social and historical development is found in the introductory material to the various sections. We have endeavored to give due weight to the tradition of social and political thought, particularly in the modern period, and have attempted, in the earlier periods, to relate it to other aspects of Indian thought. Especially in volume 1 in chapters 8, 9, 10, and 11, on Dharma, Artha, and Kama, the selections make clear that Indians, like all other peoples, have been concerned with making a living, with waging war, and with pleasure in all its varieties, including physical love, heroic valor, and aesthetic enjoyment.

As pointed out in the original preface, the use of modern religious terminology—"Jainism," "Buddhism," "Hinduism," and so forth—does not imply a commitment of the editors either to the view that Indians are peculiarly religious, or to the view that these terms denote the dominant influences in particular periods. They are used as convenient ways to categorize and classify written source material, not to describe historical epochs.

Another criticism has to do with the lack of attention to science, including astrology, and to medicine in the Indian tradition. The editors acknowledge the justness of this comment, but the available texts are so technical that, without extensive interpretation, they convey little to a nonspecialist, even to one who may have a general knowledge of the culture.

As for the relatively little attention given to the great philosophical traditions, we have tried throughout, but especially in volume 1, chapter 13, to show something of the variety of philosophical interpretations underlying the assumptions of the tradition.

The title of this book was carefully chosen. It is a collection of "sources," not *the* source. The editors wished to make the point that no claim was made to being comprehensive or definitive, either in covering the extraordinary variety of regional cultures or of encompassing all the multitude of expressions of human creativity in the subcontinent.

We are deeply grateful that the *Sources of Indian Tradition* has helped to make better known to generations of students the greatness of Indian civilization, and we trust that this new edition will continue the process. It is a matter of special pleasure that an Indian edition was widely circulated in India, and that the book has proven useful in other Asian countries.

Much of the added material consists of new translations, often by young scholars, but we have used some material recently published elsewhere and, in a few cases, older translations that still seemed useful. Since the *Sources* was first published, a new generation of American scholars in Indian studies has enriched our understanding and appreciation of Indian culture by many new and elegant translations of the classics as well as of works from modern Indian languages. We have been able to use some of these translations in this revision.

Stephen Hay

PREFACE TO THE FIRST EDITION

This book, part of a three-volume series dealing with the civilizations of Japan and China, as well as India and Pakistan, contains source readings that tell us what the peoples of India have thought about the world they lived in and the problems they faced living together. It is meant to provide the general reader with an understanding of the intellectual and spiritual traditions which remain alive in India and Pakistan today. Thus, much attention is given to religious and philosophical developments in earlier times which still form part of the Indian heritage and have experienced a considerable revival in the nineteenth and twentieth centuries. On the other hand, attention is also given to political, economic, and social thought, which other surveys, concentrating on classical Indian philosophy, have generally omitted.

Although our aim has been to combine variety with balance in the selection and presentation of materials, a few words are perhaps necessary concerning special points of emphasis. A glance at the contents will show that religion has furnished the general categories under which traditional Indian civilization is treated. This implies no judgment that religion was always the dominant factor in Indian life, but only that in the body of literature which provides us our texts, religious identities and continuities are more clearly distinguishable than are those based upon historical chronology or dynastic associations. Next, in this volume somewhat more attention is given to Theravāda Buddhism than to Mahāyāna because the latter is given fuller treatment in the volumes in this series dealing with China and Japan. In the case of Hinduism the reader will find that relatively greater emphasis is placed upon the social and devotional aspects of the religion, which have affected great numbers of Hindus, than upon the philosophical speculations which have generally commanded the first attention of educated Indians and Westerners and have already been widely reproduced in translation. In Parts One to Four, dealing with traditional Indian and Muslim civilization, most of the translations are new and many of them are of texts previously untranslated into any Western language. In the chapters on modern India and Pakistan, on the other hand, a majority of the readings are from English originals or existing translations.

Because of the unfamiliarity and complexity of many subjects not previously presented in translation, we have found it necessary to include more historical and explanatory material than is usual in a set of source readings. Nevertheless, the reader who seeks a fuller knowledge of historical and institutional background will do well to supplement this text by referring to a general survey of Indian history and culture.

Given the limitations of an introductory text, we could not hope to deal with every thinker or movement of importance, but have had to select those examples which seem best to illustrate the major patterns of Indian thought in so far as they have been expressed and preserved in writing. In the modern period the necessity for such selectivity is most apparent. Here particular prominence has been given to persons actively engaged in leading organized religious and political movements.

Compilation of this volume was originally undertaken by Dr. Andrew Yarrow in connection with the general education program in Columbia College. Before publication these readings were substantially revised by the general editor with the assistance of Dr. Royal Weiler of Columbia and supplemented by Dr. Stephen N. Hay of the University of Chicago. In making revisions for the fourth printing, the general editor was assisted by Ainslie Embree of Columbia University. It goes without saying that this volume could not have been compiled without the cooperation of our principal contributors: R. N. Dandekar of the Bhandarkar Oriental Research Institute, Poona; V. Raghavan of the University of Madras; A. L. Basham, Peter Hardy, and J. B. Harrison of the School of Oriental and African Studies, University of London; and I. H. Qureshi of the Center for Pakistan Studies, Columbia University. Their contribution is all the more appreciated because of the patience and forbearance they have shown in regard to adjustments which the general editor has had to make in order to achieve uniformity and balance in the volume as a whole. For this reason, it should be emphasized, the editor must bear primary responsibility for the selection and presentation of the materials contained here.

More material than could be included was originally prepared not only by our principal contributors but by other collaborators as well. These include Dr. Mohammad Habib and Mr. K. A. Nizami of the Muslim University, Aligarh; and Drs. Aloo Dastur, A. R. Desai, Usha Mehta, and P. R.

Brahmananda of the School of Economics and Sociology, University of Bombay. To the director of the latter institution, Dr. C. N. Vakil, an especial debt of gratitude is owed for his help in the early stages of this long project. To Professor Habib an additional debt is acknowledged by Dr. Hardy for the privilege of consulting his manuscript translations from the historian Barni. The compilers also wish to thank Mr. Arthur Michaels and Professor Holden Furber of the University of Pennsylvania for their assistance and advice in regard to the influence of British thought in India.

The final version of these readings owes much to the critical examination and comment of scholarly colleagues. Dr. Basham wishes to record his appreciation to Dr. A. K. Warder for his reading of the draft on Jainism and Buddhism. Dr. Hay is similarly indebted to Dr. Percival Spear, Professor Richard Park, and Mr. Marshall Windmiller of the University of California at Berkeley; to Professor Amiya Chakravarty of the School of Theology, Boston University; and to Dr. R. C. Majumdar, Dr. J. A. B. Van Buitenen and Mr. Sudhindranath Datta at the University of Chicago, for reading and criticizing the chapters on modern India. Dr. S. M. Ikram of the Center for Pakistan Studies, Columbia University, is also to be thanked for reading the chapters on Muslim India and Pakistan. In the editing of parts 1 and 3, Visudh Busyakul of the University of Pennsylvania gave Dr. Weiler invaluable advice and assistance, as did Marjorie A. Weiler. Hans Guggenheim performed the exacting task of preparing the chapter decorations for chapter 1–20. The remainder were drawn by Eloise Hay, who was also one of our most discerning and helpful critics. Finally, mention must be made of the indefatigable and competent service of Eileen J. Boecklen in preparing the manuscript for publication, and of our good fortune in having Joan McQuary and Eugenia Porter guide it through the Press.

This series of readings has been produced in connection with the Columbia College General Education Program in Oriental Studies, which has been encouraged and supported by the Carnegie Corporation of New York. For whatever value it may have to the general reader or college student seeking a liberal education that embraces both East and West, a great debt is owed to Dean Emeritus Harry J. Carman, Dr. Taraknath Das, and Dean Lawrence H. Chamberlain of Columbia College, who contributed much to the initiation and furtherance of this program.

Wm. Theodore de Bary
COLUMBIA UNIVERSITY 1958

ACKNOWLEDGMENTS

Without the assistance of many publishers, a book of source readings such as this is not possible, and we are grateful for the cooperation of the following:

Advaita Ashrama, Almora, India
Allen & Unwin, Ltd., London
All-Pakistan Political Science Association, Lahore
Mohammad Ashraf, Lahore
Asian Studies Center, East Lansing
Asiatic Society of Mangal, Calcutta
Sri Aurobindo Ashram, Pondichéry
Bodley Head, Ltd., London
E. J. Brill, Leiden, Netherlands
Cassell Publishing Co., London
S. Chand & Co., Ltd., New Delhi
Clarendon Press, Oxford
Current Book House, Bombay
University of Delhi, Delhi
Editions India, Calcutta
Ganesh & Co., Ltd., Madras
S. P. Gokhale, Poona
Grove Press, New York
Harper & Row, Inc., New York
Harvard University Press, Cambridge
Hero Publications, Lahore
Hind Pocket Books, Pvt. Ltd., Delhi
Ministry of Information and Broadcasting, Government of India
Indian Printing Works, Lahore
India Press, Allahabad
Intertrade Publications, Calcutta
Kitabistan, Allahabad
S. K. Lahin & Co., Calcutta

Luzac & Co., Madras
Macmillan & Co., Ltd., London and New York
al-Manar Academy, Lahore
Munshiram Manoharlal Publishers, Pvt. Ltd., New Delhi
Modern Review, Calcutta
John Murray, London, and the "Wisdom of the East" Series
The Muslim World
G. A. Natesan & Co., Madras
Natajivan Trust, Ahmedabad
P. M. Neogi, Calcutta
North Point Press, Berkeley
Orient Longmans, Ltd., Calcutta
Oxford University Press, London
Oxford University Press, Karachi
Padma Publishing, Ltd., Bombay
Pakistan Herald Press, Karachi
Panjab University Press, Lahore
Penguin Books, Ltd., London
People's Publishing House, Ltd., Bombay
Renaissance Publishers, Ltd., Calcutta
Roy and Son, Calcutta
A. W. Sahasvabuddhe, Sevagram
Sadharan Brahmo Samaj, Calcutta
Sarvodaya, Bombay
Guru Gobind Singh Foundation, Chandigarh

Sinha Publishing House, Pvt. Ltd., Calcutta
Thacker & Spink Company, Bombay
Theosophical Publishing Society, Benares
Thomas & Co., Calcutta
Thompson & Co., Ltd., Madras
R. B. Tilak, Poona

University Publishers, Jullunpur
Vedanta Society, New York
Vedic Yantralaya, Ajmer
Viking Press, New York
Visvabharati, Calcutta
West Bengal Pradesh Congress Committee, Calcutta
Writers Workshop, Calcutta

TRANSLITERATION OF PROPER NAMES

In volume 1, in the "Explanatory Note and Guide to Pronunciation," an explanation was given of the system used for the transliteration of words from the Indic, Persian, and Arabic languages. In this volume, however, much of the material was originally written in English, and in general we have preferred to use the transliterations found in the originals. This means that diacritical marks have been used very sparingly. There is a special problem with place names, many of which have been changed since the various countries of South Asia have become independent (e.g., Sri Lanka for Ceylon, Pune for Poona, etc.). Again, we have used the terms as they are found in the originals. The "Explanatory Note" of volume 1 is, however, a useful guide to the complexities of transliterating the many languages and orthographies of South Asia.

CONTRIBUTORS

In the preface to the first edition, the many scholars who had contributed to it were mentioned with gratitude, and all of these are once more thanked. Professor Stephen Hay of the University of California at Santa Barbara, who was responsible for the editing of part 6, the section on modern India and Pakistan, in the first edition, took the responsibility for its revision in volume 2. Professor David Lelyveld then of the University of Minnesota and now at Columbia, and Dr. Christopher Brunner revised part 4, the section on Islam in India. Professor Ainslie Embree of Columbia revised the other sections and acted as general editor.

Guidance on many points was offered by colleagues at Columbia, especially by those who have used the book intensively in our courses in General Education. Professor Barbara Miller gave much needed advice on many aspects of the revision and permitted the use of her translations from Sanskrit poetry and drama. Dr. Lucy Bulliet and Professor Joel Brereton offered many helpful suggestions for the revision of the first chapters and provided a number of new translations for the Vedic material. Professor David Rubin contributed translations from Hindi poets as did Neil Gross and Linda Hess (now at the University of California, Berkeley). We are especially grateful to Professor John S. Hawley, and his cotranslator, Professor Mark Juergensmeyer of the Graduate Theological Union and University of California, Berkeley, for new translations of Bhakti poetry from Hindi; the introductions and commentary owe much to their scholarly knowledge of north India's religious literature. The late Margaret Mazici helped in many editorial tasks and we regret her untimely death. Colleagues at the Southern Asian Institute, particularly Professors Stephen Rittenberg and Leonard Gordon, shared in the discussions of the revision of the material on modern India. Randolph Thornton, Peter Banos, and Susan VanKoski assisted in many editorial tasks.

From outside Columbia, numerous colleagues provided assistance. Professor W. H. McLeod of Otaga University, New Zealand, gave expert advice on the section of Sikhism, as did Professor Attar Singh of Punjab University. From the University of Chicago, Professor A. K. Ramanujan generously permitted use of his translations from Tamil and Kannada, and Professor Fazlur Rahman gave suggestions for material on Pakistan. Professor Aslam Syed of Quaid-i-Azam University offered criticism and advice on the chapter on Pakistan. Professor Eleanor Zelliot of Carleton College provided materials for volume 2, chapters 7 and 8, on Ambedkar.

In a book of this kind, the editorial services are of special importance, and we have been fortunate in having Peggy Riccardi, an Indologist, as editor; we give her grateful thanks. It was our good fortune, too, that Joan McQuary guided this edition through the Press, as she did the first edition.

This revision of the *Sources of Indian Tradition* was made possible by grants from the University Committee on General Education, the Committee on Oriental Studies, and Columbia University Press.

Ainslie T. Embree
Stephen Hay
Wm. Theodore de Bary

CHRONOLOGY

1498	Vasco da Gama rounds the southernmost tip of Africa and lands on the Malabar coast; beginning of Portuguese activity in Asia.
1600	Queen Elizabeth I grants charter to English East India Company for English trade with the East Indies.
1639	Madras founded as Fort St. George.
1668	Bombay ceded to East India Company.
1690	Calcutta founded by East India Company.
1742–1754	Dupleix serves as Governor of Pondichéry for French East India Company.
1757–1765	English East India Company gains control of Bengal.
1773	British Parliament begins supervision of East India Company.
1793	"The Permanent Settlement" in Bengal.
1799	Defeat of Tipu Sultan, Mysore ruler.
1815–1830	Rammohun Roy (c.1774–1833) active in religious controversy and social reform in Calcutta.
1817–1819	Defeat of Marathas ends Indian resistance to British in western and central India.
1833	East India Company deprived by Parliament of all commercial functions.
1835	English introduced as medium of higher education.
1839–1842	First Anglo-Afghan War.
1843	Debendranath Tagore (1817–1905) re-establishes the Brahmo Sabha as the Brahmo Samaj.
1849	Defeat of the Sikhs and annexation of Punjab.
1853	First railway and telegraph.
1857–1858	Mutinies of Indian troops and civil uprisings in North India.
1858	East India Company's rule replaced by that of a viceroy appointed by the British crown.
1875	Swami Dayananda (1824–1883) founds the Arya Samaj at

	Bombay. Syed Ahmad Khan (1817–1898) founds Mohammedan Anglo-Oriental College at Aligarh.
1877	Queen Victoria proclaimed Empress of India.
1885	Indian National Congress inaugurated in Bombay.
1893	Swami Vivekananda (1863–1902) wins renown at World Parliament of Religions in Chicago; Mohandas Karamchand Gandhi (1869–1948) begins twenty years' work as lawyer and leader of Indian community in South Africa.
1905	Partition of Bengal.
1906	Muslim League founded.
1907	Indian National Congress split by quarrel between Moderates and Extremists.
1909	Morley-Minto Reforms.
1911	Partition of Bengal annulled.
1912	Transfer of capital to Delhi.
1913	Rabindranath Tagore awarded Nobel Prize for literature.
1916	The Lucknow Pact between Congress and Muslim League.
1919	Montagu-Chelmsford Reforms provide for legislative assembly to begin in 1921. Amritsar massacre.
1919–1924	Khilāfat Movement, led by Mohammad Ali.
1920	Gandhi starts first nationwide civil disobedience movement (suspended in 1922).
1927	Simon Commission.
1930–1934	Second nationwide civil disobedience movement.
1935	Government of India Act grants measure of provincial self-government.
1940	Muslim League, under Mohammad Ali Jinnah, demands creation of separate Muslim state.
1942	"Quit India" movement.
1945–47	The British government prepares to grant India complete self-government.
1947	India, under Prime Minister Jawaharlal Nehru (1889–1964), and Pakistan, under Governor-General Mohammad Ali Jinnah (1876–1948), become independent nations.
1948	Gandhi assassinated in New Delhi. Jinnah dies in Karachi.
1950	The Constitution of India comes into effect.
1952	First general election in India.
1958	General Ayub Khan takes power in Pakistan.
1962	War between India and China.
1965	Pakistan and India at war.
1966	Indira Gandhi (1919–1984) becomes prime minister.

1971	Bangladesh secedes from Pakistan; war between India and Pakistan. Z. A. Bhutto becomes president of Pakistan.
1975–1977	"Emergency" declared in India.
1977	Janata coalition wins elections in India. General Zia takes power in Pakistan.
1980	Congress (I) Party wins elections, Indira Gandhi again becomes prime minister.
1984	Assassination of Indira Gandhi. Rajiv Gandhi becomes prime minister.

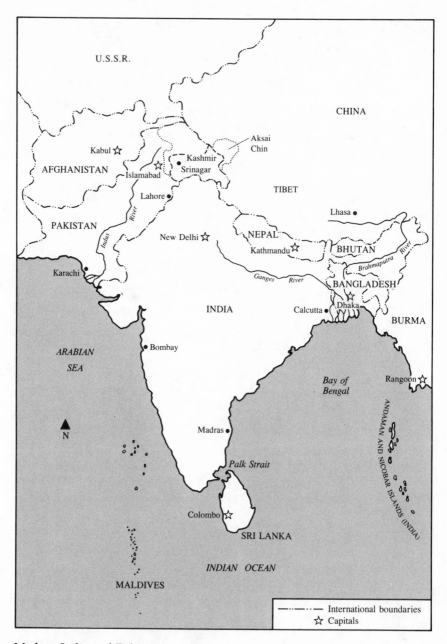

U.S.S.R.

CHINA

Aksai
Chin

Kabul ☆

Kashmir

AFGHANISTAN

Islamabad ☆

Srinagar

TIBET

Lahore ●

Lhasa ●

Indus River

PAKISTAN

New Delhi ☆

NEPAL

Kathmandu ☆

BHUTAN

Brahmaputra River

Karachi ●

Ganges River

BANGLADESH

INDIA

Calcutta ●

Dhaka ☆

BURMA

ARABIAN
SEA

Bombay ●

Bay of
Bengal

Rangoon ☆

▲
N

Madras ●

ANDAMAN AND NICOBAR ISLANDS (INDIA)

Palk Strait

Colombo ☆

SRI LANKA

INDIAN OCEAN

MALDIVES

———·———· International boundaries
☆ Capitals

Modern India and Pakistan

INTRODUCTION

This final part of *Sources of Indian Tradition* begins with a mid-eighteenth-century merchant's thoughts about life and his French employer and ends with late twentieth-century idealists' prescriptions for the future of two independent nations. In the years between these opening and closing reflections, a small European country exerted an enormous influence over the people of the Indian subcontinent. Its manner of ascending to power over the subcontinent was unprecedented: it was not by moving down from the northwest, as previous conquering groups had done, but by moving into the interior from the coasts—both eastern and western. The British came to trade and stayed to rule. Their early trading posts at Madras, Bombay, and Calcutta became the capitals of three huge provinces (called "presidencies") from which radiated inland commerce, government, technology, and British-style education. By the 1860's the British completely controlled the North Indian heartland of both Hindu and Islamic power and culture. By this time also movements to reform and revitalize these two major socioreligious communities were in full swing.

The nine chapters that follow present selections from the writings of men who initiated or carried forward efforts to improve the social, religious, educational, political, and economic life of their people. Because the English language supplanted the Persian (as Persian had earlier supplanted Sanskrit) as the main language of interregional communication, most of these men wrote and thought in English as well as in the language of their native regions. Several of those who lived in the nineteenth century spent part of their careers in the service of the government bureaucracy, and almost all of those who lived in the twentieth century absorbed European ideas and attitudes during their education in schools or colleges administered or inspected by government officials. Some twentieth-century leaders (most notable Gandhi and Jinnah) became lawyers through studying at London's Inns of Court; several others studied at Cambridge or Oxford.

In daily life, the ways of thinking and acting of growing numbers of the inhabitants of South Asia (the region now embracing the nations of India, Pakistan, and Bangladesh as well as neighboring Afganistan, Nepal, and Sri Lanka) were influenced by the technology and institutions introduced from Europe—including watches, books and newspapers, paved roads, bridges, canals, railroads, steamships, uniform currencies, courts, codes of law, an expanding market economy, and central and provincial governments with increasing non-British representation and control.

The effects of these influences from abroad varied from one person and socioreligious community to the next, but they gradually accelerated with time. Many ideas and ways were ignored or rejected, whereas others were adopted and adapted to Indian needs and circumstances. For example, Christian missionary work alienated many intellectuals and provoked them to reexamine and reinterpret classical Hindu or Islamic texts. The idea of national self-government, however, evoked growing enthusiasm along with diverse definitions of how it would function. In general, the deeper the penetration of Western influences, the more militant the religious response to them became, and the more articulate and organized the resistance to the continuation of foreign rule. In the period since 1947, when India and Pakistan won their independence, the movement of information, ideas, and technology has become more of a two-way flow to and from the world outside South Asia.

The people of India, Pakistan, and Bangladesh numbered more than 850 million in the censuses of the early 1980s and thus constitute more than one-sixth of the human race. The selections included in these chapters are drawn from the writings and speeches of some of their more prominent thinkers and leaders of the past two centuries. Many important regional leaders have had to be omitted, mainly for lack of additional space. Three particularly creative and influential leaders have received more detailed coverage than others—Rammohun Roy, Syed Ahmed Khan, and Mohandas Karamchand Gandhi.

If there is a single pattern that appears in these pages, it is the diversity of ways in which ancient, medieval, and modern ideas of Indian, Middle Eastern, and European origins have reverberated in the minds of major leaders of thought and opinion in the Indian subcontinent and have stimulated them to formulate new interpretations and syntheses of these ideas. May the reader find them of interest, and possibly of relevance to his or her own thinking in a world more and more open to such reformulations.

Stephen Hay

Chapter 1

THE OPENING OF INDIA
TO THE WEST

The spreading of European power and civilization over the entire surface of the globe in recent centuries can be viewed as a continuing series of intrusions into the cultures of the non-European world. Nowhere in Asia have the effects of this penetration been more profoundly felt than in India. Because she was the first to receive the impact of European expansion, and the only major civilization on the continent to fall directly under foreign rule, the influence of the West on her life and thought has been deep and lasting.

The first Europeans to reach India by sea were the Portuguese. Their intrepid captain, Vasco da Gama, landed on the Malabar coast in 1498. Seventy-five years later we find them received at the Mughal court by the solicitous Emperor Akbar. In the words of Akbar's biographer: "They produced many of the rarities of their country, and the appreciative Khedive [the Emperor] received each one with special favor and made inquiries about the wonders of Portugal and the manners and customs of Europe. It seemed as if he did this from a desire of knowledge, for his sacred heart is a depot of spiritual and physical sciences. But his boding soul wished that these inquiries might be the means of civilizing [istīnās, i.e., familiarity or sociability] this savage [unsocial] race."[1] Akbar later summoned Jesuit missionaries from Goa to expound the principles of their religion, in which he was much interested, but he laughingly preferred his three hundred wives to the Christian ideal of monogamy.

When the French and British East India Companies first established their tiny trading settlements along the eastern and western coasts of India in the seventeenth century, the great empire of the Mughals still held sway. A century later it had collapsed, and various Muslim and Hindu rulers were fighting among themselves for possession of its remnants. In protecting their commercial interests the sea-borne Europeans were drawn into the struggle. When in the early nineteenth century the British finally prevailed over both the local contenders and their French rivals, they found themselves masters of a population speaking fourteen different major languages, with two-ninths of them following Islam and most of the rest belonging to various Hindu castes and subcastes, and with small minorities professing Sikhism, Jainism, Buddhism, Zoroastrianism, Nestorian Christianity, and Judaism. Onto this cultural mosaic the new rulers of India imposed a pattern of their own—not a religious but a secular one: law and order, efficient government, and free trade were the new gods.

Although some Indians opposed and the majority ignored the coming of the new order, others actively abetted the opening of their country to the West. Three representative men, each of whom played a notable part in the history of this period and left to posterity written records of his thinking, are considered in this chapter—one a Hindu merchant of the 1740s and 50s, the second a Muslim aristocrat of the early nineteenth century, and the third a brāhman scholar-reformer and founder of a new religious movement. The last was active in Calcutta in the 1820s—just at the time the British were overcoming their earlier reluctance to interfere with established cultural patterns, and shortly before they took the decisive step of introducing English-style education.

Although these three men came from different religious and regional backgrounds, the question of what to do about the Westerner and his culture was in the forefront of their minds. All showed an inclination toward some aspects of the new culture and an aversion toward other aspects, but even in their likes and dislikes they differed noticeably. The attitudes that each reveals in his writings therefore give us unique insights into the complexity of Indian society in this crucial period and furnish us with valuable clues to the later evolution of Indian thought as it responded to the incessant challenge of the West.

ANANDA RANGA PILLAI: HINDU AGENT
FOR THE FRENCH

India in the eighteenth century was without any central political power. Muslim governors and Hindu chieftains vied with each other for the remnants of the Mughal empire, while most of the population pursued traditional occupations in relative indifference to the religious or regional origins of their rulers. Under these circumstances, the scattered seacoast settlements of the European trading companies attracted little attention, except from the Indian merchants who found it profitable to act as intermediaries between the foreign traders and the people of the hinterland.

The Hindu merchant Ananda Ranga Pillai (1709–1761) rose to a position of great trust and influence as chief agent for the French colony of Pondichéry. Thanks to the diary he kept faithfully for twenty-five years, we have an almost Pepysian record of the life of the tiny settlement and of its leading Indian citizen. Although most of the diary is a rather tedious chronicle of business transactions and political intrigue, we can find in it occasional glimpses of the attitude of an important Hindu toward his French masters and toward his own society.

One striking feature of *The Private Diary of Ananda Ranga Pillai* is the total absence in its author of national consciousness or sense of political loyalty to fellow Indians as opposed to Europeans. Trade was his family's hereditary occupation and he therefore entered naturally into a symbiotic relation with the merchants from across the sea. He ardently supported the empire-building ambitions of his sponsor, François Dupleix, governor of Pondichéry and commercial and political rival of the English, and identified Dupleix's fortunes with his own, regarding Dupleix, not as a foreigner, but simply as an individual with whom he enjoyed a mutually profitable connection. At the same time Ananda Ranga remained a staunch and orthodox Hindu, never violating in the slightest the rules of his religion. In this respect he is respresentative of many generations of Indians from his day down to our own whose interest in things Western remain at the level of externals, and for whom European culture and thought seemed of little importance in comparision with the time-tested value of their traditional beliefs.

On the Greatness of Dupleix

It is clear from his diary that Ananda Ranga Pillai admired the brilliant French adventurer and preferred his rule to that of the Maratha or Muslim potentates then contending for power in South India.

[From Pillai, *Private Diary*, 1: 299–301]

The English have captured the ships bound for Pondichéry, and have received a reinforcement of men-of-war from England and other places. This accounts for their activity; nevertheless they are much troubled owing to their leader, the governor, being a worthless fellow, and a man devoid of wisdom. Although Pondichéry receives no ships, her government lacks funds, the enemy has seized her vessels, she is feeble and wanting in strength, and her inhabitants are in misery; although she has all these disadvantages, no sooner is mention made of her than the nawabs [governors], and other magnates in the interior, become alarmed. When her name is uttered, her enemies tremble, and dare not stir. All this is owing to the ability, readiness, and luck of the present governor, M. Dupleix. His method of doing things is not known to any one, because none else is possessed of the quick mind with which he is gifted. In patience he has no equal. He has peculiar skill in carrying out his plans and designs; in the management of affairs, and in governing; in fitting his advice to times and persons; in maintaining at all times an even countenance; in doing things through proper agents; in addressing them in appropriate terms; and in assuming a bearing at once dignified and courteous towards all. . . .

Owing to these qualities, he has acquired such a reputation as to make all people say that he is the master, and that others are useless individuals. Because God has favored him with unswerving resolution, and because he is governing Pondichéry on an occasion when she is threatened with danger, her inhabitants are confident and fearless, and are even able to defy the people of towns opposed to them. This is due solely to the skill and administrative ability of the governor. If he did not occupy this position, and if the danger had occurred in the times of his predecessors, the inhabitants of this city would be a hundred times more disturbed and terrified than the followers of the invader: such is the general opinion regarding M. Dupleix. Besides this, if his courage, character, bearing, greatness of mind, and skill in the battlefield, were put to the test, he could be compared only with the Emperor Aurangzib, and Louis XIV; and not with any other monarch. But how am I to paint all his high and praiseworthy characteristics? I have described him only so far as my simple mind allows me. People of better capacity could do this more completely than I.

An Astrological Misfortune

Ananda Ranga was a firm believer in astrology. It struck him as a calamity, explainable only by reference to the stars, that his brother should be so unusually devoid of worldly ambition.

[From Pillai, *Private Diary*, 3: 9—10]

Although my brother is thirty-four or thirty-five years old, he has no desire to acquire wealth, and no ambition to figure conspicuously in the service of the Company. He is, further, too retiring to hold any intercourse with Europeans. Far from accusing him, however, I can only worry myself with the thought that God has created him thus, and blame my own ill-luck. The young men of these days become, from their fifth year, thoroughly filled with aspirations. The great desire for employment, coupled, as it is, with a strong craving to acquire wealth, that is evinced by them is quite extraordinary, and is beyond one's comprehension and powers of expression. The very opposite to this, my brother—who is hard on thirty-five—although naturally possessed of the gifts of high culture, excellent parts, guarded temper, winning manners, handsome presence, and fortunate birth, is not blessed with the courage and spirit of enterprise which are indispensable to raising oneself to distinction. It is this defect that induces him to cast aside all aspirations to greatness, and to prefer to remain at home in obscurity. This warp in his mind I attribute to the weak and fruitless star which, according to my horoscope, will cast its shadow over me for some months to come. I cannot but impute to this circumstance his desire to resign his post in that city of Kubera [the god of wealth], which has recently come under our rule, and to return empty-handed. This bears out the predictions of astrologers that my career, up to my thirty-eighth year, will not be marked by success. I entertain no doubt as to the truth of their statements, and shall, therefore, not lay any blame at his door.

An Improper Feast

When his arch-rival, a convert to Christianity, gave a public feast for Hindus and Christians alike, Ananda Ranga's sense of propriety was offended. The firm maintenance of Hindu custom his attitude exemplifies was to be a major stumbling-block to social reformers of the succeeding centuries.

[From Pillai, *Private Diary*, 1:293–95]

This day, there was an event worthy of record. In the village of Reddipalaiyam, to the east of Ozhukarai, a church has been constructed by Kanakarāya Mudali, and he has placed some images therein. In honor of this, he invited, without distinction, all the Brahmans, Vellāzhas, Kōmuttis, Chettis, goldsmiths, weavers, oil-mongers, and people of other castes; and all Europeans and Christians, and entertained them with a feast at Ozhukarai. Choultries [hostels] and gardens were allotted for the preparation of food by Brāhman cooks, and meals for Vellāzhas were cooked in the house of Agambadaiyans. All the arrangements were made in strict conformity with the religious scruples of each caste, and the people who attended received every attention. Meals for Europeans were prepared at Pondichéry, and brought over to Ozhukarai. Tables were procured for them to dine at, and every comfort was provided for them. The Governor, M. Dupleix, and his consort, in company with all the members of Council, repaired thither, and partook of the banquet. He remained until five in the evening, and then returned to Mortāndi Chāvadi. All the people of Pondichéry who went to Ozhukarai enjoyed themselves, and proceeded homewards in the evening. Neither in the arrangements which Kanakarāya Mudali made, nor in the supplies which he procured, was there anything wanting. Nevertheless, despite the heavy cost of the entertainment, and the elaborate nature of the preparations, there was something which detracted from the splendor, grace, and excellence of the hospitalities. Persons of every persuasion should abide by the rules prescribed for them: their conduct so regulated would look consistent. Although of a different persuasion, he followed the practice of a Hindu; assembled people of that religion; and gave them a treat which afforded room for dispraise and derision, and every man gave vent to his criticisms as he saw fit. If he wished to conform to the rules of his church, and the commands of his scriptures, he should have entertained only the Europeans, native Christians, pariahs,[2] and such others; whose associations brought them in touch with his religion. Even this would be considered derogatory to one of his position and reputation. However magnificent may be the style of any social act in which one indulges, if it be at variance with the established practice of the community concerned, it cannot redound to one's credit. If a man who has forsaken his religion, and joined another, reverts to the manners and customs of his former belief, he must inevitably draw upon himself contempt.

The Doctrine of Predestination

Commenting on Dupleix's ignominious departure from Pondichéry in 1754, Ananda Ranga revealed his belief that all a man's thoughts and actions are preordained.

[From Pillai, *Private Diary*, 9:54]

This great man has been arrested and put with his property on board ship. Such is the fate of the man who seeks his own will without the fear of God; but he who acts with circumspection, and refrains from molesting the upright, escapes falling into sin. But a man's thoughts depend upon the times and seasons. Who then can be blamed? Such is the world. He who is destined to happiness will be wise; and he who is destined to misery will be foolish. Do not the Vedas say so? What was to be has come to pass.

The Collapse of the Old Order

Toward the end of French domination over South India, an inexperienced governor appointed a man of low caste to the position formerly held by Ananda Ranga. Reflecting on the changes that the French had introduced into hierarchical Hindu society, the diarist commented bitterly.

[From Pillai, *Private Diary*, 11:318]

In times of decay, order disappears, giving place to disorder, and justice to injustice. Men no longer observe their caste rules, but transgress their bounds, so that the castes are confused and force governs. One man takes another man's wife and his property. Everyone kills or robs another. In short, there is anarchy. Who among the low is lower than a pariah beggar? And what worse can be imagined than for such a one to rule? Unless justice returns, the country will be ruined. This is what men say, and I have written it briefly.

ABU TALEB: MUSLIM TRAVELER TO THE WEST

Although Europeans had been visiting India since the days of Marco Polo, few Indians had the curiosity or the wherewithal to acquaint themselves at first hand with Europe and its culture. Hindus considered overseas travel to be defiling and automatically outcast those who ventured abroad. Muslims, on the other hand, were not only free from such restrictions but had the example of Muhammad—the great traveler—and the duty of a pilgrimage to Mecca to encourage them in venturing overseas. It is, therefore, not surprising that one of the first educated Indians to travel to Europe should be a Muslim.

Mirza Abu Taleb Khan was born in Lucknow in 1752 of Persian and Turkish descent. His mature life was spent in the service of the governors of Bengal and of Oudh, but a jealous prime minister retired him and cut off his pension. Abu Taleb then sought employment with the British, whom he had assisted in putting down a rebellious Hindu prince. He moved his family to Calcutta and seems to have learned English fairly well, but his hopes of securing a good position were disappointed. He grew very despondent, and when a Scottish friend suggested they travel to England together at his expense, he reflected, "that, as the journey was long and replete with danger, some accident might cause my death, by which I should be delivered from the anxieties of the world, and the ingratitude of mankind. I therefore accepted his friendly offer, and resolved to undertake the journey."

Despite his pessimistic frame of mind, Abu Taleb seems by his own account to have greatly enjoyed his three years in Europe. No sooner had he arrived in London than he was presented to the king and queen, dubbed "the Persian prince," and lionized by the English aristocracy. He had ample opportunity to observe his hosts and, when writing his recollections, did not hesitate to enumerate their national vices as well as their virtues.

The Travels of Mirza Abu Taleb Khan, written in Persian on his return to Calcutta, gives us a unique insight into the reactions of an aristocratic Indian Muslim to English life. For the most part a careful account of the curiosities and customs he observed, the book is remarkably barren of reflections on the cultural and religious foundations of Western civilization, leaving the impression that as a Muslim he regarded them as unworthy of serious attention. On the other hand, the lighter side of London life greatly appealed to him, as it has to other Indians since his day. Abu Taleb's comments on the English, though superficial, are important as indicative of the major differences in outlook between the Indo-Persian culture created by the Mughals and the Indo-British culture that superseded it.

Muslim Indifference to Learning About the West

Abu Taleb realized that his interest in Europe was exceptional and correctly predicted in the introduction to his book that his fellow-Muslims would continue to
ignore Western learning out of "zeal for their religion."

[From Abu Taleb, *Travels*, 1:1–6]

Glory be to God, the Lord of all worlds, who has conferred innumerable
blessings on mankind and accomplished all the laudable desires of his creatures. Praise be also to the Chosen of Mankind [Muhammad], the traveler
over the whole expanse of the heavens, and benedictions without end on
his descendants and companions.

The wanderer over the face of the earth, Abu Taleb, the son of Mohammed of Ispahan, begs leave to inform the curious in biography, that,
owing to several adverse circumstances, finding it inconvenient to remain
at home, he was compelled to undertake many tedious journeys, during
which he associated with men of all nations and beheld various wonders,
both by sea and by land.

It therefore occurred to him, that if he were to write all the circumstances of his journey through Europe, to describe the curiosities and wonders which he saw, and to give some account of the manner and customs
of the various nations he visited, all of which are little known to Asiatics,
it would afford a gratifying banquet to his countrymen.

He was also of opinion, that many of the customs, inventions, sciences,
and ordinances of Europe, the good effects of which are apparent in those
countries, might with great advantage be imitated by Mohammedans.

Impressed with these ideas, he, on his first setting out on his travels,
commenced a journal, in which he daily inserted every event, and committed to writing such reflections as occurred to him at the moment: and on
his return to Calcutta, in the year of the Hejira 1218 [A.D. 1803], having
revised and abridged his notes, he arranged them in the present form.

[Here Abu Taleb changes from the third to the first person, and laments:]
I have named this work . . . "The Travels of Taleb in the Regions of
Europe"; but when I reflect on the want of energy and the indolent dispo-
sitions of my countrymen, and the many erroneous customs which exist in
all Mohammedan countries and among all ranks of Mussulmans, I am fear-

ful that my exertions will be thrown away. The great and the rich, intoxicated with pride and luxury, and puffed up with the vanity of their possessions, consider universal science as comprehended in the circle of their own scanty acquirements and limited knowledge; while the poor and common people, from the want of leisure, and overpowered by the difficulty of procuring a livelihood, have not time to attend to their personal concerns, much less to form desires for the acquirement of information on new discoveries and inventions; although such a passion has been implanted by nature in every human breast, as an honor and an ornament to the species. I therefore despair of their reaping any fruit from my labors, being convinced that they will consider this book of no greater value than the volumes of tales and romances which they peruse merely to pass away their time, or are attracted thereto by the easiness of the style. It may consequently be concluded, that as they will find no pleasure in reading a work which contains a number of foreign names, treats on uncommon subjects, and alludes to other matters which cannot be understood at the first glance, but require a little time for consideration, they will, under pretense of zeal for their religion, entirely abstain and refrain from perusing it.

Ode to London

Shortly after his arrival in London, Abu Taleb composed a poem in praise of the city and its women. The following is a literal translation from the Persian.

[From Abu Taleb, *Travels*, 1:218–20]

> Henceforward we will devote our lives to London, and its heart-alluring Damsels:
> Our hearts are satiated with viewing fields, gardens, rivers, and palaces.
>
> We have no longing for the Toba, Sudreh, or other trees of Paradise:
> We are content to rest under the shade of these terrestrial Cypresses.
>
> If the Shaikh of Mecca is displeased at our conversion, who cares?
> May the Temple which has conferred such blessings on us, and its Priests, flourish!
>
> Fill the goblet with wine! If by this I am prevented from returning
> To my old religion, I care not; nay, I am the better pleased.

If the prime of my life has been spent in the service of an Indian Cupid,
It matters not: I am now rewarded by the smiles of the British Fair.

Adorable creatures! whose flowing tresses, whether of flaxen or of jetty
hue,
Or auburn gay, delight my soul, and ravish all my senses!

Whose ruby lips would animate the torpid clay, or marble statue!
Had I a renewal of life, I would, with rapture, devote it to your service!

These wounds of Cupid, on your heart, Taleba, are not accidental:
They were engendered by Nature, like the streaks on the leaf of a tulip.

The Evil of Western Materialism

Abu Taleb's catalogue of the vices of the English is one of the most interesting parts
of his book. In criticizing their irreligion, worldliness, and love of luxury, he antic-
ipated the argument widely used by Indian nationalists a century later, i.e., that
Westerners were incurably materialistic and therefore unfit to rule a religious country
like India. In fairness to the English, he later added a shorter list of their virtues.

[From Abu Taleb, *Travels,* 2:128–31]

The first and greatest defect I observed in the English is their want of faith
in religion, and their great inclination to philosophy [atheism]: The effects
of these principles, or rather want of principle, is very conspicuous in the
lower orders of people, who are totally devoid of honesty. They are, indeed,
cautious how they transgress against the laws, from fear of punishment; but
whenever an opportunity offers of purloining anything without the risk of
detection, they never pass it by. They are also ever on the watch to appropriate to themselves the property of the rich, who, on this account, are
obliged constantly to keep their doors shut, and never to permit an unknown person to enter them. At present, owing to the vigilance of the
magistrates, the severity of the laws, and the honor of the superior classes
of people, no very bad consequences are to be apprehended; but if ever such
nefarious practices should become prevalent and should creep in among the
higher classes, inevitable ruin must ensue.

The second defect most conspicuous in the English character is pride, or insolence. Puffed up with their power and good fortune for the last fifty years, they are not apprehensive of adversity, and take no pains to avert it. Thus, when the people of London, some time ago, assembled in mobs on account of the great increase of taxes and high price of provisions, and were nearly in a state of insurrection—although the magistrates, by their vigilance in watching them, and by causing parties of soldiers to patrole the streets day and night, to disperse all persons whom they saw assembling together, succeeded in quieting the disturbance—yet no pains were afterwards taken to eradicate the evil. Some of the men in power said it had been merely a plan of the artificers to obtain higher wages (an attempt frequently made by the English tradesmen); others were of opinion that no remedy could be applied; therefore no further notice was taken of the affair. All this, I say, betrays a blind confidence, which, instead of meeting the danger and endeavoring to prevent it, waits till the misfortune arrives, and then attempts to remedy it. Such was the case with the late king of France, who took no step to oppose the Revolution till it was too late. This self-confidence is to be found, more or less, in every Englishman; it however differs much from the pride of Indians and Persians.

Their third defect is a passion for acquiring money and their attachment to worldly affairs. Although these bad qualities are not so reprehensible in them as in countries more subject to the vicissitudes of fortune, (because, in England, property is so well protected by the laws that every person reaps the fruits of his industry, and, in his old age, enjoys the earnings or economy of his youth,) yet sordid and illiberal habits are generally found to accompany avarice and parsimony, and, consequently, render the possessor of them contemptible; on the contrary, generosity, if it does not launch into prodigality, but is guided by the hand of prudence, will render a man respected and esteemed.

The Strange Notion of Progress

Abu Taleb was surprised at the modern Western belief in progress and the infinite perfectibility of human knowledge.

[From Abu Taleb, *Travels*, 2:165–66]

The English have very peculiar opinions on the subject of *perfection*. They insist that it is merely an ideal quality, and depends entirely upon comparison; that mankind have risen, by degrees, from the state of savages to the exalted dignity of the great philosopher Newton; but that, so far from having yet attained *perfection,* it is possible that, in future ages, philosophers will look with as much contempt on the acquirements of Newton as we now do on the rude state of the arts among savages. If this axiom of theirs be correct, man has yet much to learn, and all his boasted knowledge is but vanity.

Rammohun Roy: "Father of Modern India"

Rammohun Roy (or Rammohan Ray), although he became almost friendless among Hindus in his own time, has since been seen as twentieth-century India's founding father because of his pioneering reforms in religion, morals, journalism, education, the status of women, and legal and political thought.

He was born c. 1774 into a Bengali brāhman family of the highest rank, but the foundations of his mature thought were evidently laid down by his Persian studies at home and probably also in Patna. Persian was then not only the language of government service, but also of humane letters in most of northern India. Through Persian young Rammohun became familiar with Sufi ideas, and through Persian and Arabic he became acquainted with Aristotelian logic and rhetoric, as well as with the Greco-Islamic spirit of scholarly inquiry. His mother's family, who were shaktas devoted to goddess-worship, insisted he steep himself as well in Sanskrit learning at Banaras, the Hindus' most sacred city. Rammohun apparently preferred Persian to Sanskrit culture, and with it the Islamic rejection of the use of images in worship. At sixteen he clashed with his parents over the practice of image worship. His father may have ordered him out of the house, for he then set off on his own, traveling up into Bhutan or Tibet, where he both studied the Tibetan form of Buddhism and angered its monks by criticizing their worship of lamas.

In his mid-twenties Rammohun began acquiring property in land and lending money to young British civil servants. In his thirties he entered their employ, became fluent in English, and began his investigations of European thought and politics. Napoleon's career and policies fascinated him for a while, and the enjoyment of liberty under constitutional law became his ideal. By 1815, when he was in his early forties, he had grown wealthy enough to retire from his post in the revenue service and to settle in Calcutta, the capital of the East India Company's empire in India and the main center from which British power and cultural influence were expanding into the heartland of northern India.

From 1815 to 1830 Rammohun engaged in a wide range of projects designed to enlighten the minds and improve the lot of his countrymen. First he campaigned against the worship of gods and goddesses and their images, believing such worship to be the root of all superstitious and inhumane Hindu practices. To add weight to his thesis, he rendered into Bengali and English the *Kena, Īśā, Kaṭha, and Muṇḍaka Upaniṣads,* along with other, Vedantic texts, so wording them as to emphasize the unity and power of God—a monotheistic emphasis quite different from the monism in the original Sanskrit texts. Possibly Rammohun's transcreations were influenced by the Persian versions of the Upanishads prepared at the behest of the unfortunate Mughal Prince Dārā Shikōh. Calcutta's orthodox brāhmans were outraged at Rammohun's attacks on their ways of worship and virtually ostracized him. In 1820 he published a compilation of the nontheological teachings of Jesus, because he found them "more conducive to moral principles, and better adapted for the use of rational beings, than any others which have come to my knowledge."[3] British Protestant ministers then denounced his deliberate omission of references to the divinity or miraculous powers of Jesus, and he spent three further years of research and writing in defending his *Precepts of Jesus, the Guide to Peace and Happiness.* So cogent were his arguments against the doctrine of the Trinity that he converted to Unitarianism a Baptist missionary with whom he was translating the New Testament into Bengali.

In the 1820s Rammohun became increasingly active in efforts to improve the educational, social, and political conditions of Calcutta and the surrounding region. He founded several schools, wrote textbooks, published weekly newspapers in Bengali, English, and Persian, and vigorously opposed both British plans to support impractical Sanskrit studies and the Hindu custom of burning widows alive (ostensibly so that married couples could continue together in heaven and in their subsequent incarnations). He took great interest in the spread of constitutional liberty in the United States, post-Napoleonic Europe, and Latin America, and looked forward to India's gradual evolution in this direction. On behalf of Calcutta's leading citizens, he wrote petitions protesting the 1823 ordinance restricting the freedom of the press and the 1827 Jury Act excluding Hindus and Muslims from juries in cases where Christians were the accused. (Both measures were withdrawn within a few years.) He also founded in 1828, with a group of like-minded Hindu monotheists, the Brahmo Sabha (later named the Brahmo Samaj)—the association (or society) of the worshipers of the one true God.

In the last years of his life Rammohun made the five-month sea voyage to England despite the taboo against crossing "the black waters." In London, he presented to a committee of Parliament recommendations on ways to improve the government of India, inquired about the possibility of becoming an M.P. himself, disputed with Robert Owen over Owen's antipathy to Christianity, was called on by Jeremy Bentham, honored with a dinner by the directors of the East India Company, and presented to the king. He strongly supported the passage of the 1832 Reform Bill and proposed constitutional checks on the abuse of power by the company's officials in India. Finally, ill and bankrupt, he died in Bristol in 1833 in the company of his English Unitarian friends.

Rammohun was the first Indian scholar to probe deeply into the religious and political foundations of British culture and society. In doing so, he could draw on his early studies of Islamic, Hindu, and Buddhist beliefs and practices, and, as he turned to examine the ideas and ways of the West, he was able to choose those that struck him as beneficial (the teachings of Jesus, governmental guarantees of civil and religious liberty, and modern secular knowledge), and to reject those that did not (Christian theology, and British autocratic government in India). At the same time, he singled out for attention those classical Hindu scriptures the contents of which came closest to ethical monotheism, thereby offering his fellow Indians a means of purging themselves of undesirable customs while retaining their sense of continuity with the past. For this strategic reinterpretation of Hindu religious thought, and for his many efforts to enlighten his society and improve its customs, Rammohun Roy fully deserves the epithet given him by later generations, "the father of modern India," as well as the epitaph (from the Persian poet Saʿdī) he wished to have engraved on his tombstone: "The true way of serving God is to do good to man."

How the British Took Control of India

Rammohun's statements on the decline of the Mughal Empire and the rise of the British reflected the attitudes of those in the coastal provinces (Bengal, Bombay, and Madras) who welcomed the peace, civil and religious liberties, and expansion of commerce introduced by their new rulers.

[From *Exposition of the Practical Operation of Judicial and Revenue Systems of India* 1831), and "Appeal to the King in Council" (1823), in Rammohun Roy, *English Works,* part 3, pp. 5–6, 8, part 4, pp. 11–12]

In the year 1712, the star of the Moghul ascendancy inclined towards descent, and has since gradually sunk below the horizon. The princes oftener consulted their own personal comfort than the welfare of the state, and relied for success on the fame of their dynasty, rather than on sound policy and military valour. Not only their crowns, but their lives also, depended on the good will of the nobles, who virtually assumed independence of the sovereign power, and each sought his own individual aggrandisement.

At present, all the southern and eastern, as well as several of the western provinces of the empire, have gradually fallen into the possession of the English. The army they employed chiefly consisted of the natives of India, a country into which the notion of patriotism has never made its way. Those territories were in fact transferred to British possession from the rule of a number of the rebellious nobility, while the greatest part of the northern provinces beyond the river Sutlej has fallen into the hands of Runjett [Ranjit] Singh, the chief of a tribe commonly called *Sikhs.* . . .

With regard to the circumstances under which a body of respectable English merchants (commonly known by the name of the Honourable East India Company) first obtained their Charter of Privileges in 1600, during the reign of Queen Elizabeth, to carry on trade with the East Indies; and with respect to the particulars of their success in procuring from the Emperor of Hindustan [Jahāngīr], and from several of his successors permission to establish commercial factories, as well as the enjoyment of protection, and various privileges in that country; with relation further to their conquests, which commencing about the middle of the eighteenth century have extended over the greater part of India—conquests principally owing to the dissensions and pusillanimous conduct of the native princes and chiefs, as well as to the ignorance existing in the East, of the modern improvements in the art of war, combined with the powerful assistance afforded to the Company by the naval and military forces of the crown of England—I refer the reader to the modern histories of India. . . .

The Marquis of Cornwallis [who had surrendered to Washington at Yorktown in 1781], a straight-forward honest statesman, assumed the reigns of government in Bengal in 1786. He succeeded not only in consolidating the British power in its political relations in those remote regions, but also in introducing, in 1793, material changes in every department, particularly in the revenue and judicial systems. These changes, approximating to the institutions existing in England, are calculated to operate beneficially, if regularly reduced to practice.

· · · ·

The greater part of Hindustan having been for several centuries subject to Muhammadan Rule, the civil and religious rights of its original inhabitants were constantly trampled upon, and from the habitual oppression of the conquerors, a great body of their subjects in the Southern Peninsula (Dukhin [or Deccan]), afterwards called Marhattahs [Marathas], and another body in the western parts now styled Sikhs, were at last driven to revolt; and when the Mussalman power became feeble, they ultimately succeeded in establishing their independence; but the natives of Bengal wanting vigor of body, and adverse to active exertion, remained during the whole period of the Muhammadan conquest, faithful to the existing Government, although their property was often plundered, their religion insulted, and their blood wantonly shed. Divine Providence at last, in its abundant mercy, stirred up the English nation to break the yoke of those tyrants, and to receive the oppressed Natives of Bengal under its protection. Having made Calcutta the capital of their dominions, the English distinguished this city by such peculiar marks of favour, as a free people would be expected to bestow, in establishing an English Court of Judicature, and granting to all within its jurisdiction, the same civil rights as every Briton enjoys in his native country; thus putting the Natives of India in possession of such privileges as their forefathers never expected to attain, even under Hindu Rulers. . . . Under the cheering influence of equitable and indulgent treatment, and stimulated by the example of a people famed for their wisdom and liberality, the Natives of India, with the means of amelioration set before them, have been gradually advancing in social and intellectual improvement.

Autobiographical Remarks

[From *The Athenaeum* (London), October 5, 1833, and *English Works*, part 3, p. 8]

My ancestors were Brahmans of a high order, and from time immemorial were devoted to the religious duties of their race, down to my fifth progenitor, who about 140 years ago gave up spiritual exercises for worldly pursuits and aggrandisement. His descendents ever since have followed his example, and, according to the usual fate of courtiers, with various success, sometimes rising to honour, and sometimes falling; sometimes rich and sometimes poor; sometimes excelling in success, sometimes miserable through disappointment. But my maternal ancestors being of the sacerdotal order by profession, as well as by birth, and of a family than which none holds a higher rank in that profession, have, up to the present day, uniformly adhered to a life of religious observances and devotion, preferring peace and tranquillity of mind to the excitements of ambition and all the allurements of worldly grandeur.

In conformity with the usage of my parental race, and the wish of my father, I studied the Persian and Arabic languages; these accomplishments being indispensable to those who attached themselves to the Courts of the Mohammedan princes, and agreeably to the usage of my maternal relations, I devoted myself to the study of the Sanskrit, and the theological works written in it, which contain the body of Hindu literature, law, and religion.

When about the age of sixteen, I composed a manuscript, calling in question the validity of the idolatrous system of the Hindūs. This, together with my known sentiments on the subject, having produced a coolness between me and my immediate kindred, I proceeded on my travels, and passed through different countries, chiefly within, but some beyond the bounds of Hindūstan, with a feeling of great aversion to the establishment of the British power in India. When I had reached the age of twenty, my father recalled me and restored me to his favour; after which, I first saw, and began to associate with, Europeans, and soon after made myself tolerably acquainted with their laws and form of government. Finding them generally more intelligent, more steady and moderate in their conduct, I gave up my prejudice against them and became inclined in their favour, feeling persuaded that their rule, though a foreign yoke, would lead more speedily and surely to the amelioration of the native inhabitants. I enjoyed the confidence of several of them even in their public capacity. My continued controversies with the Brahmans on the subject of their idolatry and superstition, and my interference with their custom of burning widows, and other pernicious practices, revived and increased their animosity against me with renewed force; and through their influence with my family, my father was again obliged to withdraw his countenance openly, though his limited pecuniary support was still continued to me.

After my father's death I opposed the advocates of idolatry with still greater boldness; availing myself of the art of printing, now established in India, I published various works and pamphlets against their errors, in the native and foreign languages. This raised such a feeling against me that I was at last deserted by every person, except two or three Scotch friends, to whom, and the nation to which they belong, I always feel grateful.

The ground which I took in all my controversies was not that of opposition to Brahmanism, but to a perversion of it; and I endeavoured to show that the idolatry of the Brahmans was contrary to the practice of their ancestors, and the principles of the ancient books and authorities, which they profess to revere and obey. Notwithstanding the violence of the opposition and resistance to my opinions, several highly respectable persons, both among my own relations and others, began to adopt the same sentiments.

I now felt a strong wish to visit Europe, and obtain by personal observation a more thorough insight into its manners, customs, religion, and political institutions. I refrained, however, from carrying this intention into effect until my friends, who coincided in my sentiments, should be increased in number and strength. My expectations having at length been realized, in November, 1830, I embarked for England, as the discussion of the East India Company's Charter was expected to come on, by which the treatment of the natives of India and its future government would be determined for many years to come; and an appeal to the King in Council against the abolition of the practice of burning Hindū widows, was to be heard before the Privy Council; and His Majesty the Emperor of Delhi had likewise commissioned me to bring before the authorities in England certain encroachments on his rights by the East India Company, I accordingly arrived in England in April, 1831.

. . . .

From occasionally directing my studies to the subjects and events peculiarly connected with Europe, and from an attentive though partial, practical observation in regard to some of them, I felt impressed with the idea, that in Europe literature was zealously encouraged and knowledge widely diffused; that mechanics were almost in a state of perfection, and politics in daily progress; that moral duties were, on the whole, observed with exemplary propriety notwithstanding the temptations incident to a state of high and luxurious refinement; and that religion was spreading, even amid scepticism and false philosophy.

I was in consequence continually making efforts for a series of years, to visit the Western World, with a view to satisfy[ing] myself on those subjects by personal experience. I ultimately succeeded in surmounting the obstacles to my purpose, principally of a domestic nature, and . . . arrived in England. . . . The particulars of my voyage and travels will be found in a Journal which I intend to Publish [but which is now lost]; together with whatever has appeared to me most worthy of remark and record in regard to the intelligence, riches and power, manners, customs, and especially the female virtue and excellence existing in this country.

"A Precious Gift to Those Who Believe in One God"

Rammohun gave this title in Arabic to his earliest extant religious tract, apparently borrowing it from a work by the great Delhi reformer Shāh Walī-Ullāh. The pamphlet shows the deep influence of his Indo-Persian education as well as the transreligious perspective he gained from his subsequent studies of Sanskrit texts and Buddhist beliefs and practices. One of his aims in writing it may have been to try to persuade educated Muslims to be more tolerant of other faiths, for he wrote it in Persian with a preface (translated here) in Arabic, and published it in Murshidabad, the capital of pre-British Bengal.

[From "Tuḥfat al-muwaḥḥidīn," p. iii, in *Tuḥfatu'l-muwahhidin*, trans. Obaide. Revised by Charles Wendell, with editorial explanations in brackets.]

In the Name of the Almighty

PREFACE

I have travelled in the farthest regions of the earth, both in the plains and the mountains and have found that those who live on it agree in a general way in acknowledging the existence of one source of all existing beings, who is also their Ruler. But they disagree as to the particular character of His nature, and in the variety of their credal statements regarding [both] the fundamentals of religious beliefs and the rules of what is lawful and what is forbidden.

And so, by means of this investigation I reached the conclusion that recourse (in general) to the Necessary Being was, as it were, a natural thing, shared equally by all individuals, but that each group's inclination toward a god or gods with special attributes, as well as to corresponding kinds of religious ritual and social behavior, was a supplementary quality that sprang from customs and education. And what a difference there is between that which exists by nature and that which originates in human customs!

Some believers busy themselves with demolishing the dogmas of others because of the conflicts that arise between them, basing their claims [to truth] on the validity of the sayings of their ancestors. They, however, are subject to error, sin, and contradiction just like the rest of mankind, and therefore one must say that all of them are right or [that some or all of them are] in error. In the first case it is [i.e., would be] necessary that the opposed factions agree (which is logically impossible). And in the second, we must say that falsehood exists among some of them in particular, or [among all of them] in general. If the first assumption is adopted [i.e., that falsehood exists among some religions and not others], one is of necessity opting for a preferential choice without adequate reason (which is logically inadmissible). Hence it must be that falsehood exists in all religions, without going into particulars.

The Need for a More Humane Morality and a Purer Mode of Worship

In introducing his rendering of the *Kaṭha Upaniṣad* into English and Bengali, Rammohun stated the principle he was later to put to the Christian missionaries: worship the one true God, and out of a purified heart treat others justly and kindly.

[From Rammohun Roy, *English Works*, part 2, pp. 23–24]

The advocates of idolatry and their misguided followers, over whose opinions prejudice and obstinacy prevail more than good sense and judgment, prefer custom and fashion to the authorities of their scriptures, and therefore continue, under the form of religious devotion, to practise a system which destroys, to the utmost degree, the natural texture of society, and prescribes crimes of the most heinous nature, which even the most savage nations would blush to commit, unless compelled by the most urgent necessity. I am, however, not without a sanguine hope that, through Divine Providence and human exertions, they will sooner or later avail themselves of that true system of religion which leads its observers to a knowledge and love of God, and to a friendly inclination towards their fellow-creatures, impressing their hearts at the same time with humility and charity, accompanied by independence of mind and pure sincerity. Contrary to the code of idolatry, this system defines sin as evil thoughts proceeding from the heart, quite unconnected with observances as to diet and other matters of form. At any rate, it seems to me that I cannot better employ my time than in an endeavour to illustrate and maintain truth, and to render service to my fellow-labourers, confiding in the mercy of that Being to whom the motives of our actions and secrets of our hearts are well known.

The Superiority of the Precepts of Jesus

A keen student of religions, Rammohun became deeply interested in the religious teachings being disseminated by the Christian missionaries. On reading the New Testament he formed the idea of bringing together only the ethical teachings attributed to Jesus, leaving out the theological passages (an idea that Thomas Jefferson had already carried out, but without publishing his selections). Rammohun opened his book of extracts with the following introduction.

[From Rammohun Roy, *The Precepts of Jesus, the Guide to Peace and Happiness* (1834), pp. iii-vii; *English Works*, part 5, pp. 3-4]

A conviction in the mind of its total ignorance of the nature and of the specific attributes of the Godhead, and a sense of doubt respecting the real essence of the soul, give rise to feelings of great dissatisfaction with our limited powers, as well as with all human acquirements which fail to inform us on these interesting points. On the other hand, a notion of the existence of a supreme superintending power, the Author and Preserver of this harmonious system, who has organized and who regulates such an infinity of celestial and terrestrial objects, and a due estimation of that law which teaches that man should do unto others as he would wish to be done by, reconcile us to human nature, and tend to render our existence agreeable to ourselves and profitable to the rest of mankind. The former of these sources of satisfaction, viz., a belief in God, prevails generally, being derived either from tradition and instruction, or from an attentive survey of the wonderful skill and contrivance displayed in the works of nature. The latter, although it is partially taught also in every system of religion with which I am acquainted, is principally inculcated by Christianity. This essential characteristic of the Christian religion I was for a long time unable to distinguish as such, amidst the various doctrines I found insisted upon in the writings of Christian authors, and in the conversation of those teachers of Christianity with whom I have had the honor of holding communication. . . .

I feel persuaded that by separating from the other matters contained in the New Testament, the moral precepts found in that book, these will be more likely to produce the desirable effect of improving the hearts and minds of men of different persuasions and degrees of understanding. For historical and some other passages are liable to the doubts and disputes of free-thinkers and anti-Christians, especially miraculous relations, which are much less wonderful than the fabricated tales handed down to the natives of Asia,[4] and consequently would be apt at best to carry little weight with them. On the contrary, moral doctrines, tending evidently to the maintenance of the peace and harmony of mankind at large, are beyond the reach of metaphysical perversion, and intelligible alike to the learned and to the unlearned. This simple code of religion and morality is so admirably calculated to elevate men's ideas to high and liberal notions of one GOD, who has equally subjected all living creatures, without distinction of cast, rank, or wealth, to change, disappointment, pain, and death, and has equally admitted all to be partakers of the bountiful mercies which he has lavished over nature, and is also so well fitted to regulate the conduct of the human race in the discharge of their various duties to GOD, to themselves, and to society, that I cannot but hope the best effects from its promulgation in the present form.

In Defense of Hindu Women

In a letter to an American friend, Rammohun Roy stated his willingness to support the moral principles preached by Jesus "even at the risk of my own life." Roy actually did risk his life while conducting his arduous campaign against the Hindu practice of suttee (*sati*) by which widows were encouraged to burn themselves to death on their husbands' funeral pyres. The threats of ultraconservative Hindus notwithstanding, Rammohun carried his campaign to a successful conclusion by helping the British to overcome their doubts about proscribing the custom. Having devastated his imaginary opponent by references to the highest Sanskrit authorities, he concluded his *Second Conference Between an Advocate for and an Opponent of the Practice of Burning Widows Alive* with an appeal to humanitarian standards of justice and mercy and a passionate defense of the rights of women.

[From Rammohun Roy, *English Works*, part 3, pp. 124–27]

Advocate. I alluded in page 18, line 18, to the real reason for our anxiety to persuade widows to follow their husbands, and for our endeavors to burn them pressed down with ropes: viz., that women are by nature of inferior understanding, without resolution, unworthy of trust, subject to passions, and void of virtuous knowledge; they, according to the precepts of the Sastra, are not allowed to marry again after the demise of their husbands, and consequently despair at once of all worldly pleasure; hence it is evident, that death to these unfortunate widows is preferable to existence, for the great difficulty which a widow may experience by living a purely ascetic life as prescribed by the Sastras is obvious; therefore if she do not perform Concremation [being burnt alive at her husband's cremation], it is probable that she may be guilty of such acts as may bring disgrace upon her paternal and maternal relations, and those that may be connected with her husband. Under these circumstances, we instruct them from their early life in the idea of Concremation, holding out to them heavenly enjoyments in company with their husbands, as well as the beatitude of their relations, both by birth and marriage, and their reputation in this world. From this many of them, on the death of their husbands, become desirous of accompanying them; but to remove every chance of their trying to escape from the blazing fire, in burning them we first tie them down to the pile.

Opponent. The reason you have now assigned for burning widows alive is indeed your true motive, as we are well aware; but the faults which you have imputed to women are not planted in their constitution by nature; it would be, therefore, grossly criminal to condemn that sex to death merely from precaution. By ascribing to them all sorts of improper conduct, you have indeed successfully persuaded the Hindoo community to look down upon them as contemptible and mischievous creatures, whence they have been subjected to constant miseries. I have, therefore, to offer a few remarks on this head.

Women are in general inferior to men in bodily strength and energy; consequently the male part of the community, taking advantage of their corporeal weakness, have denied to them those excellent merits that they are entitled to by nature, and afterwards they are apt to say that women are naturally incapable of acquiring those merits. But if we give the subject consideration, we may easily ascertain whether or not your accusation against them is consistent with justice. As to their inferiority in point of understanding, when did you ever afford them a fair opportunity of exhibiting their natural capacity? How then can you accuse them of want of understanding? If, after instruction in knowledge and wisdom, a person cannot comprehend or retain what has been taught him, we may consider him as deficient; but as you keep women generally void of education and acquirements, you cannot, therefore, in justice pronounce on their inferiority. On the contrary, Lilavati, Bhanumati, the wife of the prince of Karnat[aka], and that of Kalidasa, are celebrated for their thorough knowledge of all the Sastras; moreover in the Vrihadaranyaka [*Bṛhadāraṇyaka*] Upanishad of the Yajur Veda it is clearly stated that Yajnavalkya imparted divine knowledge of the most difficult nature to his wife Maitreyi, who was able to follow and completely attain it!

Secondly. You charge them with want of resolution, at which I feel exceedingly surprised. For we constantly perceive, in a country where the name of death makes the male shudder, that the female, from her firmness of mind, offers to burn with the corpse of her deceased husband; and yet you accuse those women of deficiency in point of resolution.

Thirdly. With regard to their trustworthiness, let us look minutely into the conduct of both sexes, and we may be enabled to ascertain which of them is the most frequently guilty of betraying friends. If we enumerate such women in each village or town as have been deceived by men, and such men as have been betrayed by women, I presume that the number of the deceived women would be found ten times greater than that of the betrayed men. Men are, in general, able to read and write, and manage public affairs, by which means they easily promulgate such faults as women occasionally commit, but never consider as criminal the misconduct of men towards women. One fault they have, it must be acknowledged; which is, by considering others equally void of duplicity as themselves to give their confidence too readily, from which they suffer much misery, even so far that some of them are misled to suffer themselves to be burnt to death.

In the fourth place, with respect to their subjection to the passions, this may be judged of by the custom of marriage as to the respective sexes; for one man may marry two or three, sometimes even ten wives and upwards; while a woman, who marries but one husband, desires at his death to follow him, forsaking all worldly enjoyments, or to remain leading the austere life of an ascetic.

Fifthly. The accusation of their want of virtuous knowledge is an injustice. Observe what pain, what slighting, what contempt, and what afflictions their virtue enables them to support! How many Kulin[5] Brahmans are there who marry ten or fifteen wives for the sake of money, that never see the greater number of them after the day of marriage, and visit others only three or four times in the course of their life. Still amongst those women, most, even without seeing or receiving any support from their husbands, living dependent on their fathers or brothers, and suffering much distress, continue to preserve their virtue. And when Brahmans, or those of other tribes, bring their wives to live with them, what misery do the women not suffer? At marriage the wife is recognized as half of her husband, but in after-conduct they are treated worse than inferior animals. For the woman is employed to do the work of a slave in the house, such as, in her turn, to clean the place very early in the morning, whether cold or wet, to scour the dishes, to wash the floor, to cook night and day, to prepare and serve food for her husband, father, mother-in-law, sisters-in-law, brothers-in-law, and friends and connections! (For amongst Hindoos more than in other tribes relations long reside together, and on this account quarrels are more common amongst brothers respecting their worldly affairs.) If in the prepa-ration or serving up of the victuals they commit the smallest fault, what insult do they not receive from their husband, their mother-in-law, and the younger brothers of their husband? After all the male part of the family have satisfied themselves, the women content themselves with what may be left, whether sufficient in quantity or not. Where Brahmans or Kayasthas[6] are not wealthy, their women are obliged to attend to their cows, and to prepare the cow-dung for firing. In the afternoon they fetch water from the river or tank, and at night perform the office of menial servants in making the beds. In case of any fault or omission in the performance of those la-bors, they receive injurious treatment. Should the husband acquire wealth, he indulges in criminal amours to her perfect knowledge and almost under her eyes, and does not see her perhaps once a month. As long as the hus-band is poor, she suffers every kind of trouble, and when he becomes rich, she is altogether heartbroken. All this pain and affliction their virtue alone enables them to support. Where a husband takes two or three wives to live with him, they are subjected to mental miseries and constant quarrels. Even this distressed situation they virtuously endure. Sometimes it happens that the husband, from a preference for one of his wives, behaves cruelly to another. Amongst the lower classes, and those even of the better class who have not associated with good company, the wife, on the slightest fault, or even on bare suspicion of her misconduct, is chastised as a thief. Respect to virtue and their reputation generally makes them forgive even this treat-ment. If, unable to bear such cruel usage, a wife leaves her husband's house to live separately from him, then the influence of the husband with the magisterial authority is generally sufficient to place her again in his hands; when, in revenge for her quitting him, he seizes every pretext to torment her in various ways, and sometimes even puts her privately to death. These are facts occurring every day, and not to be denied. What I lament is, that, seeing the women thus dependent and exposed to every misery, you feel for them no compassion that might exempt them from being tied down and burnt to death.

For Freedom of the Press

In 1823 the East India Company promulgated an ordinance restricting the freedom of the press by requiring all newspapers to be licensed under terms laid down by the government. Rammohun Roy responded by drawing up a memorial to the Supreme Court on behalf of the Indian community, in which he contended that their loyalty depended on the continuing enjoyment of those civil liberties which had reconciled them to British rule—an argument echoed later by many an Indian nationalist.

[From Rammohun Roy, *English Works*, part 4, pp. 7–9]

After this Rule and Ordinance shall have been carried into execution, your Memorialists are therefore extremely sorry to observe, that a complete stop will be put to the diffusion of knowledge and the consequent mental improvement now going on, either by translations into the popular dialect of this country from the learned languages of the East, or by the circulation of literary intelligence drawn from foreign publications. And the same cause will also prevent those Natives who are better versed in the laws and customs of the British Nation, from communicating to their fellow-subjects a knowledge of the admirable system of Government established by the British, and the peculiar excellencies of the means they have adopted for the strict and impartial administration of justice. Another evil of equal importance in the eyes of a just Ruler, is, that it will also preclude the Natives from making the Government readily acquainted with the errors and injustice that may be committed by its executive officers in the various parts of this extensive country; and it will also preclude the Natives from communicating frankly and honestly to their Gracious Sovereign in England and his Council, the real condition of His Majesty's faithful subjects in this distant part of his dominions and the treatment they experience from the local government; since such information cannot in future be conveyed to England, as it has heretofore been, either by the translations from the Native publications inserted in the English Newspapers printed here and sent to Europe, or by the English publications which the Natives themselves had in contemplation to establish, before this Rule and Ordinance was proposed.

After this sudden deprivation of one of the most precious of their rights, which has been freely allowed them since the establishment of the British power, a right which they are not, and cannot, be charged with having ever abused, the inhabitants of Calcutta would be no longer justified in boasting, that they are fortunately placed by Providence under the protection of the whole British Nation, or that the king of England and his Lords and Commons are their legislators, and that they are secured in the enjoyment of the same civil and religious privileges that every Briton is entitled to in England.

Your Memorialists are persuaded that the British government is not disposed to adopt the political maxim so often acted upon by Asiatic princes, that the more a people are kept in darkness, their rulers will derive the greater advantages from them; since, by reference to History, it is found that this was but a short-sighted policy which did not ultimately answer the purpose of its authors. On the contrary, it rather proved disadvantageous to them; for we find that as often as an ignorant people, when an opportunity offered, have revolted against their Rulers, all sorts of barbarous excesses and cruelties have been the consequence; whereas a people naturally disposed to peace and ease, when placed under a good Government from which they experience just and liberal treatment, must become the more attached to it, in proportion as they become enlightened and the great body of the people are taught to appreciate the value of the blessings they enjoy under its Rule.

Every good Ruler, who is convinced of the imperfection of human nature, and reverences the Eternal Governor of the world, must be conscious of the great liability to error in managing the affairs of a vast empire; and therefore he will be anxious to afford every individual the readiest means of bringing to his notice whatever may require his interference. To secure this important object, the unrestrained Liberty of Publication is the only effectual means that can be employed. And should it ever be abused, the established Law of the Land is very properly armed with sufficient powers to punish those who may be found guilty of misrepresenting the conduct or character of Government, which are effectually guarded by the same Laws to which individuals must look for protection of their reputation and good name.

Your Memorialists conclude by humbly entreating your Lordship to take this Memorial into your gracious consideration; and that you will be pleased by not registering the above Rule and Ordinance, to permit the Natives of this country to continue in possession of the civil rights and privileges which they and their fathers have so long enjoyed under the auspices of the British nation, whose kindness, and confidence, they are not aware of having done anything, to forfeit.

A Letter on Education

Having established at his own expense schools where young men could acquire through both English and Bengali the best and most modern education available, Rammohun was shocked when the government decided in 1823 to found and support a new college for Sanskritic studies. These excerpts from his letter of protest to the British governor-general of India show how highly he valued the knowledge and ways of thinking developed in Europe since the time of Francis Bacon. Twelve years later, under the urging of T. B. Macaulay, official support for Sanskrit and Arabic studies was ended and education in and through English began to be funded by the government. Macaulay used some of Rammohun's arguments, but his chief one was his own: that such education would produce "a class who may be interpreters between us and the millions whom we govern; a class of persons, Indian in blood and color, but English in taste, in opinions, in morals, and in intellect."[7]

[From Rammohun Roy, *English Works*, part 4, pp. 106–8]

The establishment of a new Sangscrit School in Calcutta evinces the laudable desire of government to improve the Natives of India by Education—a blessing for which they must ever be grateful; and every well-wisher of the human race must be desirous that the efforts made to promote it should be guided by the most enlightened principles, so that the stream of intelligence may flow in the most useful channels.

When this Seminary of learning was proposed, we understood that the Government in England had ordered a considerable sum of money to be annually devoted to the instruction of its Indian Subjects. We were filled with sanguine hopes that this sum would be laid out in employing European Gentlemen of talent and education to instruct the Natives of India in Mathematics, Natural Philosophy, Chemistry, Anatomy, and other useful Sciences, which the Natives of Europe have carried to a degree of perfection that has raised them above the inhabitants of other parts of the world.

While we looked forward with pleasing hope to the dawn of knowledge thus promised to the rising generation, our hearts were filled with mingled feelings of delight and gratitude; we already offered up thanks to Providence for inspiring the most generous and enlightened Nations of the West with the glorious ambition of planting in Asia the Arts and Sciences of modern Europe.

We find that the Government are establishing a Sangscrit school under Hindoo pandits to impart such knowledge as is already current in India. This seminary (similar in character to those which existed in Europe before the time of Lord Bacon) can only be expected to load the minds of youth with grammatical niceties and metaphysical distinctions of little or no practicable use to the possessors or to society. The pupils will there acquire what was known two thousand years ago, with the addition of vain and empty subtleties since then produced by speculative men, such as is already commonly taught in all parts of India. . . .

Neither can much improvement arise from such speculations as the following, which are the themes suggested by the Vedant: In what manner is the soul absorbed in the Deity? What relation does it bear to the Divine Essence? Nor will youths be fitted to be better members of society by the Vedantic doctrines which teach them to believe that all visible things have no real existence; that as father, brother, etc., have no actual entity, they consequently deserve no real affection, and therefore the sooner we escape from them and leave the world the better. Again, no essential benefit can be derived by the student of the Mimamsa from knowing what it is that makes the killer of a goat sinless by pronouncing certain passages of the Veds and what is the real nature and operative influence of passages of the Ved, etc.

Again, the student of the Nyaya Shastra cannot be said to have improved his mind after he has learned from it into how many ideal classes the objects in the Universe are divided, and what speculative relation the soul bears to the body, the body to the soul, the eye to the ear, etc.

In order to enable your Lordship to appreciate the utility of encouraging such imaginary learning as above characterised, I beg your Lordship will be pleased to compare the state of Science and Literature in Europe before the time of Lord Bacon with the progress of knowledge made since he wrote.

If it had been intended to keep the British nation in ignorance of real knowledge, the Baconian philosophy would not have been allowed to displace the system of the schoolmen, which was the best calculated to perpetuate ignorance. In the same manner the Sangscrit system of education would be best calculated to keep this country in darkness, if such had been the policy of the British Legislature. But as the improvement of the native population is the object of the Government, it will consequently promote a more liberal and enlightened system of instruction, embracing mathematics, natural philosophy, chemistry and anatomy, with other useful sciences, which may be accomplished with the sums proposed by employing a few gentlemen of talent and learning educated in Europe, and providing a college furnished with necessary books, instruments, and other apparatus.

In presenting this subject to your Lordship, I conceive myself discharging a solemn duty which I owe to my countrymen, and also to that enlightened Sovereign and Legislature which have extended their benevolent cares to this distant land, actuated by a desire to improve the inhabitants, and I therefore humbly trust you will excuse the liberty I have taken in thus expressing my sentiments to your Lordship.

I have the honor, etc.,

Rammohun Roy

The Future of India

With remarkable accuracy, Rammohun Roy predicted the rise of Indian nationalism in a letter of 1828 to an English friend. At the same time he indicated that by enlightened and democratic government the connection between India and Britain might be prolonged to their mutual advantage.

[From *English Works*, part 4, p. 103]

Supposing that one hundred years hence the Native character becomes elevated from constant intercourse with Europeans and the acquirement of general and political knowledge as well as of modern arts and sciences, is it possible that they will not have the spirit as well as the inclination to resist effectually any unjust and oppressive measures serving to degrade them in the scale of society? It should not be lost sight of that the position of India is very different from that of Ireland, to any quarter of which an English fleet may suddenly convey a body of troops that may force its way in the requisite direction and succeed in suppressing every effort of a refractory spirit. Were India to share one fourth of the knowledge and energy of that country, she would prove from her remote situation, her riches and her vast population, either useful and profitable as a willing province, an ally of the British Empire, or troublesome and annoying as a determined enemy.

In common with those who seem partial to the British rule from the expectation of future benefits, arising out of the connection, I necessarily feel extremely grieved in often witnessing Acts and Regulations passed by Government without consulting or seeming to understand the feelings of its Indian subjects and without considering that this people have had for more than half a century the advantage of being ruled by and associated with an enlightened nation, advocates of liberty and promoters of knowledge.

Two Poems

Rammohun's short poems, sometimes deeply religious, sometimes somber with thoughts of life's transiency, show a simple faith distilled from experience and reflection, aided by his Islamic, Buddhist, Hindu, and New Testament studies. Note the absence of any reference to life after death and his focus on kindness to others, and the felt presence of God.

[From *Rāmmohan granthābalī*, part 4, pp. 63, 64, aided by Nikiles Guha, *The Complete Songs of Rammohun Roy*, poems 25, 32]

If one day death be inevitable,
Why hope, why struggle against it?
This body so lovingly cleansed
Will one day all be dust, from skull to toe.
Grass and forest, if tended well, will last for ages;
But no such efforts can resist the body's decay.
Therefore from beginning to end, let your constant thought be this:
Be kind to other creatures, take refuge in the Real.

. . . .

Wherever I dwell, in my own or in foreign land,
Seeing you in your creation, I call out to you.
In whatever space, at whatever time, your creation is boundless.
Every instant bears witness to your majesty;
Beholding your ever-present glory and power,
I know I am not alone.

NOTES

1. Abū'l Fazl, *Akbarnāma*, 3, p. 37.
2. A low caste of Hindus in South India.
3. Rammohun Roy, *English Works*, part 4, pp. 94–95.
4. "Ugisti [the godlike rishi Agastya] is famed for having swallowed the ocean, when it had given him offence, and having restored it by urinary evacuation; at his command, also, the Vindhyu [Vindhya] range of mountains prostrated itself, and so remains." [Rammohun's footnote]
5. *Kūlīn*: an elite group found among certain Bengal brāhman and kāyastha sub-castes, whose men were much sought after as husbands. Rammohun himself was a kūlīn brāhman.
6. Kāyastha: the caste of scribes, second to brāhmans in importance in Bengal.
7. Macaulay, *Prose and Poetry*, p. 729.

Chapter 2

LEADERS OF HINDU
REFORM AND REVIVAL

Just as the Muslim conquest had injected a fresh stream of religious thought into the veins of Hindu society, so the British conquest brought with it new views of the world, man, and God. In the nineteenth century a series of creative individuals emerged from the ranks of Hindu society to respond to the combined challenge of Christian religious ideas and of modern Western rationalist and utilitarian thought.

The renaissance of Hinduism grew out of the favorable conditions created by the new rulers of India. The establishment of law and order under British administration provided Hindus with an unprecedented opportunity to improve their position vis-à-vis their former rulers, the Muslims. While the latter remained resentful of (and to a certain extent distrusted by) the new conquerers, educated Hindus entered the service of the Western power in growing numbers. They studied English, read enthusiastically the classics of English literature, and became virtually the Anglicized Indians Macaulay had intended them to become.

A few Hindus became Christians; most remained orthodox; and a third group tried to combine the best features of both religions. Rammohun Roy carefully distinguished between English virtue and English errors and defended Hinduism against the criticisms of the missionaries as vigorously as he challenged the orthodox to abandon its excrescences. Rammohun's policy of war on two fronts set the keynote for later champions of Hinduism against Christianity. The more deeply they were imbued by English education with a humanitarian outlook, the more keenly sensitive they became when faced with the missionaries' charge that Hinduism was a pagan and idolatrous religion, laden with barbarous customs. In order to defend Hinduism, therefore, they first had to reform it.

The Brahmo Samaj, founded as the Brahmo Sabha by Rammohun Roy, remained for two generations after Roy's death the focus of efforts to purify

Hinduism and to immunize it against the Christian virus by a partial incorporation of Christian ideas and practices. Debendranath Tagore first strengthened the Samaj's corporate worship and noble monotheism. Next, Keshub Chunder Sen used revivalist sermons and Brahmo missionaries to spread a gospel that became so close to Christian in its content that his conversion was thought imminent. The initiative then passed to Swami Dayananda, who based his radical social reforms entirely on the authority of the Vedas.

Amid the hubbub of these self-conscious efforts to check the advance of Christian influence, Hindu society suddenly discovered in its midst a genuine saint and mystic in Sri Ramakrishna. In the end, Ramakrishna's simple devotion to the traditional concepts and deities of his faith proved a more effective force than all the oratory of his predecessors, and, as Jesus was followed by Saint Paul, Ramakrishna had dynamic Swami Vivekananda to preach his "Gospel" to India and to the world.

The Hindu response to the Christian challenge had now come full circle from resistance, through defense by imitation, to proud self-confidence. In large part, the mounting pressure of Western secular institutions and missionary activity on Hindu society was responsible for solidifying the Hindu stand as the nineteenth century progressed. At the same time, the attention and praise that classical Indian thought was receiving from a host of European scholars added considerably to the momentum of the Hindu revival. Many Westernized Indians first took interest in the *Bhagavad Gita* and the story of the Buddha on making their acquaintance in Sir Edwin Arnold's poetic English translations. Their self-confidence turned to pride when they read the dictum of Professor Max Müller, England's foremost Sanskritist, that in India "the human mind has most fully developed some of its choicest gifts, has most deeply pondered on the greatest problems of life."[1]

Even more encouraging were the growing numbers of Europeans who rejected Western civilization and became partisans of Indian culture. In 1875 the Russian Madame Blavatsky and the American Colonel Olcott founded the Theosophical Society, which held reincarnation, karma, and other Hindu or Buddhist conceptions as central doctrines. In 1882 they moved the headquarters of the Society to Adyar, Madras. Mrs. Annie Besant, the Society's next leader, made India her permanent home from 1893 onward and took such a prominent part in Indian politics that in 1917 she became president of the Indian National Congress—the fifth and last Britisher to receive this honor. Next came Irish-borngaret Noble, Vivekananda's most fervent disciple. She settled in Calcutta, took the name of Sister Nivedita (i.e., the dedicated one), and made a deep impression on Bengali thought and culture in the first decade of this century.

In the last analysis, however, European influences—whether friendly or hostile—of necessity played but a secondary role in the renaissance of Hinduism. It was primarily through the efforts of a series of devout and devoted men that this ancient religion was able to recover in such a remarkable manner the deepest sources of its original inspiration. Even though their efforts primarily affected only the Western-educated (a tiny fraction of the total mass of Hindu society), this minority nevertheless possessed an influence far greater than its numbers would indicate. For they provided the leaders of the future—the Tagores and the Gandhis—whose understanding of their Hindu heritage was decisively shaped by that galaxy of religious thinkers who had preceded them in the nineteenth century.

DEBENDRANATH TAGORE: RE-CREATOR OF THE BRAHMO SAMAJ

The influence of Rammohun Roy on succeeding generations was kept alive by the Brahmo Samaj. After Roy's death in England, his close friend Dwarkanath Tagore, one of India's first entrepreneurial capitalists, gave the little group his financial support, but its numbers dwindled steadily. Meanwhile, Dwarkanath's eldest son Debendranath (1817–1905), who played in Rammohun's yard as a boy in Calcutta, had started a small association of his own that met monthly to discuss religious questions. In 1843 Debendranath merged his group with the remnant of Rammohun Roy's, preserving the original name but injecting a new spirit into the older organization.

Under Debendranath's devoted leadership, the Brahmo Samaj attracted numbers of Bengal's ablest young men, many of them belonging, like Debendranath, to the brāhman caste. Their spiritual center was the common worship of the one true God. Like Rammohun Roy, the Brahmos (as they came to be called) opposed both the idolatry of popular Hinduism and the teachings of the Christian missionaries. Debendranath recounts in his *Autobiography* an incident that illustrates his zeal in defense of purified Hinduism. Hearing that graduates of mission schools were becoming converts to Christianity, he called a mass meeting of the leading Hindu citizens of Calcutta and raised sufficient funds to start a free school for their children.

"Thenceforward the tide of Christian conversion was stemmed," he wrote, "and the designs of the missionaries were knocked on the head."[2]

ⓨ At heart, Debendranath's nature was more devotional than combative. When his fiery young disciple, Keshub Chunder Sen, split the Samaj by insisting that Brahmos discontinue wearing the sacred thread used by high-caste Hindus, Debendranath withdrew from active leadership of his remaining followers and spent many months traveling to places of pilgrimage or meditating in the Himalayas. His piety throughout his long life earned him the honorific title of mahārishi, "the great sage."

In addition to his work in strengthening the Brahmo Samaj, Debendranath continued the work, started by Rammohun Roy, of reviving Hindu monotheism. To find an authoritative scriptural canon for the Samaj, he sent four students to Banaras, each assigned to learn one of the four Vedas. The results of their researches being inconclusive, Debendranath came increasingly to rely on personal intuition as his authority and even composed a creed and a sacred book for the use of Brahmos. The lofty theism and deeply devotional spirit of these documents seem to spring from the same blend of Upanishadic and Christian inspirations that we find in the writings of Rammohun Roy. Debendranath Tagore's contribution to the revitalization of Hinduism was therefore a happy combination of preserving and of adding creatively to its best traditions.

The Conflict Between Sanskritic and Western Education

Debendranath tells in his *Autobiography* the story of his search for religious certainty. The following passage describes the way he resolved the conflict between the two intellectual traditions in which he was educated.

[From Debendranath Tagore, *Autobiography*, pp. 9–10]

As on the one hand there were my Sanskrit studies in the search after truth, so on the other hand there was English. I had read numerous English works on philosophy. But with all this, the sense of emptiness of mind remained just the same, nothing could heal it, my heart was being oppressed by that gloom of sadness and feeling of unrest. Did subjection to nature comprise the whole of man's existence? I asked. Then indeed are we undone. The might of this monster is indomitable. Fire, at a touch, reduces everything to ashes. Put out to sea in a vessel, whirlpools will drag you down to the bottom, gales will throw you into dire distress. There is no escape from the clutches of this Nature-fiend. If bowing down to her decree be our end and aim, then indeed are we undone. What can we hope for, whom can we trust? Again I thought, as things are reflected on a photographic plate by the rays of the sun, so are material objects manifested the mind by the senses, this is what is called knowledge. Is there any other way but this of obtaining knowledge? These were the suggestions that Western philosophy had brought to my mind. To an atheist this is enough, he does not want anything beyond nature. But how could I rest fully satisfied with this? My endeavor was to obtain God, not through blind faith but by the light of knowledge. And being unsuccessful in this, my mental struggles increased from day to day. Sometimes I thought I could live no longer.

Suddenly, as I thought and thought, a flash as of lightning broke through this darkness of despondency. I saw that knowledge of the material world is born of the senses and the objects of sight, sound, smell, touch, and taste. But together with this knowledge, I am also enabled to know that I am the knower. Simultaneously with the facts of seeing, touching, smelling, and thinking, I also come to know that it is I who see, touch, smell, and think. With the knowledge of objects comes the knowledge of the subject, with the knowledge of the body comes the knowledge of the spirit within. It was after a prolonged search for truth that I found this bit of light, as if a ray of sunshine had fallen on a place full of extreme darkness. I now realized that with the knowledge of the outer world we come to know our inner self. After this, the more I thought over it, the more did I recognize the sway of wisdom operating throughout the whole world. For us the sun and moon rise and set at regular intervals, for us the wind and rain are set in motion in the proper seasons. All these combine to fulfil the one design of preserving our life. Whose design is this? It cannot be the design of matter, it must be the design of mind. Therefore this universe is propelled by the power of an intelligent being.

I saw that the child, as soon as born, drinks at its mother's breast. Who taught it to do this? He alone, who gave it life. Again who put love into the mother's heart? Who but He that put milk into her breast. He is that God who knows all our wants, whose rule the universe obeys. When my mind's eye had opened thus far, the clouds of grief were in a great measure dispelled. I felt somewhat consoled.

One day, while thinking of these things I suddenly recalled how, long ago, in my early youth, I had once realized the Infinite as manifested in the infinite heavens. Again I turned my gaze towards this infinite sky, studded with innumerable stars and planets, and saw the eternal God, and felt that this glory was His. He is infinite wisdom. He from whom we have derived this limited knowledge of ours, and this body, its receptacle, is Himself without form. He is without body or senses. He did not shape this universe with his hands. By His will alone did He bring it into existence. He is neither the Kali[3] or Kalighat,[4] nor the family *Shalgram*.[5] Thus was laid the axe at the root of idolatry.

The Call to Renunciation

Had he followed in his father's footsteps, Debendranath could have become one of India's wealthiest men. But his innermost desire was to seek salvation through the traditional path of renunciation.

[From Debendranath Tagore, *Autobiography*, p. 41]

My father was in England. The task of managing his various affairs devolved upon me. But I was not able to attend to any business matters properly. My subordinates used to do all the work, I was only concerned with the Vedas, the Vedanta, religion, God, and the ultimate goal of life. I was not even able to stay quietly in the house. My spirit of renunciation became deeper under all this stress of work. I felt no inclination to become the owner of all this wealth. To renounce everything and wander about alone, this was the desire that reigned in my heart. Imbued with His love I would roam in such lonely places that none would know; I would see His glory on land and water, would witness His mercy in different climes, would feel His protective power in foreign countries, in danger and peril; in this enthusiastic frame of mind I could no longer stay at home.

A Decisive Dream

When his father died, Debendranath was faced with the choice of performing the customary Hindu funeral rites, in which offerings are made to various gods, or of remaining true to his vow to renounce idolatry. The decision came to him in this dream, the conclusion of which gives us a good insight into the Hindu conceptions of religion and filial piety.

[From Debendranath Tagore, *Autobiography*, pp. 48–49]

Which would triumph, the world or religion?—one could not tell—this was what worried me. My constant prayer to God was "Vouchsafe strength unto my weak heart, be Thou my refuge." All these anxieties and troubles would not let me sleep at night, my head felt dazed on the pillow. I would now doze off and again wake up. It was as if I was sleeping on the borderland between waking and sleeping. At such a time some one came to me in the dark and said "Get up," and I at once sat up. He said "Get out of bed" and I got up; he said "follow me" and I followed. He went down the steps leading out of the inner apartments, I did the same and came out into the courtyard with him. We stood before the front door. The durwans[6] were sleeping. My guide touched the door, and the two wings flew open at once. I went out with him into the street in front of the house. He seemed to be a shadowlike form. I could not see him clearly, but felt myself constrained to do immediately whatever he bade me. From thence he mounted up upwards to the sky, I also followed him. Clusters of stars and planets were shedding a bright lustre, right and left and in front of me, and I was passing through them. On the way I entered a sea of mist, where the stars and planets were no longer visible. After traversing the mist for some distance I came upon a still full moon, like a small island in that vaporous ocean. The nearer I came the larger grew that moon. It no longer appeared round, but flat like our earth. The apparition went and stood on that earth, and I did likewise. The ground was all of white marble. Not a single blade of grass was there—no flowers, no fruit. Only that bare white plain stretched all around. The moonlight there was not derived from the sun. It shone by virtue of its own light. The rays of the sun could not penetrate the surrounding mist. Its own light was very soft, like the shade we have in the daytime. The air was pleasing to the senses. In the course of my journey across this plain I entered one of its cities. All the houses and all the streets were of white marble, not a single soul was to be seen in the clean and bright and polished streets. No noise was to be heard, everything was calm and peaceful. My guide entered a house by the road and went up to the second floor, I also went with him. I found myself in a spacious room, in which there were a table and some chairs of white marble. He told me to sit down, and I sat down in one of the chairs. The phantom then vanished. Nobody else was there. I sat silent in that silent room; shortly afterwards the curtain of one of the doors in front of the room was drawn aside and my mother appeared. Her hair was down, just as I had seen it on the day of her death. When she died, I never thought that she was dead. Even when I came back from the burning ground after performing her funeral ceremonies, I could not believe that she was dead. I felt sure that she was still alive. Now I saw that living mother of mine before me. She said "I wanted to see thee, so I sent for thee. Hast thou really become one who has known Brahma? Sanctified is the family, fulfilled is the mother's desire." On seeing her, and hearing these sweet words of hers my slumber gave way before a flood of joy. I found myself still tossing on my bed.

The Brahmo Samaj and Its Relation to Orthodox Hinduism

After Keshub Chunder Sen had seceded from the Samaj, taking the majority of Brahmos with him, Debendranath pronounced in 1867 the following message on "gradualism" in matters of social reform.

[From Debendranath Tagore, *Autobiography*, pp. 152–53]

We are worshipers of Brahma, the Supreme Being. In this we are at one with Orthodox Hinduism, for all our shastras declare with one voice the supremacy of the worship of Brahma, enjoining image worship for the help of those who are incapable of grasping the highest Truth.

Our first point of distinction is in the positive aspect of our creed wherein worship is defined as consisting in "Loving Him and doing the works He loveth"—this at once differentiates us from all religions and creeds which postulate a special or verbal revelation or wherein definite forms, rites, or ceremonials are deemed essential one way or the other.

The negative aspect of our creed which prohibits the worship of any created being or thing as the Creator further distinguishes us from all who are addicted to the worship of avatars or incarnations or who believe in the necessity of mediators, symbols, or idols of any description.

We base our faith on the fundamental truths of religion, attested by reason and conscience and refuse to permit man, book, or image to stand in the way of the direct communion of our soul with the Supreme Spirit.

This message of the Brāhmo Samāj in the abstract does not materially differ from the doctrines of the pure theistic bodies all the world over. Viewed historically and socially, however, the Brāhmo Samāj has the further distinction of being the bearer of this message to the Hindu people.

This was the idea of its founder Ram Mohun Roy, this points to the duty incumbent upon all Brahmos of today, and will serve as the guiding principle in the selection of texts, forms, and ceremonials as aids to the religious life.

We are in and of the great Hindu community and it devolves upon us by example and precept to hold up as a beacon the highest truths of the Hindu shastras. In their light must we purify our heritage of customs, usages, rites, and ceremonies and adapt them to the needs of our conscience and our community. But we must beware of proceeding too fast in matters of social change, lest we be separated from the greater body whom we would guide and uplift.

While we should on no account allow any consideration of country, caste, or kinship to prevent our actions being consistent with our faith, we must make every allowance for, and abstain from, persecuting or alienating those who think differently from us. Why should we needlessly wound the feelings of our parents and elders by desecrating an image which they regard with the highest reverence, when all that our conscience can demand of us is to refrain from its adoration?

The steering of this middle course is by no means an easy task, but during my long experience I have been led greatly to hope for a brighter future by the sympathetic response of our orthodox brethren to the ideal held up before them. The amount of conformity nowadays expected by even the most orthodox, demands so little of us that a little tact and common sense will in most cases be sufficient to obviate all friction.

Nevertheless, great as are the claims of our land and our people, we must never forget that we are Brahmos first, and Indians or Hindus afterwards. We must on no account depart from our vow of renouncing the worship of images and incarnations, which is of the essence of our religion. It is a sound policy on our part to sink our minor differences, but on matters of principle no compromise is possible. Our Motherland is dear to us, but Religion is dearer, Brahma is dearest of all, dearer than son, dearer than riches, supreme over everything else.

KESHUB CHUNDER SEN AND THE INDIANIZATION OF CHRISTIANITY

The stormy career of Keshub Chunder Sen (or Keshab Chandra Sen) encompassed both the peak and the later decline of the influence of the Brahmo

Samaj on Indian intellectual life. With his great energy and oratorical skill, he brought to fulfillment the openness to Christian inspiration of Rammohun Roy and the intuitionist doctrine of Debendranath Tagore. Yet his very enthusiasm was his undoing, for by the time of his death he had shattered the Samaj into three separate organizations and damaged its prestige irrevocably.

Keshub's grandfather was a contemporary and friend of Rammohun Roy but did not share the great reformer's ideas on religion. The Sen family was one of the most Westernized in Bengal, and young Keshub grew up speaking English more fluently than Bengali. His career as a student at the Hindu College was marred by his failure in mathematics, but he took great interest in philosophy and ethics. At nineteen his religious spirit found its natural orbit in the Brahmo Samaj. Within a short time Keshub had become Debendranath's most beloved disciple. When he was excommunicated by his own family for having taken his wife to a Brahmo ceremony, Keshub found shelter in the home of his religious teacher.

With unquenchable energy, Keshub threw himself into the activities of the Brahmo Samaj, founding discussion groups and schools, organizing famine relief, advocating remarriage for widows and education for young women, writing religious tracts, and giving sermons. His fiery oratory in fluent English stirred educated audiences in many parts of India, especially in Bombay, and branches of the Samaj sprang up in cities beyond the borders of Bengal.

Keshub's zeal for social reform carried him far beyond the moderate position taken by Debendranath. When the two finally parted in 1865 over the wearing of the sacred thread, Keshub set up an independent organization that he named the Brahmo Samaj of India. From this point on, his faith in inspiration as the guide to action grew more pronounced. In 1878 another and more fatal fission took place within his own movement. Despite his prolonged advocacy of a minimum age for Brahmo marriages, and his opposition to idolatry, he was persuaded to marry his thirteen-year-old daughter to a Hindu prince, feeling that such was the will of God. Scandalized by this betrayal of his previous principles, most of his followers abandoned him and set up a third group, the Sadharan (General) Brahmo Samaj.

In the last years of his life, Keshub experimented in synthesizing elements from the world's major religions. Although he borrowed devotional and yogic practices from Hinduism, he drew even more heavily on Christian teachings and practices. The New Dispensation that he proclaimed in 1879 appropriated much from the Christian church that it claimed to supplant, including among other things a direct revelation from God, apostles, missionaries, monastic orders, and the doctrines of sin, salvation, and the divinity of Christ.

Of Keshub's work, little remained after his death in 1884 at the age of forty-five. The flaming enthusiasm that had launched him on so many enterprises, and the eloquent oratory that electrified so many audiences, left surprisingly few monuments. But the force of his example was felt in Bengal for decades, and his methods—particularly his oratorical conquests and his synthesizing of Indian and Western ideas—have been imitated by later religious leaders and nationalist politicians alike.

Enthusiasm

Two years before his death Keshub penetratingly summed up his nature and the activities into which it had plunged him.

[From Mozoomdar, *Life and Teachings of Keshub Chunder Sen,* pp. 15–16]

If I ask thee, O Self, in what creed wast thou baptized in early life? The self answers in the baptism of fire. I am a worshiper of the religion of fire, I am partial to the doctrine of enthusiasm. To me a state of being on fire is the state of salvation. My heart palpitates as soon as I perceive any coldness in my life. When the body becomes cold, it is death, when religion becomes cold, it is death also. It may take time to know whether I am a sinner or not, but it is easy to know whether I am alive or dead; I at once decide this by finding whether I am warm or cold. I live in the midst of fire, I love, embrace, and exalt fire. Every sign of heat fills me with joy, hope, zeal. As soon as I feel the fire is losing its heat, I feel as if I would jump into the sea and drown myself. When I find that a man after five years of enthusiasm is getting to be lukewarm, I at once conclude he is on the highway of a sinful life, that before long death will tread on his neck. I have always felt a cold condition to be a state of impurity. Coldness and hell have always been the same to my mind. Around my own life, around the society in which I lived, I always kept burning the flame of enthusiasm. When I succeeded in serving one body of men, I always sought another body whom I might serve. When I successfully worked in one department of life, I always sighed to work in other departments also. When I gathered truths from one set of scriptures, I have longed for others, and before finishing these I have looked out for others again, lest anything should become old or cold to me. This is my life that I am continually after new ideas, new acquirements, new enjoyments.

Loyalty to the British Nation

Keshub was only voicing the sentiments of his time when he declared British rule providential for India. His conviction that India had a reciprocal contribution to make to England was a relatively new idea, and one that was to take on increasing importance in the nationalist era. This speech was delivered in Calcutta in 1877, shortly after Queen Victoria had assumed the title of Empress of India.

[From "Philosophy and Madness in Religion," in *Keshub Chunder Sen's Lectures in India*, pp. 322–26]

Loyalty shuns an impersonal abstraction. It demands a person, and that person is the sovereign, or the head of the state, in whom law and constitutionalism are visibly typified and represented. We are right then if our loyalty means not only respect for law and the Parliament, but personal attachment to Victoria, Queen of England and Empress of India. [Applause.] What makes loyalty so enthusiastic is not, however, the presence of purely secular feelings, but of a strong religious sentiment. By loyalty I mean faith in Providence. It is this faith which gives loyalty all its sanctity and solidity, and establishes it in the individual heart and in society as a holy passion. Do you not believe that there is God in history? Do you not recognize the finger of special providence in the progress of nations? Assuredly the record of British rule in India is not a chapter of profane history, but of ecclesiastical history. [Cheers.] The book which treats of the moral, social, and religious advancement of our great country with the help of Western science, under the paternal rule of the British nation, is indeed a sacred book. There we see clearly that it is Providence that rules India through England. [Applause.] Were you present at the magnificent spectacle at Delhi, on the day of the assumption of the imperial title by our sovereign? Some men have complained that no religious ceremony was observed on the occasion, and indeed opinion is divided on this point. None, however, can gainsay the fact that the whole affair, from beginning to end

was a most solemn religious ceremony, and I rejoice I am privileged to say
this in the presence of our noble-hearted Viceroy. Was any devout believer
in Providence there? To him I appeal. Let him say whether the imperial
assemblage was not a spectacle of deep moral and religious significance. Did
not the eye of the faithful believer see that God Himself stretched His right
hand and placed the Empress' crown upon Victoria's head? [Loud cheers.]
And did he not hear the Lord God say unto her: "Rule thy subjects with
justice and truth and mercy, according to the light given unto thee and thy
advisers, and let righteousness and peace and prosperity dwell in the Empire"? [Applause.]

Would you characterize this sight and this sound as a visionary dream? Is
there no truth in the picture? Who can deny that Victoria is an instrument
in the hands of Providence to elevate this degraded country in the scale of
nations, and that in her hands the solemn trust has lately been most solemnly reposed? Glory then to Empress Victoria! [Applause.] Educated countrymen, you are bound to be loyal to your Divinely-appointed sovereign.
Not to be loyal argues base ingratitude and absence of faith in Providence.
You are bound to be loyal to the British government, that came to your
rescue, as God's ambassador, when your country was sunk in ignorance and
superstition and hopeless jejuneness, and has since lifted you to your present
high position. This work is not of man, but of God, and He has done it,
and is doing it, through the British nation. As His chosen instruments,
then, honor your sovereign and the entire ruling body with fervent loyalty.
The more loyal we are, the more we shall advance with the aid of our rulers
in the path of moral, social, and political reformation. India in her present
fallen condition seems destined to sit at the feet of England for many long
years, to learn Western art and science. And, on the other hand, behold
England sits at the feet of hoary-headed India to study the ancient literature
of this country. [Applause.] All Europe seems to be turning her attention
in these days towards Indian antiquities, to gather the priceless treasures
which lie buried in the literature of Vedism and Buddhism. Thus while we
learn modern science from England, England learns ancient wisdom from
India. Gentlemen, in the advent of the English nation in India we see a
reunion of parted cousins, the descendants of two different families of the
ancient Aryan race. Here they have met together, under an overruling
Providence, to serve most important purposes in the Divine economy. The
mutual intercourse between England and India, political as well as social, is
destined to promote the true interests and lasting glory of both nations. We

were rejoiced to see the rajahs and maharajahs of India offering their united homage to Empress Victoria and her representative at the imperial assemblage. Far greater will be our rejoicing when all the chiefs and people of India shall be united with the English nation, in a vast international assemblage, before the throne of the King of Kings and the Lord of Lords! [Loud cheers.] May England help us to draw near to that consummation, by giving us as much of the light of the West as lies in her power! That is her mission in India. May she fulfill it nobly and honorably. Let England give us her industry and arts, her exact sciences and her practical philosophy, so much needed in a land where superstition and prejudices prevail to an alarming extent. But we shall not forget our ancient sages and Rishis. Ye venerable devotees of ancient India! teach us meditation and asceticism and loving communion. Let England baptize us with the spirit of true philosophy. Let the sages of Aryan India baptize us with the spirit of heavenly madness. Let modern England teach hard science and fact; let ancient India teach sweet poetry and sentiment. Let modern England give us her fabrics; but let the gorgeous East lend her charming colors. Come then, fellow countrymen and friends, and accept this divine creed, in which you will find all that is goodliest, fairest, and sweetest, based upon a foundation scientific, strong and sound—a creed in which truth and love are harmonized. Let us have only fifty young men from our universities, trained in science and philosophy, and baptized with the spirit of madness, and let these men go forth as missionary-soldiers of God, conquering and to conquer, and in the fullness of time the banners of truth shall be planted throughout the length and breadth of the country. [Loud cheers.]

The Asiatic Christ

Whereas Rammohun Roy welcomed only the moral influence of Jesus, Keshub embraced Christ as the fulfillment of India's devotional striving. He also took Roy's assertion that Jesus was an Asian by birth and used it as an argument for better understanding between the rulers and the ruled in India.

[From "Jesus Christ: Europe and Asia," in *Keshub Chunder Sen's Lectures in India*, pp. 33–34]

Europeans and natives are both the children of God, and the ties of brotherhood should bind them together. Extend, then, to us, O ye Europeans in

India! the right hand of fellowship, to which we are fairly entitled. If, however, our Christian friends persist in traducing our nationality and national character, and in distrusting and hating Orientalism, let me assure them that I do not in the least feel dishonored by such imputations. On the contrary, I rejoice, yea, I am proud, that I am an Asiatic. And was not Jesus Christ an Asiatic? [Deafening applause.] Yes, and his disciples were Asiatics, and all the agencies primarily employed for the propagation of the Gospel were Asiatic. In fact, Christianity was founded and developed by Asiatics, and in Asia. When I reflect on this, my love for Jesus becomes a hundredfold intensified; I feel him nearer my heart, and deeper in my national sympathies. Why should I then feel ashamed to acknowledge that nationality which he acknowledged? Shall I not rather say he is more congenial and akin to my Oriental nature, more agreeable to my Oriental habits of thought and feeling? And is it not true that an Asiatic can read the imageries and allegories of the Gospel, and its descriptions of natural sceneries, of customs, and manners, with greater interest, and a fuller perception of their force and beauty, than Europeans? [Cheers.] In Christ we see not only the exaltedness of humanity, but also the grandeur of which Asiatic nature is susceptible. To us Asiatics, therefore, Christ is doubly interesting, and his religion is entitled to our peculiar regard as an altogether Oriental affair. The more this great fact is pondered, the less I hope will be the antipathy and hatred of European Christians against Oriental nationalities, and the greater the interest of the Asiatics in the teachings of Christ. And thus in Christ, Europe and Asia, the East and the West, may learn to find harmony and unity. [Deafening applause.]

An Indian National Church

With characteristic enthusiasm, Keshub saw in the simple theism of the Brahmo Samaj a platform on which the major religious traditions of India—Hindu, Muslim, Christian—could unite. The resulting faith, he thought, would sustain not only the future church of India, but would qualify India to take part in a worldwide religious brotherhood. Keshub's expectation that Hindus and Muslims would willingly merge into this national church is but one more example of his supreme optimism.

[From "The Future Church," in *Keshub Chunder Sen's Lectures in India*, pp. 155–60]

I have briefly described the general features of the church of the future—its worship, creed, and gospel. Before I conclude I must say a few words with special reference to this country. There are some among us who denounce Mahomedanism as wholly false, while others contend that Hinduism is altogether false. Such opinions are far from being correct; they only indicate the spirit of sectarian antipathy. Do you think that millions of men would to this day attach themselves so devotedly to these systems of faith unless there was something really valuable and true in them? This cannot be. There is, no doubt, in each of these creeds, much to excite to ridicule, and perhaps indignation—a large amount of superstition, prejudice, and even corruption. But I must emphatically say it is wrong to set down Hinduism or Mahomedanism as nothing but a mass of lies and abominations, and worthy of being trampled under foot. Proscribe and eliminate all that is false therein: there remains a residue of truth and purity which you are bound to honor. You will find certain central truths in these systems, though surrounded by errors, which constitute their vitality, and which have preserved them for centuries in spite of opposition, and in which hundreds of good men have always found the bread of life. It is these which form even now the mighty pillars of Hinduism and Mahomedanism, and challenge universal admiration and respect. It is idle to suppose that such gigantic systems of faith will be swept away by the fervor of youthful excitement, or the violent fulminations of sectarian bigotry, so long as there is real power in them. All the onslaughts which are being leveled against them in this age of free inquiry and bold criticism will tend, not to destroy them, but to purify them and develop their true principles. The signs of the times already indicate this process of purification and development; and I believe this process will gradually bring Hinduism and Mahomedanism, hitherto so hostile to each other, into closer union, till the two ultimately harmonize to form the future church of India.

The Hindu's notion of God is sublime. In the earliest Hindu scriptures God is represented as the Infinite Spirit dwelling in His own glory, and pervading all space, full of peace and joy. On the other hand, the Mahomedans describe their God as infinite in power, governing the universe with supreme authority as the Lord of all. Hence, the principal feature of the religion of the Hindu is quiet contemplation, while that of the religion of the Mahomedan is constant excitement and active service. The one lives in a state of quiet communion with his God of peace; the other lives as a soldier, ever serving the Almighty Ruler, and crusading against evil. These are the primary and essential elements of the two creeds, and, if blended together, would form a beautiful picture of true theology, which will be realized in the future church of this country. As the two creeds undergo development, their errors and differences will disappear, and they will harmoniously coalesce in their fundamental and vital principles. The future creed of India will be a composite faith, resulting from the union of the true and divine elements of Hinduism and Mahomedanism, and showing the profound devotion of the one and the heroic enthusiasm of the other. The future sons and daughters of this vast country will thus inherit precious legacies from Hinduism and Mahomedanism, and, while enjoying the blessings of the highest and sweetest communion with the God of love, will serve Him in the battlefield of life with fidelity to truth and unyielding opposition to untruth and sin. As regards Christianity and its relation to the future church of India, I have no doubt in my mind that it will exercise great influence on the growth and formation of that church. The spirit of Christianity has already pervaded the whole atmosphere of Indian society, and we breathe, think, feel, and move in a Christian atmosphere. Native society is being roused, enlightened, and reformed under the influence of Christian education. If it is true that the future of a nation is determined by all the circumstances and agencies which today influence its nascent growth, surely the future church of this country will be the result of the purer elements of the leading creeds of the day, harmonized, developed, and shaped under the influence of Christianity.

But the future church of India must be thoroughly national; it must be an essentially Indian church. The future religion of the world I have described will be the common religion of all nations, but in each nation it will have an indigenous growth, and assume a distinctive and peculiar character. All mankind will unite in a universal church; at the same time, it will be adapted to the peculiar circumstances of each nation, and assume a national form. No country will borrow or mechanically imitate the religion of another country; but from the depths of the life of each nation its future church will naturally grow up. And shall not India have its own national church?

DAYANANDA SARASWATI: VEDIC REVIVALIST

While Keshub Chunder Sen was preaching an Indianized version of Christianity in Bengal, a stern ascetic arose in North India who vigorously rejected all religions, Indian or foreign—except the one he believed to have been practiced by the ancient Aryans. Swami Dayananda Saraswati (1824–

1883) was an even more ardent reformer than Keshub, yet he drew his inspiration purely from indigenous sources. Standing foursquare on his interpretation of the Vedas, he fearlessly denounced the evils of post-Vedic Hinduism.

Dayananda was born into a brahman family in a princely state of Gujarat, a section of western India relatively untouched by British cultural influence. His well-to-do father instructed him in Sanskrit and Shaivism from the age of five, but Dayananda revolted against idol-worship at fourteen and, to avoid being married, ran away from home at nineteen to become a sannyāsī (religious mendicant) of the Saraswati order. He spent the next fifteen years as a wandering ascetic, living in jungles, in Himalayan retreats, and at places of pilgrimage throughout northern India. A tough, blind old teacher completed his education by literally beating into him a reverence for the four Vedas and a disdain for all later scriptures.

For the rest of his life Dayananda lectured in all parts of India on the exclusive authority of the Vedas. Time after time he challenged all comers to religious debates, but few could withstand his forceful forensic attack. Idol-worship is not sanctioned by the Vedas, he pointed out, nor is untouchability, nor child marriage, nor the subjection of women to unequal status with men. The study of the Vedas should be open to all, not just to brāhmans, and a man's caste should be in accordance with his merits. Such revolutionary teachings evoked the wrath of the orthodox, and numerous attempts were made on Dayananda's life. His great physical strength saved him from swordsmen, thugs, and cobras, but the last of many attempts to poison him succeeded. Like John the Baptist, he accused a princely ruler of loose living, and the woman in question (so we are told) demanded his death.

Dayananda's energetic and sometimes acrimonious method of disputation signaled the shift among those Hindu religious leaders who were aware of the challenge of Christianity from an assimilative or defensive attitude to an active, aggressive one. His claims were sometimes extravagant, however, as, for example, his assertion that firearms were made and used in ancient India. His followers dubbed him "the Luther of India," an analogy that is quite apt, considering the fervor of his reforms, the great importance he attached to the Vedas as a holy "book," and his stress on doing good works as well as adhering to the true faith. The Arya Samaj (the Society of the Āryas, or "noble men"), which he established at Bombay in 1875 and refounded at Lahore in 1877, has since reflected the militant character of its founder and, from its stronghold in the Punjab, has contributed to the militancy of Hindu nationalism.

Of Mice and Idols

A major turning point in Dayananda's life came when he was fourteen and observed for the first time a special all-night fast and vigil in honor of the god Shiva. What his father accepted unthinkingly caused in him a revulsion that led him, four years later as he meditated on the death of his sister, to decide to "violently break, and for ever, with the mummeries of external mortification and penances, and the more to appreciate the inward efforts of the soul."[7]

[From *Autobiography of Swami Dayanand Saraswati*, pp. 12–16]

My family belonged to the *Shaiva*[8] sect, and they very much wished to see me initiated into its religious mysteries. In consequence, I was taught to worship the uncouth piece of clay representing *Shiva*'s emblem—the *Parthiva Lingam*. But as there was a good deal of fasting and various hardships connected with this worship, and I had the habit of taking early meals, my mother, fearing that it might tell upon my health, opposed it. But my father seriously insisted upon it and this eventually became a source of acrimonious quarrel between my parents.

Meanwhile, I studied Sanskrit grammar and learnt some *Vedic* text by heart. I accompanied my father to the shrines, temples and other places where *Shiva* was worshipped. My father's conversation always touched upon one topic: the highest devotion and reverence must be paid to *Shiva* for he was the most divine of all gods.

It went on thus until I had reached my fourteenth year (A.D. 1838) when having learnt by heart the whole of the *Yajurveda*, parts of other *Vedas* and grammar works, such as *Shabdarupawaii*,[9] I completed my education.

In that year—1838—my father, unmindful of my mother's remonstrances, ordered that I should begin practising *Parthiva pujanam*.[10] Accordingly, when the great day of fasting, called *Shivaratri*[11] came, my father after reciting the sacred legend on the *Magha Badi* 13 (Jan.–Feb. 1838) commanded me to observe fast and to participate in the night long vigil in the temple of *Shiva*. I obeyed him and went to the temple where the townspeople were going with their children.

The *Shivaratri* vigil is divided into four *praharas* of three hours each. After the first two *praharas* I saw that the *pujaris* (the priests) and some lay devotees had left the temple and lay asleep outside it. Having been taught for years that by sleeping on that particular night, the worshipper lost all charm of his devotion, I tried to refrain from sleeping by washing my eyes now and then with cold water. My father was, however, less fortunate in this respect. He fell asleep, leaving me to watch alone a miracle which happened just then: a mouse came out of its hide-out and began to wander around the idol of *Shiva*. Not only that, it even climbed on the idol and ate away the *akshata* (offerings) too.

Now thoughts upon thoughts and questions upon questions crowded upon and disturbed my mind. "Is it possible", I asked myself, "that he was the same *Mahadeva*,[12] the semblance of man, the idol of a personal god that I see bestriding his bull before me, and who, according to religious accounts, walks about, eats, sleeps, and drinks, and who holds a trident in his hand, beats his *dumroo* (drum) and pronounces curses upon men? Is he the one who is invoked as the Lord of *Kailasha*,[13] the supreme being and the divine hero of all the stories we read of him in the *Puranas.*"

Unable to resist such thoughts any longer, I awoke my father and asked him to tell me whether the hideous emblem of *Shiva* in the temple was identical with the *Mahadeva* of the scriptures? "Why do you ask this?" enquired my father. "I feel it is impossible", I replied, "to reconcile to the idea of an omnipotent, living god, with this idol which allows the mice to run over his body and thus suffers his image to be polluted without the slightest protest."

My father tried to explain to me that this stone representation of the *Mahadeva* of *Kailasha*, having been consecrated by the holy *Brahmans*, became in consequence the god himself, and is worshipped and regarded as such. As *Shiva* cannot be perceived, he further added, in this *Kali-Yuga*,[14] we have the idol in which the *Mahadeva* of *Kailasha* is imagined by his votaries. This kind of worship pleases the great deity as much as if instead of the emblem he were there himself. But the explanation fell short of satisfying me. I could not help suspecting misinterpretation and sophistry in all this. Feeling weak with hunger and fatigue I begged to be allowed to go home. My father consented to it, and sent me away with a sepoy, reiterating that I should not break my fast. But when once home, I told my mother of my hunger, she fed me with sweetmeats, and I fell into a profound sleep.

In the morning, when my father returned home and learned that I had broken my fast, he felt very angry. He tried to impress me with the enormity of my sin. But I could not make myself believe that the idol and *Mahadeva* were one and the same god, and, therefore, could not comprehend why I should be made to fast for and worship the former. I had, however, to conceal my lack of faith, and bring forward as an excuse for abstaining from regular worship my study, which really left me little or no time for anything else. In this I was strongly supported by my mother and my uncle, who pleaded my case so well that my father had to yield. I was allowed to devote my whole attention to my studies.

A Debate with a Christian and a Muslim

Dayananda loved to engage in religious debates, usually with orthodox Hindus, but occasionally with representatives of other faiths. The following summary of his 1877 debate with a Christian minister and a Muslim *maulvi*[15] gives a good picture of his harshly critical attitude toward their respective religions—an attitude that led his later followers into intermittent friction with India's Muslims.

[From Har Bilas Sarda, *Life of Dayanand Saraswati*, pp. 170–72]

As time was short, after some talk it was decided that the question "What is salvation and how to attain it," should be discussed. As both the Christians and the Muslims declined to open the debate, Swamiji opened it. He said:

"Mukti or salvation means deliverance, in other words, to get rid of all suffering, and to realize God, to remain happy and free from rebirth. Of the means to attain it, the first is to practice truth, that is truth which is approved both by one's conscience and God. That is truth, in uttering which, one gets encouragement, happiness, and fearlessness. In uttering untruth, fear, doubt, and shame are experienced. As the third mantra of the fortieth chapter of Yajurveda says, those who violate God's teachings, that is, those who speak, act, or believe against one's conscience are called Asur, Rakkhshas, wicked and sinful. The second means to attain salvation is to acquire knowledge of the Vedas and follow truth. The third means is to associate with men of truth and knowledge. The fourth is by practicing Yoga, to eliminate untruth from the mind and the soul, and to fix it in truth. The fifth is to recite the qualities of God and meditate on them. The sixth is to pray to God to keep one steadfast in truth (gyana), realization of the reality and dharma, to keep one away from untruth, ignorance and adharma, and to free one from the woes of birth and death and obtain mukti. When a man worships God wholeheartedly and sincerely, the merciful God gives him happiness. Salvation, dharma, material gain and fulfillment of desires, and attainment of truth are the results of one's efforts, and not otherwise. To act according to the teaching of God is dharma and violation of it is adharma. Only rightful means should be adopted to attain success and prosperity. Injustice, untruth and unrighteous means should not be made use of to gain happiness."

Rev. Scott said:

"Salvation does not mean deliverance from woes. Salvation only means to be saved from sins and to obtain Heaven. God had created Adam pure, but he was misled by Satan and committed sin which made all his descendants sinful. Man commits sin of his own accord as the clock works by itself, that is to say, one cannot avoid committing sin by one's own effort and so cannot get salvation. One can obtain salvation only by believing in Christ. Wherever Christianity spreads, people are saved from sin. I have attained salvation by believing in Christ."

Maulvi Muhammad Hasim said:

"God does what he wishes to do; whom He wishes He gives salvation, just as a judge acquits those with whom he is pleased and punishes those with whom he is displeased. God does what He likes. He is beyond our control. We must trust whoever is the ruler for the time being. Our Prophet is the ruler of the present time. We can get salvation by putting our trust in Him. With knowledge we can do good work, but moksha or salvation lies in His hands."

Swamiji replied that:

"Suffering is the necessary result of sin; whoever avoids sin will be saved from suffering. The Christians believe God to be powerful; but to believe that Satan misled Adam to commit sin is to believe that God is not All powerful; for, if God had been All powerful, Satan could not have misled Adam, who had been created pure by God. No sensible man can believe that Adam committed sin and all his descendants became sinful. *He alone undergoes suffering who commits sin; no one else.* You say that Satan misleads everyone, I therefore ask you who misled Satan. If you say no one misled him, then as Satan misled himself, so must Adam have done it. Why believe in Satan then? If you say, somebody else must have misled Satan, then the only one who could have done it was God. In that case when God himself misleads and gets others to commit sin, then how can He save people from sin. Satan disturbs and spoils God's creation, but God neither punishes him nor imprisons him, nor puts him to death. This proves that God is powerless to do so. Those who believe in Satan cannot avoid committing sins, for they believe that Satan gets them to commit sin and they themselves are not sinful. Again, when God's only son suffered crucifixion for the sins of all people, then the people need not be afraid of being punished for their sins and they can go on committing sins with impunity. The illustration of the clock given by the Padree sahib is also inappropriate. "The clock works only as its *maker has given it the power* to do. The clock cannot alter it. Then again how can you continue to live in Paradise. Adam was misled there by Satan into eating wheat. Will you not eat wheat and be expelled from Paradise? You gentlemen believe God to be like a man. Man has limited knowledge and does not know everything, he therefore stands in need of recommendation of someone who possesses knowledge. But God is All-knowing and All-powerful. He does not stand in need of any recommendation or help from any prophet or anyone else; otherwise, where would be the difference between God and man? Nor does He according to you remain just, for He does not do justice, if he pardons the culprit on the recommendations of anybody. If God is present everywhere, He cannot have a body; for if he has a body, He will be subject to limitation and will not be infinite, and then he must be subject to birth and death. Is God incapable of saving his worshipers without Christ's intervention? Nor has God any need of a prophet. It is true that where there are good people in a country, people improve because of good men's teachings. As regards the Maulvi sahib, he is wrong in saying that God does what He likes, because then He does not remain just. As a fact, he gives salvation only to those whose works deserve it. Without sin and righteousness there can be no suffering and no happiness. God is the ruler for all time. If God gives salvation on the recommendation of others, he becomes dependent. God is All-powerful. It is a matter of surprise that though the Mussalmans believe God to be one and without a second, yet they made the prophet take part with God in bestowing salvation."

The Parable of the Preceptor and His Two Disciples

Dayananda frequently condemned the followers of the various Hindu sects for their irreverent theological quarrels.

[From Dayananda, *The Light of Truth*, pp. 431–32]

A hermit had two disciples. They massaged the feet of their preceptor. For convenience's sake, they had distributed their work. One had the charge of one leg and the other of the other. One day it so happened that one of the disciples had gone to the market and the other was massaging the leg in his charge. As the preceptor changed sides the leg assigned to the absent disciple happened to fall on the leg under massage. The disciple took a cudgel and gave a blow to that leg. The preceptor cried, "O villain! what hast thou done?" The disciple answered, "What business had this leg to fall on the leg assigned to me?" In the meantime the other disciple who had gone for shopping returned. He began to massage the foot assigned to him. But when he saw swelling on the leg he asked, "Preceptor, how is this leg of mine swollen?" The preceptor told the story. That fool also said nothing, but instantly getting hold of a stick, gave a strong stroke to the other leg of the preceptor. The preceptor began to cry. The disciples belaboured his legs one after another. The noise attracted the neighbours. They came and asked, "Well father! what is the matter?" A wise man among them somehow disentangled the disciples and explained to them that both the feet belonged to the preceptor; the main object of their serving the preceptor was to give him pleasure; it was he who suffered on account of their foolish deed.

The analogy holds good in the case of these cults of Shaivism, Vaisnavism etc., which run down each other not knowing the correct meaning of these words visnu, rudra etc., which are really speaking different names of the same indivisible, infinite, supreme being. These foolish people do not at all think that Visnu, Rudra, Shiva etc., are the names signifying various aspect of the qualities, and nature of the same lord of the universe who is all governing, all pervading, one-without-the-second. How can such fools escape the displeasure of God?

Against the Hindu Reform Movements of the Nineteenth Century

[From Dayananda, *The Light of Truth*, pp. 548–49]

Q.—The Brāhma Samāja and Prārthanā Samāja are all good. Their principles are very good.

A.—1. They are not good in all respects. How can the principles of these who are unaware of the Vedic lore be all good. They saved many persons from the clutches of Christianity, they removed idolatory also to a certain extent, and they protected people from the snares of certain spurious scriptures. These are all good points. But they are lacking in patriotism. They have borrowed much from Christianity in their way of living. They have also changed the rules of marriage etc.

2. Instead of praising their country and glorifying their ancestors, they speak ill of them. In their lectures they eulogize Christians and Englishmen. They do not even mention the names of old sages, Brahmā etc. But they say that there was never a learned man like the English people from the very creation of the world, that Indians have all along remained ignorant, and that they never made any progress.

3. Not only do they not respect the Vedas etc. but they do not desist from condemning them. The books of the Brāhma Samāja include among the saints Christ, Moses, Mohammad, Nānāka and Chaitanyā. They do not mention even the name of ṛshis and sages of ancient India. This shows that their religion also derives its tenets from the personages whose names have been mentioned in their books. When they are born in the Aryāvartta,[16] they have eaten food and drunk water of this country, and are still doing the same, it does not behove them to abandon the path of their ancestors and incline to alien faiths. The Brāhma Samājīsts and Prāthanā Samājīsts call themselves educated, though they have no knowledge of the literature of their own country, i.e., Sanskṛta. No permanent sort of reform is expected from those who, in their pride for English education, are ready to launch a new religion.

4. They observe no restrictions on interdining with Englishmen, Moslems and low class people. They are perhaps under the impression that they and their country would be regenerated simply by removing the restriction of food and caste.

The Virtues of Europeans

Even though he disliked Christianity, Swami Dayananda was impressed by the moral qualities of India's Christian rulers.

[From Dayananda, *The Light of Truth*, pp. 549–50]

Q.—We see that the Europeans have made so much progress because they wear round-toed shoes, coats, pants etc. and eat in hotels, food cooked by any person.

A.—You are mistaken. Moslems and low caste people eat food cooked by any one, yet they have made no progress. The advancement of the Eu-

ropeans is due to the following points; absence of early marriage; good education of boys and girls; marriage according to the choice of the married
couple; no preaching by undesirable persons; they educate themselves and
do not fall into the snares of anybody; whatever they do is done with mutual consultation; they devote their body, soul and wealth to the well-being
of their country; they are not indolent and work very hard; they allow into
their offices and courts only English shoes and not Indian shoes. This one
point is sufficient to show how patriotic they are—they respect the shoes of
their country more than they respect the men of other countries. These
Europeans have come into this country for a little more than a hundred
years, yet wear coarse clothes as they do in their own country. They have
not forsaken the way of their country. Many of you have copied their ways.
This shows that they are wise and you are foolish. Copying is not a sign of
wisdom. These Europeans are very dutiful and well disciplined. They always
help the trade of their country. These qualifications and deeds have contributed to their advancement, and not round toed shoes, coat, pant; eating
in hotels, or other evils.

And see, they have class distinction also. When a European marries a
foreign girl or a European girl marries a foreign man, however big and respectable they may be, they cease to be invited to dinners by other Europeans. What is it if not a class distinction? They exploit your simplicity
when they say that they have no class-distinctions, and you readily believe
them owing to your simplicity. Therefore, whatever is done should be done
after full consideration, so that one may not regret afterwards.

A Summary of His Beliefs

In the final section of his Hindi masterwork,[17] Dayananda restated his religious
beliefs and his ideals for the man of active virtue—ideals very similar to those his
fellow Gujarati M. K. Gandhi was later to adopt as his own guide through life.

From Dayananda, *The Light of Truth*, pp. 846–47

The Sanātan Dhārma or Eternal Religion is that set of universal doctrines
which belong to all countries and all men, which were accepted in the past,
are being accepted in the present, and shall be accepted in future by everybody and which it is impossible for anybody to go against. Wise men never
conform with anything promulgated by those who are ignorant or misled by

the teachings of a particular faith. All persons should accept as their beliefs only those principles which are inculcated by men of profound learning (adepts), i.e. the persons who think the truth, speak the truth and do the truth and are philanthropic and impartial. Similarly their disbelief should consist of those things which such persons reject as unworthy of acceptance. I declare before all right-thinking people that I believe in all those things (God etc.) which are accepted by the Vedas and other true scriptures and which have been the beliefs of all persons from Brahmā down to the sage Jaimini.[18] My beliefs are only those which should be uniformly acceptable to all men in all ages (three times, past, present and future). I have no intention whatever to introduce a new thing or to found a new religion. My wish is to accept and to ask others to accept what is truth; and to reject and to ask others to reject what is untruth. Had I been partial, I would have clung to any one of faiths prevalent in the Āryāvartta. But neither I accept the demerits of different faiths whether Indian or alien, nor reject what is good in them. In fact it does not behove a man to do so. Only he is entitled to be called 'man' who thinks and looks upon the happiness, unhappiness, loss and profit of other men as his own, who is not afraid of a strong man if he is unjust, and fears a virtuous man even though he is weak. Not only this. He should always try to support the case of the virtuous people even if they are helpless, weak and untalented, and to discourage, suppress and even destroy the vicious, even if he is the mightiest sovereign of the whole world and very clever. That is, he should spare no pains to make the vicious weak and the virtuous strong. To achieve this end, he should bear all sufferings and even sacrifice his life but he should not quit his duty.

SHRI RAMAKRISHNA: MYSTIC AND SPIRITUAL TEACHER

Shri Ramakrishna (1836–1886) was among the most saintly of the many religious leaders to whom modern India has given birth. A son of Bengal, like Debendranath and Keshub, he was, unlike them, a child of the soil and never lost his rustic simplicity. Like Dayananda, he personified the rebirth of an ancient tradition in the midst of an era of increasing Westernization and modernization. But, unlike that militant Gujarati, he practiced and preached a gentle faith of selfless devotion to God and of ultimate absorption in Him.

Ramakrishna imbibed from his boyhood days as the son of a village priest the spirit of devotion to Kālī, the Divine Mother, which the songs of Rāmaprasād had made popular in rural Bengal in the eighteenth century. (See volume 1, chapter 12) Ecstatic communion with the Divine, an aspect of this tradition, came naturally to the attractive young brāhman, and at the age of seven he experienced his first mystical trance. He received no formal education in Sanskrit or English and could read and write Bengali only moderately well. Yet this "God-intoxicated" man attained to wisdom that was the envy of many of his enlightened, English-educated contemporaries.

His elder brother took him at sixteen to Calcutta, where they were eventually installed as priests of a new temple on the Hooghly River, a branch of the Ganges. For the next twelve years Ramakrishna put himself through every known type of spiritual discipline in an agonized search for God. Finally his efforts were rewarded with a series of mystical experiences during which he saw God in a variety of manifestations—as a Divine Mother, as Sītā, as Rāma, as Krishna, as Muhammad, as Jesus Christ, and worshiped Him in the manner of Muslims, Jains, and Buddhists—in each case suiting his dress, food, and meditation to the particular religious tradition concerned.

Through the aid of Keshub Chunder Sen, who greatly admired him, Ramakrishna began to attract disciples from among the Westernized middle class of Calcutta. His keen insight into the hearts of men made him an excellent teacher, and his natural simplicity and purity made a profound impression on these young men. From him they learned to draw strength from the living traditions of popular Hinduism; through them his teachings became known to all India and the world at large.

The World As Seen by a Mystic

Ramakrishna lived in a state of consciousness so close to continual meditation that he was able to see great meaning in the smallest incidents. One of his disciples collected his sayings and anecdotes as he related them. They show us the world as he saw it—a world permeated by the presence of the Divine.

[From *The Gospel of Ramakrishna*, pp. 207–14]

I practiced austerities for a long time. I cared very little for the body. My longing for the Divine Mother was so great that I would not eat or sleep. I would lie on the bare ground, placing my head on a lump of earth, and cry out loudly: "Mother, Mother, why dost Thou not come to me?" I did not know how the days and nights passed away. I used to have ecstasy all the time. I saw my disciples as my own people, like children and relations, long before they came to me. I used to cry before my Mother, saying: "O Mother! I am dying for my beloved ones (Bhaktas); do Thou bring them to me as quickly as possible."

At that time whatever I desired came to pass. Once I desired to build a small hut in the Panchavati[19] for meditation and to put a fence around it. Immediately after I saw a huge bundle of bamboo sticks, rope, strings, and even a knife, all brought by the tide in front of the Panchavati. A servant of the Temple, seeing these things, ran to me with great delight and told me of them. There was the exact quantity of material necessary for the hut and the fence. When they were built, nothing remained over. Everyone was amazed to see this wonderful sight.

When I reached the state of continuous ecstasy, I gave up all external forms of worship; I could no longer perform them. Then I prayed to my Divine Mother: "Mother, who will now take care of me? I have no power to take care of myself. I like to hear Thy name and feed Thy Bhaktas and help the poor. Who will make it possible for me to do these things? Send me someone who will be able to do these for me." As the answer to this prayer came Mathura Bābu,[20] who served me so long and with such intense devotion and faith! Again at another time I said to the Mother: "I shall have no child of my own, but I wish to have as my child a pure Bhakta, who will stay with me all the time. Send me such an one." Then came Rākhāl (Brahmānanda).

Those who are my own are parts of my very Self.

In referring to the time of joyous illumination that immediately followed His enlightenment, He exclaimed:

II

What a state it was! The slightest cause aroused in me the thought of the Divine Ideal. One day I went to the Zoological Garden in Calcutta. I desired especially to see the lion, but when I beheld him, I lost all sense-consciousness and went into samādhi.[21] Those who were with me wished to show me the other animals, but I replied: "I saw everything when I saw the king of beasts. Take me home." The strength of the lion had aroused in me the consciousness of the omnipotence of God and had lifted me above the world of phenomena.

Another day I went to the parade ground to see the ascension of a balloon. Suddenly my eyes fell upon a young English boy leaning against a tree. The very posture of his body brought before me the vision of the form of Krishna and I went into samādhi.

Again I saw a woman wearing a blue garment under a tree. She was a harlot. As I looked at her, instantly the ideal of Sītā[22] appeared before me! I forgot the existence of the harlot, but saw before me pure and spotless Sītā, approached Rāma, the Incarnation of Divinity, and for a long time I remained motionless. I worshiped all women as representatives of the Divine Mother. I realized the Mother of the universe in every woman's form.

Mathura Bābu, the son-in-law of Rāshmoni, invited me to stay in his house for a few days. At that time I felt so strongly that I was the maidservant of my Divine Mother that I thought of myself as a woman. The ladies of the house had the same feeling; they did not look upon me as a man. As women are free before a young girl, so were they before me. My mind was above the consciousness of sex.

What a Divine state it was! I could not eat here in the Temple. I would walk from place to place and enter into the house of strangers after their meal hour. I would sit there quietly, without uttering a word. When questioned, I would say: "I wish to eat here." Immediately they would feed me with the best things they had.

III

Once I heard of a poor Brāhmin who was a true devotee and who lived in a small hut in Bāghbāzār. I desired to see him, so I asked Mathura Bābu to take me to him. He consented, immediately ordered a large carriage, and drove me there. The Brāhmin's house was so small that he scarcely had room to receive us, and he was much surprised to see me coming with such a rich man in such a carriage!

At another time I wished to meet [Debendranath] Tagore. He is a very rich man, but in spite of his enormous wealth he is devoted to God and repeats His Holy Name. For this reason I desired to know him. I spoke about him to Mathura Bābu. He replied: "Very well, Bābā,[23] I will take Thee to him; he was my classmate." So he took me and introduced me to

him, saying: "This holy man has come to see you. He is mad after God." I
saw in him a little pride and egotism. It is natural for a man who has so
much wealth, culture, fame, and social position. I said to Mathura Bābu:
"Tell me, does pride spring from true wisdom or from ignorance? He who
has attained to the highest knowledge of Brāhman cannot possess pride or
egotism, such as 'I am learned,' 'I am wise,' 'I am rich,' and so on." While
I was speaking with [Debendranath] Tagore, I went into a state from where
I could see the true character of every individual. In this state the most
learned pandits and scholars appear to me like blades of grass. When I see
that scholars have neither true discrimination nor dispassion, then I feel
that they are like straws; or they seem like vultures who soar high in the
heavens, but keep their minds on the charnel-pits below on the earth. In
[Debendranath] I found both spiritual knowledge and worldly desire. He has
a number of children, some of whom are quite young. A doctor was present.
I said: "When you have so much spiritual knowledge, how can you live
constantly in the midst of so much worldliness? You are like Rājā Janaka;[24]
you can keep your mind on God, remaining amid worldly pleasures and
luxury. Therefore I have come to see you. Tell me something of the Divine
Being." [Debendranath] then read some passages from the Vedas and said:
"This world is like a chandelier, and each Jiva (individual soul) is like a
light in it." Long ago, when I spent nearly all my time meditating at the
Panchavati, I saw the same thing. When [Debendranath's] words harmonized with my experience, I knew that he must have attained to some true
knowledge. I asked him to explain. He said: "Who would have known this
world? God has created man to manifest His glory. If there were no light
in the chandelier, it would be all dark. The chandelier itself would not be
visible." After a long conversation [Debendranath] Tagore begged me to
come to the anniversary of the Brāhmo-Samāj. I answered: "If it be the will
of the Lord. I go wherever He takes me."

Fix Your Mind on God

During one of his visits with Keshub Chunder Sen and his disciples, Ramakrishna
advised the Brahmos to cultivate the liberating powers of the mind.

[From *The Gospel of Ramakrishna*, pp. 158–60]

A Brāhmo: Revered Sir, is it true that God cannot be realized without
giving up the world?

The Bhagavān,[25] smiling: Oh no! You do not have to give up everything. You are better off where you are. By living in the world you are enjoying the taste of both the pure crystallized sugar and of the molasses with all its impurities. You are indeed better off. Verily I say unto you, you are living in the world, there is no harm in that; but you will have to fix your mind on God, otherwise you cannot realize Him. Work with one hand and hold the Feet of the Lord with the other. When you have finished your work, fold His feet to your heart with both your hands.

Everything is in the mind. Bondage and freedom are in the mind. You can dye the mind with any color you wish. It is like a piece of clean white linen: dip it in red and it will be red, in blue it will be blue, in green it will be green, or any other color. Do you not see that if you study English, English words will come readily to you? Again, if a pandit studies Sanskrit, he will readily quote verse from Sacred Books. If you keep your mind in evil company, your thoughts, ideas, and words will be colored with evil; but keep in the company of Bhaktas, then your thoughts, ideas and words will be of God. The mind is everything. On one side is the wife, on the other side is the child; it loves the wife in one way and the child in another way, yet the mind is the same.

By the mind one is bound; by the mind one is freed. If I think I am absolutely free, whether I live in the world or in the forest, where is my bondage? I am the child of God, the son of the King of kings; who can bind me? When bitten by a snake, if you assert with firmness: "There is no venom in me," you will be cured. In the same way, he who asserts with strong conviction: "I am not bound, I am free," becomes free.

Some one gave me a book of the Christians. I asked him to read it to me. In it there was only one theme—sin and sin, from the beginning to the end. (To Keshub) In your Brāhmo-Samāj the main topic is also sin. The fool who repeats again and again: "I am bound. I am bound," remains in bondage. He who repeats day and night: "I am a sinner, I am a sinner," becomes a sinner indeed.

Beware of the Wicked

Ramakrishna's advice to his disciples was often of a very practical nature, as this example shows.

[From *The Gospel of Ramakrishna*, pp. 42–44]

One of the devotees present said: But when a person is annoyed with me, Bhagavān, I feel unhappy. I feel that I have not been able to love everyone equally.

Rāmakrishna: When you feel that way, you should have a talk with that person and try to make peace with him. If you fail after such attempts, then you need not give it further thought. Take refuge with the Lord. Think upon Him. Do not let your mind be disturbed by any other thing.

Devotee: Christ and Chaitanya have both taught us to love all mankind.

Rāmakrishna: You should love everyone because God dwells in all beings. But to wicked people you should bow down at a distance. (To Bijoy, smiling): Is it true that people blame you because you mix with those who believe in a Personal God with form? A true devotee of God should possess absolute calmness and never be disturbed by the opinions of others. Like a blacksmith's anvil, he will endure all blows and persecutions and yet remain firm in his faith and always the same. Wicked people may say many things about you and blame you; but if you long for God, you should endure with patience. One can think on God even dwelling in the midst of wicked people. The sages of ancient times, who lived in forests, could meditate on God although surrounded by tigers, bears, and other wild beasts. The nature of the wicked is like that of a tiger or bear. They attack the innocent and injure them. You should be especially cautious in coming in contact with the following: First, the wealthy. A person who possesses wealth and many attendants can easily do harm to another if he so desires. You should be very guarded in speaking with him; sometimes it may even be necessary to agree with him in his opinion. Second, a dog. When a dog barks at you, you must not run, but talk to him and quiet him. Third, a bull. When a bull chases you, you should always pacify him by talking to him. Fourth, a drunkard. If you make him angry, he will call you names and swear at you. You should address him as a dear relative, then he will be happy and obliging.

When wicked people come to see me, I am very careful. The character of some of them is like that of a snake. They may bite you unawares. It may take a long time and much discrimination to recover from the effects of that bite. Or you may get so angry at them that you will wish to take revenge. It is necessary, however, to keep occasionally the company of holy men. Through such association right discrimination will come.

Parables and Sayings

There is much in Ramakrishna's homely yet charming wisdom that is based on experiences from everyday life, experiences that are used to illustrate profound moral and religious truths.

[From *Teachings of Sri Ramakrishna*, pp. 31–94, 351]

The vegetables in the cooking pot move and leap till the children think they are living beings. But the grown-ups explain that they are not moving of themselves; if the fire be taken away they will soon cease to stir. So it is ignorance that thinks "I am the doer." All our strength is the strength of God. All is silent if the fire be removed. A marionette dances well, while the wires are pulled; but when the master's hand is gone, it falls inert. [p. 31]

The guru said: "Everything that exists is God," and the disciple understood this literally. Passing along the road, he met an elephant. The driver shouted from his high place: "Move away, move away!" But the disciple thought: "Why should I move away? I am God and so is the elephant. What fear can God have of himself?" Thinking thus he did not move. At last the elephant took him by his trunk and dashed him aside. He was severely hurt, and going back to his guru, he told his story. The guru said: "It is quite true that you are God. It is true that the elephant is God too, but God was also in the form of the elephant-driver. Why did you not listen to the God on top?" [p. 46]

At a game of chess the onlookers can tell what is the correct move better than the players themselves. Men of the world think they are very clever; but they are attached to things of this world—money, honors, pleasure, etc. Being actually engaged in the play it is hard for them to hit upon the right move. Holy men who have given up the world are not attached to it. They are like the onlookers at a game of chess. They see things in their true light and can judge better than the men of the world. [p. 68]

As a nail cannot be driven into a stone, yet it enters easily into the earth, so the advice of the pious does not affect the soul of a worldly man, while it pierces deep into the heart of a believer. [p. 94]

A man woke up at midnight and desired to smoke. He wanted a light, so he went to a neighbor's house and knocked at the door. Someone opened the door and asked him what he wanted. The man said: "I wish to smoke. Can you give me a light?" The neighbor replied: "Bah! What is the matter with you? You have taken so much trouble to come and [awaken] us at this hour, when in your hand you have a lighted lantern!" What a man wants is already within him; but he still wanders here and there in search of it. [p. 351]

[From Müller, *Ramakrishna, His Life and Sayings*, pp. 134–80]

A disciple, having firm faith in the infinite power of his guru, walked over a river even by pronouncing his name. The guru, seeing this, thought within himself: "Well, is there such a power even in my name? Then I must be very great and powerful, no doubt!" The next day he also tried to walk over the river pronouncing "I, I, I," but no sooner had he stepped into the waters than he sank and was drowned. Faith can achieve miracles, while vanity or egoism is the death of man. [p. 134]

A man after fourteen years of hard asceticism in a lonely forest obtained at last the power of walking over the waters. Overjoyed at this acquisition, he went to his guru, and told him of his grand feat. At this the master replied: "My poor boy, what thou hast accomplished after fourteen years' arduous labor, ordinary men do the same by paying a penny to the boatman." [p. 154]

When a wound is perfectly healed, the slough falls off itself; but if the slough be taken off earlier, it bleeds. Similarly, when the perfection of knowledge is reached by a man, the distinctions of caste fall off from him, but it is wrong for the ignorant to break such distinctions. [p. 147]

The light of the gas illumines various localities with various intensities. But the life of the light, namely, the gas, comes from one common reservoir. So the religious teachers of all climes and ages are but as many lampposts through which is emitted the light of the spirit flowing constantly from one source, the Lord Almighty. [p. 148]

The difference between the modern Brāhmaism [of the Brāhmo Samāj] and Hinduism is like the difference between the single note of music and the whole music. The modern Brahmas are content with the single note of Brahman, while the Hindu religion is made up of several notes producing a sweet and melodious harmony. [p. 153]

As it is very difficult to gather together the mustard-seeds that escape out of a torn package, and are scattered in all directions; so, when the human mind runs in diverse directions and is occupied with many things in the world, it is not a very easy affair to collect and concentrate it. [p. 167]

He who would learn to swim must attempt swimming for some days. No one can venture to swim in the sea after a single day's practice. So if you want to swim in the sea of Brahman, you must make many ineffectual attempts at first, before you can successfully swim therein. [p. 175]

As the village maidens carry four or five pots of water placed one over the other upon their heads, talking all the way with one another about their own joys and sorrows, and yet do not allow one drop of water to be spilt, so must the traveler in the path of virtue walk along. In whatever circumstances he may be placed, let him always take heed that his heart does not swerve from the true path. [p. 177]

When an elephant is let loose, it goes about uprooting trees and shrubs, but as soon as the driver pricks him on the head with the goad he becomes quiet; so the mind when unrestrained wantons in the luxuriance of idle thoughts, but becomes calm at once when struck with the goad of discrimination. [p. 180].

Know thyself, and thou shalt then know the non-self and the Lord of all. What is my ego? Is it my hand, or foot, or flesh, or blood, or muscle, or tendon? Ponder deep, and thou shalt know that there is no such thing as I. As by continually peeling off the skin of the onion, so by analyzing the ego it will be found that there is not any real entity corresponding to ego. The ultimate result of all such analysis is God. When egoism drops away, Divinity manifests itself. [p. 180]

SWAMI VIVEKANANDA: HINDU MISSIONARY
TO THE WEST

Among Sri Ramakrishna's disciples was a young Calcutta-born student on whom he showered special attention and praise. This boy, Narendranath Datta (1863–1902), came from a kāyastha[26] family of lawyers and received a good Western-style education. When he first visited Ramakrishna, he was planning to study law in England and then follow the profession that was the high road to success in British India. Within a year's time, his interviews with the master mystic had changed the course of his life. He resolved to give up worldly pursuits and adopt the life of sannyāsī. After twelve years of ascetic discipline, he became famous as Swami Vivekananda, the apostle to the world of his master's philosophy of God-realization.

Vivekananda's meteoric career as missionary of Vedantic Hinduism to the West began in 1893 when he addressed the First World Parliament of Religions at Chicago. After four years of lecturing in America and England he returned to India a national hero and took up the task of regenerating his fellow countrymen. He literally burned himself out in their service, dedicating the Ramakrishna Mission to both social work and religious education, and rousing young men with his fiery speeches to devote themselves to uplifting the poor and starving millions of India.

Although he died at thirty-nine, Vivekananda's example had a powerful impact on the thinking of his own and later generations. Despite his scorn for politics, his success in preaching to the world the greatness of Hinduism gave his countrymen an added sense of dignity and pride in their own culture. His zeal to serve the downtrodden masses opened a new dimension of activity to Indian nationalist leaders, whose Western outlook had heretofore isolated them from the vast majority of their countrymen. Gandhi, the greatest to work in this new field, acknowledged his debt to the Swami in this respect.

Vivekananda called India to become great by realizing her own possibilities and by living up to her own highest ideals. The heart and soul of his teaching was the message of his beloved master, Ramakrishna: That each man was potentially divine, and so should both work to unleash the infinite power within himself, and should help other men to do the same.

Man Is God

In his series of lectures entitled "Practical Vedanta," delivered in London in 1896, Vivekananda set forth the teachings of his master, Ramakrishna. The central point of his message was that God is within man, that in his inmost being, man is God.

[From *The Complete Works of the Swami Vivekananda*, 2:324–25]

Do you not remember what the Bible says: "If you cannot love your brother whom you have seen, how can you love God whom you have not seen?" If you cannot see God in the human face, how can you see Him in the clouds, or in images made of dull, dead matter, or in mere fictitious stores of your brain? I shall call you religious from the day you begin to see God in men and women and then you will understand what is meant by turning the left cheek to the man who strikes you on the right. When you see man as God, everything, even the tiger, will be welcome. Whatever comes to you is but the Lord, the Eternal, the Blessed One, appearing to us in various forms, as our father, and mother, and friend, and child; they are our own soul playing with us.

As our human relationships can thus be made divine so our relationship with God may take any of these forms and we can look upon Him as our father or mother or friend or beloved. Calling God Mother is a higher idea than calling Him Father, and to call Him Friend is still higher, but the highest is to regard Him as the Beloved. The highest point of all is to see no difference between lover and beloved. You may remember, perhaps, the old Persian story, of how a lover came and knocked at the door of the beloved and was asked: "Who are you?" He answered: "It is I," and there was no response. A second time he came, and exclaimed: "I am here," but the door was not opened. The third time he came, and the voice asked from inside: "Who is there?" He replied: "I am thyself, my beloved," and the door opened. So is the relation between God and ourselves. He is in everything, He is everything. Every man and woman is the palpable, blissful, living God. Who says God is unknown? Who says He is to be searched after? We have found God eternally. We have been living in Him eternally. He is eternally known, eternally worshiped.

The Rationale of Caste and Idol-Worship

In contrast with the Brahmo reformers and Dayananda, Vivekananda justified the caste system as good, and the worship of idols as useful for those who need them.

[From *The Complete Works of the Swami Vivekananda*, 3:245–46, 460]

Caste is a natural order. I can perform one duty in social life, and you another; you can govern a country, and I can mend a pair of old shoes, but there is no reason why you are greater than I, for can you mend my shoes? Can I govern the country? I am clever in mending shoes, you are clever in reading Vedas, but there is no reason why you should trample on my head; why if one commits murder should he be praised, and if another steals an apple why should he be hanged! This will have to go. Caste is good. That is the only natural way of solving life. Men must form themselves into groups, and you cannot get rid of that. Wherever you go there will be caste. But that does not mean that there should be these privileges. They should be knocked on the head. If you teach Vedanta to the fisherman, he will say, I am as good a man as you, I am a fisherman, you are a philosopher, but I have the same God in me as you have in you. And that is what we want, no privileges for any one, equal chances for all; let every one be taught that the Divine is within, and every one will work out his own salvation. . . .

This external worship of images has, however, been described in all our Shastras as the lowest of all the low forms of worship. But that does not mean that it is a wrong thing to do. Despite the many iniquities that have found entrance into the practices of image-worship as it is in vogue now, I do not condemn it. Aye, where would I have been, if I had not been blessed with the dust of the holy feet of that orthodox, image-worshiping Brahmana [Ramakrishna]!

Those reformers who preach against image-worship, or what they denounce as idolatry—to them I say: "Brothers! If you are fit to worship God-without-Form discarding any external help, do so, but why do you condemn others who cannot do the same? A beautiful large edifice, the glorious relic of a hoary antiquity has, out of neglect or disuse, fallen into a dilapidated condition; accumulations of dirt and dust may be lying everywhere within it; may be, some portions are tumbling down to the ground. What will you do to it? Will you take in hand the necessary cleansing and repairs and thus restore the old, or will you pull the whole edifice down to the ground and seek to build another in its place, after a sordid modern plan whose permanence has yet to be established? We have to reform it, which truly means to make ready or perfect by necessary cleansing and repairs, not by demolishing the whole thing. There the function of reform ends."

India and the West

Vivekananda developed the idea, put forth by Keshub, that India should take practical knowledge from Europe, and in exchange should teach religious wisdom to the world. In a speech about Ramakrishna delivered in New York he stated most emphatically his claim that the Orient (by which he primarily meant India) was superior to the West in spiritual matters.

[From *The Complete Works of the Swami Vivekananda*, 4:150–52]

"Whenever virtue subsides and vice prevails, I come down to help mankind," declares Krishna, in the *Bhagavad-Gītā*. Whenever this world of ours, on account of growth, on account of added circumstances, requires a new adjustment, a wave of power comes, and as man is acting on two planes, the spiritual and the material, waves of adjustment come on both planes. On the one side, of the adjustment on the material plane, Europe has mainly been the basis during modern times, and of the adjustment on the other, the spiritual plane, Asia has been the basis throughout the history of the world. . . . What avails it if you have power over the whole of the world, if you have mastered every atom in the universe? That will not make you happy unless you have the power of happiness in yourself, until you have conquered yourself. Man is born to conquer Nature, it is true, but the Occidental means by "Nature" only the physical or external Nature. It is true that external Nature is majestic, with its mountains, and oceans, and rivers, and with the infinite powers and varieties. Yet there is a more majestic internal Nature of man, higher than the sun, moon, and the stars, higher than this earth of ours, higher than the physical universe, transcending these little lives of ours; and it affords another field of study. There the Orientals excel, just as the Occidentals excel in the other. Therefore it is fitting that, whenever there is a spiritual adjustment, it should come from the Orient. It is also fitting that when the Oriental wants to learn about machine-making, he should sit at the feet of the Occidental and learn from him. When the Occidental wants to learn about the spirit, about God, about the soul, about the meaning and the mystery of this universe, he must sit at the feet of the Orient to learn.

Indian Thought to Conquer the World

In a lecture in Madras, Swami Vivekananda challenged his audience to conquer the West with India's spirituality. Through such speeches as this he instilled a feeling

of self-confidence in the youth of the country, thus contributing to the later movement for national independence.

[From *The Complete Works of the Swami Vivekananda,* 33:276–77]

This is the great ideal before us, and every one must be ready for it—the
conquest of the whole world by India—nothing less than that, and we must
all get ready for it, strain every nerve for it. Let foreigners come and flood
the land with their armies, never mind. Up, India, and conquer the world
with your spirituality! Aye, as has been declared on this soil first, love must
conquer hatred, hatred cannot conquer itself. Materialism and all its miseries can never be conquered by materialism. Armies when they attempt to
conquer armies only multiply and make brutes of humanity. Spirituality
must conquer the West. Slowly they are finding out that what they want is
spirituality to preserve them as nations. They are waiting for it, they are
eager for it. Where is the supply to come from? Where are the men ready
to go out to every country in the world with the messages of the great sages
of India? Where are the men who are ready to sacrifice everything, so that
this message shall reach every corner of the world? Such heroic souls are
wanted to help the spread of truth. Such heroic workers are wanted to go
abroad and help to disseminate the great truths of the Vedanta. The world
wants it; without it the world will be destroyed. The whole of the Western
world is on a volcano which may burst tomorrow, go to pieces tomorrow.
They have searched every corner of the world and have found no respite.
They have drunk deep of the cup of pleasure and found it vanity. Now is
the time to work so that India's spiritual ideas may penetrate deep into the
West. Therefore, young men of Madras, I specially ask you to remember
this. We must go out, we must conquer the world through our spirituality
and philosophy. There is no other alternative, we must do it or die. The
only condition of national life, of awakened and vigorous national life, is
the conquest of the world by Indian thought.

America and India's Poor

While he was preaching the philosophy of the Vedanta to the people of the West,
Vivekananda was worrying about the poverty of his own countrymen. In 1894 he
wrote from Chicago to the Maharaja of Mysore, one of India's most enlightened
princes, giving his opinion of American materialism, and asking for help in his new-
found ambition to educate India's poor.

[From *The Complete Works of the Swami Vivekananda*, 4:307–9]

Sri Narayana bless you and yours. Through your Highness' kind help it has been possible for me to come to this country. Since then I have become well-known here, and the hospitable people of this country have supplied all my wants. It is a wonderful country and this is a wonderful nation in many respects. No other nation applies so much machinery in their every-day work as do the people of this country. Everything is machine. Then again, they are only one-twentieth of the whole population of the world. Yet they have fully one-sixth of all the wealth of the world. There is no limit to their wealth and luxuries. Yet everything here is so dear. The wages of labor are the highest in the world; yet the fight between labor and capital is constant.

Nowhere on earth have women so many privileges as in America. They are slowly taking everything into their hands and, strange to say, the number of cultured women is much greater than that of cultured men. Of course, the higher geniuses are mostly from the rank of males. With all the criticism of the Westerners against our caste, they have a worse one—that of money. The almighty dollar, as the Americans say, can do anything here.

No country on earth has so many laws, and in no country are they so little regarded. On the whole our poor Hindu people are infinitely more moral than any of the Westerners. In religion they practice here either hypocrisy or fanaticism. Sober-minded men have become disgusted with their superstitious religions and are looking forward to India for new light. Your Highness cannot realize without seeing, how eagerly they take in any little bit of the grand thoughts of the holy Vedas, which resist and are unharmed by the terrible onslaughts of modern science. The theories of creation out of nothing, of a created soul, and of the big tyrant of a God sitting on a throne in a place called heaven, and of the eternal hell-fires, have disgusted all the educated; and the noble thoughts of the Vedas about the eternity of creation and of the soul, and about the God in our own soul, they are imbibing fast in one shape or other. Within fifty years the educated of the world will come to believe in the eternity of both soul and creation, and in God as our highest and perfect nature, as taught in our holy Vedas. Even now their learned priests are interpreting the Bible in that way. My conclusion is that they require more spiritual civilization, and we, more material.

The one thing that is at the root of all evils in India is the condition of the poor. The poor in the West are devils; compared to them ours are angels, and it is therefore so much the easier to raise our poor. The only service to be done for our lower classes is, to give them education, *to develop their lost individuality*. That is the great task between our people and princes. Up to now nothing has been done in that direction. Priest-power and foreign conquest have trodden them down for centuries, and at last the poor of India have forgotten that they are human beings. They are to be given ideas; their eyes are to be opened to what is going on in the world around them, and then they will work out their own salvation. Every nation, every man, and every woman must work out their own salvation. Give them ideas—that is the only help they require, and then the rest must follow as the effect. Ours is to put the chemicals together, the crystallization comes in the law of nature. Our duty is to put ideas into their heads, they will do the rest. This is what is to be done in India. It is this idea that has been in my mind for a long time. I could not accomplish it in India, and that was the reason of my coming to this country. The great difficulty in the way of educating the poor is this. Supposing even your Highness opens a free school in every village, still it would do no good, for the poverty in India is such, that poor boys would rather go to help their fathers in the fields, or otherwise try to make a living, then come to the school. Now if the mountain does not come to Mahomet, Mahomet must go to the mountain. If the poor boy cannot come to education, education must go to him. There are thousands of single-minded, self-sacrificing Sannyasins in our own country, going from village to village, teaching religion, If some of them can be organized as teachers of secular things also, they will go from place to place, from door to door, not only preaching but teaching also. Suppose two of these men go to a village in the evening with a camera, a globe, some maps, etc. They can teach a great deal of astronomy and geography to the ignorant. By telling stories about different nations, they can give the poor a hundred times more information through the ear than they can get in a lifetime through books. This requires an organization, which again means money. Men enough there are in India to work out this plan, but alas! they have no money. It is very difficult to set a wheel in motion, but when once set, it goes on with increasing velocity. After seeking help in my own country and failing to get any sympathy from the rich, I came over to this country through your Highness' aid. The Americans do not care a bit whether the poor of India die or live. And why should they, when our own people never think of anything but their own selfish ends?

My noble prince, this life is short, the vanities of the world are transient, but they alone live who live for others, the rest are more dead than alive. One such high, noble-minded, and royal son of India as your Highness can do much towards raising India on her feet again, and thus leave a name to posterity which shall be worshiped.

That the Lord may make your noble heart feel intensely for the suffering millions of India sunk in ignorance, is the prayer of—

Vivekananda

Modern India

In one of his last essays, written in Bengali in 1899, Vivekananda declared India's independence of Western standards. Scouting blind imitation of foreign models as unmanly, he called on his compatriots to take pride in their past and to unite rich and poor, high and low castes, in order to make their nation strong.

[From *The Complete Works of the Swami Vivekananda*, 4:408–13]

It has been said before that India is slowly awakening through her friction with the outside nations, and, as the result of this little awakening is the appearance, to a certain extent, of free and independent thought in modern India. On one side is modern Western science, dazzling the eyes with the brilliance of myriad suns, and driving in the chariot of hard and fast facts collected by the application of tangible powers direct in their incision; on the other are the hopeful and strengthening traditions of her ancient fore-fathers, in the days when she was at the zenith of her glory—traditions that have been brought out of the pages of her history by the great sages of her own land and outside, that run for numberless years and centuries through her every vein with the quickening of life drawn from universal love, tra-ditions that reveal unsurpassed valor, superhuman genius, and supreme spir-ituality, which are the envy of the gods—these inspire her with future hopes. On one side, rank materialism, plenitude of fortune, accumulation of gigan-tic power, and intense sense pursuits, have through foreign literature caused a tremendous stir; on the other, through the confounding din of all these discordant sounds, she hears, in low yet unmistakable accents, the heart-rending cries of her ancient gods, cutting her to the quick. There lie before her various strange luxuries introduced from the West—celestial drinks, costly well-served food, splendid apparel, magnificent palaces, new modes of conveyance—new manners, new fashions, dressed in which moves about the well-educated girl in shameless freedom; all these are arousing unfelt desires in her; again, the scene changes and in its place appear, with stern presence, Sītā, Sāvitrī,[26] austere religious vows, fastings, the forest retreat, the matted locks and orange garb of the semi-naked Sannyasin, Samadhi, and the search after the Self. On one side, is the independence of Western societies based on self-interest; on the other, is the extreme self-sacrifice of the Aryan society. In this violent conflict, is it strange that Indian society should be tossed up and down? Of the West, the goal is—individual independence, the language—money-making education, the means—politics; of India, the goal is—Mukti [or *mokṣa*, release], the language—the Veda, the means—renunciation. For a time, modern India thinks, as it were: I am running this worldly life of mine in vain expectation of uncertain spiritual welfare hereafter, which has spread its fascination over me; and again, lo! spellbound she listens: "Here, in this world of death and change, O man, where is thy happiness?"

On one side, New India is saying: "We should have full freedom in the selection of husband and wife; because, the marriage in which are involved the happiness and misery of all our future life, we must have the right to determine, according to our own free will." On the other, Old India is dictating: "Marriage is not for sense enjoyment, but to perpetuate the race. This is the Indian conception of marriage. By the producing of children, you are contributing to, and are responsible for, the future good or evil of the society. Hence, society has the right to dictate whom you shall marry and whom you shall not. That form of marriage obtains in society, which is conducive most to its well-being; do you give up your desire of individual pleasure for the good of the many."

On one side New India is saying: "If we only adopt Western ideas, Western language, Western food, Western dress and Western manners, we shall be as strong and powerful as the Western nations"; on the other, Old India is saying: "Fools! By imitation, other's ideas never become one's own—nothing, unless earned, is your own. Does the ass in the lion's skin become the lion?"

On one side, New India is saying: "What the Western nations do are surely good, otherwise how did they become so great?" On the other side, Old India is saying: "The flash of lightning is intensely bright, but only for a moment; look out, boys, it is dazzling your eyes. Beware!"

Have we not then to learn anything from the West? Must we not needs try and exert ourselves for better things? Are we perfect? Is our society entirely spotless, without any flaw? There are many things to learn, we must struggle for new and higher things till we die—struggle is the end of human life. Sir Rāmakrishna used to say: "As long as I live, so long I learn." That man or that society which has nothing to learn is already in the jaws of death. Yes, learn we must many things from the West, but there are fears as well.

A certain young man of little understanding used always to blame Hindu Shastras before Sri Rāmakrishna. One day he praised the *Bhagavad-Gītā*, on which Sri Rāmakrishna said: "Methinks some European pandit has praised the *Gītā*, and so he has also followed suit."

O India, this is your terrible danger. The spell of imitating the West is getting such a strong hold upon you, that what is good or what is bad is no longer decided by reason, judgment, discrimination, or reference to the Shastras. Whatever ideas, whatever manners the white men praise or like, are good; whatever things they dislike or censure are bad! Alas! What can be a more tangible proof of foolishness than this?

The Western ladies move freely everywhere—therefore, that is good; they choose for themselves their husbands—therefore, that is the highest step of advancement; the Westerners disapprove of our dress, decorations, food, and ways of living—therefore, they must be very bad; the Westerners condemn image-worship as sinful—surely then, image-worship is the greatest sin, there is no doubt of it!

The Westerners say that worshiping a single Deity is fruitful of the highest spiritual good—therefore, let us throw our Gods and Goddesses into the river Ganges! The Westerners hold caste distinctions to be obnoxious—therefore, let all the different castes be jumbled into one! The Westerners say that child-marriage is the root of all evils—therefore, that is also very bad, of a certainty it is!

We are not discussing here whether these customs deserve countenance or rejection; but if the mere disapproval of the Westerners be the measure of the abominableness of our manners and customs, then it is our duty to raise our emphatic protest against it. . . .

Oh India! With this mere echoing of others, with this base imitation of others, with this dependence on others, this slavish weakness, this vile detestable cruelty, wouldst thou, with these provisions only, scale the highest pinnacle of civilization and greatness? Wouldst thou attain, by means of thy disgraceful cowardice, that freedom deserved only by the brave and the heroic? Oh India! Forget not that the ideal of thy womanhood is Sītā, Sāvitrī, Damayanti;[27] forget not that the God thou worshipest is the great Ascetic of ascetics, the all-renouncing Shankara, the Lord of Uma;[28] forget not that thy marriage, thy wealth, thy life are not for sense-pleasure, are not for thy individual personal happiness; forget not that thou art born as a sacrifice to the *Mother's* altar; forget not that thy social order is but the reflex of the Infinite Universal Motherhood; forget not that the lower classes, the ignorant, the poor, the illiterate, the cobbler, the sweeper, are thy flesh and blood, thy brothers. Thou brave one, be bold, take courage, be proud that thou art an Indian, and proudly proclaim: "I am an Indian, every Indian is my brother." Say: "The ignorant Indian, the poor and destitute Indian, the Brāhman Indian, the Pariah Indian, is my brother." Thou too clad with but a rag round thy loins proudly proclaim at the top of thy voice: "The Indian is my brother, the Indian is my life, India's gods and goddesses are my God, India's society is the cradle of my infancy, the pleasure-garden of my youth, the sacred heaven, the *Vārānasi,*[29] of my old age." Say, brother: "The soil of India is my highest heaven, the good of India is my good," and repeat and pray day and night: "O Thou Lord of Gauri,[30] O Thou Mother of the Universe, vouchsafe manliness unto me! O Thou Mother of Strength, take away my weakness, take away my unmanliness, and—*Make me a Man!*"

NOTES

1. F. Max Müller: *India, What Can It Teach Us?* p. 6.
2. Debendranath Tagore, *The Autobiography of Maharshi Devendranath Tagore,* p. 39.
3. Kālī—the Great Goddess.
4. The temple of Kālī in Calcutta.
5. Sacred stone used in Vaishnava domestic worship.
6. Doorkeepers.
7. *Autobiography of Swami Dayanand Saraswati,* p. 17.
8. Devoted to Shiva.
9. A small book of elementary Sanskrit grammar.
10. Devotional worship invoking Shiva's presence in the clay emblem.
11. Shiva's night.
12. Great God, a name of Shiva.
13. The Himalayan peak on which Shiva is thought to dwell in meditation.
14. Age of physical and spiritual deterioration.
15. A Muslim learned in Islamic law and theology.

16. "Abode of the noble," i.e., of the ancient Aryans in northern India.
17. Dayananda, *Satyarth Prakash (The Light of Truth)*.
18. Believed to have founded the Mīmāmsa school of philosophy, c. 200 B.C.
19. Five sacred trees planted together to form a grove used for contemplation.
20. A wealthy disciple. "Bābu" is a respectful Bengali form of address.
21. Intense meditation.
22. The consort of Rāma, hero of the *Rāmāyana*. She exemplifies the Hindu ideal of womanhood.
23. An affectionate form of address.
24. King Janaka, the father of Sītā.
25. Blessed One.
26. High caste in Bengal, traditionally associated with clerical work.
27. Sāvitrī, famed in Indian legend for having saved her doomed husband from the God of Death.
28. Damayanti, celebrated in Indian legend for her devotion to her husband Nala.
29. Umā, a name of the wife of Shiva or Shankara (the Gracious One).
30. Banaras.
31. A name for the wife of Shiva.

Chapter 3

NATIONALISM TAKES ROOT:
THE MODERATES

Before the British conquest, the concept of membership in a stable political order embracing and involving them all seems to have been unknown to the inhabitants of India. Dynasties rather than nations were the centers of political power and the foci of personal loyalties. Powerful rulers like Ashoka, Samudragupta, and Harsha had indeed succeeded in bringing large parts of the subcontinent under their sway, but their empires dissolved with the death of the last strong ruler in each reigning line. Thanks largely to the genius of Akbar (1542–1605), the Mughal empire created a somewhat more durable administrative order, but internal dissensions and Persian-Afghan invasions led to the empire's dismemberment after the passing of the militant Aurangzeb (1619–1707). For a time the Marathas gave promise of re-establishing Hindu dominion, but again their rule could not unite all of India around their standard, let alone bridge the gap between India's two major religious traditions.

A new chapter opened when British arms and diplomacy placed the whole of the subcontinent under one paramount power for the first time in history. They imposed not only unity on India, but a relatively efficient administrative machinery as well. Gradually the sinews of a new polity were strengthened by the introduction of printing and journalism, railroads, a postal and telegraph system, and by the growth of an all-India economy centering in large modern cities accessible to ocean-going ships.

The new political and economic order attracted able Indians anxious to improve their status and increase their wealth by entering its service. A new class emerged to mediate between the foreign rulers or traders and the mass of the people. Using their knowledge of English as the key to advancement, Indian clerks and functionaries found employment in government posts; Indian lawyers pleaded in British-style courts; Indian businessmen dealt with foreign firms; and Indian teachers imparted to their countrymen the language and culture of the conquerors. This rising middle class demonstrated a loyalty to the British that outweighed the angry discontent of the old elite—both Muslim and Hindu. The suppression of the latter in the Mutiny and Rebellion of 1857–1858 only confirmed the entrenched position of their successors.

But the English education that provided so many willing collaborators for the British in India eventually proved the undoing of their empire. For one thing, the members of the new middle class—whether from the South or the North, from Bengal or from Maharashtra—could all communicate with each other through the medium of a common language. Equally important, their reading of the English classics instilled in them Western ideals of justice, freedom, and love of country. As their numbers grew they found the good government jobs too few, with the best ones reserved for Europeans. To economic frustration was added the bitter sting of racial discrimination, for "the Mutiny" of 1857 had sharpened British suspicions of Indian loyalty, and the late nineteenth-century doctrines of Social Darwinism and aggressive imperialism combined to increase the white man's feeling of inherent superiority over his darker-skinned subjects. Ignoring the sympathetic statements made in Parliament and the conciliatory proclamation of Queen Victoria in 1858, Britishers in India saw little reason to grant Indians a greater measure of control over their own affairs.

Under these circumstances, it was not long before the seed-idea of nationalism implanted by their reading of Western books began to take root in the minds of intelligent and energetic Indians. Allan Octavian Hume, a Scotsman sympathetic to their aspirations, made possible the first meeting (in 1885) of the Indian National Congress, which was intended to serve as a forum for the discussion of political reforms and patriotic projects. From this beginning as a safety-valve through which the upper classes could air their grievances, the Congress quickly transformed itself into an all-India nationalist organization.

The Moderates, the first men to come forward as leaders of the nationalist movement, shared a great many assumptions with those liberal Englishmen who advised and encouraged them. They believed in the providential character of British rule and in the gradual evolution of India toward enlightenment and self-government under that rule. They regretted the backwardness of Hindu society and worked to bring about the reform of its grosser evils. The poverty of the people depressed them, and they therefore concerned themselves with plans for India's economic improvement. Although they were not men devoid of religious faith, they accepted the divorce of religion from government and maintained a secular view of politics that contrasted markedly with the religious outlook of the Extremists, who later posed a serious challenge to their leadership.

Having become, as Macaulay had predicted, "English in taste, in opinions, in morals, and in intellect," the Indian Moderates gained certain advantages but at the same time ran certain risks in guiding the nationalist movement. Their familiarity with British culture enabled them to appeal to the best instincts of their rulers, from whom they demanded the same rights and liberties that all Britons took for granted. Their knowledge of the gradual rise of democratic government in English history furnished them with useful ammunition, and they repeatedly harked back to the assurances given by Parliament and Queen Victoria that Indians would be allowed to compete freely with Europeans for positions in the Indian Civil Service.

In relation to their rivals, the Extremists, however, the position of the Moderates was bound to be somewhat vulnerable for several reasons. Their heavy reliance on British good faith embarrassed them whenever the concessions they asked for were refused or postponed. Moreover, the more Anglicized they became in their thinking, the further they removed themselves from emotional rapport with the bulk of the population—the illiterate, poverty-stricken, and religious-minded peasantry.

In one respect the Moderates did yeoman's service in tending to the needs of the peasantry. Unwilling to attack British rule for the political and social reforms it had introduced, they focused their attention on the obvious disparity between Britain's prosperity and India's poverty. Dadabhai Naoroji, an Indian businessman resident in London, placed the blame for his country's plight on foreign rule, and in doing so was seconded by English socialist theoreticians. The Bengali leader Surendranath Banerjea accepted Dadabhai's thesis, and M. G. Ranade sought a constructive solution in rapid industrialization under government auspices. Ranade's disciple G. K. Gokhale left the theorizing to others and bent his efforts to reducing the load of taxation burdening the Indian people. R. C. Dutt, through his economic writings, had a profound influence on the nationalist movement.

Those four men were probably the most outstanding Moderate leaders in the opening decades of the nationalist movement. It is significant that all were scholarly in temperament and spent part of their early careers as teachers in colleges imparting English education to Indian students. Each possessed a flawless command of the English language and was able to hold his own in debates with Englishmen. Four of them—Naoroji, Banerjea, Dutt, and Gokhale—made speaking tours in Great Britain to impress the British electorate with the importance of greater self-government for India. The same four were also elected presidents of the Congress, and all five were deeply involved in its work.

Although the Extremist leaders could muster far greater support by appealing to popular Hindu symbols and traditions, it is doubtful that they could have succeeded in freeing India without the patient, more diplomatic efforts of the Moderates. Their greater willingness to cooperate with the British in instituting administrative reforms kept the nationalist movement from "going off the rails" into senseless violence, which could only lead to severe reprisals and political deadlock. Their contribution to the achievement of self-government has largely been forgotten by subsequent generations, but independent India's dedication to parliamentary democracy, economic development, and social progress stands as mute testimony to their farsighted wisdom.

DADABHAI NAOROJI: ARCHITECT OF INDIAN NATIONALISM

In retrospect the rise of Indian nationalism may seem to have been inevitable under the conditions created by British rule, but its emergence would have been impossible without the strenuous efforts of devoted national leaders. The first of a long series of such men, Dadabhai Naoroji drew the plans and laid the foundations for India's self-government.

This architect of Indian nationalism was neither Hindu nor Muslim, but a descendant of the followers of Zoroaster who had fled Persia after the Muslim conquest of that country. Settling as refugees along the western coast of India, the Zoroastrians became known as Parsis (Persians). When the British came to trade, they emerged as the group most willing to do business, for they were bound neither by caste rules nor by prejudice against taking interest on loans, and as a minority group they had little to lose and much to gain by dealing with the Europeans. As a result of their trading contacts, the Parsis became the most Westernized and the wealthiest single community in India.

Dadabhai Naoroji was born in Bombay in 1825, the son of a Zoroastrian priest. His family name, Dordi, was little used; but the original meaning of the word (twisted rope made of coconut husk) had a symbolic significance for Dadabhai, who was absolutely inflexible once he had made up his mind.

"You may burn a *dordi,*" he once said, "but you can never take the twist out of it. So it is with me. When once I form a decision, nothing will dislodge me from it."[1]

Tenacity of purpose was indeed his chief characteristic. He so distinguished himself in his studies at the Elphinstone Institution (Bombay's leading college) that he became at twenty-seven its Professor of Mathematics—the first Indian to attain such an academic rank. At thirty he left India to become a partner in the first Indian firm to do business in England. His aim in moving permanently to London, the heart of the empire, was not to gain wealth, but to enable himself to appeal directly to the British public for a better understanding of India's problems. For fifty years Dadabhai delivered papers on Indian subjects to numerous learned societies, submitted memoranda and petitions to British officials concerned with India, and agitated both privately and publicly—all in the service of one cause: that Indians should be granted the same rights and privileges as other British subjects.

With his famous theory of "the drain" of India's wealth to Britain, Dadabhai Naoroji sounded the keynote of Indian economic nationalism. But for all his bitter condemnation of the costliness of foreign government to his country, he never advocated violent action as a solution. His loyalty to the parliamentary system of government was rewarded in 1892 with his election to the British House of Commons on the Liberal ticket. The first Indian member of Parliament, he served both his London constituency and the interests of India for three years, succeeding in his attempt to have a parliamentary commission investigate the financial administration of British India.

Dadabhai punctuated his long residence in England with frequent visits to India. In 1873–1874 he served as chief minister to the Indian state of Baroda to prevent it from being annexed by the British crown (the usual penalty for misgovernment in the princely states). He took a prominent part in the first session of the Indian National Congress in 1885 and was thrice elected its president—in 1886, 1893, and 1906. The younger generation of nationalist leaders all looked up to the patriarchal patriot for advice, and both Gandhi and Jinnah revered him. He died in Bombay in 1917, but to this day the affectionate title "the Grand Old Man of India" is associated with his name.

The Pros and Cons of British Rule

In the discussion following the presentation of a paper on India to a learned society in London in 1871, Dadabhai drew up an impromptu account of the advantages and disadvantages of British rule to India. It shows both his fairness in recognizing the good the British had done, and his persistent criticism of the crushing cost to India of their rule.

[From Naoroji, *Essays, Speeches, Addresses, and Writings,* pp. 131–36]

Credit—*In the Cause of Humanity:* Abolition of suttee and infanticide.

Destruction of Dacoits, Thugs, Pindarees,[2] and other such pests of Indian society.

Remarriage of Hindoo widows, and charitable aid in time of famine.

Glorious work all this, of which any nation may well be proud, and such as has not fallen to the lot of any people in the history of mankind.

In the Cause of Civilization: Education, both male and female. Though yet only partial, an inestimable blessing as far as it has gone, and leading gradually to the destruction of superstition, and many moral and social evils. Resuscitation of India's own noble literature, modified and refined by the enlightenment of the West.

The only pity is that as much has not been done as might have been in this noble work; but still India must be, and is, deeply grateful.

Politically: Peace and order. Freedom of speech and liberty of the press. Higher political knowledge and aspirations. Improvement of government in the native States. Security of life and property. Freedom from oppression caused by the caprice or avarice of despotic rulers, and from devastation by war. Equal justice between man and man (sometimes vitiated by partiality to Europeans). Services of highly educated administrators, who have achieved the above-mentioned good results.

Materially: Loans for railways and irrigation. (I have been particularly charged with ignoring this, but I consider it one of the greatest benefits you have conferred upon India, inasmuch as it has enabled us to produce more than we could before, though there is not yet enough for all India's ordinary wants, and I have said this in my paper.) I cannot ascertain the exact amount of investments in irrigation works, but I take them to be about £10,000,000, making the total £110,000,000. The development of a few valuable products, such as indigo, tea, coffee, silk, &c. Increase of exports. Telegraphs.

Generally: A slowly growing desire of late to treat India equitably, and as a country held in trust. Good intentions.

No nation on the face of the earth has ever had the opportunity of achieving such a glorious work as this. I hope in this credit side of the account I have done no injustice, and if I have omitted any item which anyone may think of importance, I shall have the greatest pleasure in inserting it. I appreciate, and so do my countrymen, what England has done for India, and I know that it is only in British hands that her regeneration can be accomplished. Now for the debit side.

Debit—In the Cause of Humanity: Nothing. Everything, therefore, is in your favor under this head.

In the Cause of Civilization: As I have said already, there has been a failure to do as much as might have been done, but I put nothing to the debit. Much has been done, or I should not be standing here this evening.

Politically: Repeated breach of pledges to give the natives a fair and reasonable share in the higher administration of their own country, which has much shaken confidence in the good faith of the British word. Political aspirations and the legitimate claim to have a reasonable voice in the legislation and the imposition and disbursement of taxes, met to a very slight degree, thus treating the natives of India not as British subjects, to whom representation is a birthright.

(I stop here a moment to say a word as to a mistake into which my friend, Mr. Hyde Clarke, fell, in supposing that I desired the government of India to be at once transferred to the natives. In my belief a greater calamity could not befall India than for England to go away and leave her to herself.)

Consequent on the above, an utter disregard of the feelings and views of the natives. The great moral evil of the drain of the wisdom and practical administration and statesmanship, leaving none to guide the rising generation. (Here, again, have I been misunderstood. I complain not of Englishmen returning to their own country, but of the whole administration being kept entirely in English hands, so that none of the natives are brought up to and taught the responsibilities and duties of office, so that we have none amongst ourselves to guide us as our elders and to teach us our duties as citizens and as moral beings. A foster mother or nurse will never supply the place of the real mother, and the natives will therefore naturally follow their own leaders, unless you prove more kind, humane, and considerate.

Draw these leaders on your side.) The indifference to India, even of a large portion of those who have had an Indian career, and who are living on Indian pensions. The culpable indifference of a large portion of the people, the public press, and Parliament of this country to the interests of India; therefore, periodical committees of inquiry are absolutely necessary, for the knowledge that such will take place would be a check on careless administration. With regard to the native states, though their system is improving, it is most unjust that their cases should be decided in secret. The frequent change of officials is a constant source of disturbance in policy, and though it may be unavoidable, it is none the less hard upon India.

Financially: All attention is engrossed in devising new modes of taxation, without any adequate effort to increase the means of the people to pay; and the consequent vexation and oppressiveness of the taxes imposed, imperial and local. Inequitable financial relations between England and India, i.e., the political debt of £100,000,000 clapped on India's shoulders, and all home charges also, though the British exchequer contributes nearly £3,000,000 to the expenses of the colonies. The crushing and economically rude and unintelligent policy of making the present generation pay the whole cost of public works for the benefit of the future, instead of making the political like all other machinery, and distributing the weight so as to make a small power lift a large weight by the aid of time. The results of trying to produce something out of nothing, of the want of intelligent adaptation of financial machinery, and of much reckless expenditure; ending in financial embarrassments, and deep discontent of the people.

Materially: The political drain,[3] up to this time, from India to England, of above £500,000,000, at the lowest computation, in principal alone, which with interest would be some thousands of millions. The further continuation of this drain at the rate, at present, of above £12,000,000, with a tendency to increase. (I do not mean this as a complaint; you must have a return for the services rendered to India, but let us have the means of paying. If I have a manager to whom I pay £1,000 a year, and he only makes the business produce £400, so that £600 a year must be paid him out of capital, any man of business can see what will be the result. Peace and order will soon be completely established by the closing of the concern.)

The consequent continuous impoverishment and exhaustion of the country, except so far as it has been very partially relieved and replenished by the railway and irrigation loans, and the windfall of the consequences of the American war, since 1850. Even with this relief, the material condition of India is such that the great mass of the poor people have hardly 2d a day and a few rags, or a scanty subsistence.

The famines that were in their power to prevent, if they had done their duty, as a good and intelligent government. The policy adopted during the last fifteen years of building railways, irrigation works, etc., is hopeful, has already resulted in much good to your credit, and if persevered in, gratitude and contentment will follow.

[An] increase of exports [without adequate compensation]; [a] loss of manufacturing industry and skill. Here I end the debit side. . . .

To sum up the whole, the British rule has been—morally, a great blessing; politically peace and order on one hand, blunders on the other, materially, impoverishment (relieved as far as the railway and other loans go). The natives call the British system "Sakar ki Churi," the knife of sugar. That is to say there is no oppression, it is all smooth and sweet, but it is the knife, notwithstanding. I mention this that you should know these feelings. Our great misfortune is that you do not know our wants. When you will know our real wishes, I have not the least doubt that you would do justice. The genius and spirit of the British people is fair play and justice. The great problems before the English statesmen are two: 1) To make the foreign rule self-supporting, either by returning to India, in some shape or other, the wealth that has been, and is being, drawn from it, or by stopping that drain in some way till India is so far improved in its material condition as to be able to produce enough for its own ordinary wants and the extraordinary ones of a costly distant rule. If you cannot feel yourself actuated by the high and noble ambition of the amelioration of 200,000,000 of human beings let your self-interest suggest to you to take care of the bird that gives the golden egg of £12,000,000 a year to your nation, and provisions to thousands of your people of all classes. In the name of humanity, I implore our rulers to make up their minds not to prevent the restoration of the equilibrium, after the continuous exhaustion by drain and by horrible famines. I do not in the least grudge any legitimate benefit England may derive for its rule in India. On the contrary, I am thankful for its invaluable moral benefits; but it is the further duty of England to give us such a government, and all the benefit of its power and credit, as to enable us to pay, without starving or dying by famine, the tribute or price for the rule; 2) How to satisfy reasonably the growing political aspirations and just rights of a people called British subjects to have a fair share in the administration and legislation of their own country. If the Select Committee solve these two problems, before which all other difficulties, financial or others, are as nothing, they will deserve the blessings of 200,000,000 of the human race.

The Blessings of British Rule

Dadabhai's presidential address at the second session of the Congress in 1886 rings with protestations of loyalty and gratitude to British rule for the unity, peace, civil liberties and education it brought to the Indian people.

[From Naoroji, *Essays, Speeches, Addresses, and Writings*, pp. 332–33]

The assemblage of such a Congress is an event of the utmost importance in Indian history. I ask whether in the most glorious days of Hindu rule, in the days of Rajahs like the great Vikram,[4] you could imagine the possibility of a meeting of this kind, where even Hindus of all different provinces of the kingdom could have collected and spoken as one nation. Coming down to the later empire of our friends, the Mahomedans, who probably ruled over a larger territory at one time than any Hindu monarch, would it have been, even in the days of the great Akbar himself, possible for a meeting like this to assemble composed of all classes and communities, all speaking one language, and all having uniform and high aspirations of their own?

Well, then, what is it for which we are now met on this occasion? We have assembled to consider questions upon which depend our future, whether glorious or inglorious. It is our good fortune that we are under a rule which makes it possible for us to meet in this manner. [Cheers.] It is under the civilizing rule of the Queen and people of England that we meet here together, hindered by none, and are freely allowed to speak our minds without the least fear and without the least hesitation. Such a thing is possible under British rule and British rule only. [Loud cheers.] Then I put the *question* plainly: Is this Congress a nursery for sedition and rebellion against the British Government [cries of "no, no"]; or is it another stone in the foundation of that stability of that Government [cries of "yes, yes"]? There could be but one answer, and that you have already given, because we are thoroughly sensible of the numberless blessings conferred upon us, of which the very existence of this Congress is a proof in a nutshell. [Cheers.] Were it not for these blessings of British rule I could not have come here, as I have done, without the least hesitation and without the least fear that my children might be robbed and killed in my absence; nor could you have come from every corner of the land, having performed, within a few days, journeys which in former days would have occupied as many months. [Cheers.] These simple facts bring home to all of us at once some of those great and numberless blessings which British rule has conferred upon us. But there remain even greater blessings for which we have to be grateful. It is to British rule that we owe the education we possess; the people of England were sincere in the declarations made more than half a century ago that India was a sacred charge entrusted to their care by Providence, and that they were bound to administer it for the good of India, to the glory of their own name, and the satisfaction of God. [Prolonged cheering.] When we have to acknowledge so many blessings as flowing from British rule—and I could descant on them for hours, because it would simply be recounting to you the history of the British empire in India—is it possible that an assembly like this, every one of whose members is fully impressed with the knowledge of these blessings, could meet for any purpose inimical to that rule to which we owe so much? [Cheers.]

The thing is absurd. Let us speak out like men and proclaim that we are loyal to the backbone [cheers]; that we understand the benefits English rule has conferred upon us; that we thoroughly appreciate the education that has been given to us, the new light which has been poured upon us, turning us from darkness into light and teaching us the new lesson that kings are made for the people, not people for their kings; and this new lesson we have learned amidst the darkness of Asiatic despotism only by the light of free English civilization. [Loud cheers.]

The Moral Impoverishment of India

The frustration felt by the swelling ranks of educated Indians who were excluded from government positions is well expressed in Dadabhai's memorandum of 1880. Note the veiled threat with which this selection concludes.

[From Naoroji, *Essays, Speeches, Addresses, and Writings,* pp. 465–67]

In this Memorandum I desire to submit for the kind and generous consideration of His Lordship the Secretary of State for India, that from the same cause of the deplorable drain, besides the material exhaustion of India, the moral loss to her is no less sad and lamentable.

With the material wealth go also the wisdom and experience of the country. Europeans occupy almost all the higher places in every department of government, directly or indirectly under its control. While *in* India they acquire India's money, experience, and wisdom, and when they go, they carry both away with them, leaving India so much poorer in material and moral wealth. Thus India is left without, and cannot have, those elders in wisdom and experience, who in every country are the natural guides of the rising generations in their national and social conduct, and of the destinies of their country—and a sad, sad loss this is!

Every European is isolated from the people around him. He is not their mental, moral or social leader, or companion. For any mental or moral influence or guidance or sympathy with the people, he might just as well be living in the moon. The people know not him, and he knows not, nor cares for the people. Some honorable exceptions do, now and then, make an effort to do some good they can, but in the very nature of things, these efforts are always feeble, exotic, and of little permanent effect. These men are not always in the place, and their works die away when they go.

The Europeans are not the natural leaders of the people. They do not belong to the people. They cannot enter into their thoughts and feelings; they cannot join or sympathize with their joys or griefs. On the contrary, every day the estrangement is increasing. Europeans deliberately and openly widen it more and more. There may be very few social institutions started by Europeans in which natives, however fit and desirous to join, are not deliberately and insultingly excluded. The Europeans are and make themselves strangers in every way. All they effectually do is to eat the substance of India, material and moral, while living there, and when they go, they carry away all they have acquired, and their pensions and future usefulness besides.

This most deplorable moral loss to India needs most serious consideration, as much in its political as in its national aspect. Nationally disastrous as it is, it carries politically with it its own nemesis. Without the guidance of elderly wisdom and experience of their own natural leaders, the education which the rising generations are now receiving is naturally leading them (or call it misleading them, if you will) into directions which bode no good to the rulers, and which, instead of being the strength of the rulers as it ought to and can be, will turn out to be their great weakness. The fault will be of the rulers themselves for such a result. The power that is now being raised by the spread of education, though yet slow and small, is one that in time must, for weal or woe, exercise great influence. In fact it has already begun to do so. However strangely the English rulers, forgetting their English manliness and moral courage, may, like the ostrich, shut their eyes by gagging acts or otherwise, to the good or bad influences they are raising around them, this good or evil is rising nevertheless. The thousands that are being sent out by the universities every year find themselves in a most anomalous position. There is no place for them in their motherland. They may beg in the streets or break stones on the roads, for aught the rulers seem to care for their natural rights, position, and duties in their own country. They may perish or do what they like or can, but scores of Europeans must go from this country to take up what belongs to them, and that, in spite of every profession for years and years past and up to the present day, of English statesmen, that they must govern India for India's good, by solemn acts and declarations of Parliament, and above all, by the words of the August Sovereign Herself. For all practical purposes all these high promises have been hitherto, almost wholly, the purest romance, the reality being quite different.

The educated find themselves simply so many dummies, ornamented with the tinsel of school education, and then their whole end and aim of life is ended. What must be the inevitable consequence? A wild, spirited horse, without curb or reins, will run away wild, and kill and trample upon every one that came in his way. A misdirected force will hit anywhere and destroy anything. The power that the rulers are, so far to their credit, raising, will, as a nemesis recoil against themselves, if with this blessing of education they do not do their whole duty to the country which trusts to their righteousness, and thus turn this good power to their own side. The nemesis is as clear from the present violence to nature, as disease and death arise from uncleanliness and rottenness. The voice of the power of the rising education is, no doubt, feeble at present. Like the infant, the present dissatisfaction is only crying at the pains it is suffering. Its notions have not taken any form or shape or course yet, but it is growing. Heaven only knows what it will grow to! He who runs may see, that if the present material and moral destruction of India continued, a great convulsion must inevitably arise, by which either India will be more and more crushed under the iron heel of despotism and destruction, or may succeed in shattering the destroying hand and power. Far, far is it from my earnest prayer and hope that such should be the result of the British rule.

SURENDRANATH BANERJEA: BENGALI MODERATE

The Hindu renaissance in nineteenth-century Bengal was accompanied by a gradual political awakening in that province. Politics, however, unlike religion, came as a comparatively new category of thought to Bengali Hindus after centuries of domination by Muslim rulers. Following the example set by Rammohun Roy, a growing number of men emerged from the English-speaking middle class infused by their Western-style education with new ideals of patriotism and public service.

To this group Allan Octavian Hume appealed with his letter of 1883, addressing the graduates of Calcutta University. "You are the salt of the land," he wrote. "And if amongst even you, the elite, fifty men cannot be found with sufficient power of self-sacrifice, sufficient love for and pride in their country, sufficient genuine and unselfish heart-felt patriotism to take the initiative, and if needs be, devote the rest of their lives to the Cause—then there is no hope for India."[5]

To one Calcutta University graduate, Hume's appeal was entirely superfluous, for Surendranath Banerjea (1848–1926) had already cast himself into the stormy sea of national service. A brāhman and the son of a doctor, Surendranath had been one of the first Indians to be admitted to the select Indian Civil Service, the so-called "steel frame" of British administration; but his failure to correct a false report prepared in his name by a subordinate had caused him to be dismissed—a punishment far more severe than English members of the I.C.S. received for similar oversights. Undaunted, Surendranath journeyed to London to appeal his case. When the appeal was denied, he appeared for bar examinations, only to be refused again. With the two swiftest roads to success—the civil service and the law—closed to him, Surendranath returned to Calcutta, convinced that "the personal wrong done to me was an illustration of the impotency of our people" and determined to spend his life "redressing our wrongs and protecting our rights, personal and collective."[6]

The rest of his long life was only the acting out of this resolve. Starting as a teacher, he soon founded a patriotic association, then a newspaper, then a college. As Keshub Chunder Sen had captivated audiences in many parts of the land with his revivalist sermons, so Surendranath used his oratorical gifts to rouse Indians from Bengal to the Punjab to a greater sense of loyalty to their country. When he was jailed for criticizing a British judge, he started the tradition of welcoming imprisonment in order to demonstrate the injustice of a governmental law or policy.

Surendranath's career dramatizes the change of heart in countless educated Indians from blind loyalty to British rule to stubborn resistance against its evils. Despite his sufferings at the hands of the authorities, Surendranath insisted that only constitutional means be used in the struggle for self-government. When the Extremists cried for more drastic measures against the foreigner, he opposed them as firmly as he opposed the British. Twice president of the Congress, he left it in 1918 to head the All-India Liberal Federation when the younger Congress leaders threatened to obstruct the introduction of the important Montagu-Chelmsford Reforms. His persistence in his chosen course earned him the respect of Indians and British alike and won him the aptly coined nickname of "Surrender-not" Banerjea.

The Need for Indian Unity

Understanding between Hindus and Muslims formed a major plank in the Moderates' platform. In one of Surendranath's earliest speeches (in 1878) he exhorted the young men of the country to strive for unity as a patriotic duty.

[From Banerjea, *Speeches and Writings,* pp. 227–31]

Young men, whom I see around me in such large numbers, you are the hopes of your families. May I not also say, you are the hopes of your country? Your country expects great things from you. Now I ask, how many of you are prepared, when you have finished your studies at the college, to devote your lives, to consecrate your energies to the good of your country? I repeat the question and I pause for a reply. [Here the speaker paused for a few seconds. Cries of "all, all" from all sides of the gallery.] The response is in every way worthy of yourselves and of the education which you are receiving. May you prove true to your resolve, and carry out in life the high purposes which animate your bosoms.

Gentlemen, I have a strong conviction and an assured belief that there comes a time in the history of a nation's progress, when every man may verily be said to have a mission of his own to accomplish. Such a time has now arrived for India. The fiat has gone forth. The celestial mandate has been issued that every Indian must now do his duty, or stand condemned before God and man. There was such a time of stirring activity in the glorious annals of England, when Hampden offered up his life for the deliverance of his own country, when Algernon Sydney laid down his head on the block to rid his country of a hated tyrant, when English bishops did not hesitate in the discharge of their duty to their Fatherland to descend from the performance of their ecclesiastical functions and appear as traitors before the bar of a Criminal Court. These are glorious reminiscences in England's immortal history, which Englishmen to this day look back upon with pride and satisfaction. It is not indeed necessary for us to have recourse to violence in order to obtain the redress of our grievances. Constitutional agitation will secure for us those rights, the privileges which in less favoured countries are obtained by sterner means. But peaceful as are the means to be enforced, there is a stern duty to be performed by every Indian. And he who fails in that duty is a traitor before God and man.

In holding up for your acceptance the great principle of Indian unity, I do not lay claims to originality. Three hundred years ago, in the Punjab, the immortal founder of Sikhism, the meek, the gentle, the blessed Nānak preached the great doctrine of Indian unity and endeavoured to knit together Hindus and Musulmans under the banner of a common faith. That attempt was eminently successful. Nānak became the spiritual founder of the Sikh empire. He preached the great doctrine of peace and good will between Hindus and Musulmans. And standing in the presence of his great example, we too must preach the great doctrine of peace and good will between Hindus and Musulmans, Christians and Parsees, aye between all sections of the great Indian community. Let us raise aloft the banner of our country's progress. Let the word "Unity" be inscribed there in characters of glittering gold. We have had enough of past jealousies, past dissensions, past animosities. The spirits of the dead at Paniput[7] will testify to our bloody strifes. The spirits of the dead in other battlefields will testify to the same fact. There may be religious differences between us. There may be social differences between us. But there is a common platform where we may all meet, the platform of our country's welfare. There is a common cause which may blind [bind] us together, the cause of Indian progress. There is a common Divinity, to whom we may uplift our voices in adoration, the Divinity who presides over the destinies of our country. In the name then of a common country, let us all, Hindus, Musulmans, Christians, Parsees, members of the great Indian community, throw the pall of oblivion over jealousies and dissensions of bygone times and embracing one another in fraternal love and affection, live and work for the benefit of a beloved Fatherland. Under

English auspices there is indeed a great future for India. I am confident of the great destinies that are in store for us. You and I may not live to see that day. These eyes of ours may not witness that spectacle of ineffable beauty. It may not be permitted to us to exclaim Simeonlike, "Now Lord, lettest thou thy servant depart in peace." It may not be permitted to us to exclaim like the Welsh Bard on the heights of Snowdon, "Visions of glory, spare my aching sight." But is it nothing to know when you are dying, when you are about to take leave of this world, of its joys and sorrows, when the past of your life is unfurled before you, when eternity opens wide its portals, is it nothing to know at that last awful, supreme moment of your lives, that you have not lived in vain, that you have lived for the benefit of others, that you have lived to help in the cause of your country's regeneration? Let us all lead worthy, honorable, and patriotic lives, that we may all live and die happily and that India may be great. This is my earnest and prayerful request. May it find a response in your sympathetic hearts.

Faith in England

The backbone of the Moderates' creed was faith that the British would grant self-government to India when she was prepared for it. Surendranath enunciated this creed in the peroration of his presidential address to the Congress in 1895.

[From Banerjea, *Speeches and Writings*, pp. 93–96]

We feel that in this great struggle in which we are engaged, the moral sympathies of civilized humanity are with us. The prayers of the good and the true in all parts of the world follow us. They will welcome as glad tidings of great joy the birth of an emancipated people on the banks of the Ganges. For, have they not all read about our ancient civilization; how, in the morning of the world, before the Eternal City had been built upon the Seven Hills, before Alexander had marched his army to the banks of the Tigris, before Babylonian astronomers had learnt to gaze upon the starry world, our ancestors had developed a great civilization, and how that civilization has profoundly influenced the course of modern thought in the highest concerns of man? Above all, we rely with unbounded confidence on the justice and generosity of the British people and of their representatives in Parliament. . . .

Nevertheless we feel that much yet remains to be done, and the impetus must come from England. To England we look for inspiration and guidance.

To England we look for sympathy in the struggle. From England must come the crowning mandate which will enfranchise our peoples. England is our political guide and our moral preceptor in the exalted sphere of political duty. English history has taught us those principles of freedom which we cherish with our lifeblood. We have been fed upon the strong food of English constitutional freedom. We have been taught to admire the eloquence and genius of the great masters of English political philosophy. We have been brought face to face with the struggles and the triumphs of the English people in their stately march towards constitutional freedom. Where will you find better models of courage, devotion, and sacrifice; not in Rome, not in Greece, not even in France in the stormy days of the Revolution—courage tempered by caution, enthusiasm leavened by sobriety, partisanship softened by a large-hearted charity—all subordinated to the one predominating sense of love of country and love of God.

We should be unworthy of ourselves and of our preceptors—we should, indeed, be something less than human—if, with our souls stirred to their inmost depths, our warm Oriental sensibilities roused to an unwanted pitch of enthusiasm by the contemplation of these great ideals of public duty, we did not seek to transplant into our own country the spirit of those free institutions which have made England what she is. In the words of Lord Lansdowne, a wave of unrest is passing through this country. But it is not the unrest of discontent or disloyalty to the British government—it is the unrest which is the first visible sign of the awakening of a new national life. It is the work of Englishmen—it is the noblest monument of their rule—it is the visible embodiment of the vast moral influence which they are exercising over the minds of the people of India. Never in the history of the world have the inheritors of an ancient civilization been so profoundly influenced by the influx of modern ideas. In this Congress from year to year we ask England to accomplish her glorious work. The course of civilization following the path of the sun has traveled from East to West. The West owes a heavy debt to the East. We look forward to the day when that debt will be repaid, not only by the moral regeneration, but by the political enfranchisement of our people.

Faith in Social Progress

In concluding his memoirs in his old age, Surendranath looked back at the changes that had taken place in Hindu society during his lifetime and summed up that faith in gradual reform which is one of the hallmarks of a Moderate.

[From Banerjea, A Nation in Making, pp. 397–98]

I feel that if we have to advance in social matters, we must, so far as practicable, take the community with us by a process of steady and gradual uplift, so that there may be no sudden disturbance or dislocation, the new being adapted to the old, and the old assimilated to the new. That has been the normal path of progress in Hindu society through the long centuries. It would be idle to contend that Hindu society is today where it was two hundred years ago. It moves slowly, perhaps more slowly than many would wish, but in the words of Galileo "it does move," more or less according to the lines of adaptation that I have indicated. The question of sea-voyage, or child-marriage, or even enforced widowhood, is not today where it was in the latter part of the last century. Fifty years ago I was an outcaste (being an England-returned Brahmin) in the village where I live. Today I am an honored member of the community. My public services have, perhaps, partly contributed to the result. But they would have been impotent, as in the case of Ram Mohun Roy for many long years after his death, if they were not backed by the slow, the silent, the majestic forces of progress, working noiselessly but irresistibly in the bosom of society, helping on the fruition of those ideas which have been sown in the public mind. Remarkable indeed have been, in many respects, the relaxations and the removal of restrictions of caste. Dining with non-Hindus, which was an abomination not many years ago, is now connived at, if not openly countenanced. A still more forward step towards loosening the bonds of caste has been taken within the last few years. The barriers of marriage between some sub-castes have been relaxed, and marriages between hitherto prohibited subcastes of Brahmins and Kayasthas are not infrequent, and I have had some personal share in this reform. Beneficent are the activities of the Brāhmo Samāj, but behind them is the slower but larger movement of the general community, all making towards progress.

MAHADEV GOVIND RANADE: PIONEER MAHARASHTRIAN REFORMER

Western cultural influence came, as did British rule itself, to different parts of India at different times. The coastal ports founded in the seventeenth centuries—Madras, Bombay, Calcutta—became and remain today the centers of the new order of life and thought. The spread of this order into the hinterland, however, was a slow and irregular process. Bengal, the home of

a number of thinkers considered thus far, was the first province to fall entirely under British sway and therefore the first to react to the impact of
Western ways and ideas.

On the opposite side of the Indian subcontinent, protected by their
mountain fortresses in the Western Ghats, the proud kingdoms of Maharashtra were among the last to surrender to foreign rule. The leadership that
made this prolonged resistance possible came notably from two caste groups.
The fighting Maratha-Kunbi castes under Shivaji (1630?–1680) and his descendants provided most of the military force, while the small but influential Chitpāvan brāhman caste provided the peshwas (prime ministers) and
the intellectual leaders of later times. Even after the final defeat of the
peshwa's government in 1818 the city of Poona remained the center of
Maharashtrian intellectual life. In the closing decades of the nineteenth
century, the Chitpāvan brāhman caste produced three leaders whose names
are to be inscribed in Indian nationalism's hall of fame—Ranade, Gokhale,
and Tilak.

Mahadev Govind Ranade (1842–1901), the eldest of three children, was
born into a strictly orthodox household. An extremely serious student, he
begged his father to send him to school in Bombay to complete his English
education. At fourteen he entered the Elphinstone Institution and at seventeen took his place in the first class to enroll in the new Bombay University. He distinguished himself by his diligence and originality of thought
and became a teacher of economics and later of history and literature at his
alma mater. He chose, however, to make his career in law, and before he
was thirty he had received his first appointment as a subordinate judge in
the government courts at Poona.

During his thirty years as a judge, Ranade gently but firmly worked for
the reform of such social evils as child marriage, the nonremarriage of widows, and the seclusion of women. In many ways his efforts resembled those
of Rammohun Roy, whom he admired as a patriot and as a godly man.
Ranade was one of the early members of the Prarthana Samaj (Prayer Society, modeled after the Brahmo Samaj), whose founding in 1867 was sparked
by Keshub Chunder Sen's earlier visits to Bombay. Under Ranade's judi-
cious guidance the Prarthana Samaj did not cut itself off from the rest of
Hindu society, but strove gradually to bring the orthodox around to its
position. Despite the vociferous and sometimes violent opposition of Tilak
and his school, Ranade's policy of moderation in social reform met with
increasing success.

Disqualified from entering active politics by his judgeship, Ranade's contribution to the nationalist movement was largely in the realm of social and economic reform. In 1887, he founded the Indian National Social Conference as a separate organization that met concurrently with the annual Congress sessions, and in 1890 he inaugurated the Industrial Association of Western India. Ranade's views on economics grew out of his long and patient study of Indian problems. He concluded that their constructive solution lay in a vigorous policy of industrial and commercial development under British government auspices.

Ranade's infinite capacity for taking pains, his saintly disposition, and his devotion to the welfare of India inspired to greater patriotic endeavor the hundreds of younger men with whom he maintained contact in person or through correspondence. He was a Moderate in the best sense of the term—scholarly, patient, practical, constructive, never wasting his time in denouncing those who held other views. After his death in 1901 his memory continued to inspire the leaders of Western India—Gokhale and, after him, Gandhi, carrying on the tradition he initiated of social and economic reform as an integral part of selfless public service.

Revivalism versus Reform

The impracticability of reviving ancient traditions merely because they were ancient was tellingly demonstrated by Ranade in his 1897 Social Conference address. Having explained why he rejected the suggestion of the Brahmo and Arya Samajists that all social reformers should convert to those faiths, he went on to analyze the four basic causes of the degeneration of Indian society.

[From Chintamani, *Indian Social Reform*, part 2, pp. 89–95]

While the new religious sects condemn us for being too orthodox, the extreme orthodox section denounce us for being too revolutionary in our methods. According to these last, our efforts should be directed to revive, and not to reform. I have many friends in this camp of extreme orthodoxy, and their watchword is that revival, and not reform, should be our motto. They advocate a return to the old ways, and appeal to the old authorities and the old sanction. Here also, as in the instance quoted above, people speak without realizing the full significance of their own words. When we are asked to revive our institutions and customs, people seem to be very much at sea as to what it is they seem to revive. What particular period of our history is to be taken as the old? Whether the period of the Vedas, of the Smritis, of the Puranas or of the Mahomedan or modern Hindu times? Our usages have been changed from time to time by a slow process of growth, and in some cases of decay and corruption, and we cannot stop at a particular period without breaking the continuity of the whole. When my revivalist friend presses his argument upon me, he has to seek recourse in some subterfuge which really furnishes no reply to the question—what shall we revive? Shall we revive the old habits of our people when the most sacred of our caste indulged in all the abominations as we now understand them of animal food and drink which exhausted every section of our country's zoology and botany? The men and the gods of those old days ate and drank forbidden things to excess in a way no revivalist will now venture to recommend. Shall we revive the twelve forms of sons, or eight forms of marriage, which included capture, and recognized mixed and illegitimate intercourse? Shall we revive the Niyoga system of procreating sons on our brother's wives when widowed? Shall we revive the old liberties taken by the Rishis and by the wives of the Rishis with the marital tie? Shall we revive the hecatombs of animals sacrificed from year's end to year's end, and in which human beings were not spared as propitiatory offerings? Shall we revive the Shakti worship of the left hand with its indecencies and practical debaucheries? Shall we revive the sati and infanticide customs, or the flinging of living men into the rivers, or over rocks, or hookswinging, or the crushing beneath Jagannath car?[8] Shall we revive the internecine wars of the Brahmins and Kshatriyas, or the cruel persecution and degradation of the aboriginal population? Shall we revive the custom of many husbands to one wife or of many wives to one husband? Shall we require our Brahmins to cease to be landlords and gentlemen, and turn into beggars and dependants upon the king as in olden times? These instances will suffice to show that the plan of reviving the ancient usages and customs will not work our salvation, and is not practicable. If these usages were good and beneficial, why were they altered by our wise ancestors? If they were bad and injurious, how can any claim be put forward for their restoration after so many ages? Besides, it seems to be forgotten that in a living organism, as society is, no revival is possible. The dead and the buried or burnt are dead, buried, and burnt once for all, and the dead past cannot therefore be revived except by a reformation of the old materials into new organized beings. If revival is impossible, reformation is the only alternative open to sensible people, and now it may be asked what is the principle on which this reformation must be based? People have very hazy ideas on this subject. It seems to many that it is the outward form which has to be changed, and if this change can be made, they think that all the difficulties in our way will vanish. If we change our outward manners and customs, sit in a particular way, or walk in a particular fashion, our work according to them is accomplished. I cannot but think that much of the prejudice against the reformers is due to this misunderstanding. It is not the outward form, but the inward form, the thought and the idea which determines the outward form, that has to be changed if real reformation is desired.

Now what have been the inward forms or ideas which have been hastening our decline during the past three thousand years? These ideas may be briefly set forth as isolation, submission to outward force or power more than to the voice of the inward conscience, perception of fictitious differences between men and men due to heredity and birth, passive acquiescence in evil or wrong doing, and a general indifference to secular well-being, almost bordering upon fatalism. These have been the root ideas of our ancient social system. They have as their natural result led to the existing family arrangements where the woman is entirely subordinated to the man and the lower castes to the higher castes, to the length of depriving men of their natural respect for humanity. All the evils we seek to combat result from the prevalence of these ideas. They are mere corollaries to these axiomatic assumptions. They prevent some of our people from realizing what they really are in all conscience, neither better nor worse than their fellows, and that whatever garb men may put on, they are the worse for assuming dignities and powers which do not in fact belong to them. As long as these ideas remain operative on our minds, we may change our outward forms and institutions, and be none the better for the change. These ideas have produced in the long course of ages their results on our character, and we must judge their good or bad quality, as Saint Paul says, by the fruits they have borne. Now that these results have been disastrous, nobody disputes or doubts, and the lesson to be drawn for our guidance in the future from this fact is that the current of these ideas must be changed, and in the place of the old worship we paid to them, we must accustom ourselves and others to worship and reverence new ideals. In place of isolation, we must cultivate the spirit of fraternity or elastic expansiveness. At present it is everybody's ambition to pride himself upon being a member of the smallest community that can be conceived, and the smaller the number of those with whom you can dine, or marry, or associate, the higher is your perfection and purity, the purest person is he who cooks his own food, and does not allow the shadow of even his nearest friend to fall upon his cooked food. Every caste and every sect has thus a tendency to split itself into smaller castes and smaller sects in practical life. Even in philosophy and religion, it is a received maxim that knowledge is for the few, and that salvation is only possible for the esoteric elect with whom only are the virtues of sanctity and wisdom, and that for the rest of mankind, they must be left to wander in the wilderness, and grovel in superstition and even vice, with only a coloring of so-called religion to make them respectable. Now all this must be changed. The new mold of thought on this head must be, as stated above, cast on the lines of fraternity, a capacity to expand outwards, and to make more cohesive inwards the bonds of fellowship. Increase the circle of your friends and associates, slowly and cautiously if you will, but the tendency must be towards a general recognition of the essential equality between man and man. It will beget sympathy and power. It will strengthen your own hands, by the sense that you have numbers with you, and not against you, or as you foolishly imagine, below you.

The next idea which lies at the root of our helplessness is the sense that we are always intended to remain children, to be subject to outside control and never to rise to the dignity of self-control by making our conscience and our reason the supreme, if not the sole, guide to our conduct. All past history has been a terrible witness to the havoc committed by this misconception. We are children no doubt but the children of God, and not of man, and the voice of God is the only voice [to] which we are bound to listen. Of course, all of us cannot listen to this voice when we desire it, because from long neglect and dependence upon outside help, we have benumbed this faculty of conscience in us. With too many of us, a thing is true or false, righteous or sinful, simply because somebody in the past has said that it is so. Duties and obligations are duties and obligations, not because we feel them to be so, but because somebody reputed to be wise has laid it down that they are so. In small matters of manners and courtesies, this outside dictation is not without its use. But when we abandon ourselves entirely to this helpless dependence on other wills, it is no wonder that we become helpless as children in all departments of life. Now the new idea which should take up the place of this helplessness and dependence is not the idea of a rebellious overthrow of all authority, but that of freedom responsible to the voice of God in us. Great and wise men in the past, as in the present, have a claim upon our regards, but they must not come between us and our God—the Divine principle enthroned in the heart of every one of us high or low. It is this sense of self-respect, or rather respect for the God in us, which has to be cultivated. It is a very tender plant which takes years and years to make it grow. But there is the capacity and the power, and we owe it as a duty to ourselves to undertake the task. Revere all human authority, pay your respects to all prophets and all revelations, but never let this reverence and respect come in the way of the dictates of conscience, the Divine command in us.

Similarly there is no doubt that men differ from men in natural capacities, and aptitudes, and that heredity and birth are factors of considerable importance in our development. But it is at the same time true they are not the only factors that determine the whole course of our life for good or for evil, under a law of necessity. Heredity and birth explain many things, but this Law of Karma does not explain all things! What is worse, it does not explain the mystery that makes man and woman what they really are, the reflection and the image of God. Our passions and our feelings, our pride and our ambition, lend strength to these agencies, and with their help the Law of Karma completes our conquest, and in too many cases enforces our surrender. The new idea that should come in here is that this Law of Karma can be controlled and set back by a properly trained will, when it is made subservient to a higher will than ours. This we see in our everyday life, and Necessity, or the Fates are, as our own texts tell us, faint obstacles in the way of our advancement if we devote ourselves to the Law of Duty. I admit that this misconception is very hard to remove, perhaps the hardest of the old ideas. But removed it must be, if not in this life or generation, in many lives and generations, if we are ever to rise to our full stature.

The fourth old form or idea to which I will allude here is our acquiescence in wrong or evil doing as an inevitable condition of human life, about which we need not be very particular. All human life is a vanity and a dream, and we are not much concerned with it. This view of life is in fact atheism in its worst form. No man or woman really ceases to be animal who does not perceive or realize that wrong or evil-doing, impurity and vice, crime and misery, and sin of all kinds, is really our animal existence prolonged. It is the beast in us which blinds us to impurity and vice, and makes them even attractive. There must be nautches[9] in our temples, say our priests, because even the Gods cannot do without these impure fairies. This is only a typical instance of our acquiescence in impurity. There must be drunkenness in the world, there must be poverty and wretchedness and tyranny, there must be fraud and force, there must be thieves and the law to punish them. No doubt these are facts, and there is no use denying their existence, but in the name of all that is sacred and true, do not acquiesce in them, do not hug these evils to your bosom, and cherish them. Their contact is poisonous, not the less deadly because it does not kill, but it corrupts men. A healthy sense of the true dignity of our nature, and of man's high destiny, is the best corrective and antidote to this poison. I think I have said more than enough to suggest to your reflecting minds what it is that we have to reform. All admit that we have been deformed. We have lost our stature, we are bent in a hundred places, our eyes lust after forbidden things, our ears desire to hear scandals about our neighbors, our tongues lust to taste forbidden fruit, our hands itch for another man's property, our bowels are deranged with indigestible food. We cannot walk on our feet, but require stilts or crutches. This is our present social polity, and now we want this deformity to be removed; and the only way to remove it is to place ourselves under the discipline of better ideas and forms such as those I have briefly touched above. Now this is the work of the Reformer. Reforms in the matter of infant marriage and enforced widowhood, in the matter of temperance and purity, intermarrige between castes, the elevation of the low castes, and the readmission of converts, and the regulation of our endowments and charities, are reforms only so far and no further as they check the influence of the old ideas and promote the growth of the new tendencies. The Reformer has to infuse in himself the light and warmth of nature, and he can only do it by purifying and improving himself and his surroundings. He must have his family, village, tribe, and nation recast in other and new molds, and that is the reason why Social Reform becomes our obligatory duty, and not a mere pastime which might be given up at pleasure. Revival is, as I have said, impossible; as impossible as mass-conversion into other faiths. But even if it were possible, its only use to us would be if the reforms elevated us and our surroundings, if they made us stronger, braver, truer men with all our faculties of endurance and work developed, with all our sympathies fully awakened and refined, and if with our heads and hearts acting in union with a purified and holy will, they made us feel the dignity of our being and the high destiny of our existence, taught us to love all, work with all, and feel for all.

India's Need: State Guidance of Economic Development

In his essay of 1892 on "Indian Political Economy," Ranade first showed that English *laissez faire* doctrines were being challenged by more recent theories of the science of economics and were not necessarily relevant to India's problems, then continued with a diagnosis of the Indian economy.

[From Ranade, Essays on Indian Economics, pp. 22–25, 33–36]

This resumé of the past and contemporary history of the growth of economic Sciences in England, France, Germany, Italy, and America will satisfy the student that modern European thought does not at all countenance the view of the English writers of the Ricardian School, that the principles of the science, as they have enunciated them in their textbooks, are universally and necessarily true for all times and places, and for all stages of advancement. Modern thought is veering to the conclusion that the individual and his interests are not the center round which the theory should revolve, that the true center is the body politic of which that individual is a member, and that collective defense and well-being, social education and discipline, and the duties, and not merely the interests, of men, must be taken into account, if the theory is not to be merely utopian. The method to be followed is not the deductive but the historical method, which takes account of the past in its forecast of the future; and relativity, and not absoluteness, characterizes the conclusions of economical science. There are those who seek to get over this difficulty by differentiating the science from what they are disposed to call the art of economy. This divorce of theory and practice is, however, a mischievous error, which relegates the science to the sterility of an ideal dream or a puzzle, and condemns the art to the position of a rule of the thumb. Theory is only enlarged practice, practice is theory studied in its relation to proximate causes. The practice is predetermined by the theory which tests its truth, and adapts it to different conditions by reason of its grasp of the deep-seated, permanent, and varied basal truths. I hope thus to have shown that the nature of the subject itself as a branch of social science, which is best studied historically and not deductively, the actual practice of the most civilized nations and the history of the growth of its theory given above alike establish the doctrine of relativity, and the predominant claim of collective welfare over individual interests, as the principal features in which the highest minds of the present day chiefly differ from the economical writers of the old school, with their a priori conclusions based on individual self-interest and unrestricted competition.

   We have next to consider the bearings of this enlarged view of the science in its Indian aspects. The characteristics of our social life are the prevalence of status over contract, of combination over competition. Our habits of mind are conservative to a fault. The aptitudes of climate and soil facilitate the production of raw materials. Labor is cheap and plentiful, but unsteady, unthrifty, and unskilled. Capital is scarce, immobile, and unenterprising. Cooperation on a large scale of either capital or labor is unknown. Agriculture is the chief support of nearly the whole population, and this agriculture is carried on under conditions of uncertain rainfall. Commerce and manufactures on a large scale are but recent importations, and all industry is carried on, on the system of petty farming, retail dealing, and job working by poor people on borrowed capital. There is an almost complete absence of a landed gentry or wealthy middle class. The land is a monopoly of the State. The desire for accumulation is very weak, peace and security having been almost unknown over large areas for any length of time till within the last century. Our laws and institutions favour a low standard of life, and encourage subdivision and not concentration of wealth. The religious ideals of life condemn the ardent pursuit of wealth as a mistake to be avoided as far as possible. These are old legacies and inherited weaknesses. Stagnation and dependence, depression and poverty—these are written in broad characters on the face of the land and its people. To these must be added the economical drain of wealth and talents, which foreign subjection has entailed on the country. As a compensation against all these depressing influences, we have to set off the advantage of a free contact with a race which has opened the country to the commerce of the world, and by its superior skill and resources has developed communications in a way previously unknown. If we wish to realize our situation fully, we may not overlook this factor, because, it represents the beam of light which alone illumines the prevailing darkness. It cannot well be a mere accident that the destinies of this country have been entrusted to the guidance of a nation whose characteristic strength is opposed to all our weaknesses, whose enterprise, chiefly in commerce and manufactures, knows no bounds, whose capital overflows the world, among whom contract has largely superseded status, and competition and cooperation play a predominant part, whose view of life is full of hope, and whose powers of organization have never been surpassed.

Ranade next advanced several reasons why industrial enterprise should be encouraged, and urged government action to populate untilled lands, protect peasants against excessive taxation, and prevent exploitation by landlords or moneylenders. In his conclusion he argued that the state should play a more active role in the economic development of the country.

Lastly comes the great department of governmental interference. The meddlesomeness of the mercantile system provoked a reaction against state control and guidance towards the end of the last century in favor of natural liberty. The doctrines of this negative school have now in their turn been abused by a too logical extension of its principles. There is a decided reaction in Europe against the *laissez faire* system. Even in England, the recent factory legislation, the qualified recognition by law of Trades-Unionism, the poor law system, and the Irish Land Settlement, are all instances which indicate the same change of view. Speaking roughly, the province of state interference and control is practically being extended so as to restore the good points of the mercantile system without its absurdities. The State is now more and more recognized as the national organ for taking care of national needs in all matters in which individual and cooperative efforts are not likely to be so effective and economic as national effort. This is the correct view to take of the true functions of a state. To relegate them to the simple duty of maintaining peace and order is really to deprive the community of many of the advantages of the social union. Education, both liberal and technical, post and telegraphs, railway and canal communications, the pioneering of new enterprise, the insurance of risky undertakings—all these functions are usefully discharged by the state. The question is one of time, fitness, and expediency, not one of liberty and rights. In our own country the State has similarly enlarged its functions with advantage. The very fact that the rulers belong to a race with superior advantages imposes this duty on them of attempting things which no native rulers, past or present, could as well achieve, or possibly even think of. This obligation is made more peremptory by the fact that the State claims to be the sole landlord, and is certainly the largest capitalist in the country. While the State in India has done much in this way in the working of iron and coal fields, and in the experiments made about cotton and tobacco, and in tea and coffee and cinchona Plantations, it must be admitted that, as compared with its resources and the needs of the country, these attempts are as nothing by the side of what has been attempted with success in France, Germany, and other countries, but which, unhappily, has not been attempted in this country. Even if political considerations forbid independent action in the matter of differential duties, the pioneering of new enterprises is a duty which the government might more systematically undertake with advantage. In truth, there is no difference of principle between lending such support and guidance, by the free use of its credit and superior organization, in pioneering industrial undertaking or subsidizing private cooperative effort, and its guaranteeing minimum interest to railway companies. The building up of national, not merely state, credit on broad foundations by helping people to acquire confidence in a free and largely ramified banking system, so advantageously worked in Europe under different forms, has also not been attempted here. There is, lastly, the duty cast on it of utilizing indigenous resources, and organizing them in a way to produce in India in state factories all products of skill which the state departments require in the way of stores. These are only a few of the many directions in which, far more than exchange and frontier difficulties, the highest statesmanship will have a field all its own for consideration and action. They will, no doubt, receive such consideration if only the minds of the rulers were once thoroughly freed from the fear of offending the so-called maxims of rigid economical science. It is time that a new departure should take place in this connection, and it is with a view to drawing public attention to this necessity that I have ventured to place before you the results of modern economic thought. In this, as in other matters, the conditions of Indian life are more faithfully reproduced in some of the continental countries and in America than in happy England, proud of its position, strong in its insularity, and the home of the richest and busiest community in the modern industrial world. If the attempt I have made leads to a healthy and full discussion of the change of policy I advocate, I shall regard myself amply repaid for my trouble.

GOPAL KRISHNA GOKHALE: SERVANT OF INDIA

The work of reform begun by Ranade was ably shouldered by his younger friend and colleague Gopal Krishna Gokhale (1866–1915). So close was the personal relationship between the two men during Ranade's lifetime—for years they met weekly to discuss their ideas and projects—that Gokhale's excursions into active politics can be regarded as the logical extension of his teacher's endeavors. Sprung from the same proud Maharashtrian stock, both leaders nevertheless clung to the policy of cooperation with the government and of moderate opposition to its evils. Gokhale, however, had to endure the merciless attacks of the Extremists during the stormiest decade in Indian politics up to that time.

Gokhale dedicated his life to public service at the age of nineteen, on his graduation from Elphinstone College, by joining the Deccan Education Society in Poona. Members of the Society took a vow of poverty for twenty years in order to devote their time exclusively to educating their fellow-countrymen. For his part, Gokhale became a teacher of English and mathematics in the Fergusson College founded by the Society in 1885. He soon met Justice Ranade and began his long and fruitful apprenticeship under him—examining documents, weighing evidence, analyzing fiscal data, and preparing comprehensive memoranda on public questions.

Gokhale attracted public attention with the sagacity of his carefully prepared speeches and in 1899 was elected a member of the recently formed Legislative Council for the state of Bombay. When only thirty-six, he became the Indian representative of this state on the Imperial Legislative Council, despite its limited powers the highest law-making body in India. For the last thirteen years of his life he wore himself out with his efforts to secure government cooperation in granting much needed financial and administrative reforms for India. "No taxation without representation," was the essence of his demand, and his annual speeches on the imperial budget effected many concessions from harassed ministers of finance.

In 1905 Gokhale founded the Servants of India Society in Poona, modeling it after the lay and monastic orders of the Catholic Church. Famine relief, education, Hindu-Muslim unity, and the elevation of the lowest castes were among the fields in which it carried on the work begun by its founder. Gokhale also took great interest in the problems of Indian emigrants to South Africa, giving freely of his advice and encouragement to their leader, M. K. Gandhi. Although bitterly reviled by Tilak and other supporters of violent action to end foreign rule, Gokhale's readiness to cooperate with the British in introducing gradual reforms helped to pave the way for the eventual peaceful transfer of power to an independent India.

Taxation Without Representation

Soon after taking his place in the Imperial Legislative Council, Gokhale made the first of his annual budget speeches. His attacks on the government's taxation policy are representative of the Moderates' preoccupation with the economic shortcomings of British rule.

[From Gokhale, *Speeches*, pp. 1–2, 8–11]

Your Excellency, I fear I cannot conscientiously join in the congratulations which have been offered to the Hon'ble Finance Member on the huge surplus which the revised estimates show for the last year. A surplus of seven crores[10] of rupees is perfectly unprecedented in the history of Indian finance, and coming as it does on the top of a series of similar surpluses realized when the country has been admittedly passing through very trying times, it illustrates to my mind in a painfully clear manner the utter absence of a due correspondence between the condition of the people and the condition of the finances of the country. Indeed, my Lord, the more I think about this matter the more I feel—and I trust Your Lordship will pardon me for speaking somewhat bluntly—that these surpluses constitute a double wrong to the community. They are a wrong in the first instance in that they exist at all—that government should take so much more from the people than is needed in times of serious depression and suffering; and they are also a wrong, because they lend themselves to easy misinterpretation and, among other things, render possible the phenomenal optimism of the Secretary of State for India, who seems to imagine that all is for the best in this best of lands. A slight examination of these surpluses suffices to show that they are mainly, almost entirely, currency surpluses, resulting from the fact that government still maintain the same high level of taxation which they considered to be necessary to secure financial equilibrium when the rupee stood at its lowest. . . .

A taxation so forced as not only to maintain a budgetary equilibrium but to yield as well "large, continuous, progressive surpluses"—even in years of trial and suffering—is, I submit, against all accepted canons of finance. In European countries, extraordinary charges are usually met out of borrowings, the object being to avoid, even in times of pressure, impeding the even, normal development of trade and industry by any sudden or large additions to the weight of public burdens. In India, where the economic side of such questions finds such scant recognition, and the principle of meeting the charges of the year with the resources of the year is carried to a logical extreme, the anxiety of the Financial Administration is not only to make both ends meet in good and bad years alike, but to present large surpluses year after year. . . . Taxation for financial equilibrium is what we all can understand, but taxation kept up in the face of the difficulties and misfortunes of a period of excessive depression and for "large, continuous and progressive surpluses" is evidently a matter which requires justification. At all events, those who have followed the course of the financial history of the period will admit that the fact viewed *per se* that "such large, continuous, and progressive surpluses" have occurred during the period—as a result not of a normal expansion of fiscal resources but of a forced up and heavy taxation—does not connote, as Lord George Hamilton contends, an advancing material prosperity of the country or argue any marvelous recuperative power on the part of the masses—as the Hon'ble Sir Edward Law urged last year. To them, at any rate, the apparent paradox of a suffering country and an overflowing treasury stands easily explained and is a clear proof of the fact that the level of national taxation is kept unjustifiably high, even when government are in a position to lower that level.

Improving the Lot of Low-Caste Hindus

One of Gokhale's chief concerns in the realm of social reform was the lot of the so-called "Untouchables." The appeal launched in this speech to a social conference in 1903 was answered after his death by Gandhi's devotion to their cause.

[From Gokhale, *Speeches*, pp. 740–47]

Mr. President and Gentlemen: The proposition which has been entrusted to me runs thus—"That this Conference holds that the present degraded condition of the low castes is, in itself and from the national point of view, unsatisfactory, and is of opinion that every well-wisher of the country should consider it his duty to do all he can to raise their moral and social condition by trying to rouse self-respect in these classes and placing facilities for education and employment within their reach."

   Gentlemen, I hope I am not given to the use of unnecessarily strong language and yet I must say that this resolution is not as strongly worded as it should have been. The condition of the low castes—it is painful to call them low castes—is not only unsatisfactory as this resolution says, it is so deeply deplorable that it constitutes a grave blot on our social arrangements; and, further, the attitude of our educated men towards this class is profoundly painful and humiliating. I do not propose to deal with this subject as an antiquarian; I only want to make a few general observations from the standpoint of justice, humanity, and national self-interest. I think all fair-minded persons will have to admit that it is absolutely monstrous that a class of human beings, with bodies similar to our own, with brains that can think and with hearts that can feel, should be perpetually condemned to a low life of utter wretchedness, servitude, and mental and moral degradation, and that permanent barriers should be placed in their way so that it should be impossible for them ever to overcome them and improve their lot. This is deeply revolting to our sense of justice. I believe one has only to put oneself mentally into their place to realize how grievous this injustice is. We may touch a cat, we may touch a dog, we may touch any other animal, but the touch of these human beings is pollution! And so complete is now the mental degradation of these people that they themselves see nothing in such treatment to resent, that they acquiesce in it as though nothing better than that was their due.

I remember a speech delivered seven or eight years ago by the late Mr. Ranade in Bombay, under the auspices of the Hindu Union Club. That was a time when public feeling ran high in India on the subject of the treatment which our people were receiving in South Africa. Our friend, Mr. Gandhi, had come here on a brief visit from South Africa and he was telling us how our people were treated in Natal and Cape Colony and the Transvaal—how they were not allowed to walk on footpaths or travel in first-class carriages on the railway, how they were not admitted into hotels, and so forth. Public feeling, in consequence, was deeply stirred, and we all felt that it was a mockery that we should be called British subjects, when we were treated like this in Great Britain's colonies. Mr. Ranade felt this just as keenly as any one else. He had been a never-failing adviser of Mr. Gandhi, and had carried on a regular correspondence with him. But it was Mr. Ranade's peculiar greatness that he always utilized occasions of excitement to give a proper turn to the national mind and cultivate its sense of proportion. And so, when every one was expressing himself in indignant terms about the treatment which our countrymen were receiving in South Africa, Mr. Ranade came forward to ask if we had no sins of our own to answer for in that direction. I do not exactly remember the title of his address. I think it was "Turn the searchlight inwards," or some such thing. But I remember that it was a great speech—one of the greatest that I have ever been privileged to hear. He began in characteristic fashion, expressing deep sympathy with the Indians in South Africa in the struggle they were manfully carrying on. He rejoiced that the people of India had awakened to a sense of the position of their countrymen abroad, and he felt convinced that this awakening was a sign of the fact that the dead bones in the valley were once again becoming instinct with life. But he proceeded to ask: "Was this sympathy with the oppressed and downtrodden Indians to be confined to those of our countrymen only who had gone out of India? Or was it to be general and to be extended to all cases where there was oppression and injustice?" It was easy, he said, to denounce foreigners, but those who did so were bound in common fairness to look into themselves and see if they were absolutely blameless in the matter. He then described the manner in which members of low caste were treated by our own community in different parts of India. It was a description which filled the audience with feelings of deep shame and pain and indignation. And Mr. Ranade very justly asked whether it was for those who tolerated such disgraceful oppression and injustice in their own country to indulge in all that denunciation of the people of South Africa. This question, therefore, is, in the first place, a question of sheer justice.

Next, as I have already said, it is a question of humanity. It is sometimes urged that if we have our castes, the people in the West have their classes, and after all, there is not much difference between the two. A little reflection will, however, show that the analogy is quite fallacious. The classes of the West are a perfectly elastic institution, and not rigid or cast-iron like our castes. Mr. Chamberlain, who is the most masterful personage in the British empire today, was at one time a shoemaker and then a screwmaker. Of course, he did not make shoes himself, but that was the trade by which he made money. Mr. Chamberlain today dines with royalty, and mixes with the highest in the land on terms of absolute equality. Will a shoemaker ever be able to rise in India in the social scale in a similar fashion, no matter how gifted by nature he might be? A great writer has said that castes are eminently useful for the preservation of society, but that they are utterly unsuited for purposes of progress. And this I think is perfectly true. If you want to stand where you were a thousand years ago, the system of castes need not be modified in any material degree. If, however, you want to emerge out of the slough in which you have long remained sunk, it will not do for you to insist on a rigid adherence to caste. Modern civilization has accepted greater quality for all as its watchword, as against privilege and exclusiveness, which were the root-ideas of the old world. And the larger humanity of these days requires that we should acknowledge its claims by seeking the amelioration of the helpless condition of our downtrodden countrymen.

Finally, gentlemen, this is a question of national self-interest. How can we possibly realize our national aspirations, how can our country ever hope to take her place among the nations of the world, if we allow large numbers of our countrymen to remain sunk in ignorance, barbarism, and degradation? Unless these men are gradually raised to a higher level, morally and intellectually, how can they possibly understand our thoughts or share our hopes or cooperate with us in our efforts? Can you not realize that so far as the work of national elevation is concerned, the energy, which these classes might be expected to represent, is simply unavailable to us? I understand that that great thinker and observer—Swami Vivekananda—held this view very strongly. I think that there is not much hope for us as a nation unless the help of all classes, including those that are known as low castes, is forthcoming for the work that lies before us. Moreover, is it, I may ask, consistent with our own self-respect that these men should be kept out of our houses and shut out from all social intercourse as long as they remain within the pale of Hinduism, whereas the moment they put on a coat and a hat and a pair of trousers and call themselves Christians, we are prepared to shake hands with them and look upon them as quite respectable? No sensible man will say that this is a satisfactory state of things. Of course, no one expects that these classes will be lifted up at once morally and intellectually to a position of equality with their more-favored countrymen.

This work is bound to be slow and can only be achieved by strenuous exertions for giving them education and finding for them honourable employment in life. And, gentlemen, it seems to me that, in the present state of India, no work can be higher or holier than this. I think if there is one question of social reform more than another that should stir the enthusiasm of our educated young men and inspire them with an unselfish purpose, it is this question of the degraded condition of our low castes. Cannot a few men—five percent, four percent, three, two, even one percent—of the hundreds and hundreds of graduates that the university turns out every year, take it upon themselves to dedicate their lives to this sacred work of the elevation of low castes? My appeal is not to the old or the middle-aged— the grooves of their lives are fixed—but I think I may well address such an appeal to the young members of our community—to those who have not yet decided upon their future course and who entertain the noble aspiration of devoting to a worthy cause the education which they have received. What the country needs most at the present moment is a spirit of self-sacrifice on the part of our educated young men, and they may take it from me that they cannot spend their lives in a better cause than raising the moral and intellectual level of these unhappy low castes and promoting their general well-being.

ROMESH CHUNDER DUTT: PIONEER ECONOMIC HISTORIAN

From his own experience as a government official in rural Bengal from 1871 to 1897, Romesh Chunder Dutt (1848–1909) felt deeply the poverty of India's villagers. After taking an early retirement, he wrote two volumes on India's economic history under British rule which attacked those policies that had led, in his opinion, to the poverty of the vast majority of his countrymen.

Dutt was born in Calcutta, the son of a surveyor in government service, and started school at the age of four. He saw a good deal of Bengal's countryside over the next eight years as his father was posted from one rural town to another. He remembered that in 1858 "great cheers" and "cries of 'Long live the Queen' in English and Bengali rent the air" when Victoria was proclaimed queen of India.[11] The following year his mother died, his father two years after that, and an affectionate uncle raised him until his marriage at fifteen. At sixteen he entered college. At nineteen, he and a friend left their homes secretly at night, joined young Surendranath Banerjea, and all sailed to London to study for the prestigious Indian Civil Service. As usual, he came out near the top of the list. He passed his bar exams as well and returned to India to take up his duties on a low rung of the civil service ladder.

By dint of hard work and good judgment he reached the post of divisional commissioner, the highest level an Indian had attained in the civil service. In 1895–1896 he had charge of the entire area that today is the State of Orissa. At intervals in this busy career he found time to write books about Bengal peasant life and Bengali literature, as well as two social and four historical novels in Bengali. In addition he applied his literary skill to the task of making both his countrymen and the Western world more aware of the greatness of ancient India's civilization. First he outraged orthodox Brahmans by rendering the sacred hymns of the *Rig Veda* into Bengali, then he published selections from them in English. He also wrote a three-volume *History of Civilization in Ancient India* with a patriotic purpose in mind. As he stated in his introduction: "No study has so potent an influence in forming a nation's mind, a nation's character, as a critical and careful study of its past history. And it is by such study alone that an unreasoning and superstitious worship of the past is replaced by a legitimate and manly admiration." [12] In addition, he selected and translated into English verse narrative passages from the *Mahābhārata* and *Rāmāyana*.

Romesh Dutt's services to his countrymen took new forms after retirement freed him to travel, give public speeches, and concentrate his writing on the relationship between India and Britain and how it might be improved. A series of terrible famines struck several areas of the country in 1896–1897 and 1900–1901, and Dutt's concern about how such catastrophes could be averted in the future was reflected in his presidential address to the Indian National Congress in 1899 and in his books *England and India, Famines in India, The Economic History of India Under Early British Rule,* and *India in the Victorian Age: An Economic History of the People.* In each he prescribed measures for making the government of India more sensitive to the needs of the peasantry and for lessening their tax burdens.

In his last five years, from 1904 to 1909, he resumed his career as an administrator by entering the service of the Gaekwar of Baroda, an Indian ruler in Gujarat. There he introduced some of the reforms he had implored the British to adopt in British India. From 1906 to 1909 he reasoned with Lord Morley, (then Secretary of State for India) privately and persuasively, in person and by mail, for that greater Indian participation in the provincial and central governments which parliament embodied in the Government of India Act of 1909. Later in that year he died, remembered by those who know his work as *garīb kā dost*—"the friend of the poor."

The Causes of India's Poverty

Romesh Chunder Dutt attributed India's poverty to Britain's failings on four counts: the discouragement of hand-woven cloth production; heavy and unpredictable taxes on agriculture; the outflow of money from India to pay its foreign debt and some of its administrative costs; and the absence of Indian representatives at the highest levels of government. Although his arguments on the first and third counts were countered to some extent in *The Economic Transition in India* (1911) by Theodore Morison, who noted that the "industrial transformation" of Canada, Argentina, Japan, and so forth, was also accompanied by the decline of "archaic" modes of production and considerable foreign indebtedness, Dutt's underlying assumption that India became impoverished under British rule remained a popular theme with nationalist leaders, including Gandhi and Nehru.

[From Dutt, *The Economic History of India Under Early British Rule*, pp. v–ix, xi–xvi, xxi–xxii]

Excellent works on the military and political transactions of the British in India have been written by eminent historians. No history of the people of India, of their trades, industries, and agriculture, and of their economic condition under British administration, has yet been compiled.

Recent famines in India have attracted attention to this very important subject, and there is a general and widespread desire to understand the condition of the Indian people—the sources of their wealth and the causes of their poverty. A brief Economic History of British India is therefore needed at the present time.

Englishmen can look back on their work in India, if not with unalloyed satisfaction, at least with some legitimate pride. They have conferred on the people of India what is the greatest human blessing—Peace. They have introduced Western Education, bringing an ancient and civilised nation in touch with modern thought, modern sciences, modern institutions and life. They have built up an Administration which, though it requires reform with the progress of the times, is yet strong and efficacious. They have framed wise laws, and have established Courts of Justice, the purity of which is as absolute as in any country on the face of the earth. These are results which no honest critic of British work in India regards without high admiration.

On the other hand, no open-minded Englishman contemplates the material condition of the people of India under British rule with equal satisfaction. The poverty of the Indian population at the present day is unparalleled in any civilised country; the famines which have desolated India within the last quarter of the nineteenth century are unexampled in their extent and intensity in the history of ancient or modern times. By a moderate calculation, the famines of 1877 and 1878, of 1889 and 1892, of 1897 and 1900, have carried off fifteen millions of people. The population of a fair-sized European country has been swept away from India within twenty-five years. A population equal to half of that of England has perished in India within a period which men and women, still in middle age, can remember.

What are the causes of this intense poverty and these repeated famines in India? Superficial explanations have been offered one after another, and have been rejected on close examination. It was said that the population increased rapidly in India and that such increase must necessarily lead to famines; it is found on inquiry that the population has never increased in India at the rate of England, and that during the last ten years it has altogether ceased to increase. It was said that the Indian cultivators were careless and improvident, and that those who did not know how to save when there was plenty, must perish when there was want; but it is known to men who have lived all their lives among these cultivators, that there is not a more abstemious, a more thrifty, a more frugal race of peasantry on earth. It was said that the Indian money-lender was the bane of India, and by his fraud and extortion kept the tillers of the soil in a chronic state of indebtedness; but the inquiries of the latest Famine Commission have revealed that the cultivators of India are forced under the thraldom of money-lenders by the rigidity of the Government revenue demand. It was said that in a country where the people depended almost entirely on their crops, they must starve when the crops failed in years of drought; but the crops in India, as a whole, have never failed, there has never been a single year when the food supply of the country was insufficient for the people, and there must be something wrong, when failure in a single province brings on a famine, and the people are unable to buy their supplies from neighbouring provinces rich in harvests. . . .

It is, unfortunately, a fact which no well-informed Indian official will ignore, that, in many ways, the sources of national wealth in India have been narrowed under British rule. India in the eighteenth century was a great manufacturing as well as a great agricultural country, and the products of the Indian loom supplied the markets of Asia and of Europe. It is, unfortunately, true that the East Indian Company and the British Parliament, following the selfish commercial policy of a hundred years ago, discouraged Indian manufacturers in the early years of British rule in order to encourage the rising manufactures of England. Their fixed policy, pursued during the last decades of the eighteenth century and the first decades of the nineteenth, was to make India subservient to the industries of Great Britain, and to make the Indian people grow raw produce only, in order to supply material for the looms and manufactories of Great Britain. This policy was pursued with unwavering resolution and with fatal success; orders were sent out, to force Indian artisans to work in the Company's factories; commercial residents were legally vested with extensive powers over villages and communities of Indian weavers; prohibitive tariffs excluded Indian silk and cotton goods from England; English goods were admitted into India free of duty or on payment of a nominal duty.

The British manufacturer, in the words of the historian H. H. Wilson, "employed the arm of political injustice to keep down and ultimately strangle a competitor with whom he could not have contended on equal terms;" millions of Indian artisans lost their earnings; the population of India lost one great source of their wealth. It is a painful episode in the history of British rule in India; but it is a story which has to be told to explain the economic condition of the Indian people, and their present helpless dependence on agriculture. The invention of the power-loom in Europe completed the decline of the Indian industries; and when in recent years the power-loom was set up in India, England once more acted towards India with unfair jealousy. An excise duty has been imposed on the production of cotton fabrics in India which disables the Indian manufacturer from competing with the manufacturer of Japan and China, and which stifles the new steam-mills of India.

Agriculture is now virtually the only remaining source of national wealth in India, and four-fifths of the Indian people depend on agriculture. But the Land Tax levied by the British Government is not only excessive but, what is worse, it is fluctuating and uncertain in many provinces.

It will appear from the facts stated above that the Land Tax in India is not only heavy and uncertain, but that the very principle on which it is raised is different from the principle of taxation in all well-administered countries. In such countries the State promotes the accumulation of wealth, helps the people to put money into their pockets, likes to see them prosperous and rich, and then demands a small share of their earnings for the expenses of the State. In India the State virtually interferes with the accumulation of wealth from the soil, intercepts the incomes and gains of the tillers, and generally adds to its land revenue demand at each recurring settlement, leaving the cultivators permanently poor. In England, in Germany, in the United States, in France and other countries, the State widens the income of the people, extends their markets, opens out new sources of wealth, identifies itself with the nation, grows richer with the nation. In India, the State has fostered no new industries and revived no old industries for the people; on the other hand, it intervenes at each recurring land settlement to take what it considers its share out of the produce of the soil. Each new [land tax] settlement in Bombay and in Madras is regarded by the people as a wrangle between them and the State as to how much the former will keep and how much the latter will take. It is a wrangle decided without any clear limits fixed by the law—a wrangle in which the opinion of the revenue officials is final, and there is no appeal to judges or Land Courts. The revenue increases and the people remain destitute.

Taxation raised by a king, says the Indian poet, is like the moisture of the earth sucked up by the sun, to be returned to the earth as fertilising rain; but the moisture raised from the Indian soil now descends as fertilising rain largely on other lands, not on India. Every nation reasonably expects that the proceeds of taxes raised in the country should be mainly spent in the country. Under the worst governments that India had in former times, this was the case. The vast sums which Afghan and Moghal Emperors spent on their armies went to support great and princely houses, as well as hundreds of thousands of soldiers and their families. The gorgeous palaces and monuments they built, as well as the luxuries and displays in which they indulged, fed and encouraged the manufacturers and artisans of India. Nobles and Commanders of the army, Subadars, Dewans, and Kazis,[13] and a host of inferior officers in every province and every district, followed the example of the Court; and mosques and temples, roads, canals and reservoirs, attested to their wide liberality, or even to their vanity. Under wise rulers as under foolish kings, the proceeds of taxation flowed back to the people and fructified their trade and industries. . . .

For one who has himself spent the best and happiest years of his life in the work of Indian administration, it is an ungracious and a painful task to dwell on the weak side of that administration, the financial and economic policy of the Indian government. I have undertaken this duty because at the present moment the economic story of British India has to be told, and the deep-seated cause of the poverty of the Indian people has to be explained. Place any other country under the same condition, with crippled industries, with agriculture subject to a heavy and uncertain Land Tax, and with financial arrangements requiring one-half of its revenues to be annually remitted out of the country, and the most prosperous nation on earth will soon know the horrors of famine. A nation prospers if the sources of its wealth are widened, and if the proceeds of taxation are spent among the people, and for the people. A nation is impoverished if the sources of its wealth are narrowed, and the proceeds of taxation are largely remitted out of the country. These are plain, self-evident economic laws, which operate in India, as in every other country, and the Indian statesman and administrator must feel that the poverty of India cannot be removed until Indian industries are revived, until a fixed and intelligible limit is placed on the Indian Land Tax, and until the Indian revenues are more largely spent in India. . . .

Nor are Indian administrators strong in the support of the Indian people. The Indian Government means the Viceroy and the Members of the Executive Council, viz., the Commander-in-Chief, the Military Member, the Public Works Member, the Finance Member, and the Legal Member. The people are not represented in this Council; their agriculture, their landed interests, their trades and industries, are not represented; there is not, and never has been, a single Indian member in the Council. All the Members of the Council are heads of spending departments, as was lately explained by Sir Auckland Colvin and Sir David Barbour before the Royal Commission on Indian expenditure. The Members are high English officials, undoubtedly interested in the welfare of the people, but driven by the duties of their office to seek for more money for the working of their departments; there are no Indian Members to represent the interests of the people. The forces are all arrayed on the side of expenditure, there are none on the side of retrenchment. . . .

"The government of a people by itself," said John Stuart Mill, "has a meaning and a reality; but such a thing as government of one people by another does not, and cannot exist. One people may keep another for its own use, a place to make money in, a human cattle-farm to be worked for the profits of its own inhabitants."

There is more truth in this strongly worded statement than appears at first sight. History does not record a single instance of one people ruling another in the interests of the subject nation. Mankind has not yet discovered any method for safeguarding the interests of a subject nation without conceding to that nation some voice in controlling the administration of their own concerns. . . .

The wisest administrators in the past, like Munro, Elphinstone, and Bentinck, . . . sought to promote the welfare of the people by accepting the co-operation of the people, as far as was possible, in their day. What is needed to-day is a continuance and development of the same policy, not a policy of exclusiveness and distrust. What is needed to-day is that British rulers, who know less of India to-day than their predecessors did fifty years ago, should descend from their dizzy isolation, and should stand amidst the people, work with the people, make the people their comrades and collaborators, and hold the people responsible for good administration. The cooperation of the people is essential to successful administration in every civilised country; the co-operation of the people is more needful in India than anywhere else on earth.

The dawn of a new century finds India deeper in distress and discontent than any preceding period of history. A famine, wider in the extent of country affected than any previous famine, has desolated the country. In parts of India, not affected by this famine, large classes of people attest to semi-starvation by their poor physique; numbers of them suffer from a daily insufficiency of food; and the poorer classes are trained by life-long hunger to live on less food than is needed for proper nourishment. In the presence of facts like these, party controversy is silenced; and every Englishman and every Indian, experienced in administration and faithful to the British Empire, feel it their duty to suggest methods for the removal of the gravest danger which has ever threatened the Empire of India.

NOTES

1. R. P. Masani, *Dadabhai Naoroji: The Grand Old Man of India*, p. 25.
2. Armed thieves, highway murderers, robber bands.
3. Dadabhai refers to the export from India of the savings and pensions of British officials, and to other costs of British rule such as supplies and military expenditures.
4. Vikramāditya, a great and good king in Indian legend.
5. William Wedderburn, *Allan Octavian Hume, C.B.*, pp. 51–52.
6. Surendranath Banerjea, *A Nation in Making, Being the Reminiscences of Fifty Years in Public Life*, p. 33.
7. Panipat, the site of numerous pitched battles in Indian history. It lies about fifty miles north of Delhi.
8. A huge cart used to carry the idol of Jagannath, "the Lord of the Universe," in the city of Puri. In fits of frenzy devotees would hurl themselves in front of its wheels. The word "juggernaut" derives from this source.
9. Women attached to temples as dancers (and sometimes as prostitutes).
10. One crore equals ten million rupees.
11. J. N. Gupta, *Life and Works of Romesh Chunder Dutt, C.I.E.*, p. 13.
12. *Ibid.*, pp. 123–24.
13. Provincial governors, chief ministers, and judges.

Chapter 4

THE MARRIAGE OF POLITICS AND RELIGION: THE EXTREMISTS

In much the same way as the opening of India to Western cultural influence stimulated the renaissance of Hinduism, so the imposition of foreign rule inevitably evoked powerful indigenous reactions in the political sphere. The militant xenophobia that had found expression in scattered resistance to British conquest, and in the unorganized uprisings of 1857–1858, finally crystallized in the late nineteenth century with the group of zealous nationalists known to others as the Extremists. This group possessed two weapons unavailable to previous militant opponents of British rule. First, they shared with their Moderate rivals the use of a common "national" language, English, and through it enjoyed the opportunities for political agitation provided by the press, the schools, and the Indian National Congress. Second, they were able to draw on the newly formulated ideals of renascent Hinduism and to create a potent ideology out of the marriage between these ideals and the imported concepts of patriotism and national unity.

Impatient to throw off the foreign yoke, the Extremists concentrated on building up mass support for the nationalist movement. To create this support and to unify the Westernized elite with the Hindu peasantry and townspeople, they appealed to three principal ties common to both the educated and the uneducated—language, history, and religion. Casting off the use of English wherever possible, they wrote and spoke in the regional languages understood by the common people. As a means of heightening patriotic fervor, they fostered pride in a glorious past, when Hindu kings and warriors ruled the land. Most effective of all, because it had the broadest appeal, was the use of religious symbolism and terminology to instill in all Hindus a fervent devotion to the Motherland.

In contrast to the Moderates, the Extremists regarded such tasks as social reform and Hindu-Muslim cooperation as mere side issues draining energies from the political struggle and weakening Hindu solidarity. At times their anger at Muslim collaboration with the British spurred them to engage openly in anti-Muslim activity, heedless of the fact that in so doing they were ruining the chances of creating an independent but undivided India. The 1905 partition of Bengal into Hindu and Muslim majority areas drove a further wedge between the two religious communities, for it encouraged prominent Muslims to enter into a tacit alliance with the British against Hindu ambitions (the Muslim League was founded in 1906, and its demand for separate electorates was granted in 1909). The danger that the more numerous and better-educated Hindu community would preempt the positions of power and influence in a self-governing India gave many Muslims a pressing reason to convert to friendship their traditional hostility to the British.

Both Moderates and Extremists insisted that divided Bengal be reunited, but the latter urged that radical measures be taken to coerce the ruling power. In essence, their program was much like the one Gandhi introduced fifteen years later, being based on the principle of reducing Indian dependence on the British in every possible way. Its principal aims were the boycott of foreign goods, the use of Indian-made articles (or swadeshi—"of one's own country"), the strengthening of an indigenous system of education, and, in time, the creation of a parallel government of, by, and for the Indian people.

Such a bold stand, coupled with the religious ideology that motivated it, captured the imagination of younger men more readily than did the cautious policies of the Moderates, and the following of the Extremists increased rapidly in numbers after 1905. Their abortive attempt to gain control of the Congress led to a schism in that body at the 1907 session. For the next decade most of the Extremist leaders were either in jail, in exile, or in retirement, but the continuance of terrorist activity—climaxing in an attempt on the viceroy's life in 1912—showed that their memory was still honored in their absence. The rescinding of the partition of Bengal in 1911 and the altered situation produced by the First World War made it possible for the Moderates and the Extremists to patch up their quarrel in 1916. The death of the Extremists' greatest leader, Tilak, in 1920, marked the end of an era. In that same year the Congress submitted to Gandhi's unique form of leadership.

Although the heyday of the Extremists was short-lived, their chief contribution to modern Indian thought—the creation of a Hindu nationalism combining religious with political ideas—paved the way for the decades of

Gandhi's dominance, as well as for the emergence of the two major non-Congress parties that he would try, in vain, to reconcile—the Muslim League and the Hindu Mahasabha.

BANKIM CHANDRA CHATTERJEE: NATIONALIST AUTHOR

Gokhale's saying, "What Bengal thinks today, all India thinks tomorrow," is nowhere more applicable than in the case of the Bengali writer Bankim Chandra Chatterjee (1838–1894). Bankim, although he took no part in politics, first employed the triple appeal of language, history, and religion that enabled Hindu nationalism to win widespread support in the opening decade of the twentieth century. His historical novels in Bengali reminded his readers that their glorious past should inspire them to achieve an equally glorious future, and demonstrated the power of the pen as an instrument for stirring up patriotic emotions in times when overt political action was impossible.

Bankim was born near Calcutta, the son of a brāhman landlord and local deputy collector of revenue. A brilliant student, he passed through the anglicized educational system with distinction and was in 1858 one of two in Calcutta University's first graduating class. He was immediately offered a position as deputy magistrate in the Bengal civil service, and for all but one year held this rank until his retirement in 1891—a mute comment on the opportunities for advancement given to Indians in government service. Fortunately he found an outlet for his natural talent in another direction. Throughout his career as an official, he used his spare time to write stories and novels that captured the imagination of literate Bengal. Bankim employed a new prose style that combined the virtues of Sanskritized Bengali and the vigor of the common speech and that, for the first time since the introduction of English education, made it respectable for Bengalis to write in their own mother tongue.

Nationalism in all parts of the world has often been associated with attachment to a common language and its accompanying literary heritage. Bankim could thus be credited with quickening a Bengali, as distinct from an all-Indian, nationalism. But this distinction was rendered largely superfluous after 1905, when the agitation against the partition of Bengal took on a nationwide character. By the same token, the poem *Bande Mātaram*

(Hail to the Mother), which first appeared in one of his novels, soon became the *Marseillaise* of the nationalist movement throughout the country.

Bankim's original concept, "the Mother" of *Bande Mātaram*, referred at the same time to the land of Bengal and to the female aspect of the Hindu deity. From this fusion of the hitherto separate objects of patriotic and religious devotion sprang the central concept of modern Hindu nationalism. The concept of the divine Motherland, equating as it did love of country with love of God, made an instinctive appeal to the devout Hindu peasantry, for whom the secular reformism and Westernized nationalism of the Moderate leaders remained beyond comprehension.

For all the strength of dedication and mass appeal it generated, Hindu nationalism acted as a regressive force both in hindering social reform and in exacerbating the latent hostility between Hindus and Muslims. Bankim's novels faithfully reflect these two shortcomings, for with rare exceptions they picture well-meaning reformers as fools and Muslims as knaves. Nevertheless, his magic blend of religious sentiment, glorification of the Hindu past, and a beautiful style assured Bankim of lasting popularity among Bengalis and exerted a far-reaching influence on the rise of extremist Hindu nationalism throughout India.

The Language of the Masses

In a letter to the editor of a new English-language periodical, Bankim explained why he, too, was founding a review—in Bengali. His concluding remarks illustrate the linguistic complexity of India as a whole, and remain almost as true today as when they were written.

[From "Letter from Bankim Chandra Chatterjee," in *Bengal: Past and Present*, vol. 8, part 2 (April–June, 1914), pp. 273–74]

I wish you every success in your project. I have myself projected a Bengali magazine with the object of making it the medium of communication and sympathy between the educated and the uneducated classes. You rightly say that English for good or evil has become our vernacular; and this tends daily to widen the gulf between the higher and the lower ranks of Bengali society. This I think is not exactly what it ought to be; I think that we ought to *disanglicize* ourselves, so to speak, to a certain extent, and to speak to the masses in the language which they understand. I therefore project a Bengali magazine. But this is only half the work we have to do. No purely vernacular organ can completely represent the Bengali culture of the day. Just as we ought to address ourselves to the masses of our own race and country, we have also to make ourselves intelligible to the other Indian races, and to the governing race. There is no hope for India until the Bengali and the Punjabi understand and influence each other, and can bring their joint influence to bear upon the Englishman. This can be done only through the medium of the English, and I gladly welcome your projected periodical.

Hail to the Mother

In *Ānandamath (The Abbey of Bliss)*, his most famous novel, Bankim took as his theme the Sannyāsī Rebellion in Bengal of the 1779s, attributing to these raiding ascetics a sort of religious nationalism whose focus was God in the form of the Mother. He neatly avoided the charge of disloyalty to British rule by making the Muslims (still the titular rulers of Bengal) the villains of the piece. In this excerpt, Bhavananda, one of the sannyāsīs, reveals to a new disciple the group's mission and the mystique that sustains it.

[From *Abbey of Bliss*, pp. 31–37; *Bande Mātaram* translation in Ghose, *Collected Poems and Plays*, 2:227–28]

In that smiling moonlit night, the two silently walked across the plain. Mahendra [the disciple] was silent, sad, careless, and a little curious.

Bhavananda suddenly changed his looks. He was no more the steady and mild anchorite, nor wore any more the warlike hero's face—the face of the slayer of a captain of forces. Not even was there in his mien the proud disdain with which he had scolded Mahendra even now. It seemed as if his heart was filled with joy at the beauteous sight of the earth, lulled in peace and beaming under the silvery moon, and of the glory in her wilds and woods and hills and streams, and grew cheery like the ocean smiling with the rise of the moon. Bhavananda grew chatty, cheerful, cordial, and very eager to talk. He made many an attempt to open a conversation with his companion but Mahendra would not speak. Having no option left, he then began to sing to himself:

Mother, I bow to thee!
Rich with thy hurrying streams,
Bright with thy orchard gleams,
Cool with thy winds of delight,
Dark fields waving, Mother of might,
Mother free.

Mahendra was a little puzzled to hear the song; he could not grasp anything. Who could be the mother, he thought.

Rich with thy hurrying streams,
Bright with orchard gleams.
Cool with thy winds of delight,
Dark fields waving, Mother of might,
Mother free.

He asked, "Who is the mother?" Bhavananda did not answer but sang
on:

Glory of moonlight dreams
Over the branches and lordly streams,
Clad in thy blossoming trees, ⸱
Mother, giver of ease,
Laughing low and sweet!
Mother, I kiss thy feet,
Speaker sweet and low!
Mother, to thee I bow.

"It is the country and no mortal mother," cried Mahendra. "We own no
other mother," retorted Bhavananda; "they say, 'the mother and the land
of birth are higher than heaven.' We think the land of birth to be no other
than our mother herself. We have no mother, no father, no brother, no
wife, no child, no hearth or home, we have only got the mother—

Rich with hurrying streams,
Bright with orchard gleams.

Mahendra now understood the song and asked Bhavananda to sing again.

He sang:

Mother, I bow to thee!
Rich with thy hurrying streams,
Bright with thy orchard gleams,
Cool with thy winds of delight,
Dark fields waving, Mother of might,
Mother free.
Glory of moonlight dreams
Over thy branches and lordly streams,
Clad in thy blossoming trees,
Mother, giver of ease,
Laughing low and sweet!
Mother, I kiss thy feet,
Speaker sweet and low!
Mother, to thee I bow.
Who hath said thou art weak in thy lands,
When the swords flash out in twice seventy million hands
And seventy million voices roar[1]
Thy dreadful name from shore to shore?
With many strengths who are mighty and stored,
To thee I call, Mother and Lord!
Thou who savest, arise and save!
To her I cry who ever her foemen drave
Back from plain and sea
And shook herself free.
Thou art wisdom, thou art law,
Thou our heart, our soul, our breath,
Thou the love divine, the awe
In our hearts that conquers death.
Thine the strength that nerves the arm,
Thine the beauty, thine the charm.
Every image made divine
In our temples is but thine.
Thou art Durga,[2] Lady and Queen,
With her hands that strike and her swords of sheen,
Thou art Lakshmi[3] lotus-throned,
And the Muse a hundred-toned.
Pure and Perfect without peer,

Mother, lend thine ear.
Rich with thy hurrying streams,
Bright with thy orchard gleams,
Dark of hue, O candid-fair
In thy soul, with jewelled hair
And thy glorious smile divine,
Loveliest of all earthly lands,
Showering wealth from well-stored hands!
Mother, mother mine!
Mother sweet, I bow to thee
Mother great and free!

Mahendra saw that the outlaw was weeping as he sang. He then asked in wonder, "Who may you be, please?"

Bhavananda answered, "We are the Children."

"Children! Whose children are you?"

"Our mother's."

"Well, but does a child worship its mother with the proceeds of robbery?"

"We do nothing of the sort."

"Presently you looted a cart."

"Was that robbery? Whom did we rob?"

"Why, of course the king!"

"The king! What right has he to take this money?"

"It is the royal portion which goes to the king."

"How do you call him a king who does not rule his kingdom?"

"I fear you will be blown up before the sepoy's cannons one of these days."

"We have seen plenty of sepoys; even today we have had some."

"You haven't yet known them aright, you will know them one day however."

"What then? One never dies more than once."

"But why should you willingly invite death?"

"Mahendra Sinha, I thought you to be a man amongst men, but I now see there is little to choose between you and the rest of your lot—you are only the sworn consumer of milk and butter. Just think of the snake. It creeps on the ground; I cannot think of any creature lower and meaner than it; but put your foot on its neck and it will spread its fangs to bite you. But can nothing disturb *your* equanimity? Look round and see, look at Magadha, Mithila, Kasi, Kanchi,[4] Delhi, Kashmir—where do you find such misery as here? Where else do the people eat grass for want of better food? Where do they eat thorns and white-ants' earth and wild creepers? Where do men think of eating dogs and jackals and even carcasses? Where else can you find men getting so anxious about the money in their coffers, the *salgram*[5] in their temples, the females in the Zenana,[6] and the child in the mother's womb? Yes, here they even rip open the womb! In every country the bond that binds a sovereign to his subjects is the protection that he gives; but our Mussulman king—how does he protect us? Our religion is gone; so is our caste, our honor and the sacredness of our family even! Our lives even are now to be sacrificed. Unless we drive these tipsy longbeards away, a Hindu can no longer hope to save his religion."

"Well, but how can you drive them away?"

"We will beat them."

"Alone, will you? With a slap, I presume."

The outlaw sang:

Who hath said thou art weak in thy lands,
When the swords flash out in twice seventy million hands
And seventy million voices roar
Thy dreadful name from shore to shore?

M: "But I see you are alone."

Bh: "Why, only now you saw two hundred of us."

M: "Are they all children?"

Bh: "They are, all of them."

"How many more are there?"

"Thousands of them; we will have more by and by."

"Suppose you get ten or twenty thousands. Could you hope to depose the Mussulman king with them?"

"How many soldiers had the English at Plassey?"

"Tut! to compare the English with the Bengali!"

"Why not? Physical strength does not count for much; the bullet won't be running faster, I ween, if I am stronger."

"Then why this great difference between the English and the Mussulman?"

"Because an Englishman would die sooner than fly; the Mussulman will fly with the first breath of fire and look about for *sherbet.*[7] Secondly, the English have determination: what they want to do they will see done. The

Mussulman soldiers come to die for pay, and even that they don't always get. Lastly there is courage. A cannon ball falls only on one spot and cannot kill two hundred men together. Yet, when such a ball falls before the Mussulmans, they fly away in a body, while no Englishman would even fly before a shower of balls."

"Have you these qualities?"

"No, but you don't pluck them like ripe fruits from trees; they come by practice."

"What is your practice?"

"Don't you see we are all anchorites? Our renunciation is for the sake of this practice alone. When our mission is done or the practice is completed, we shall go back to our homes. We too have wives and children."

"You have left them all? How could you break the ties of family life?"

"A Child must not lie! I will not brag in vain to you. Nobody can ever cut the bond. He who says that he never cares for the family bonds either did never love or merely brags. We don't get rid of the bonds but simply keep our pledge. Will you enter our order?"

"Till I hear of my wife and child, I can say nothing."

"Come and you will see them."

So saying they began to walk along. Bhavananda sang the song "Hail Mother" again. Mahendra had a good voice and had some proficiency in music which he loved; so he joined Bhavananda in his song. He found that it really brought tears to the eye. "If I have not got to renounce my wife and daughter," said he, "you may initiate me into your order."

"He who takes this vow," said Bhavananda, "has to give up his wife and children. If you take it, you need not see your wife and daughter. They will be well kept, but till the mission is fulfilled, you are not to see their face[s]."

"I don't care to take your vow," blurted out Mahendra.

Mahendra does take the vow, but is later reunited with his wife and daughter.

Why the British Came to Rule India

In the final chapter of Ānandamath, after the sannyāsīs have routed both the Muslims and the British, Bankim has a supernatural figure explain to their leader Satyānanda, that the British have been forced to rule in India in order that Hinduism might regain its pristine power.

[From *Anandamath*, part 4, ch. 8, trans. by T. W. Clark]

S: Come, I'm ready. But, my lord, clear up this doubt in my mind. Why at the very moment in which I have removed all barriers from before our eternal Faith, do you order me to cease?

He: Your task is accomplished. The Muslim power is destroyed. There is nothing else for you to do. No good can come of needless slaughter.

S: The Muslim power has indeed been destroyed, but the dominion of the Hindus has not yet been established. The British still hold Calcutta.

He: Hindu dominion will not be established now. If you remain at your work, men will be killed to no purpose. Therefore come.

S: (greatly pained) My lord, if Hindu dominion is not going to be established, who will rule? Will the Muslim kings return?

He: No. The English will rule.

S: (turning tearfully to the image of her who symbolized the land of his birth) Alas, my Mother! I have failed to set you free. Once again you will fall into the hands of infidels. Forgive your son. Alas, my Mother! Why did I not die on the battlefield?

He: Grieve not. You have won wealth; but it was by violence and robbery, for your mind was deluded. No pure fruit can grow on a sinful tree. You will never set your country free in that way. What is going to happen now is for the best. If the English do not rule, there is no hope of a revival of our eternal Faith. I tell you what the wise know. True religion is not to be found in the worship of 33 crores of gods; that is a vulgar, debased religion, which has obscured that which is true. True Hinduism consists in knowledge not in action. Knowledge is of two kinds, physical and spiritual. Spiritual knowledge is the essential part of Hinduism. If however physical knowledge does not come first, spiritual knowledge will never comprehend the subtle spirit within. Now physical knowledge has long since disappeared from our land, and so true religion has gone too. If you wish to restore true religion, you must first teach this physical knowledge. Such knowledge is unknown in this country because there is no one to teach it. So we must learn it from foreigners. The English are wise in this knowledge, and they are good teachers. Therefore we must make the English rule. Once the people of India have acquired knowledge of the physical world from the English, they will be able to comprehend the nature of the spiritual. There will then be no obstacle to the true Faith. True religion will then shine forth again of itself. Until that happens, and until Hindus are wise and virtuous and strong, the English power will remain unbroken. Under the English our people will be happy; and there will be no impediment to our teaching our faith. So, wise one, stop fighting against the English and follow me.

S: My lord, if it was your intention to set up a British government, and if at this time a British government is good for the country, then why did you make use of me to fight this cruel war?

He: At the present moment the English are traders. Their minds are set on amassing wealth. They have no desire to take up the responsibilities of government. But as a result of the rebellion of the Children, they will have to; because they will get no money if they do not. The rebellion took place to make the English ascend the throne. Come with me now. Know and you will understand.

S: My lord, I do not desire knowledge. It cannot help me. I have vowed a vow and I must keep it. Bless me, and let me not be shaken in my devotion to my Mother.

He: Your vow is fulfilled. You have brought fortune to your Mother. You have set up a British government. Give up your fighting. Let the people take to their plows. Let the earth be rich with harvest and the people rich with wealth.

S: (weeping hot tears) I will make my Mother rich with harvest in the blood of her foes.

He: Who is the foe? There are no foes now. The English are friends as well as rulers. And no one can defeat them in battle.

S: If that is so, I will kill myself before the image of my Mother.

He: In ignorance? Come and know. There is a temple of the Mother in the Himalayas. I will show you her image there.

So saying, He took Satyānanda by the hand. What incomparable beauty! In the dim light, in the deep recesses of Vishnu's temple, two human forms radiant with light stood before a mighty four-armed figure. One held the other by the hand. Who held the hand; and whose was the hand be held? Knowledge was holding Devotion by the hand; Faith that of Action; Self-sacrifice that of Glory; Heavenly Joy that of Earthly Peace. Satyānanda was the Earthly Peace; He was Heavenly Joy. Satyānanda was Glory; He was Self-sacrifice.

And Self-sacrifice led away Glory.

BAL GANGADHAR TILAK: "FATHER OF INDIAN UNREST"

Impressed by his grandfather's recollections of the days before British rule reached Mahārāshtra, and of the Mutiny and Rebellion of 1857–1858, it is not surprising that Bal Gangadhar Tilak (1856–1920) should have grown up questioning the right of the British to govern his land. Like Ranade and Gokhale (with whom he fought a running political duel for many years) Tilak was descended from the Chitpāvan brāhman caste, but unlike them he maintained an uncompromising hostility to foreign domination.

In addition to the Maratha history he imbibed at his grandfather's knee, Tilak learned Sanskrit and English from his father, a schoolteacher and deputy inspector of education in a small town on India's western seacoast. When he was ten, the family moved to Poona, but at sixteen Tilak was an orphan. A self-reliant but weak-bodied youth, he devoted a year to building up his physique with exercises. After receiving his B.A., he took a Bachelor of Laws degree but refused to enter government service, the usual haven of educated Indians in those days. Instead, with a few like-minded friends he started a school and two newspapers in order to spread Western knowledge among the people of their native region of Maharashtra. Tilak helped to found the Deccan Education Society and Fergusson College but, opposing the reform program of Agarkar and Gokhale, he resigned from the group in 1890.

Tilak now purchased from the group the Marathi weekly Kesarī (The Lion), which he had named and helped to edit, and its English counterpart, The Mahratta.[8] Henceforth he poured his energies into educating the people of his province through the columns of these newspapers. His Marathi style was particularly effective and made a direct appeal to villagers, who would gather to have it read to them. Tilak also promoted in his papers the cele-bration of two new annual festivals—one dedicated to the Hindu god Ga-nesh, the other honoring the Maratha hero Shivaji. His purpose in organiz-ing these festivals was to develop in the Maharashtrian people a sense of pride in their common history and religion; however, the Muslim commu-nity could not ignore the fact that one of them was made to coincide with their own festival of Muharram, and the other extolled the Mughal empire's fiercest enemy. As eaters of beef, Muslims were further alarmed at the anti-cowkilling agitation that had been started by Dayananda, and which Tilak continued to sponsor.

Tilak's success in arousing popular enthusiasm through these activities began to worry the government after the assassination in 1897 of two British officials in Poona. Tilak was accused of fanning hatred for the officials with his *Kesarī* articles and was sentenced to jail for eighteen months. Imprisonment only whetted his fighting spirit, and the Bengal agitation of 1905 found him in the front lines of the fray. "Militancy—not mendicancy" was the slogan the Extremist faction used to disparage the Moderates, and his cry "Freedom is my birthright and I will have it" swept the country. When the Extremists failed to wrest control of the Congress from the Moderates at the 1907 session, Tilak defied the chairman (who had refused to recognize him), whereupon the meeting degenerated into a riot in which shoes and chairs flew through the air.

Shortly afterward Tilak was again arrested and tried for countenancing political assassination in his speeches and writings. He was sentenced to six years' rigorous confinement in Mandalay, Upper Burma. Books helped him to pass the time, and he returned to his Sanskrit studies. Earlier he had written two books arguing that the Vedas were over six thousand years old. His *magnum opus*, written in prison, was his lengthy commentary on the *Bhagavad Gītā*.

Tilak's interpretation of the *Gītā*, emphasizing as it does the importance of action in this world, gives us the key to his own character and to the influence he has had on political thought in twentieth-century India. He stressed that Hinduism's most popular sacred poem preached political as well as religious activity and hinted that violence in a righteous cause was morally justifiable. His followers, however, cut themselves loose from the known but foreign standards to which the Moderates remained attached and drifted into the uncharted depths of revolutionary violence and terrorism. Tilak himself never used such methods, but when others used them he maintained a silence that implied assent. The "father of Indian unrest," as the British journalist Valentine Chirol called him, was not the man to reprimand his own offspring.

In 1916 Tilak rejoined the Congress and, as their most popular leader, insisted on the compromises that made possible the united demand for self-government agreed to at Lucknow by the Congress and the Muslim League. By the time of his death in 1920 he had tempered his opposition to British rule sufficiently to favor contesting the elections provided for under the Montagu-Chelmsford Reforms of 1919—in contrast to the younger Gandhi, who wished to boycott them. But Tilak's example of fearless defiance was

remembered by those who came after him, and the title of "Lokamānya"—
"Honored by the People"—is still used as a reminder of his efforts to transform the nationalist cause from an upper-class into a truly popular movement.

The Gītā versus the Penal Code

In a speech at the 1897 festival honoring the eighteenth-century warrior-king Shivaji, Tilak boldly declared that the Bhagavad Gītā sanctioned the killing of enemies
for unselfish and benevolent reasons. (Shivaji had enticed his Muslim opponent
Afzal Khan into a private conference and in a struggle had murdered him with a
concealed weapon.) One week after his and other speeches appeared in the Kesarī,
a young brāhman killed a British official who had offended public opinion. Tilak
himself was soon tried, sentenced, and jailed for encouraging sedition against the
government. A half century later, Gandhi's assassin used at his trial a similar interpretation of the Gītā.

[From The Political Awakening in India, ed. by John R. McLane, p. 56]

It is needless to make fresh historical researches in connection with the
killing of Afzal Khan. Let us even assume that Shivaji first planned and
then executed the murder of Afzal Khan. Was this act of the Maharaja
[Shivaji] good or bad? This question which has to be considered should not
be viewed from the standpoint of the Penal Code or even the Smritis [law
books] of Manu or Yajnavalkya, or even the principles of morality laid down
in the Western and Eastern ethical systems. The laws which bind society
are for common men like yourselves and myself. No one seeks to trace the
genealogy of a Rishi [a legendary sage], nor to fasten guilt upon a king.
Great men are above the common principles of morality. These principles
fail in their scope to reach the pedestal of great men. Did Shivaji commit
a sin in killing Afzal Khan? The answer to this question can be found in
the Mahabharata itself. Shrimat Krishna's teaching in the Bhagavad Gita is
to kill even our teachers and our kinsmen. No blame attaches to any person
if he is doing deeds without being motivated by a desire to reap the fruit of
his deeds. Shri Shivaji Maharaja did nothing with a view to fill the small
void of his own stomach [from selfish motives]. With benevolent intentions
he murdered Afzal Khan for the good of others. If thieves enter our house
and we have not sufficient strength in our wrists to drive them out, we
should shut them up and burn them alive. God has not conferred upon the

Mlecchas [barbarians, foreigners] the grant inscribed on a copperplate[9] of the kingdom of Hindustan. The Maharaja strove to drive them away from the land of his birth; he did not thereby commit the sin of coveting what belonged to others. Do not circumscribe your vision like a frog in a well. Get out of the Penal Code, enter into the extremely high atmosphere of the *Bhagavad Gita,* and then consider the actions of great men.

The Tenets of the New Party

At the end of the Congress session of 1906, it was clear that the gap between the Moderates and the Extremists had been bridged only temporarily by the mediation of Dadabhai Naoroji. At this juncture Tilak delivered an address summarizing the aims and methods of the new party of which he was the leader.

[From Tilak, *Writings and Speeches,* pp. 55–57, 61, 63–67]

Calcutta, 2d January, 1907

Two new words have recently come into existence with regard to our politics, and they are *Moderates* and *Extremists.* These words have a specific relation to time, and they, therefore, will change with time. The Extremists of today will be Moderates tomorrow, just as the Moderates of today were Extremists yesterday. When the National Congress was first started and Mr. Dadabhai's views, which now go for Moderates, were given to the public, he was styled an Extremist, so that you will see that the term Extremist is an expression of progress. We are Extremists today and our sons will call themselves Extremists and us Moderates. Every new party begins as Extremists and ends as Moderates. The sphere of practical politics is not unlimited. We cannot say what will or will not happen 1,000 years hence— perhaps during that long period, the whole of the white race will be swept away in another glacial period. We must, therefore, study the present and work out a program to meet the present condition.

It is impossible to go into details within the time at my disposal. One thing is granted, namely, that this government does not suit us. As has been said by an eminent statesman—the government of one country by another can never be a successful, and therefore, a permanent government. There is no difference of opinion about this fundamental proposition between the old and new schools. One fact is that this alien government has ruined the country. In the beginning, all of us were taken by surprise. We were almost dazed. We thought that everything that the rulers did was for our good and that this English government has descended from the clouds to save us from the invasions of Tamerlane and Chingis Khan, and, as they say, not only from foreign invasions but from internecine warfare, or the internal or external invasions, as they call it. We felt happy for a time, but it soon came to light that the peace which was established in this country did this, as Mr. Dadabhai has said in one place—that we were prevented from going at each other's throats, so that a foreigner might go at the throat of us all. *Pax Britannica* has been established in this country in order that a foreign government may exploit the country. That this is the effect of this *Pax Britannica* is being gradually realized in these days. It was an unhappy circumstance that it was not realised sooner. We believed in the benevolent intentions of the government, but in politics there is no benevolence. Benevolence is used to sugar-coat the declarations of self-interest and we were in those days deceived by the apparent benevolent intentions under which rampant self-interest was concealed. That was our state then. But soon a change came over us. English education, growing poverty, and better familiarity with our rulers, opened our eyes and our leaders; especially, the venerable leader who presided over the recent Congress was the first to tell us that the drain from the country was ruining it, and if the drain was to continue, there was some great disaster awaiting us. So terribly convinced was he of this that he went over from here to England and spent twenty-five years of his life in trying to convince the English people of the injustice that is being done to us. He worked very hard. He had conversations and interviews with secretaries of state, with members of Parliament—and with what result?

He has come here at the age of eighty-two to tell us that he is bitterly disappointed. Mr. Gokhale, I know, is not disappointed. He is a friend of mine and I believe that this is his honest conviction. Mr. Gokhale is not disappointed but is ready to wait another eighty years till he is disappointed like Mr. Dadabhai. . . .

You can now understand the difference between the old and the new parties. Appeals to the bureaucracy are hopeless. On this point both the new and old parties are agreed. The old party believes in appealing to the British nation and we do not. That being our position, it logically follows we must have some other method. There is another alternative. We are not going to sit down quiet. We shall have some other method by which to achieve what we want. We are not disappointed, we are not pessimists. It is the hope of achieving the goal by our own efforts that has brought into existence this new party.

There is no empire lost by a free grant of concession by the rulers to the ruled. History does not record any such event. Empires are lost by luxury, by being too much bureaucratic or overconfident or from other reasons. But an empire has never come to an end by the rulers conceding power to the ruled. . . .

We have come forward with a scheme which if you accept [it], shall better enable you to remedy this state of things than the scheme of the old school. Your industries are ruined utterly, ruined by foreign rule; your wealth is going out of the country and you are reduced to the lowest level which no human being can occupy. In this state of things, is there any other remedy by which you can help yourself? The remedy is not petitioning but boycott. We say prepare your forces, organize your power, and then go to work so that they cannot refuse you what you demand. A story in *Mahabharata* tells that Sri Krishna was sent to effect a compromise, but the Pandavas and Kauravas were both organizing their forces to meet the contingency of failure of the compromise. This is politics. Are you prepared in this way to fight if your demand is refused? If you are, be sure you will not be refused; but if you are not, nothing can be more certain than that your demand will be refused, and perhaps, forever. We are not armed, and there is no necessity for arms either. We have a stronger weapon, a political weapon, in boycott. We have perceived one fact, that the whole of this administration, which is carried on by a handful of Englishmen, is carried on with our assistance. We are all in subordinate service. This whole government is carried on with our assistance and they try to keep us in ignorance of our power of cooperation between ourselves by which that which is in our own hands at present can be claimed by us and administered by us. The point is to have the entire control in our hands. I want to have the key of my house, and not merely one stranger turned out of it. Self-government is our goal; we want a control over our administrative machinery. We don't want to become clerks and remain [clerks]. At present, we are clerks and willing instruments of our own oppression in the hands of an alien government, and that government is ruling over us not by its innate strength but by keeping us in ignorance and blindness to the perception of this fact. Professor Seely[10] shares this view. Every Englishman knows that they are a mere handful in this country and it is the business of every one of them to befool you in believing that you are weak and they are strong.

This is politics. We have been deceived by such policy so long. What the new party wants you to do is to realize the fact that your future rests entirely in your own hands. If you mean to be free, you can be free; if you do not mean to be free, you will fall and be for ever fallen. So many of you need not like arms; but if you have not the power of active resistance, have you not the power of self-denial and self-abstinence in such a way as not to assist this foreign government to rule over you? This is boycott and this is what is meant when we say, boycott is a political weapon. We shall not give them assistance to collect revenue and keep peace. We shall not assist them in fighting beyond the frontiers or outside India with Indian blood and money. We shall not assist them in carrying on the administration of justice. We shall have our own courts, and when time comes we shall not pay taxes. Can you do that by your united efforts? If you can, you are free from tomorrow. Some gentlemen who spoke this evening referred to half bread as against the whole bread. I say I want the whole bread and that immediately. But if I can not get the whole, don't think I have no patience.

I will take the half they give me and then try for the remainder. This is the line of thought and action in which you must train yourself. We have not raised this cry from a mere impulse. It is a reasoned impulse. Try to understand that reason and try to strengthen that impulse by your logical convictions. I do not ask you to blindly follow us. Think over the whole problem for yourselves. If you accept our advice, we feel sure we can achieve our salvation thereby. This is the advice of the new party. Perhaps we have not obtained a full recognition of our principles. Old prejudices die very hard. Neither of us wanted to wreck the Congress, so we compromised, and were satisfied that our principles were recognized, and only to a certain extent. That does not mean that we have accepted the whole situation. We may have a step in advance next year, so that within a few years our principles will be recognized, and recognized to such an extent that the generations who come after us may consider us Moderates. This is the way in which a nation progresses, and this is the lesson you have to learn from the struggle now going on. This is a lesson of progress, a lesson of helping yourself as much as possible, and if you really perceive the force of it, if you are convinced by these arguments, then and then only is it possible for you to effect your salvation from the alien rule under which you labor at this moment.

There are many other points but it is impossible to exhaust them all in an hour's speech. If you carry any wrong impression come and get your doubts solved. We are prepared to answer every objection, solve every doubt, and prove every statement. We want your cooperation; without your help we cannot do anything singlehanded. We beg of you, we appeal to you, to think over the question, to see the situation, and realize it, and after realizing it to come to our assistance, and by our joint assistance to help in the salvation of the country.

The Message of the Bhagavad Gītā

Differing from the nondualistic interpretation of the Gītā as pointing the path to renunciation of the world, Tilak held that it preached a life of desireless action *in* the world. In the conclusion to his *Mystic Import of the Bhagavad Gītā*, he linked this message with the revival of India's political fortunes.

[From Tilak, *Srīmad Bhagavadgītā Rahasya*, 2:712–13]

The religion of the Gītā, which is a combination of spiritual knowledge, devotion, and action, which is in all respects undauntable and comprehensive, and is further perfectly equable, that is, which does not maintain any distinction, but gives release to everyone in the same measure, and at the same time shows proper forbearance towards other religions, is thus seen to be the sweetest and immortal fruit of the tree of the Vedic religion. In the Vedic religion, higher importance was given in the beginning principally to the sacrifice of wealth or of animals, that is to say, principally to action in the shape of ritual; but, when the knowledge expounded in the Upanishads taught later on that this ritualistic religion of the Shrutis was inferior, Sānkhya philosophy came into existence out of it. But as this knowledge was unintelligible towards abandonment of action, it was not possible for ordinary people to be satisfied merely by the religion of the Upanishads, or by the unification of the Upanishads and the Sānkhya philosophy in the Smritis. Therefore, the Gītā religion fuses the knowledge of the Brahman contained in the Upanishads, which is cognoscible only to the intelligence, with the "king of mysticisms" (*rāja-guhya*) of the worship of the perceptible which is accessible to love, and consistently with the ancient tradition of ritualistic religion, it proclaims to everybody, though nominally to Arjuna, that, "[to] perform lifelong your several worldly duties according to your respective positions in life, desirelessly, for the universal good, with a self-identifying vision, and enthusiastically, and thereby perpetually worship the deity in the shape of the Paramātman (the Highest Ātman), which is eternal, and which uniformly pervades the body of all created things as also the cosmos; because, therein lies your happiness in this world and in the next"; and on that account, the mutual conflict between action, spiritual knowledge (jnāna), and love (devotion) is done away with, and the single *Gītā* religion, which preaches that the whole of one's life should be turned into a sacrifice (yajna), contains the essence of the entire Vedic religion. When hundreds of energetic noble souls and active persons were busy with the benefit of all created things, because they looked upon that as their duty, as a result of their having realized this eternal religion, this country was blessed with the favor of the Parameshvara,[11] and reached the height not only of knowledge but also of prosperity; and it need not be said in so many words, that when this ancient religion, which is beneficial in this life and in the next, lost following in our country, it (our country) reached its present fallen state. I, therefore, now pray to the Parameshvara, at the end of this book, that there should come to birth again in this our country such noble and pure men as will worship the Parameshvara according to this equable and brilliant religion of the *Gītā*, which harmonizes devotion, spiritual knowledge, and energism.

AUROBINDO GHOSE: MYSTIC PATRIOT

The agitation against the partition of Bengal drew into public life one of the most fascinating figures modern India has produced—a completely Westernized intellectual who became a fanatical nationalist and ended his days an accomplished yogi. Aurobindo Ghose (1872–1950)—or Sri Aurobindo, as he is known to his followers—spent only four years in active politics, but in that brief span his passionate devotion to the national cause won him renown as an Extremist leader second only to Tilak in nationwide popularity.

Aurobindo's father, an England-educated Bengali doctor, was so determined to give his son a completely European education that he sent him to a convent school at five and to England at seven. Isolated from Indian influences, Aurobindo studied in England until he was twenty. Leaving Cambridge University, he returned to India in 1893 to enter the civil service of the progressive princely state of Baroda. Sensing himself "denationalized" by his foreign education, he turned his attention to Indian culture and politics. He was inspired by the writings of Ramakrishna, Vivekananda, and the novels of Bankim Chandra Chatterjee, and, after studying Sanskrit, he was able to appreciate in the original the Upanishads and the *Gītā*.

His fascination with Hindu culture, when combined with the sense of patriotism he had imbibed along with the rest of his English education, led Aurobindo to sympathize with the Extremist politicians. Despite the fact that he was unusually shy, during the agitation against the partition of Bengal he gave up his post as vice-principal of Baroda College and threw himself into the maelstrom of Bengal politics. His articles in the English-language weekly *Bande Mātaram* made him famous, especially after the government tried and failed to prove seditious their deftly phrased innuendos. In 1907 Aurobindo led a large Bengali delegation to the crucial Congress session at Tilak's request and served as Lokamanya's right-hand man during the stormy days of the split between the Moderates and the Extremists.

Shortly afterward Aurobindo consulted a Hindu holy man who advised him to void his mind of all thought so as to be able to receive supra-mental inspiration. He followed this advice faithfully, and, while in prison as a suspected member of a bombing plot, he heard the voice of Vivekananda guiding him in his practice of yoga and saw all men as incarnations of God. After his release, Aurobindo gradually withdrew from political life. In 1910 he abandoned Bengal—and his wife—for the French settlement of Pondichéry, where he spent his remaining forty years doing spiritual exercises and writing. All efforts to bring him back into the political arena proved ineffectual.

Brief as his political career was, Aurobindo defined the essence of religious nationalism in a manner that for sheer passion has never been surpassed. Because of his prolonged absence from India, Aurobindo came to idealize both his native land and its ancestral faith and to identify one with the other in a way no previous thinker had dared to do. The very fervor of his faith in "India" helped his Hindu countrymen to transcend the many differences of caste, language, and custom that had hindered the development among them of allegiance to one nation.

Although free of the region-centered nationalism that limited the effectiveness of a Bengali like Bankim or a Maharashtrian like Tilak, Aurobindo failed (as they had) to perceive that the greater the zeal of the Hindu nationalists became, the more difficult it would be to assuage the fears of Indian Muslims regarding their future in an independent Hindu-dominated India. In his later, postpolitical years, however, Aurobindo envisioned the coming of a global spiritual consciousness, "a spiritual religion of human-ity," enabling all persons to live in freedom and inner unity, oblivious of national or religious affiliations.

The Doctrine of Passive Resistance

In a series of articles penned in April 1907, Aurobindo outlined the doctrine of passive resistance, the Extremists' program of national self-reliance. Both the nega-tive and the positive aspects of this program were later utilized by Gandhi.

[From Ghose, The Doctrine of Passive Resistance, pp. 73–74, 77–79]

We desire to put an end to petitioning until such a strength is created in the country that a petition will only be a courteous form of demand. We wish to kill utterly the pernicious delusion that a foreign and adverse inter-est can be trusted to develop us to its own detriment, and entirely to do away with the foolish and ignoble hankering after help from our natural adversaries. Our attitude to bureaucratic concession is that of Laocoon: "We fear the Greeks even when they bring us gifts." Our policy is self-develop-ment and defensive resistance. But we would extend the policy of self-de-velopment to every department of national life; not only Swadeshi and Na-tional Education, but national defense, national arbitration courts, sanitation, insurance against famine or relief of famine—whatever our hands find to do or urgently needs doing, we must attempt ourselves and no longer look to the alien to do it for us. And we would universalize and extend the policy of defensive resistance until it ran parallel on every line with our self-de-velopment. We would not only buy our own goods, but boycott British goods; not only have our own schools, but boycott government institutions; not only organize our league of defense, but have nothing to do with the bureaucratic executive except when we cannot avoid it. At present even in Bengal where boycott is universally accepted, it is confined to the boycott of British goods and is aimed at the British merchant and only indirectly at the British bureaucrat. We would aim it directly both at the British mer-chant and at the British bureaucrat who stands behind and makes possible exploitation by the merchant. . . .

The double policy of self-development and defensive resistance is the common standing-ground of the new spirit all over India. Some may not wish to go beyond its limits, others may look outside it; but so far all are agreed. For ourselves we avow that we advocate passive resistance without wishing to make a dogma of it. In a subject nationality, to win liberty for one's country is the first duty of all, by whatever means, at whatever sacrifice; and this duty must override all other considerations. The work of national emancipation is a great and holy yajna[12] of which boycott, Swadeshi, national education, and every other activity, great and small, are only major or minor parts. Liberty is the fruit we seek from the sacrifice and the Motherland the goddess to whom we offer it; into the seven leaping tongues of the fire of the yajna we must offer all that we are and all that we have, feeding the fire even with our blood and lives and happiness of our nearest and dearest; for the Motherland is a goddess who loves not a maimed and imperfect sacrifice, and freedom was never won from the gods by a grudging giver. But every great yajna has its Rakshasas[13] who strive to baffle the sacrifice, to bespatter it with their own dirt, or by guile or violence put out the flame. Passive resistance is an attempt to meet such disturbers by peaceful and self-contained *Brahmatej;*[14] but even the greatest Rishis of old could not, when the Rakshasas were fierce and determined, keep up the sacrifice without calling in the bow of the Kshatriya. We should have the bow of the Kshatriya ready for use, though in the background. Politics is especially the business of the Kshatriya, and without Kshatriya strength at its back, all political struggle is unavailing.

Vedantism accepts no distinction of true or false religions, but considers only what will lead more or less surely, more or less quickly to moksha, spiritual emancipation and the realization of the Divinity within. Our attitude is a political Vedantism. India, free, one and indivisible, is the divine realization to which we move, emancipation our aim; to that end each nation must practice the political creed which is the most suited to its temperament and circumstances; for that is the best for it which leads most surely and completely to national liberty and national self-realization. But whatever leads only to continued subjection must be spewed out as mere vileness and impurity. Passive resistance may be the final method of salvation in our case or it may be only the preparation for the final sadhana.[15] In either case, the sooner we put it into full and perfect practice, the nearer we shall be to national liberty.

Nationalism Is the Work of God

Addressing a Bombay audience soon after the Moderate-Extremist split, Aurobindo made his mind a blank and spoke as the spirit moved him. The result was a startling declaration of the religious significance of Indian nationalism.

[From Ghose, *Speeches*, pp. 7–9]

There is a creed in India today which calls itself Nationalism, a creed which has come to you from Bengal. This is a creed which many of you have accepted when you called yourselves Nationalists. Have you realized, have you yet realized what that means? Have you realized what it is that you have taken in hand? Or is it that you have merely accepted it in the pride of a superior intellectual conviction? You call yourselves Nationalists. What is Nationalism? Nationalism is not a mere political program; Nationalism is a religion that has come from God; Nationalism is a creed which you shall have to live. Let no man dare to call himself a Nationalist if he does so merely with a sort of intellectual pride, thinking that he is more patriotic, thinking that he is something higher than those who do not call themselves by that name. If you are going to be a nationalist, if you are going to assent to this religion of Nationalism, you must do it in the religious spirit. You must remember that you are the instruments of God. What is this that has happened in Bengal? You call yourselves Nationalists, but when this happens to you, what will you do? This thing is happening daily in Bengal, because, in Bengal, Nationalism has come to the people as a religion, and it has been accepted as a religion. But certain forces which are against that religion are trying to crush its rising strength. It always happens when a new religion is preached, when God is going to be born in the people, that such forces rise with all their weapons in their hands to crush the religion. In Bengal too a new religion, a religion divine and sattwic[16] has been preached, and this religion they are trying with all the weapons at their command to crush. By what strength are we in Bengal able to survive? Nationalism is not going to be crushed. Nationalism survives in the strength of God and it is not possible to crush it, whatever weapons are brought against it. Nationalism is immortal; Nationalism cannot die; because it is no human thing, it is God who is working in Bengal. God cannot be killed, God cannot be sent to jail. When these things happen among you, I say to you solemnly, what will you do? Will you do as they do in Bengal? [Cries of "Yes."] Don't lightly say "yes." It is a solemn thing; and suppose that God puts you this question, how will you answer it? Have you got a real faith? Or is it merely a political aspiration? Is it merely a larger kind of selfishness? Or is it merely that you wish to be free to oppress others, as you are being oppressed? Do you hold your political creed from a higher source? Is it God that is born in you? Have you realized that you are merely the instruments of God, that your bodies are not your own? You are merely instruments of God for the work of the Almighty. Have you realized that? If you have realized that, then you are truly Nationalists; then alone will you be able to restore this great nation. In Bengal it has been realized clearly by some, more clearly by others, but it has been realized and you on this side of the country must also realize it. Then there will be a blessing on our work, and this great nation will rise again and become once more what it was in the days of its spiritual greatness.

India's Mission: The Resurrection of Hinduism

In a memorable speech to the Society for the Protection of Religion after his release from prison in 1908, Aurobindo relayed to his countrymen the messages that had mystically come to him during his confinement. First of all he was to dedicate himself to God's work. Second, through her national revival, India was to spread the universal truth of Hinduism throughout the world.

[From Ghose, *Speeches*, pp. 76–80]

This then is what I have to say to you. The name of your society is "Society for the Protection of Religion." Well, the protection of the religion, the protection and upraising before the world of the Hindu religion, that is the work before us. But what is the Hindu religion? What is this religion which we call Sanatan, eternal? It is the Hindu religion only because the Hindu nation has kept it, because in this Peninsula it grew up in the seclusion of the sea and the Himalayas, because in this sacred and ancient land it was given as a charge to the Aryan race to preserve through the ages. But it is not circumscribed by the confines of a single country, it does not belong peculiarly and forever to a bounded part of the world. That which we call the Hindu religion is really the eternal religion, because it is the universal religion which embraces all others. If a religion is not universal, it cannot be eternal. A narrow religion, a sectarian religion, an exclusive religion can live only for a limited time and a limited purpose. This is the one religion that can triumph over materialism by including and anticipating the discoveries of science and the speculations of philosophy. It is the one religion which impresses on mankind the closeness of God to us and embraces in its compass all the possible means by which man can approach God. It is the one religion which insists every moment on the truth which all religions acknowledge that He is in all men and all things and that in Him we move and have our being. It is the one religion which enables us not only to understand and believe this truth but to realize it with every part of our being. It is the one religion which shows the world what the world is, that it is the Lila of Vasudeva.[17] It is the one religion which shows us how we can best play our part in that Lila, its subtlest laws and its noblest rules. It is the one religion which does not separate life in any smallest detail from religion, which knows what immortality is and has utterly removed from us the reality of death.

This is the word that has been put into my mouth to speak to you today. What I intended to speak has been put away from me, and beyond what is given to me I have nothing to say. It is only the word that is put into me that I can speak to you. That word is now finished. I spoke once before with this force in me and I said then that this movement is not a political movement and that nationalism is not politics but a religion, a creed, a faith. I say it again today, but I put it in another way. I say no longer that nationalism is a creed, a religion, a faith; I say that it is the Sanatan Dharma which for us is nationalism. This Hindu nation was born with the Sanatan Dharma, with it it moves and with it it grows. When the Sanatan Dharma declines, then the nation declines, and if the Sanatan Dharma were capable of perishing, with the Sanatan Dharma it would perish. The Sanatan Dharma, that is nationalism. This is the message that I have to speak to you.

Divinizing This World Through Integral Yoga

In his forty years of residence in the tiny French colony of Pondichéry, Aurobindo lived a largely private life. In 1920 he was joined by a French woman with similar interests, and the Sri Aurobindo Ashram they established together became a major center of spiritual endeavor. Drawing on both the Judeo-Christian heritage he had experienced as a chapel-going student in England and on the Hindu heritage in which he had steeped himself after returning to his homeland, he advanced to new insights in the mystical, spiritual life. These excerpts from his letters to his disciples give glimpses into his personal experiences of the inward and upward movements of his consciousness, the transforming descent of what he called the Divine Peace, Power, Light, and Bliss, and the readiness to act in the world as an instrument of the Divine Will.

[From *Letters on Yoga* and other volumes in the *Sri Aurobindo Birth Centenary Library*. Volume and page references follow each quotation.]

Yoga means union with the Divine—a union either transcendental (above the universe) or cosmic (universal) or individual or, as in our yoga, all three together. [24:1149]

This is the entire definition of the aim of integral Yoga; it is the rendering in personal experience of the truth which universal Nature has hidden in herself and which she travails to discover. It is the conversion of the human soul into the divine soul and of natural life into divine living. [20:57]

It is the soul, the psychic being in you, behind the heart, that is awake and wants to concentrate the mind on the Divine. [24:1117]

It is not possible to make a foundation in yoga if the mind is restless. The first thing needed is quiet in the mind. Also to merge the personal consciousness is not the first aim of the yoga: the first aim is to open it to a higher spiritual consciousness and for this also a quiet mind is the first need. [23:635]

The piercing of the veil between the outer consciousness and the inner being is one of the crucial movements in yoga. For yoga means union with the Divine, but it also means awaking first to your inner self and then to your higher self,—a movement inward and a movement upward. It is, in fact, only through the awakening and coming to the front of the inner being that you can get into union with the Divine. . . .

There are two mutually complementary movements; in one the inner being comes to the front and impresses its own normal motions on the outer consciousness to which they are unusual and abnormal; the other is to draw back from the outer consciousness, to go inside into the inner planes, enter the world of your inner self and wake in the hidden parts of your being. When that plunge has once been taken, you are marked for the yogic, spiritual life and nothing can efface the seal that has been put upon you. [23:991]

Until we know the Truth (not mentally but by experience, by change of consciousness) we need the soul's faith to sustain us and hold on to the

Truth—but when we live in the knowledge, this faith is changed into knowledge.

Of course, I am speaking of direct spiritual knowledge. Mental knowledge cannot replace faith, so long as there is only mental knowledge, faith is still needed. [23:576]

Yoga, however, is scientific to this extent that it proceeds by subjective experiment and bases all its findings on experience; mental intuitions are admitted only as a first step and are not considered as realisation—they must be confirmed by being translated into and justified by experience. [22:189]

There are many ways of opening to this Divine Consciousness or entering into it. My way which I show to others by a constant practice is to go inward into oneself, to open by aspiration to the Divine and once one is conscious of it and its action, to give oneself to it entirely. This self-giving means not to ask for anything but the constant contact or union with the Divine Consciousness, to aspire for its peace, power, light and felicity, but to ask nothing else and in life and action to be its instrument only for whatever work it gives one to do in the world. If one can once open and feel the Divine Force, the Power of the Spirit working in the mind and heart and body, the rest is a matter of remaining faithful to it, calling for it always, allowing it to do its work when it comes and rejecting every other and inferior force that belongs to the lower consciousness and the lower nature. [27:416]

The descent of Peace, the descent of Force or Power, the descent of Light, the descent of Ananda [Bliss], these are the four things that transform the nature. [24:1170]

The Force descends for two things:
1. To transform the nature.
2. To carry on the work through the instrument. [24:1173]

I mean by action work done for the Divine and more and more in union with the Divine—for the Divine alone and nothing else. Naturally that is not easy at the beginning, any more than deep meditation and luminous knowledge are easy or even true love and bhakti are easy. But like others it has to be begun in the right spirit and attitude, with the right will in you, then all the rest will come.

. . . One becomes aware of one's inner being and sees the outer as an instrument; one feels the universal Force doing one's works and the Self or Purusha watching or witness but free; one feels all one's works taken from one and done by the universal or supreme Mother or by the Divine Power controlling and acting from behind the heart. By constant referring of all one's will and works to the Divine, love and adoration grow, the psychic being comes forward. By the reference to the Power above, we can come to feel it above and its descent and the opening to an increasing consciousness and knowledge. Finally, works, bhakti and knowledge go together and self-perfection becomes possible—what we call the transformation of the nature.

These results certainly do not come all at once; they come more or less slowly, more or less completely according to the condition and growth of the being. There is no royal road to the divine realisation. [23:528–29]

As to the sexual impulse. Regard it not as something sinful and horrible and attractive at the same time, but as a mistake and wrong movement of the lower nature. Reject it entirely, not by struggling with it, but by drawing back from it, detaching yourself and refusing your consent; look at it as something not your own, but imposed on you by a force of Nature outside you. If anything in your vital [nature] consents, insist on that part of you withdrawing its consent. Call in the Divine Force to help you in your withdrawal and refusal. If you can do this quietly and resolutely and patiently, in the end your inner will will prevail against the habit of the outer Nature. [24:1531]

There is a love in which the emotion is turned towards the Divine in an increasing receptivity and growing union. What it receives from the Divine it pours out on others, but freely without demanding a return—if you are capable of that, then that is the highest and most satisfying way to love. [23:815]

The aspiration should be for the full descent of the Truth and victory over falsehood in the world. [23:564]

The Divine Truth is greater than any religion or creed or scripture or idea or philosophy—so you must not tie yourself to any of these things. [24:1281]

The interpenetration of the planes [material, vital, mental, and Supra-mental] is indeed for me a capital and fundamental part of spiritual experi-ence without which yoga as I practise it and its aim could not exist. For that aim is to manifest, reach or embody a higher consciousness upon earth and not to get away from earth into a higher world or some supreme Ab-solute. The old yogas (not quite all of them) tended the other way—but that was, I think, because they found the earth as it is a rather impossible place for any spiritual being and the resistance to change too obstinate to be borne; earth-nature looked to them in Vivekananda's simile like the dog's tail which, every time you straighten it, goes back to its original curl. [22:177–78]

From Inner Awareness of Spiritual Reality to a Lasting Human Unity

Believing (like Teilhard de Chardin) in the evolution of human consciousness into ever higher forms, Aurobindo predicted the coming union of the world's peoples, held together not so much by political and administrative ties as by the growing, nonsectarian awareness of the spiritual, divine Reality "in which we are all one."

[From *The Ideal of Human Unity* in the *Sri Aurobindo Birth Centenary Library*, 15:548, 554–55]

In other words,—and this is the conclusion at which we arrive,—while it is possible to construct a precarious and quite mechanical unity by political and administrative means, the unity of the human race, even if achieved, can only be secured and can only be made real if the religion of humanity, which is at present the highest active ideal of mankind, spiritualises itself and becomes the general inner law of human life.

A spiritual religion of humanity is the hope of the future. By this is not meant what is ordinarily called a universal religion, a thing of creed and intellectual belief and dogma and outward rite. Mankind has tried unity by that means; it has failed and deserved to fail, because there can be no universal religious system, one in mental creed and form. The inner spirit is indeed one, but more than any other the spiritual life insists on freedom and variation in its self-expression and means of development. A religion of humanity means the growing realisation that there is a secret Spirit, a divine Reality, in which we are all one, that humanity is its highest present vehicle on earth, that the human race and the human being are the means by which it will progressively reveal itself here. It implies a growing attempt to live out this knowledge and bring about a kingdom of this divine Spirit upon earth. By its growth within us oneness with our fellow-men will become the leading principle of all our life, not merely a principle of cooperation but a deeper brotherhood, a real and an inner sense of unity and quality and a common life. There must be the realisation by the individual that only in the life of his fellow-men is his own life complete. There must be the realisation by the race that only on the free and full life of the individual can its own perfection and permanent happiness be founded. There must be too a discipline and a way of salvation in accordance with this religion, that is to say, a means by which it can be developed by each man within himself, so that it may be developed in the life of the race. To go into all that this implies would be too large a subject to be entered upon here; it is enough to point out that in this direction lies the eventual road. No doubt, if this is only an idea like the rest, it will go the way of all ideas. But if it is at all a truth of our being, then it must be the truth to which all is moving and in it must be found the means of a fundamental, an inner, a complete, a real human unity which would be the one secure base of a unification of human life. A spiritual oneness which would create a psychological oneness not dependent upon any intellectual or outward uniformity and [would] compel a oneness of life not bound up with its mechanical means of unification, but ready always to enrich its secure unity by a free inner variation and a freely varied outer self-expression, this would be the basis for a higher type of human existence.

LAJPAT RAI: "LION OF THE PUNJAB"

After Bengal and Bombay, the province of North India to contribute the most volunteers for the more militant wing of the Congress was "the land of the five rivers," the Punjab (so named from the Persian words *panj*, "five," and *āb*, "water, river"). Here the marriage of politics and religion initially took the form of the militant, Hinducentric nationalism of the Arya Samaj, brought to Lahore in 1877 by Swami Dayananda Saraswati. Punjab's Hindus were outnumbered by Muslims and threatened by conversions to the smaller but caste-free Sikh community, or to Christianity. Dayananda's message appealed to young men anxious to reform and strengthen their community and to bring it into revitalizing touch with its ancient heritage.

One such young man was Lala Lajpat Rai (1865–1928). His openness to a new religious perspective resembled that of his parents: his father's father was a Jain, his father a Hindu who taught Persian and Urdu and much admired Islamic culture; his mother's ancestors had been Sikhs, but after her marriage she followed Hindu devotional practices. Lajpat Rai received his elementary education mainly from his father and always did well at the schools he attended. At fifteen he easily passed the entrance examination to the Punjab University College at Lahore and entered it at sixteen. As his father was quite poor, he lived very frugally. He worked so hard in his first year that he fell ill. After a second year, he obtained a license to practice as a law clerk and left college to begin supporting himself and helping his family. Three years later he passed a higher legal examination and commenced a career that was to make him a wealthy man in a few more years.

In 1881, in his first year in college, Lajpat Rai joined the local Brahmo Samaj, but in the following year he was drawn into the Arya Samaj by college friends and by his growing love for ancient Hindu culture. From then on, he worked to enlarge and strengthen the Samaj, particularly by giving speeches, writing letters to newspapers, and raising and contributing funds for it. His favorite project was the Dayananda Anglo-Vedic School and College, founded at Lahore in 1886 and 1889 respectively. Its plan resembled, structurally, that of Syed Ahmed Khan's Anglo-Mohammedan College at Aligarh (see chapter 5). Each combined instruction in English and Western learning with the study of the classical language, literature, and religion of the community that founded it, and each was established in a region where that community was a minority. Lajpat Rai settled in Lahore in 1892 to continue his law practice and thereafter gave himself increasingly to the service of the Samaj and the college. In 1901 he resolved that whatever he earned would be devoted to public work.

By this time Lajpat Rai had won wide respect among his educated countrymen for his writings in Urdu and English and his speeches at the 1888 and 1893 meetings of the Indian National Congress. In the 1890s he wrote a series of Urdu biographies of heroic leaders: Mazzini (whom he made his political guru), Garibaldi, Shivaji, Dayananda, and Shri Krishna. He also did relief work during the famine years that closed the century, helped found orphanages for Hindu children, and publicized the need for agricultural development, technical education, and national industry and banking.

In the next decade, Lajpat Rai rose to national prominence as a militant nationalist. He had met and admired Tilak at the Lahore Congress sessions of 1893 and 1900, and when he founded a new English-language newspaper, *The Punjabee*, in 1904, he appointed as its editor a journalist from Poona recommended to him by Tilak. At the 1905 Congress, Lajpat Rai stirred his younger listeners with his call for greater manliness in the face of government repression. In both 1906 and 1907 he tried to mediate between the Extremists and the Moderates in the Congress. Then his arrest and six-month deportation to Burma without trial in 1907 made him a national hero. Denying the Extremists' offer to elect him Congress president in 1907, he remained with the Moderate faction after the two factions split. His interest in national politics then declined, and he again focused his mind on the problems of the poor, the uneducated, and on the Untouchables. In some of these concerns, as well as in his 1905 advocacy of passive resistance and his 1907 endorsement of a stoppage of all work to protest an injustice *(hartal)*, he preceded Gandhi and may have influenced him.

When the First World War broke out, Lajpat Rai was in London as a member of a Congress delegation. Rather than risk re-arrest in wartime India, he chose to go into exile in the United States. There, and in Japan for six months, he wrote and spoke about the nationalist movement in India but steadfastly refused to join the Indian revolutionaries who tried to recruit him. The British would not give him a visa to return to India until the end of 1919, but when he finally landed in February 1920, he was warmly greeted at a crowded public reception chaired by Muhammed Ali Jinnah, with Tilak and Mrs. Annie Besant on the platform. He accepted the presidency of the special Congress session in September of that eventful year and correctly predicted that Gandhi's noncooperation program would not win sufficient response to achieve his objective of "swaraj in one year." Jailed for sedition in 1922, he wrote both gratefully and critically of Gandhi, who had just called off the movement.

In the next few years, Lajpat Rai continued on his practical path of work for both national and Hindu interests. In a series of articles on "The Hindu-Muslim Problem," which appeared in leading Indian newspapers in 1924, he proposed "a clear partition of India into a Muslim India and a non-Muslim India,"[18] with Bengal and the Punjab to be bisected (as in fact they were in 1947). He joined, and in 1925 presided over, the newly formed

Hindu Mahasabha and was elected to the Central Legislative Assembly. His health was already failing when in 1928 he led a demonstration in front of the Lahore railway station against the all-British commission to consider modifications in India's constitution. He braved the policemen threatening the demonstration and was beaten in the chest. Eighteen days later he was dead, having earned once more the sobriquet, "the lion of the Punjab."

An Open Letter to Syed Ahmed Khan

In 1888, at the age of twenty-three, Lajpat Rai attacked the Muslim leader Syed Ahmed Khan (see chapter 5) for opposing the demands for political reforms made by the newly organized Indian National Congress. His four peppery letters to a Lahore Urdu newspaper were translated into English and circulated among delegates to the 1888 Congress session, where they won immediate notice for young Lajpat Rai.

[From Lajpat Rai, *Writings and Speeches*, 1:1–4]

Would you excuse me if I encroach upon your valuable time for a short while? Before I address you on the subject matter of discussion I think it advisable to state for your information that I have been a constant reader and admirer of your writings. From childhood, I was taught to respect the opinions and the teachings of the white-bearded Syed of Aligarh. Your *Social Reformer* was constantly read to me by my fond father, who looked upon you as no less than a prophet of the nineteenth century. Your writings in the *Aligarh Institute Gazette* and your speeches in Council and other public meetings, were constantly studied by me and preserved as a sacred trust by my revered parent. It was thus that I came to know that you once approved of the contents of John Stuart Mill's book on "Liberty," . . . Is it strange then that I have been astonished to read what you now speak and write about the "National Congress"? Any person, in my circumstances, would shout out. Times have changed and with them convictions! Flattery and official cajoleries have blinded the eyes of the most far-seeing; cowardice has depressed the souls of the foremost of seekers after truth, and high sounding titles and the favours of worldly governors have extinguished the fire of truth burning in many a noble heart. It is not a sad spectacle to the men whose days are numbered, whose feet are almost in the grave, trying to root out all the trees planted with their own hands!

Under these circumstances, Syed Sahib, it is, surely, not strange if I ask what has been the cause of this lamentable change in you. Old age and exhaustion of faculties may, perhaps, have some share in causing you to forget what you once wrote and spoke. Has your memory lost its retentiveness, or is it the blindness of dotage which has permitted you to stray into your present unhappy position?

If the former, I from amongst your old admirers will take upon myself the duty of reminding you of what, in moments of wisdom, was recorded and published by your pen and tongue, and this duty, I promise, I will fulfil with the utmost pleasure and with feelings of the highest satisfaction.

I will begin with your book on the "Causes of the Indian Revolt", which was written in 1858. . . . In this book, after having tried to prove that the Mutiny of 1857 was no "religious war," nor the result of a preconcerted conspiracy, you say that "most men, I believe, agree in thinking that it is highly conducive to the welfare and prosperity of Government—indeed, that it is essential to its stability—that the people should have a voice in its Councils. It is from the voice of the people that Government can learn whether its projects are likely to be well received. The voice of the people can alone check errors in the bud and warn us of dangers before they burst upon and destroy us." To make the matter more clear you go on saying that "this voice, however, can never be heard, and this security never acquired, unless the people are allowed a share in the consultations of Government. The security of a government, it will be remembered, is founded on its knowledge of the character of the governed as well as on its careful observance of their rights and privileges." These are noble words, nobly spoken; words of sterling honesty and independence of spirit. Can they bear any other meaning than that which attaches to that resolution of the National Congress which prays for the introduction of a representative element into the constitution of our Legislative Councils? . . . How can the people of a country have their voice constantly heard if not through representatives? . . . Nay, further, not to leave any doubts in the matter, and to prove that in your book you even go to the length of saying that your countrymen should be selected to form an assembly like the English Parliament (which demand, at the time you advanced it, was certainly more premature than it now is, though the National Congress, with all the advantages that the country has had in the way of education and enlightenment since that miserable year of 1858, only advocates the partial introduction of a representative element in the Legislative Councils), I shall give some more extracts from the same work.

There you say: "I do not want to enter here into the question as to how the ignorant and uneducated natives of Hindustan could be allowed a share in the deliberations of the Legislative Council, or as to how they should be selected to form an assembly like the English Parliament. These are knotty points. All I wish to prove is that such a step is not only advisable but absolutely necessary, and that the disturbances are due to the neglect of such a measure." Could clearer words be used that what have been quoted above? . . .

Sir Syed, does it not sound strange that the writer of the words above quoted should put himself forward as the leader of the anti-Congress movement? Is it not one more proof of India's misfortune that the writer of the above words should impute bad motives to the supporters of the National Congress, mainly because they advocate the introduction of some sort of representation in the Legislative Councils of India? Is not your charge of sedition against the promoters of the Congress, in the face of these, a mere mockery, a contradiction in terms? Thirty years ago, you advocated the institution of a Parliament, and yet you chide us saying that we want an Indian Parliament, notwithstanding that we protest that for the present, and for a long time to come, we do not claim any such thing? Mark the difference. India is no longer what it was thirty years ago. In the course of this period it has made a marked advance towards a higher civilization. The natives of India are no longer, with *very* few exceptions, ignorant or uneducated. The rays of education are penetrating and shedding their wholesome light inside most Indian homes; hundreds of thousands of Indians are as well educated as any average English gentleman, and we see scores of our countrymen every year crossing the "black waters" to witness with their own eyes the proceedings of the great British Parliament and personally familiarize themselves with the political institutions of the English nation. Can you in face of these facts still call us "seditious"? According to your writings, we are the most loyal subjects of the Government, and if, notwithstanding what you have written, you still deserve to be called "the ablest of our loyal Mahomedan gentlemen," why [do] we deserve not to be styled "as the ablest of the most loyal subjects of the English Government."

Reform versus Revival

In his 1904 article, "Reform or Revival?," Lajpat Rai deftly turned the tables on the reformers by suggesting that the model toward which they wanted to change India was a foreign one and then asking whether they wanted to adopt foreign vices as well. In the end he thought the differences between the two schools not great enough to be worth arguing about.

[From Lajpat Rai, *Writings and Speeches* 1:46–47, 50–51, 53–54]

One class of people who have already established a name for themselves do not like to give up the name they have patented and by which they have gained distinction. These latter gentlemen call themselves reformers and insist upon certain social changes being introduced in the name of "reform" and reform only. The other class who have lately come into prominence call themselves "revivalists," and they swear that any change in the social customs and institutions of the community can only be introduced under the shadow of revival. They think they cannot tolerate reform. The result is that while the former taunt the latter as "revivalists and reactionaries" the latter mock the former as "reformers and revolutionists." Both classes contain amongst them great and good men, men with pure motives and noble intentions. Both classes are to all appearances sincere in their convictions and efforts, but to the great misfortune of the country and the nation they cannot join their heads and work amicably. The wordy weapons are sometimes changed, and while the reformers take their stand on "reform on rational lines" the revivalists plead for "reform on national lines." Here for once at least they seem to agree on reform, as the force of the difference is centered on the words "rational" and "national." . . .

We may be pardoned for pointing out that to us the fight seems to be generally on the same lines and on the same grounds which marked the polemics of the old class of Pandits. The real truth is that the so-called reformers are mostly in faith and in religion Brahmos. They were the earliest in the field and fought for reform when the revivalists had not yet come into existence. The revivalists are the products of a wider diffusion of Sanskrit literature which has taken place principally within the last quarter of a century. This study has afforded them sufficient and strong evidence of their ancestors having enjoyed a great and glorious civilization from which most of the present evil practices and customs that are the bane of modern Hinduism were absent. They, therefore, naturally look to the past for light and guidance and plead that a revival might lead them into that haven of progress which is the object of all. . . . [Lajpat Rai then referred to M. G. Ranade's 1897 Social Conference address, which is given above, pp. 104–9]

Now, if it be permissible for a comparatively young and inexperienced man without laying himself open to a charge of disrespect for one of our revered leaders whose great wisdom, deep learning, and general judicial-mindedness are accepted all around, I will, with due deference to the late Mr. Ranade, beg to point out the injustice of the observations quoted above. Cannot a revivalist, arguing in the same strain, ask the reformers into what they wish to reform us? Whether they want us to be reformed on the pattern of the English or the French? Whether they want us to accept the divorce laws of Christian society or the temporary marriages that are now so much in favour in France or America? Whether they want to make men of our women by putting them into those avocations for which nature never meant them? Whether they want us to substitute the legal *niyoga*[19] of the Mahabharata period with the illegal and immoral *niyoga* that is nowadays rampant in European society? Whether they want us to reform into Sunday drinkers of brandy and promiscuous eaters of beef? In short, whether they want to revolutionise our society by an outlandish imitation of European customs and manners and an undiminished adoption of European vice? The revivalists do not admit that the institutions which they want to revive are dead, burnt and gone. The very fact that they wish to revive them goes to show that they believe that there is still some life left in them and that given the proper remedy, their present unhealthy and abnormal state is sure to disappear and result in the bringing about of the normal and healthy condition of affairs. In fact, in an earlier part of the same address, Mr. Ranade summed up the position of the revivalists in a few well chosen and apt words when he admitted that, "In the case of our society especially, the usages which at present prevail amongst us are admittedly not those which obtained in the most glorious periods of our history. On most of the points which are included in our programme, our own record of the past shows that there has been a decided change for the worse and it is surely within the range of practical possibilities for us to hope that we may work up our way back to a better state of things without stirring up the rancorous hostilities which religious differences have a tendency to create and foster." It is exactly this working up our way back which the revivalists aim at. No revivalist has ever pleaded for the institutions selected by Mr. Justice Ranade as the butt end of his attack against them.

The real significance of these words—"reform" and "revival", if any, seems to be in the authority or authorities from which the reformers and the revivalists respectively seek their inspiration for guidance in matters social. The former are bent on relying more upon reason and the experience of European society, while the latter are disposed to primarily look at their Shastras and the past history, and the traditions of their people and the ancient institutions of the land which were in vogue when the nation was at the zenith of its glory. On our part we here in the Punjab are prepared to take our inspiration from both these sources, though we prefer to begin with the latter and call in the assistance of the former mainly to understand and explain what is not clear and ambiguous in the latter. But so long as our conclusions are principally the same, I think the fight is not worth being continued and may be dropped for good.

The Coming Political Struggle

In a fiery speech seconding the 1905 Congress resolution in protest against the government's repressive measures, Lajpat Rai denounced these "Russian methods" and called for his countrymen to act in a "manly and vigorous" way toward their rulers.

[From Lajpat Rai, *Writings and Speeches*, 1:97–100]

I am afraid I cannot deliver a speech in the strain which we have been hearing on the resolution on the "Partition of Bengal" and the present resolution before you. I give it my heartiest support on two grounds. You have been hearing of the misfortunes of our brethren of Bengal. I am rather inclined to congratulate them on the splendid opportunity to which an all-wise Providence, in his dispensation, has afforded to them by heralding the dawn of a new political era for this country. I think the honour was reserved for Bengal, as Bengal was the first to benefit by the fruits of English education. Bengal, up to this time—excuse me for saying that—the Bengal lion, by some cause, had degenerated into a jackal, and I think Lord Curzon has done us a great service by provoking the lion in his own den and rousing him to a sense of consciousness of his being a lion. I think no greater service could have been done to India, to the cause of India or to Bengal, by any other statesman. There are times, gentlemen, when I am inclined to pray that from time to time God might be pleased to send Viceroys like

Lord Curzon to this country, in order to awaken the people of this country to a sense of their responsibility in this matter. Gentlemen, I believe, and I believe earnestly, that the political struggle has only commenced and it was only in the fitness of things that when the Congress attained its majority, the attaining of that majority should have been preceded by a manly and vigorous protest on the part of the people of this country. It is only in the fitness of things that the movement's coming to age of majority should have been preceded by a vigorous and manly declaration of its approaching manhood. I think in the circumstances like ours, in conditions like ours, we are perfectly justified in taking the attitude that our brethren of Bengal have taken. What else was left for you? It has been explained that all possible things that could be done in the name of constitutional agitation have been exhausted. What was the example given to you by your fellow-subjects in the other parts of the Empire? Englishmen have been our teachers in all branches of human knowledge. Englishmen have given us constitutional rights. Was it not perfectly right to take a page from the book of the Englishman on the methods of constitutional agitation and adopt those methods which will be appreciated by themselves? Now, let us see what Englishmen in England do. I do not say that our conditions allow of our exactly copying or imitating them, but surely we have a right to adopt that spirit, understand that spirit and follow it. Let me tell you what are the methods adopted by Englishmen in England when they have a grievance to be listened to by Government. The method which is perfectly legitimate, perfectly constitutional and perfectly justifiable, is the method of passive resistance. Although I am not at the present moment quoting any social democrat or labourman, I must admire them; I have great respect for them. I must tell you that the message which the people of England wanted to send to you through me was the message that in our utterances, in our agitations and in our fight and struggle for liberty, we ought to be more manly than we have been heretofore (cheers). An Englishman hates or dislikes nothing like beggary. I think a beggar deserves to be hated. Therefore, it is our duty to show to the Englishmen that we have risen to the sense of consciousness, that we are no longer beggars and that we are subjects of an Empire where people are struggling to achieve that position which is their right by right of natural law. Gentlemen, at every stage people were arbiters of their destiny, but we are not so at the present moment. We are perfectly justified in trying to become arbiters of our own destiny and in trying to obtain freedom. I think the people of Bengal ought to be congratulated on being leaders of that march in the van of progress. I rather envy them. I am rather jealous of them; at the same time I am proud of them. They have begun the battle, they have begun the fight and they have begun it in right manly style. They have effaced all those taunts, they have effaced all those insinuations against them of being timid and cowardly; they have exhibited a manliness, they have exhibited a spirit in this battle which has to be commended to other Provinces of India. If the other Provinces of India will just follow their example, I say the day is not far from distant sights. But if you simply go there as a beggar without the consciousness of your power, of your right to demand your rights, you go there simply to be rejected. If, therefore, you want to be heard, and you want to be heard with respect, you must approach with determination, with evidences of determination, with signs that you are determined to achieve your rights at any cost. Unless you do that, the goddess of liberty is very jealous. She shall never allow you to approach her, and she shall never allow you to enter her portals. You must remain outside because you are profane; you cannot enter because you are not sufficiently pure; you must purify yourselves through the ordeals of fire and self-sacrifice. The goddess of liberty is the most sacred goddess in the world, and before you can approach her, you should show by your life, life of self-denial, that you are fit to enter her temple (cheers). What have we been doing to be fit to approach that temple. I am afraid that our record is extremely poor and extremely humiliating; it is extremely bad to look at. But there are signs of the rising sun. And if the people of India will just learn that lesson from the people of Bengal, I think the struggle is not hopeless. We are just awakening to a sense of our duty and a sense of responsibility to the motherland. It may be that with the consciousness of that strength we may tread the right way, the right path in the struggle for freedom. . . .

I see the time is going fast (cries of "go on"). No, I am not going to break the rule. I think I have already exceeded the limits. There is only one word I should like to say. If you have adopted this manly and vigorous policy, be prepared for the logical consequence. Don't conceal your heads, don't behave like cowards. Once having adopted that manly policy, stick to it till the last. Glorify yourselves as I have told you. Is it not a matter of shame for us that this National Congress in the last twenty-one years should not have produced at least a number of political Sanyasis that could sacrifice their lives for the political regeneration of the country? Now that the Congress has come to a stage when it could become a father, a parent, I earnestly appeal to you to let it have its legitimate offsprings: a band of earnest missionaries to work out the political regeneration of the country. There is no use of our talking aloud, there is not much use of our showing signs of discontent and disaffection, unless we are true to ourselves, true to our noble country, true to the motherland, true to the cause of political regeneration and political agitation. If you show, in a few years, to our rulers that we are steadfast in our determination, that we are steadfast in our devotion to our cause, I assure you there is no power in the world that can prevent you from going forward.

Untouchability Must Go

In line with the Arya Samaj's opposition to caste distinctions, Lajpat Rai in a 1909 article forcefully stated the case for ending the age-old practice of treating certain castes as untouchable.

[From Lajpat Rai, *Writings and Speeches,* 1:166–67]

There can be no denying the fact that the rigidity of the Hindu caste system is the bane of Hindu society. It is a great barrier in the way of the social and national progress of the Hindus. It confronts them at every step and slackens the speed with which, otherwise, the nation would climb up to the heights of national solidarity. The condition of the "low" castes, sometimes described as "untouchables", at other times as the "depressed classes," is nothing short of disgraceful. It is a disgrace to our humanity, our sense of justice, and our feeling of social affinity. It is useless to hope for any solidarity so long as the depressed classes continue to be so low in the social scale as they are. The intellectual and moral status of the community as a whole cannot be appreciably raised without the co-operation of *all* the classes forming the community. So long then, as there are *classes* amongst us who are untouchable by the so-called superior classes, because of their having been born of certain parents, the moral and intellectual elevation of the community as a whole can only proceed by slow, very slow, degrees. The condition of the depressed classes is a standing blot on our social organisation, and we must remove that blot if we are really desirous of securing the efficiency of our social organism. All the parts of a whole must be raised, not necessarily to the same level but to a level from which they can, by their individual efforts, talents and achievements, rise to the highest possible position within the reach of the members of the social organism.

The present arrangement is a cruel and unjust arrangement. Besides, it is both economically and politically unsound. A community which allows so much valuable human material to rot in a state of utter depression and helplessness, cannot be said to be economically wise. As to the political danger involved by the continuance of these classes in their present condition, one need only look at the arguments advanced by our friends of the Muslim League in support of their contention for a larger representation on the Legislative Councils than they are entitled to by virtue of their numerical strength. Quite ignoring the fact that they are as much affected by these classes as the Hindus, they make it a point to say that in counting the Hindus for the purposes of representation the untouchables enumerated with them should be excluded. Whatever may be the value of this argument for the purpose for which it is used, there can be no doubt that the existence of these classes in their present deplorable condition is a menace to the power and influence of the Hindu community. The line of argument adopted by our Muslim friends and also by some missionary critics of the Reform Scheme, ought to open the eyes of the Hindus to the absolute necessity and urgency of raising the social status of their fellow-religionists, called and known as the members of the depressed classes. Thus from every point of view, whether that of humanity, justice or fairplay, or that of self-interest, it is the bounden duty of the so called high-caste Hindus to give a helping hand to their brothers of the "low castes" and raise them socially as well as intellectually. We are living in a democratic age. The tendencies of democracy are towards the leveling down of all inequalities.

NOTES

1. When used as a national anthem, this figure was changed to 300 million.
2. The Mother Goddess, much worshiped in Bengal.
3. The Goddess of Wealth.
4. Names of ancient Indian cities and kingdoms, used here in lieu of modern place-names.
5. Family idol.
6. The rooms of a house in which women are secluded.
7. A chilled sweet drink.
8. The old spelling for Maratha.
9. The kings of ancient India had their grants or charters to subordinates engraved on large copper or bronze rectangular plates.

10. Sir John Robert Seeley, author of *The Expansion of England* (London, 1895).
11. The Highest God.
12. Ritual sacrifice.
13. Demons.
14. Divine power.
15. Spiritual discipline leading to attainment of the highest good.
16. Pure, holy.
17. The play or sport of God.
18. Lajpat Rai, *Writings and Speeches*, 2: p. 213.
19. Intercourse between a childless widow and her husband's kinsman in order to bear children considered as her husband's.

Chapter 5

LEADERS OF ISLAMIC REVIVAL, REFORM, AND NATIONALISM IN PRE-INDEPENDENT INDIA

The coming of the British and of the civilization then evolving in Western Europe and North America had somewhat different repercussions within the Hindu and Muslim communities of India. The British impact was felt first in the coastal regions, most intensely in the port cities of Bombay, Madras, and Calcutta. As we have seen, many upper-class Hindus in these regions responded to the new situation with both an eagerness to learn from the British whatever would contribute to their own advancement and a deep desire to revitalize (with the help of European Sanskritists) what seemed of highest value in their own religious heritage. To these ends, and to secure the economic benefits of trading with, collecting land revenues for, or working in the offices of the English, many upper class Hindus in the coastal provinces (and the Zoroastrian Parsis on the western coast) quickly learned the language of their rulers and cooperated in building their expanding commercial, military, and governmental empire.

The last parts of the Indian subcontinent to come under the full sway of the British were precisely those areas where Muslim power and culture had reached their greatest height under the empire of the Mughals. The decline and fall of that empire, from financial weakness, internal disunity, invasions from Persia and Afghanistan, and the rise of the Maratha empire and the Sikh kingdom in the Punjab, put upper-class Muslims in an extremely vulnerable position. The East India Company's troops (most of them Indian soldiers under British officers) took over Delhi from the Marathas in 1803, though the emperor was kept on his throne as titular ruler of the country. Some attempts were made to introduce Western learning through translations into Hindustani (the regional language, written in Arabic script), but

North India's Muslims remained attached to Islamic studies and to the memories of their ancestors' empires.

Compared to the eighteenth century's turbulence, the settled conditions of the Company's government might have seemed an improvement to educated Muslims. This was more true at Lucknow—capital of the kingdom of Oudh, left unconquered by the Company until 1856—than elsewhere in the North Indian plains. Lahore had fallen to the Sikh power. Delhi lay in between, geographically as well as politically. There, the leading scholar Shāh Walī-Ullāh's son ʿAbd al-ʿAzīz took an ambivalent position toward British rule, ruling that Muslims living under it were, in theory, living in a zone of war with infidels (*dār al ḥarb*), though they were free to study at English schools and take jobs in the Company's spreading administrative network. Some did one or both, whereas others remained unreconciled to their new, non-Muslim overlords.

The smoldering resentment burst into flames in three areas of India. In the northwest, Sayyid Ahmad Barelwi, a disciple of Shah ʿAbd al-ʿAziz, waged a holy war (*jihād*) against Sikh rule over Muslims from 1826 until his death in 1831. In East Bengal (the other Muslim-majority region to become in the twentieth century a part of the new nation of Pakistan), Dudhu Miyan led attacks by Muslim farm workers on Hindu and British estate owners in the 1830s and 1840s. Then came the most violent outbreak of all—the 1857 mutinies by the Company's troops in north-central India and the subsequent civil uprisings in the countryside around Delhi and Lucknow. Although Hindus in the coastal cities voiced their support for the British cause (and some, like Debendranath Tagore, who were caught in the rebellious area, feared for their lives), no genuine unity emerged within the ranks of the rebels. Numerous manifestos were issued; some favored restoration of the Mughal Empire, others did not. British-led forces, swelled by Sikh troops from the Punjab and Gurkhas from Nepal, recaptured Delhi and Lucknow and crushed (sometimes brutally) all resistance. The aging emperor's sons were executed and he himself was sent into exile in Burma, where he died. Thus ended the last military effort aimed at driving the British out of India.

In the last half of the nineteenth century, two major movements attempted to rescue Islam in India from further disintegration. Both made their headquarters within a hundred-mile radius of the now devastated city of Delhi. At Deoband, a group of scholars founded a new center for the transmission of the old faith, in the purified form initiated by Shah Walī-Ullah. At Aligarh, a civil servant of the government, Syed Ahmed Khan, opened a school that became a college (and later a university) where the modern Western knowledge was taught side by side with traditional Islamic learning. Greatly impressed by the level of civilized life he found in England, Syed Ahmed also tried, independently of his educational efforts, to show that the message of Islam was in complete harmony with the discoveries of modern science. As the Indian National Congress launched its long campaign to transfer more and more power to Indian hands, Syed Ahmed warned his fellow Muslims to boycott it and to look to the British for the defense of their interests—a policy that led after his death to the 1906 founding of the All-India Muslim League and the granting of a separate voting system to Muslims when partly elected legislatures were introduced in 1909. These separate, or "communal," electorates were to become the hub of controversies and negotiations between Muslim League and Congress leaders in the following decades.

In Syed Ahmed's last years, younger members of the Aligarh faculty gave voice to more romantic views of their Islamic heritage. The most notable among these faculty members were the poet Hali and the historian Shibli, whose celebrations of earlier Muslims' deeds can be compared to Bankim's praise of his Hindu predecessors. Soon the graduates of the college began to express themselves in fluent English on the issues of the day. The most articulate among the alumni was Mohamed Ali, who went on to Oxford University and a brief career in journalism. His visions of pan-Islamic unity stirred him to give up Syed Ahmed's pro-British policy and to support the cause of Ottoman Turkey and its caliph, both during the Balkan Wars in 1911 and during World War I, when the Turks sided with Germany and Austria-Hungary against Britain, France, Italy, and Russia. After the war Mohamed Ali and his brother, Shaukat, became the leaders of the Khilāfat movement, which attempted to unite Indian Muslims against what was regarded as an attack by the British on the Caliph (Khalīfa) of the Ottoman Empire. With the Muslim journalist, Abul Kalam Azad, they worked with M. K. Gandhi in an unsuccessful attempt to bring about unity between Muslims and Hindus. The more mystical and scholarly Azad (his pen name meaning "free") stayed with the Congress, but Mohamed Ali became disillusioned with its program and in 1930 denounced Gandhi as "fighting for the supremacy of Hinduism and the submergence of Muslims." [1]

Perhaps the most famous of all the spokesmen for the revival of Islam in India was the philosopher and poet Muhammad Iqbal. Like Syed Ahmed Khan and Mohamed Ali, in the earlier part of his life he had believed that

Hindus and Muslims could live together in one nation. Later, as the pace of political change quickened, Iqbal and other leaders doubted that Islam could long survive under Hindu-majority rule.

After World War I, it became clear that India would eventually free itself from foreign rule. Tensions mounted and tempers flared, however, over the various social, economic, and constitutional problems to be solved, both before and after independence. The most burning of these issues in the three decades before independence concerned the future status of the minority groups, especially the Muslims, who formed about 25 percent of the population.

By the nature of their faith, Muslims felt a greater sense of solidarity with one another (apart from differences between Shīʿas and Sunnis, which sometimes led to riots) than the far more segmented members of other minority groups, such as the untouchable caste groups. They were also more literate and had, in their gatherings for Friday prayers and the sermons of their learned men, the means for rapid communication with one another. The great mosques, forts, and tombs of their medieval ancestors stood as daily reminders of the empires Muslims had once created. The Muslims also had many leaders of great ability. What role would they play when British overlordship came to an end?

Mohamed Ali at first believed the answer lay in cooperation between Muslims and Hindus, preferably on the basis of a religious federation. His faith faded as differences arose between him and Gandhi over the causes and effects of a spiraling number of Hindu-Muslim riots and killings. He died in 1930 with no resolution in sight to the problem of unity between the two communities.

Muhammad Iqbal came forward in that same year with a solution that his fellow Punjabi Lala Lajpat Rai had mentioned as early as 1901: let those areas where Muslims had lived for the longest time, and where they now made up the majority of the inhabitants, set up their own government. Iqbal expected that such a government would be a part of a larger federation of states but made it clear that within this area (the northwestern region of India) Muslims would be free to live according to their own religious laws, rather than according to a secular legal system developed in Europe.

Then Muhammed Ali Jinnah, a Muslim who deeply believed in the British system of laws, gradually became convinced that a separate Muslim state or states was necessary in order to protect as many of India's Muslims as possible from permanent domination by a Hindu constitutional majority.

Jinnah's ideal was a secular state, and from 1940 to 1946 he used constitutional methods to organize support for a larger state than Iqbal had wanted, including in it the Muslim-majority areas of eastern India.

Many Muslims, however, deplored the idea that the country would be partitioned, however. One of them, Maulana Abul Kalam Azad, a devoutly religious Muslim who was president of the Indian National Congress from 1940 to 1946, reasserted the Congress's traditional policy that it represented all the citizens of India, without regard to their religion. After the division of British-ruled India into India and Pakistan, he lamented the harm wrought by the partition. The following readings trace some of the major currents of thought in the Indo-Islamic world before 1947.

An Attempted Mughal Restoration: The Azamgarh Proclamation

In the summer of 1857, with much of north-central India in rebellion against British rule, the Azamgarh Proclamation was allegedly issued by one of the grandsons of the king of Delhi, the descendant of the great Mughal emperors of the sixteenth and seventeenth centuries. The various appeals made to rally support commingle grievances against the British (chiefly religious and economic), promises to those who would join to root the British out, and threats to those who would not. A few weeks after the proclamation was made, the king was taken prisoner at Delhi.

[From Ball, *The History of the Indian Mutiny*, 2:630–32]

It is well known to all that in this age the people of Hindostan,[2] both Hindoos and Mohammedans, are being ruined under the tyranny and oppression of the infidel and treacherous English. It is therefore the bounden duty of those who have any sort of connexion with any of the Mohammedan royal families, and are considered the pastors and masters of the people, to stake their lives and property for the well-being of the public. With the view of effecting this general good, several princes belonging to the royal family of Delhi have dispersed themselves in the different parts of India, Iran, Turan [Turkestan], and Afghanistan, and have been long since taking measures to compass their favourite end; and it is to accomplish this charitable object that one of the aforesaid princes has, at the head of an army of Afghanistan, etc., made his appearance in India; and I, who am the grandson of Abul Muzuffer Sarajuddin Bahadur Shah Ghazee, king of India, having in the course of circuit come here to extirpate the infidels residing in the eastern part of the country, and to liberate and protect the

poor helpless people now groaning under their iron rule, have, by the aid
of the Majahdeens [*mujāhidīn*, "fighters for Islam against infidels"] . . . erected
the standard of Mohammed, and persuaded the orthodox Hindoos who had
been subject to my ancestors, and have been and are still accessories in the
destruction of the English, to raise the standard of Mahavir.[3]

Several of the Hindoo and Mussulman chiefs, who have long since quit-
ted their homes for the preservation of their religion, and have been trying
their best to root out the English in India, have presented themselves to
me, and taken part in the reigning Indian crusade, and it is more than
probable that I shall very shortly receive succours from the west. Therefore,
for the information of the public, the present Ishtahar [proclamation], consisting of several sections, is put in circulation, and it is the imperative duty
of all to take it into their careful consideration, and abide by it. Parties
anxious to participate in the common cause, but having no means to provide for themselves, shall receive their daily subsistence from me; and be it
known to all, that the ancient works, both of the Hindoos and the Mohammedans, the writings of the miracle-workers, and the calculations of the
astrologers, pundits, and rammals [fortune-tellers], all agree in asserting that
the English will no longer have any footing in India or elsewhere. . . .

No person, at the misrepresentation of the well-wishers of the British
government, ought to conclude from the present slight inconveniences usually attendant on revolutions, that similar inconveniences and troubles should
continue when the Badshahi [royal] government is established on a firm
basis; and parties badly dealt with by any sepoy [soldier] or plunderer, should
come up and represent their grievances to me, and receive redress at my
hands; and for whatever property they may lose in the reigning disorder,
they will be recompensed from the public treasury when the Badshahi government is well fixed.

Section I.—Regarding Zemindars [landholders].—It is evident that the
British government, in making zemindary settlements, have imposed exor-
bitant jummas [taxes], and have disgraced and ruined several zemindars, by
putting up their estates to public auction for arrears of rent, insomuch that
on the institution of a suit by a common ryot [cultivator], a maidservant,
or a slave, the respectable zemindars are summoned into court, arrested, put
in gaol, and disgraced. In litigations regarding zemindaries, the immense
value of stamps, and other unnecessary expenses of the civil courts, which
are pregnant with all sorts of crooked dealings, and the practice of allowing
a case to hang on for years, are all calculated to impoverish the litigants.

Besides this, the coffers of the zemindars are annually taxed with subscriptions for schools, hospitals, roads, etc. Such extortions will have no manner of existence in the Badshahi government; but, on the contrary, the jummas will be light, the dignity and honour of the zemindars safe, and every zemindar will have absolute rule in his own zemindary.[4] The zemindary disputes will be summarily decided according to the Shurrah [*Sharīʿa*] and the Shasters [*śāstras*], without any expense; and zemindars who will assist in the present war with their men and money, shall be excused for ever from paying half the revenue. . . .

Section II.—Regarding Merchants.—It is plain that the infidel and treacherous British government have monopolised the trade of all the fine and valuable merchandise, such as indigo, cloth, and other articles of shipping, leaving only the trade of trifles to the people, and even in this they are not without their share of the profits, which they secure by means of customs and stamp fees, etc., in money suits, so that the people have merely a trade in name. . . . When the Badshahi government is established, all these aforesaid fraudulent practices shall be dispensed with, and the trade of every article, without exception, both by land and water, shall be open to the native merchants of India, who will have the benefit of the government steam-vessels and steam carriages for the conveyance of the merchandise gratis; and merchants having no capital of their own shall be assisted from the public treasury. . . .

Section III.—Regarding Public Servants.—It is not a secret thing, that under the British government, natives employed in the civil and military services, have little respect, low pay, and no manner of influence; and all the posts of dignity and emolument in both the departments, are exclusively bestowed on Englishmen. . . . But under the Badshahi government, . . . the posts . . . which the English enjoy at present . . . will be given to the natives . . . together with jagheers [landed estates], khilluts [ceremonial dress], inams [tax-free lands], and influence. Natives, whether Hindoos or Mohammedans, who fall fighting against the English, are sure to go to heaven; and those killed fighting for the English, will, doubtless, go to hell. Therefore, all the natives in the British service ought to be alive to their religion and interest, and, abjuring their loyalty to the English, side with the Badshahi government and obtain salaries of 200 or 300 rupees per month for the present, and be entitled to high posts in future. . . .

Section IV.—Regarding Artisans.—It is evident that the Europeans, by the introduction of English articles into India, have thrown the weavers, the cotton-dressers, the carpenters, the blacksmiths, and the shoemakers, &c., out of employ, and have engrossed their occupations, so that every description of native artisan has been reduced to beggary. But under the Badshahi government the native artisans will exclusively be employed in the services of the kings, the rajahs, and the rich; and this will no doubt insure their prosperity. Therefore the artisans ought to renounce the English services, and assist the Majahdeens [the faithful] . . . engaged in the war, and thus be entitled both to secular and eternal happiness.

Section V.—Regarding Pundits, Fakirs, and other learned persons.—The pundits and fakirs being the guardians of the Hindoo and Mohammedan religions respectively, and the Europeans being the enemies of both religions, and as at present a war is raging against the English on account of religion, the pundits and fakirs are bound to present themselves to me, and take their share in this holy war, otherwise they will stand condemned according to the tenor of the Shurrah and the Shasters; but if they come, they will, when the Badshahi government is well established, receive rent-free lands.

Lastly, be it known to all, that whoever, out of the above-named classes, shall, after the circulation of this Ishtahar, still cling to the British government, all his estates shall be confiscated, and his property plundered, and he himself, with his whole family, shall be imprisoned, and ultimately put to death.

SYED AHMED KHAN: MUSLIM REFORMER AND EDUCATOR

The career of Syed Ahmed (or Sayyid Ahmad) Khan (1817–1898) parallels in many ways that of Rammohun Roy. Both were born into families of the high social rank, and both were educated in the Persian and Arabic learning required of entrants into the service of the Mughal Empire—well after that empire had been replaced by another. Both came to know and trust British officials and to appreciate the advanced knowledge and new form of government they brought to India. Both rejected the Christian doctrines being preached by missionaries and made their own independent studies of the Christian scriptures. Both searched for the central messages at the core of the religions of their ancestors, then sought to purge those religions of superstitions and medieval accretions, reinterpreting them in such ways as to give their ancient meanings new vitality in the present. Both edited periodicals, enriched with their writings the languages of their regions, and founded schools to make Western learning available to young people. (Syed Ahmed far outdid Rammohun in the amount of time and money he devoted to educational work.) Both occasionally took stands critical of their rulers and traveled to England to learn from, and offer advice to, its inhabitants. Both suffered bitter attacks from their coreligionists, and yet each in the twentieth century has been hailed as the founding father of his community's "modern" world view. The religious ideas they were trying to defend and revitalize, however, and the geographic and sociopolitical contexts in which they operated, were quite different.

Syed Ahmed as a boy might have seen Rammohun in his customary Persian-style gown, shawl, and turban presenting himself to the powerless Mughal emperor before setting off for London as his majesty's ambassador; Syed Ahmed's family was attached to the Delhi court, his mother's father having twice served the emperor as his prime minister. This grandfather was also on good terms with the British, having been principal of the Calcutta Madrasa (school of Islamic learning) and an attaché with an embassy sent to the king of Persia by the East India Company. His example and personal influence (for his grandson grew up in his house) prepared young Syed Ahmed for a distinguished career of dual allegiance to India's Muslims and to their British rulers.

Syed Ahmed's mother was a devoted follower or ʿAbd al-ʿAziz (d. 1823), who had expanded the reformist work of his father Shāh Walī-Ullāh by writing on the Qurʾān for the first time in Urdu, the everyday language of the Muslims of North India. When Syed Ahmed's father, a reclusive mystic with whom he seems to have had relatively little contact, died in 1838, it was time for the twenty-one-year-old to find a job. Through his mother's brother, a subjudge in the East India Company's service, he obtained a clerkship in the judicial branch and did so well he rose to be a subjudge himself within a few years. He made good use of his free time by writing and editing historical works on Islamic rulers in India, and he commented admiringly on the heroic campaigns and 1831 death of Sayyid Ahmad Barelwi (a disciple of ʿAbd al-ʿAziz) who had tried to free the Punjab's Muslims from Sikh rule.

The great shock of Syed Ahmed's life, which changed him from an observer to an active worker in defense of Muslims and of Islam in India, was the 1857 outbreak of military mutinies and civil strife in northern India. Syed Ahmed's immediate response was to save the lives of the British fam-

ilies of the district in which he was stationed as subjudge and then to try to
keep the peace until the Company's forces arrived. He failed in this because
of fighting between Hindu and Muslim factions.

After criticizing the East India Company in an Urdu pamphlet (he never
learned enough English to write confidently in it) for their insensivity to
their subjects' opinions, he recommended that a few Indians be appointed
to the governor-general's legislative council, a practice that was initiated in
1861, with Syed Ahmed himself holding such an appointment from 1878
to 1883. But what worried him most in the next decade were indications
that the British were placing the blame for the mutinies and rebellions on
the Muslims, and that in consequence his already disadvantaged community
would be rendered even more helpless than before.

Syed Ahmed's strategy was twofold: to persuade the British that the Muslims of India were loyal and worthy of help, and to teach his own community that they would only benefit by cooperating with and learning from
the West. He managed to achieve both aims, but the first more easily than
the second. Even though several high officials (including the viceroy) were
assassinated by Muslims in the 1860s and 1870s, Syed Ahmed's educational
initiatives quickly won British support. After founding several schools, a
"scientific society" for promoting the translation of modern Western knowledge into Urdu, and a weekly magazine printed in English and Urdu on
facing columns, he took leave from his judicial work in order to see England
for himself. He was well received, much impressed, and stayed for seventeen months, developing plans to found a college modeled after Harrow and
Cambridge but where both Islamic and modern Western studies could be
offered. Five years later he was able to open a school on these lines, then
retire from government service. In 1877 the viceroy came to lay the foundation stone of the Mohammedan Anglo-Oriental College at Aligarh. For
the next two decades, Syed Ahmed remained the heart and soul of his new
creation, while delegating its administration to a series of British educators.
Muslim students came from all parts of India to enroll, and Hindu students
were also welcomed and their dietary customs respected.

Some orthodox Muslims objected to the college on the grounds that Syed
Ahmed had gone too far in accepting Western ideas and ways of living. But
what particularly aroused them was his new interpretation of Islam, set forth
in various lectures and in his series of essays on the Qur'ān (1876–1891).
Rejecting the authority of traditional scholars, and of the sayings (*Hadīth*)
attributed to the prophet Muhammad, Syed Ahmed relied on his own judg-

ment as he examined and compared the actual words in the Qur'ān itself. Further, in his enthusiasm for the progress of the natural sciences, he declared that nothing in the Qur'ān, when rightly understood, contradicted the laws of nature. His critics seized upon the word "nature" and called him and his followers *Nechārīs* ("naturists"), but scholars in subsequent generations have seen him as a pioneer in using independent experience and judgment to arrive at a truer understanding of the words that came into the heart of the prophet. To ensure the success of his college, Syed Ahmed carefully kept his own theological views out of its curriculum, made sure that both Sunni and Shī'ī instruction were offered, and required Muslim students to pray facing toward Mecca five times each day.

In the final years of his life, Syed Ahmed broadened the scope of his efforts to serve and defend the interests of the Muslims of India, founding in 1886 the annual Muhammadan Educational Conference and in 1888 the United India Patriotic Association. He urged both Hindus and Muslims to boycott the newly formed Indian National Congress, in part because he felt that its antigovernment agitation would turn Muslims away from the modern Western learning that was essential to their progress. Muslims at that time formed only 20 percent of India's population and in education, wealth, and positions in the government service had fallen far behind Hindus. Because of his call to stay out of the Congress, Syed Ahmed has been seen as a forefather of the movement to establish the Muslim-majority nation of Pakistan. In addition, Muslims both there and in India claim him as the father of their modern outlook on education—and to some extent on religion as well.

Advice to the People of Bijnor After the 1857–1858 Uprising

After serving in the judicial branch of the East India Company's government for almost twenty years, Syed Ahmed Khan felt no sympathy for the military mutinies and civil rebellions in north-central India in 1857–1858. He reprimanded those in his district who had participated in and suffered from them.

[From Ahmed Khan, *History of the Bijnor Rebellion*, pp. 107–9]

A man should think about those events which happen in the world and strive to instruct himself from a study of their consequences. The turmoil of violence which happened was only a punishment for the ungratefulness of the Hindustanis [inhabitants of India, and particularly of north-central India]. . . . In Hindustan, people are not at all accustomed to learn about former times from the facts of history, nor from reading books. It is for this reason that you people were not acquainted with the injustice and oppression that used to take place in the days of past rulers. Whether rich or poor, a person in those times could never be at ease. If you had been acquainted with the injustice and excesses of those past days you would have appreciated the value of English rule and given thanks to God. But you were never grateful to God and remained always discontented. . . .

Think how the Muslims, both in the beginning and at the end, grew strong in the District, and those who were called traditional governors [nawābs] ruled as if it had been only their elders and no one else who had established the District. Take a view of their rule and recollect how the Hindus of the District were ruined, murdered, and plundered. Great landlords of the District were ruined and driven into exile. Scores of innocent Hindus were seized and killed while their property, effects, and houses were all looted. The Muslims, for their part, might well ponder the question of why those Nawabs did not harm them. Even this was only a matter of political expediency, for the wretches were only interested in keeping the Muslims on their side. God forbid if their Government had stabilized itself just a little; then you Muslims would have seen how your co-religionists could be cruel and unjust to you.

In the interval between the [first and second] time when the Nawabs were in the ascendant, the Hindus became strong enough to dominate for a few days, so that the Hindu landlords were able to rule the District. You could then taste the Government of the Hindus and see what Muslims experienced at Hindu hands: how many houses looted, how many villages razed, and even your own womenfolk ravaged. Speak truthfully then. The English ruled fifty-four years in this District. Did any person, Hindu or Muslim, experience any trouble or annoyance then? Can you not recollect what were the disasters brought down on your head by this Hindustani Government in those times of the rebellion? Go to the history books on the rule of the former great emperors to measure the extent of the cruelties and disasters borne by the common folk of those days of organized governments.

Not even one hundred-thousandth part of the ease was present then which fell to your lot in English times. Look how Hindus and Muslims are living with all ease and in peace under English rule. The strong cannot tyrannize the weak now. Each worships God and his Creator according to the requirements of his religion. There is an atmosphere of live-and-let-live. The Hindu builds temples in which to worship; the Muslim builds mosques where prayers are read and the call to prayer is uttered. There is no one to stop and no one to forbid. The merchant pursues his trading affairs, entrusting goods worth thousands to an infirm and aged agent, who is sent thousands of miles to earn a profit; and there is no fear of dacoit [armed robber] or thug. And roads—how perfectly secure they are; women, adorned with jewelry worth thousands of rupees, may ride at night in horse-drawn carriages from stage to stage, all quite free of anxiety. The owner-cultivator is busy in the fields; no one takes an iota more than the appointed rent [revenue] for these fields. . . .

It has been customary in Hindustan that when any mighty person gained control of some country, the common people accepted the obligation to obey him; everyone became his companion and supporter. When he departed and someone else came, the newcomer was also obeyed by all; try to understand this matter. It is not improper to associate the English Government with this tradition. The common people did not enjoy liberty under former Hindustani Governments; the rulers of the day kept them crushed under all kinds of injustice and violence and improper Government. Their property, in truth, was the property of those tyrants who seized what they wanted and levied fines on whomever they pleased without regard to fault. In direct contrast to our English rule, the common people enjoyed no rights under such Government.

Now the people have obtained freedom, and each person is master of his own thing, he does as he wishes. To the extent that the English Government protects its own right, to the same extent does it also protect the rights of the people. If the lowly Chamar[5] subject of the Government knows that the Government has unjustly taken even his paisa [the cheapest coin], he can bring an action against his own Government to obtain justice. It is as though the people and the authorities were partners in the Government. Under this kind of Government, there is one duty that falls on the subject, that each person must necessarily and properly fulfill. This duty requires that the subject must take the side of his Government. . . . and do his duty by the Government. . . . In this regard, you people were found negligent. On the contrary, even more than negligent, for you have brought dishonor on all your fellow countrymen. Would that you had not done so! For would the evil days at [the time of] retribution [when the East India Company's forces reconquered the District] which fell to your lot have then come? Even now you ought to do your duty by the Government, so that you may wash away with the cool water of obedience and sincere assistance to the Government the dishonor which was your lot, and so that you may find the upshot to be good.

Impressions of England and Her Civilization

In 1869 Syed Ahmed Khan made a trip to England to enter his son at Cambridge University and to study the institutions of the country by whom India was then governed. In his frank letter to the Scientific Society at Aligarh (which he had founded in 1866 for the diffusion of modern knowledge in Urdu translations), he attributed the higher state of civilization in England to the education of both men and women there.

[From Graham, *Life and Work of Sir Syed Ahmed Khan* as corrected by Hafeez Malik), pp. 125–27, 129–30, 131–32.]

It is nearly six months since I arrived in London, and [I] have been unable to see many things I should have liked, been able to see a good deal, and have been in the society of lords and dukes at dinners and evening parties. Artisans and the common working-man I have seen in numbers. I have visited famous and spacious mansions, museums, engineering works, ship-building establishments, gun-foundries, ocean-telegraph companies which connect continents, vessels of war (in one of which I walked for miles, the Great Eastern steamship), have been present at the meetings of several societies, and have dined at clubs and private houses. The result of all this is, that although I do not absolve the English in India of discourtesy, and of looking upon the natives of that country as animals and beneath contempt, I think they do so from not understanding us; and I am afraid I must confess that they are not far wrong in their opinion of us. Without flattering the English, I can truly say that the natives of India, high and low, merchants and petty shopkeepers, educated and illiterate, when contrasted with the English in education, manners, and uprightness, are as like them as a dirty animal is to an able and handsome man. The English have reason for believing us in India to be imbecile brutes. Although my countrymen will consider this opinion of mine an extremely harsh one, and will wonder what they are deficient in, and in what the English excel, to cause me to write as I do, I maintain that they have no cause for wonder, as they are ignorant of everything here, which is really beyond imagination and conception. . . . I am not thinking about those things in which, owing to the specialties of our respective countries, we and the English differ. I only remark on politeness, knowledge, good faith, cleanliness, skilled workmanship, accomplishments, and thoroughness, which are the results of education and civilisation. All good things, spiritual and worldly, which should be found in man, have been bestowed by the Almighty on Europe, and especially on England. By spiritual good things I mean that the English carry out all the details of the religion which they believe to be the true one, with a beauty and excellence which no other nation can compare with. This is entirely due to the education of the men and women, and to their being united in aspiring after this beauty and excellence. If Hindustanis can only attain to civilisation, it will probably, owing to its many excellent natural powers, become, if not the superior, at least the equal of England. . . .

I am extremely pleased that my Bengal and Parsi brethren have begun to some extent to promote civilisation, but their pace is so fast that there is danger of their falling. The fatal shroud of complacent self-esteem is wrapt around the Mohammedan community: they remember the old tales of their ancestors, and think that there are none like themselves. The Mohammedans of Egypt and Turkey are daily becoming more civilised. . . .

Look at this young girl Elizabeth Matthews [a servant in the house in which he was living], who, in spite of her poverty, invariably buys a halfpenny paper called the "Echo" and reads it when at leisure. If she comes across a "Punch," in which there are pictures of women's manners and customs, she looks at them, and enjoys the editor's remarks thereon. All the shops have the names of their occupants written in front in splendid golden letters, and servants requiring anything have only to read and enter. Cabmen and coachmen keep a paper or a book under their seats and after taking the passenger to his destination, or in case the coach has to wait, they take out their newspaper and start reading. Remember that the rank of a cabman corresponds to that of the *ekhawallas* [*ikkāvāla:* driver of two-wheeled horse carriage] of Benares.

Until the education of the masses is pushed on as it is here, it is impossible for a native to become civilised and honoured.

The cause of England's civilisation is that all the arts and sciences are in the language of the country. . . . Those who are really bent on improving and bettering India must remember that the only way of compassing this is by having the whole of the arts and sciences translated into their own language. I should like to have this written in gigantic letters on the Himalayas, for the remembrance of future generations. If they be not translated, India can never be civilised. This is [the] truth, this is the truth, this is the truth! Government has a difficult task. When the governing tongue is not that of the country, the people do not care to study their own language, because up to the present no one studies for the sake of science, but only to get service. O well-wishers of Hindustan, do not place your dependence on anyone! Spread abroad, relying on yourselves and your subscriptions, translations of the arts and sciences: and when you have mastered these and attained to civilisation, you will think very little of going into Government service. I hope and trust that such a day may soon come.

The Importance of Modern Western Education

As in Japan, China, and other countries, so in nineteenth-century India, the introduction of modern Western education was strongly resisted by those in charge of transmitting and interpreting the received teachings of their ancestors. Syed Ahmed insisted, as did his counterparts in other societies, that the new knowledge from abroad must be absorbed, not only to prevent the obliteration of his people and their culture, but also to enable the deepest truths of that culture to shine forth more brightly than before.

[From a letter to Mawlawi Tasadduq, in *Sir Syed ke chand nadir khutut*]

I have been accused by people, who do not understand, of being disloyal to the culture of Islam, even to Islam itself. There are men who say that I have become a Christian. All this I have drawn upon myself because I advocate the introduction of a new system of education which will not neglect the Islamic basis of our culture, nor, for that matter, the teaching of Islamic theology itself, but which will surely take account of the changed conditions in this land. Today there are no Muslim rulers to patronize those who are well versed in the old Arabic and Persian learning. The new rulers insist upon a knowledge of their language for all advancement in their services and in some of the independent professions like practising law as well. If the Muslims do not take to the system of education introduced by the British, they will not only remain a backward community but will sink lower and lower until there will be no hope of recovery left to them. Is this at all a pleasing prospect? Can we serve the cause of Islam in this way?

Shall we then be able to ward off the obliteration of all that we hold dear for any length of time?

If the choice were to lie between giving up Islam itself or saving ourselves from apostasy, I should have unhesitatingly chosen the latter even it it had meant utter destruction for myself and my people. That, however, is not the choice. The adoption of the new system of education does not mean the renunciation of Islam. It means its protection. We are justly proud of the achievements of our forefathers in the fields of learning and culture. We should, however, remember that these achievements were possible only because they were willing to act upon the teachings of the Prophet upon whom be peace and blessings of God. He said that knowledge is the heritage of the believer, and that he should acquire it wherever he can find it. He also said that the Muslims should seek knowledge even if they have to go to China to find it. It is obvious that the Prophet was not referring to theological knowledge in these sayings; China at that time was one of the most civilized countries of the world, but it was a non-Muslim country and could not teach the Muslims anything about their own religion. Islam, Islamic culture, and the Muslims themselves prospered as long as the Prophet was followed in respect of these teachings; when we ceased to take interest in the knowledge of others, we began to decline in every respect. Did the early Muslims not take to Greek learning avidly? Did this in any respect undermine their loyalty to Islam?

It is not only because the British are today our rulers, and we have to recognize this fact if we are to survive, that I am advocating the adoption of their system of education, but also because Europe has made such remarkable progress in science that it would be suicidal not to make an effort to acquire it. Already the leeway between our knowledge and that of Europe is too great. If we go on with our present obstinacy in neglecting it, we shall be left far behind. How can we remain true Muslims or serve Islam, if we sink into ignorance? The knowledge of yesterday is often the ignorance of tomorrow, because knowledge and ignorance are, in this context, comparative terms. The truth of Islam will shine the more brightly if its followers are well educated, familiar with the highest in the knowledge of the world; it will come under an eclipse if its followers are ignorant and backward.

The Muslims have nothing to fear from the adoption of the new education if they simultaneously hold steadfast to their faith, because Islam is not irrational superstition; it is a rational religion which can march hand in hand with the growth of human knowledge. Any fear to the contrary betrays lack of faith in the truth of Islam.

Islam in the Light of Modern Knowledge

As Syed Ahmed's educational campaign advanced, he became aware (with the assistance of many critics) that the spread of modern scientific knowledge among young Muslims might undermine their faith in Islam. He therefore sought in various lectures and writings to show that in its essence the Qurʾān, the word of God, was entirely consistent with the laws of nature (including those of human nature), which God had created in the beginning.

[From Baljon, *The Reforms and Religious Ideas of Sir Sayyid Ahmad Khan*, pp. 77, 114, and Dar, *Religious Thought of Sayyid Ahmad Khan*, pp. 176, 149–50]

Today we are, as before [i.e., when Islamic thinkers were influenced by Greek science and philosophy], in need of a modern ʿilm al-kalām [knowledge and method of scholastic theology], by which we should either refute the doctrines of [the] modern sciences or undermine their foundations, or show that they are in conformity with the articles of Islamic faith. . . . When I endeavour to propagate those sciences amongst the Muslims which, [as] I have just stated, disagree with [the tenets of] present-day Islam, then it is my duty to defend as much as I can the religion of Islam, right or wrong, and to reveal to the people the original bright face of Islam. My conscience tells me that if I should not do so, I would stand as a sinner before God.

. . . . .

Revelation is that which has been given to the Prophet by God, but former interpreters did not explain this "has been given" in the right way; they thought that God and the Prophet were like a king and a minister. These explanations of our ʿUlama [learned Muslims] in former days are an object of mockery for people of today, and on account of such explanations they consider the Qurʾān and Islam as nonsense. . . . One ought, however, to understand that prophethood is a natural phenomenon which is present in the prophets like other innate faculties. . . . The heart of the prophet is the mirror in which the splendour of the divine glory is reflected, it is the instrument which echoes the words of God, it is the ear which hears the letterless and soundless words of God.

. . . .

[To judge whether or not a prophet is a true one] We will compare his moral code with the law of Nature. We will judge it in the light of [the] knowledge, reason and experience that man has been able to gain. If the moral code is quite true to Nature, we shall accept the prophet as true. . . . A French scholar has said that nobody was as truthful as the Prophet Muhammad, who neither showed any miracle nor claimed a rank for himself which is beyond human nature to attain. He only claimed to be a moral preacher who taught right conduct and warned us of [the] wrong path. For these things, he is above all comparison. His religion is a religion of Nature.

. . . .

Neither an atheist nor a believer can deny the fact that man's constitution is such (or, we may say, God has bestowed upon him the powers) that he is able to do certain works and not able to do certain others; and, therefore, he must choose for himself a most suitable vocation in life wherein his internal and external qualities render the service for which he was born. So the only touchstone of a true religion can be this: If that religion is in conformity with human nature or with Nature in general, then it is true. It would be a clear proof that this religion is from the hands of God, the Author of Nature both in man and outside [him]. If that religion is against human nature and [man's] constitution, and against his powers and the rights which follow from these powers, and stands in the way of putting them to useful purposes, then undoubtedly that religion cannot be claimed to issue forth from the hands of the Author of Nature, for religion, after all, is made for men. . . . I am fully confident that the guidance which He has given us is absolutely in conformity with our constitution and our nature, and this is the only touchstone of its truth. It would be clearly absurd to assert that God's action is different from His words. All creation including man is the work of God and religion is His Word, so there cannot be any contradiction between the two.

Hindu-Muslim Peaceful Coexistence Possible Only Under British Rule

Speaking from personal knowledge of the hostilities between Hindus and Muslims during the 1857–1858 mutinies and civil revolts, and fearing that even greater troubles would occur if the British were to leave India to govern herself, Syed Ahmed Khan vigorously opposed the nationalist aims of the Indian National Congress (founded in 1885). Maximum progress, he believed, could only be achieved through harmonious relations between Muslims and Hindus under prolonged British rule.

[From Ahmed Khan, *Writings and Speeches*, pp. 159–60, 184–86, *Akhari Madamin*, pp. 46–50]

(1883) Friends, in India there live two prominent nations which are distinguished by the names of Hindus and Mussulmans. Just as a man has some principal organs, similarly these two nations are like the principal limbs of India. To be a Hindu or a Muslim is a matter of internal faith which has nothing to do with mutual relationship and external conditions. How good is the saying, whoever may be its author, that a human being is composed of two elements—his faith which he owes to God and his moral sympathy which he owes to his fellow-being. Hence leave God's share to God and concern yourself with the share that is yours.

Gentlemen, just as many reputed people professing Hindu faith came to this country, so we also came here. The Hindus forgot the country from which they had come; they could not remember their migration from one land to another and came to consider India as their homeland, believing that their country lies between the Himalayas and the Vindhyachal. Hundreds of years have lapsed since we, in our turn, left the lands of our origin. We remember neither the climate nor the natural beauty of those lands, neither the freshness of the harvests nor the deliciousness of the fruits, nor even do we remember the blessings of the holy deserts. We also come to consider India as our homeland and we settled down here like the earlier immigrants. Thus India is the home of both of us. We both breathe the air of India and take the water of the holy Ganges and the Jamuna. We both consume the products of the Indian soil. We are living and dying together. By living so long in India, the blood of both have changed. The colour of both have become similar. The faces of both, having changed, have become similar. The Muslims have acquired hundreds of customs from the Hindus and the Hindus have also learned hundreds of things from the Mussulmans. We mixed with each other so much that we produced a new language—Urdu, which was neither our language nor theirs. Thus if we ignore that aspect of ours which we owe to God, both of us, on the basis of being common inhabitants of India, actually constitute one nation; and the progress of this country and that of both of us is possible through mutual cooperation, sympathy and love. We shall only destroy ourselves by mutual disunity and animosity and ill-will to each other. It is pitiable to see those who do not understand this point and create feeling of disunity among these two nations and fail to see that they themselves will be the victims of such a situation, and inflict injury to themselves. My friends, I have repeatedly said and say it again that India is like a bride which has got two beautiful and lustrous eyes—Hindus and Mussulmans. If they quarrel against each other that beautiful bride will become ugly and if one destroys the other, she will lose one eye. Therefore, people of Hindustan you have now the right to make this bride either squint eyed or one eyed.

Undoubtedly, what to say of Hindus and Mussulmans, a quarrel among human beings is a natural phenomenon. Within the ranks of the Hindus or Mussulmans themselves, or even between brothers as also between fathers and sons, mothers and daughters there are dissensions. But to make it perennial is a symptom of decay of the family, the country, and of the nation. How blessed are those who repent, and step forward to unite the knot which has by chance, marred their mutual relations and do not allow it to get disrupted. O! God, let the people of India change to this way of thinking.

. . . . .

(1888)Now, suppose that all the English and the whole English army were to leave India, taking with them all their cannon and their splendid weapons and everything, then who would be rulers of India? Is it possible that under these circumstances two nations—the Mohammedans and the Hindus—could sit on the same throne and remain equal in power? Most certainly not. It is necessary that one of them should conquer the other and thrust it down. To hope that both could remain equal is to desire the impossible and the inconceivable. At the same time you must remember that although the number of Mohammedans is less than that of the Hindus, and although they contain far fewer people who have received a high English education, yet they must not be thought insignificant or weak. Probably they would be by themselves enough to maintain their own position. But suppose they were not. Then our Mussalman brothers, the Pathans, would come out as a swarm of locusts from their mountain valleys, and make rivers of blood to flow from their frontier on the north to the extreme end of Bengal. This thing—who after the departure of the English would be conquerors—would rest on the will of God. But until one nation had conquered the other and made it obedient, peace cannot reign in the land. This conclusion is based on proofs so absolute that no one can deny it.

Now, suppose that the English are not in India and that one of the nations of India has conquered the other, whether the Hindus the Mohammedans, or the Mohammedans the Hindus. At once some other nation of Europe, such as the French, the Germans, the Portuguese, or the Russians, will attack India. Their ships of war, covered with iron and loaded with flashing cannon and weapons, will surround her on all sides. At that time who will protect India? Neither Hindus can save nor Mohammedans; neither the Rajputs nor my brave brothers the Pathans. And what will be the result? The result will be this—that foreigners will rule India, because the state of India is such that if foreign powers attack her, no one has the power to oppose them. From this reasoning it follows of necessity that an empire, not of any Indian race, but of foreigners, will be established in India. Now, will you please decide which of the nations of Europe you would like to rule over India? I ask if you would like Germany, whose subjects weep for heavy taxation and the stringency of their military service? Would you like the rule of France? Stop! I fancy you would, perhaps, like the rule of the Russians, who are very great friends of India and of Mohammedans, and under whom the Hindus will live in great comfort, and who will protect with the tenderest care the wealth and property which they have acquired under English rule? (Laughter). Everybody knows something or other about these powerful kingdoms of Europe. Everyone will admit that their governments are far worse, nay, beyond comparison worse, than the British Government. It is, therefore, necessary that for the peace of India and for the progress of everything in India the English Government should remain for many years— in fact for ever!

.   .   .

Long before the idea of founding the Indian National Congress was mooted, I had given thought to the matter whether representative government is suited to the conditions of India. I studied John Stuart Mill's views in support of representative government. He has dealt with this matter exceedingly well in great detail. I reached the conclusion that the first requisite of a representative government is that the voters should possess the highest degree of homogeneity. In a form of government which depends for its functioning upon majorities, it is necessary that the people should have no differences in the matter of nationality, religion, ways of living, customs, mores, culture, and historical traditions. These things should be common among a people to enable them to run a representative government properly. Only when such homogeneity is present can representative government work or prove beneficial. It should not even be thought of when these conditions do not exist. . . .

In a country like India where homogeneity does not exist in any one of these fields, the introduction of representative government can not produce any beneficial results; it can only result in interfering with the peace and prosperity of the land.

The aims and objects of the Indian National Congress are based upon an ignorance of history and present-day realities; they do not take into consideration that India is inhabited by different nationalities; they presuppose that the Muslims, the Marathas, the Brahmins, the Kshatriyas, the Banias, the Sudras, the Sikhs, the Bengalis, the Madrasis, and the Peshawaris can all be treated alike and all of them belong to the same nation. The Congress thinks that they profess the same religion, that they speak the same language, that their way of life and customs are the same, that their attitude to History is similar and is based upon the same historical traditions. . . . For the successful running of a democratic government it is essential that the majority should have the ability to govern not only themselves but also unwilling minorities. . . . I consider the experiment which the Indian National Congress wants to make fraught with dangers and suffering for all the nationalities of India, specially for the Muslims. The Muslims are in a minority, but they are a highly united minority. At least traditionally they are prone to take the sword in hand when the majority oppresses them. If this happens, it will bring about disasters greater than the ones which came in the wake of the happenings of 1857. . . . The Congress cannot rationally prove its claim to represent the opinions, ideals, and aspirations of the Muslims.

MOHAMED ALI: PATRIOT AND DEFENDER OF THE FAITH

The Muslims of British-ruled India found it increasingly difficult to remain faithful to Sir Syed Ahmed Khan's policy of loyal support to their rulers. This was partly because of the quickening spirit of nationalism in other parts of the Islamic world as well as in India, and partly because of the progressive dismemberment of the Ottoman Empire by European nations and the consequent Ottoman decision in October 1914 to enter World War I on the side of Germany and Austria-Hungary. Growing sympathy among

Indian Muslims for the Ottoman sultan was based on the tradition that the head of the strongest Islamic state was also the head of Muslims everywhere. Thus, nascent national feeling among Muslims in India for a time took the form of looking abroad for their symbolic leader. In this period, which ended in 1924 when the new Turkish government abolished the institution of the caliphate, the most vigorous English-speaking defender of the rights of the Ottoman caliph was Mohamed Ali (1878–1931).

Mohamed Ali was born into a highly respected family in the Muslim-ruled principality of Rampur, about one hundred miles east of Delhi. He was the youngest son of a youngest son and was raised in a conservative social, cultural, and political world just beginning to be influenced by the Western ways of the British. Following the example of his elder brother Shaukat Ali, and with the approval of their widowed mother, Mohamed Ali broke with family tradition by studying English at local schools and by leaving at the age of twelve for Aligarh, there to spend eight years (the last eight years of Syed Ahmed's life) absorbing the unique amalgam of modern Western and Islamic learning offered by the Mohammedan Anglo-Oriental School and College. Because he stood higher on his final examinations than any other student in the United Provinces, his brother raised sufficient funds to send him to Oxford University. There he graduated with honors in history in 1902, having taken special interest in the early Muslim conquests and empires.

Thoroughly anglicized (as Gandhi had been on his return to India nine years earlier), Mohamed Ali on his return worked as an official in the service of the princely state of Baroda in Gujarat, entering that service just as Aurobindo Ghose was about to leave it. Indian political developments soon awakened his attention, and he joined the Muslim League on its founding in 1906 and helped in drawing up its constitution. In 1907 he used his pellucid English prose to write his *Thoughts on the Present Discontent,* an appeal to the British to come down from their Olympian heights and win the affections of educated Indians by dealing with them more courteously. In 1910 he left Baroda, moved to Calcutta to start a weekly newspaper, the *Comrade,* in order to assist India's Muslims "to make their proper contribution to territorial patriotism without abating a jot of the fervour of their extraterritorial sympathies which is the quintessence of Islam."[6] His own anguish over the conquest of Ottoman territory in the Balkans drove him to contemplate suicide and to help organize a medical mission to aid the beleaguered Turks. The news that the Ottoman Empire had joined Germany and Austria-Hungary, thus becoming Britain's enemy in World War I, brought tears to his eyes. The British, suspicious of his pan-Islamic sentiments, removed him and his brother to a small town in central India and interned them there until the war was over.

Even before World War I ended, Gandhi made efforts to secure the release from internment of Mohamed Ali and his brother Shaukat. Only when the Ottoman Empire, whose cause they had defended, surrendered, were they set free, to find the realms of the caliph further diminished by the loss of all non-Turkish territory. They soon became the leaders of the Khilāfat movement, which called for the preservation of the Ottoman caliph's sovereignty over the holy places of Islam—Mecca, Medina, and Jerusalem. Motivated in part by a romantic attachment to the last great Islamic empire, in part by suspicion that the new Arab rulers of the homelands of Islam were puppets of the British, and above all by fears that Islam itself was in grave danger, many Indian Muslims quickly responded to the calls for action made by Mohamed and Shaukat Ali and other leaders. The Ali brothers accepted Gandhi's plan that they join with the Congress in a nonviolent movement of noncooperation with British institutions in India. Hopes were high in 1920 and 1921 that this alliance would grow into a solid and permanent unity between Hindus and Muslims, but outbreaks of violence cause Gandhi to cancel the movement and the alliance to break down.

To the end of his life Mohamed Ali wanted a united and independent India, but neither he nor any other leader could find a practical way to reconcile the differences that divided Muslims and Hindus. Muslims were infuriated, for example, when Hindu religious processions with loudly beating drums passed mosques during the times of prayer, and Hindus were outraged at Muslim killings of cows or bulls. In the long history of conflict and reluctant coexistence between the two communities, Mohamed Ali, Shaukat Ali, and M. K. Gandhi created a miraculous moment of hearty cooperation, but in the process they awakened religious passions that drove the wedge of division ever deeper. Mohamed Ali died a disappointed but not a despairing man in 1931. He was buried in Jerusalem—one of the cities he had sought, in vain, to keep under the protection of the Turkish caliph.

"The Communal Patriot"

In the following 1912 *Comrade* article, Mohamed Ali explained why politically conscious Muslims had recoiled at the upsurge of Hinducentric or "communal" nationalism in the preceding decade. The difficult task ahead was to move from these opposing Hindu and Muslim communal patriotisms to a common national consciousness.

[From Mohamed Ali, *Select Writings and Speeches*, 2: 66–70]

The Hindu "communal patriot" sprang into existence with "Swaraj" as his war-cry. He refuses to give quarter to the Muslims unless the latter quietly shuffles off his individuality and becomes completely Hinduized. He knows, of course, the use of the words like "India" and "territorial nationality," and they form an important part of his vocabulary. But the Muslims weigh on his consciousness all the same, as a troublesome irrelevance; and he would thank his stars if some great exodus or even a geological cataclysm could give him riddance.

The Muslim "communal patriot" owes his origin to a very different set of circumstances. His community lagged behind in the race by moodily sulking in its tents and declining, for a considerable time, to avail itself of the facilities for intellectual and material progress. When it made up its mind to accept the inevitable and move with the times, it suddenly found itself face to face with a community vastly superior to it in number, in wealth, in education, in political organization and power, in a word a united community uttering new accents and pulsating with a new hope. The spectacle of a go-ahead Hinduism, dreaming of self-government and playing with its ancient gods, clad in the vesture of democracy, dazed the conservative Muslim, who was just shaking himself free from the paralyzing grip of the past. He realized that the spirit of the fight had changed. The weapons were new and so were the ways to use those weapons. He felt as if he was being treated as an alien, as a meddlesome freak, who had wantonly interfered with the course of Indian history. Strange incidents were raked up from his long and eventful career, which he was called upon to justify. He had come as a conqueror and had freely given to India the best that was in him. With the loss of empire he felt as if he were to lose his self-respect as well. The "communal patriots" amongst the Hindus treated him as a prisoner in the dock, and loudly complained of him as an impossible factor in the scheme of India's future. Then, again, the new conditions of political success alarmed him. It was to him a painful education to learn that wisdom consisted in lung-power multiplied by the millions and political strength lay in the counting of heads. His community was small in numbers, ignorant, and poor. He was a negligible quantity in the visions of the Hindu "patriot." His religion and history had given him an individuality which he was very loth to lose. As a consequence he drew within his shell and nursed ideals of communal patriotism. He has been scared into this attitude in self-defense. The Hindu "communal patriot" has an advantage over him in the choice of his formulas. While the former boldly walks a road in the garb of India's champion, the latter, less mobile and more unfortunate, formulates even his unimpeachable right to live in terms of apology. . . .

Cows have been responsible for many riots in the country and many riotous campaigns in the Press. If only the Muslims gave up eating beef, we are told by many well-meaning persons, the Hindu-Muslim relations would grow in good will and cordiality at a bound. . . . It is sometimes forgotten that to a non-Hindu a cow is an ordinary quadruped and no more. A Muslim who eats beef does so on the score of its comparative cheapness. It is not possible that the Hindu, while retaining all his reverence for the animal, should leave others to their own notions of its utility, as long as they are not wantonly offensive? The educated Hindu who assures us that cow-killing lies at the root of racial bitterness makes rather a large demand on our credulity. India may be in varying stages of development from the twelfth century onward, but the sense of proportion of her educated sons is surely quite abreast of the twentieth's.

We need not multiply instances to show how the attitude of the Hindu "communal patriots" has alarmed the Muslims and driven them into a comparative isolation. The walls of separation can be broken down only if a radical change takes place in the conceptions of communal duty and patriotism. The responsibility of the Hindus is much greater in the matter, because they are more powerful and have sometimes used their strength with strange disregard to consequences. The Muslims stand aloof because they are afraid of being completely swallowed up. Any true patriot of India working for the evolution of Indian nationality will have to accept the communal individuality of the Muslims as the basis of his constructive effort. This is the irreducible factor of the situation, and the politician who ignores it has no conception of the task that awaits India's statesmen. . . . The communal sentiment and temper must change, and interests must grow identical before the Hindus and the Muslims can be welded into a united nationality. The problem is great, in fact, one of the greatest known to history. None, however, need despair, as the influences of education, and the leveling, liberalizing tendencies of the times are bound to succeed in creating political individuality out of the diversity of creed and race. Any attempt to impose artificial unity is sure to end in failure, if not in disaster.

The Expanded Horizon of Young Muslim Men

While in prison from 1921 to 1923 Mohamed Ali wrote his autobiography and began a study of the causes of the misunderstanding between the Islamic and Western worlds. His comment on the changes in outlook of Westernized young Muslims (or Musalmans, to use the Persian term) shows how some of them had turned away from Western models, discovered their classical heritage, and come into closer touch with their fellow religionists—a pattern not dissimilar to that followed by young Hindus like Vivekananda a generation earlier, and one that young people in other Muslim lands would follow in future generations.

[From Mohamed Ali, *My Life: A Fragment*, pp. 49–51]

There is no doubt that there has been an almost complete transformation in the mental outlook and mode of life of so many of the younger Musalmans of India during the last decade. The reaction has extended very far and has taken such unexpected forms that regular "cnuts" ["nuts," or dandies] who used to dream of nothing but what would be the "mode" in the *next* century A.C. have begun to hunt in the *Sunnah* or Tradition of the Prophet for the fashion plates of Year 1 A.H.! [i.e., 622]. Young dandies who were on the look-out for the latest toilet preparations like European women of the smartest of smart sets, and were [as] "fondly proud of a well-trimmed moustache as a European girl of her curls, are now to be seen in some cases with the most ungainly beards turning grey with the dust of an Indian summer." But it must not be imagined that there has been any fanatical and irrational revulsion against everything Western. On the contrary no one values more what the West has taught them in the way of *real* progress than these men. They feel more eager than ever to multiply the facilities for imparting to their co-religionists and fellow-countrymen an instruction in the best that Europe has yet to teach them, and particularly for the rapid diffusion of its scientific knowledge throughout the East. Their newly awakened spirituality has not driven them into an unthinking hostility towards the material progress of Europe. Only they want its material progress without the gross materialism that would one day spell its ruin. They have for their guide the sane and sound philosophy of their broad-minded Prophet who had taught them to "leave the foul, and take the clean," to "seek knowledge even if it be in China," and to regard wisdom wherever they found it, as their own "lost patrimony" to which they were entitled even more than those with whom they found it. It would, therefore, be perhaps more accurate to say that instead of a transformation of their outlook, there was rather an enlargement of the field of their vision. Their mental and spiritual horizon has suddenly expanded and they have been brought into the closest touch, on the one side, with the old world conservatism and orthodoxy, and on the other, with the masses whose troubles they now began to share as comrades in arms, and no longer as commanders who only deigned to issue instructions to them—"for their good." A general levelling up has taken place in the Muslim community which has made it a power in the land such as it had never been before, and that without any dependence of the use or force or external authority.

To Self-Government Through Hindu-Muslim Unity, Nonviolence, and Sacrifice

In his 1923 presidential address to the Indian National Congress, Mohamed Ali voiced the aspirations that had led him to join the Congress and work with Gandhi in the 1920–1922 noncooperation movement.

[From Mohamed Ali, *Select Writings and Speeches*, 2: 117–18, 141–42, 145, 188]

I had long been convinced that here in this country of hundreds of millions of human beings, intensely attached to religions, and yet infinitely split up into communities, sects and denominations, Providence had created for us the mission of solving a unique problem and working out a new synthesis, which was nothing less than a Federation of Faiths. As early as 1904, when I had been only two years in India after my return from Oxford, I had given to this ideal a clear, if still somewhat hesitating expression, in an address delivered at Ahmedabad on the "Proposed Mohammedan University." "Unless some new force"—this is what I had said on that occasion—"unless some new force, *other than the misleading unity of opposition,* unites this vast continent of India, it will either remain a geographical misnomer, or what I think it will ultimately do, become a Federation of Religions." . . . For more than twenty years I have dreamed the dream of a federation, grander, nobler and infinitely more spiritual than the United States of America, and to-day when many a political Cassandra prophesies a return to the bad old days of Hindu-Muslim dissensions, I still dream that old dream of "United *Faiths* of India." It was in order to translate this dream into reality that I had launched my weekly newspaper, and had significantly called it *The Comrade*—"comrade of all and partisan of none." . . .

Jesus counselled the upholders of the *lex talionis* [law of retaliation] who claimed an eye for an eye and a tooth for a tooth that he who had been smitten on one cheek should turn the other cheek also to the smiter. So much for the foreign tyrant. As for his own countryman, the Jew, who, falling a victim to his own weakness and a fear of the Gentile masters of Judea, had become a publican or tax-collector on behalf of the foreigner, he too could easily claim a share in the abounding love of Jesus. The idea of being all-powerful by suffering and resignation, and of triumphing over force by purity of heart, is as old as the days of Abel and Cain, the first progeny of Man. But since it so eminently suited the conditions of the times of Jesus, and the record of his ministry, however inadequate or defective, has still preserved for us this part of his teachings in some detail, it has come to be regarded by Christians, and even by many non-Christians as an idea peculiar to Jesus.

Be that as it may, it was just as peculiar to Mahatma Gandhi also; but it was reserved for a Christian government to treat as a felon the most Christ-like man of our times and to penalise as a disturber of the public peace the one man engaged in public affairs who comes nearest to the Prince of Peace. The political conditions of India just before the advent of the Mahatma resembled those of Judea [under foreign rule] on the eve of the advent of Jesus, and the prescription that he offered to those in search of a remedy for the ills of India was the same that Jesus had dispensed before in Judea. Self-purification through suffering; a moral preparation for the responsibilities of government; self-discipline as the condition precedent of Swaraj—this was the Mahatma's creed and conviction; and those of us who have been privileged to have lived in the glorious year that culminated in the Congress session at Ahmedabad [in 1921] have seen what a remarkable and what a rapid change he wrought in the thoughts, feelings and actions of such large masses of mankind. . . .

Friends, I have said all that I could say on the Hindu-Muslim question and if after all this lengthy dissertation I leave any Hindu or Muslim still unconvinced of the necessity of co-operation among ourselves and non-co-operation with our foreign masters, I can say no more and must acknowledge myself beaten. One thing is certain, and it is this that neither can the Hindus exterminate the Muslims to-day nor can the Muslims get rid of the Hindus. If the Hindus entertain any such designs they must know that they lost their opportunity when Mohammad bin Qasim landed on the soil of Sind twelve hundred years ago. Then the Muslims were few, and to-day they number more than seventy millions. And if the Muslims entertain similar notions, they too have lost their opportunity. They should have wiped out the whole breed of Hindus when they ruled from Kashmir to Cape Comorin and from Karachi to Chittagong. And as the Persian proverb says, the blow that is recalled after the fight must be struck on one's own jaw. If they cannot get rid of one another, the only thing to do is to settle down to co-operate with one another, and while the Muslims must remove all doubts from the Hindu minds about their desire for Swaraj for its own sake and their readiness to resist all foreign aggression [i.e., from Afghani-stan], the Hindus must similarly remove from the Muslim minds all apprehensions that the Hindu majority is synonymous with Muslim servitude. . . .

Warfare, according to the Quran, is an evil; but persecution is a worse evil, and may be put down with the weapons of war. When persecution ceases, and every man is free to act with the sole motive of securing divine goodwill, warfare must cease. These are the limits of violence in Islam, as I understand it, and I cannot go beyond these limits without infringing the Law of God. But I have agreed to work with Mahatma Gandhi, and our compact is that as long as I am associated with him I shall not resort to the use of force even for purposes of self-defence. And I have willingly entered into this compact because I think we can achieve victory without violence; that the use of violence for a nation of three hundred and twenty millions of people should be a matter of reproach to it; and, finally, that victory achieved with violence must be not the victory of all sections of the nation, but mainly of the fighting classes, which are more sharply divided in India from the rest of the nation than perhaps anywhere else in the world. Our Swaraj [self-government] must be the Raj [government] of all, and, in order to be that, it must have been won through the willing sacrifice of all. If this is not so, we shall have to depend for its maintenance as well on the prowess of the fighting classes, and this we must do. Swaraj must be won by the minimum sacrifice of the maximum number and not by the maximum sacrifice of the minimum number.

A Final Appeal for Islam and India

Before leaving for London in 1930 for the first of several "round table" conferences between British and Indian leaders, Mohamed Ali denounced Gandhi as a tool of the Hindu Mahasabha. At the conference, shortly before he died, he championed the two causes closest to his heart: the "supernationalist" freedom of India, and the integrity of the world of Islam.

[From Mohamed Ali, *Select Speeches and Writings*, 2, pp. 350, 355–57, 361]

. . . The one purpose for which I came [to speak] is this—that I want to go back to my country if I can go back with the substance of freedom in my hand. Otherwise I will not go back to a slave country. I would even prefer to die in a foreign country so long as it is a free country, and if you do not give us freedom in India you will have to give me a grave here. . . .

The real problem which is upsetting us all the time has been . . . the Hindu-Muslim problem; but that is no problem at all. The fact is that the Hindu-Muslim difficulty . . . is of your own creation. But not altogether. It is the old maxim of "divide and rule." But there is a division of labour here. We divide and *you* rule. The moment we decide not to divide you will not be able to rule as you are doing to-day. . . .

I belong to two circles of equal size, but which are not concentric. One is India, and the other is the Muslim world. When I came to India in 1920 at the head of the Khilafat Delegation [to defend the traditional position of the Turkish caliph], my friends said: "You must have some sort of a crest for your stationery." I decided to have it with two circles on it. In one circle was the word "India"; in the other circle was Islam, with the word "Khilafat." We as Indian Muslims came in both circles. We belong to these two circles, each of more than 300 millions, and we can leave neither. We are not nationalists but supernationalists, and I as a Muslim say that "God made man and the Devil made the nation." Nationalism divides; our religion binds. No religious wars, no crusades, have seen such holocausts and have been so cruel as your last war, and that was a war of your nationalism. . . .

I now take my seat and I hope I shall not be called upon to speak again in the Plenary Conference until you announce, Mr. Chairman, that India is as free as England.

MUHAMMAD IQBAL: POET AND PHILOSOPHER
OF THE ISLAMIC REVIVAL

Syed Ahmed had brought rationalism and the desire for knowledge and progress to the Indian Muslims; Muhammad Iqbal brought them inspiration and a philosophy. Next to the Qurʾān, there is no single influence upon the consciousness of the Pakistani intelligentsia so powerful as Iqbal's poetry. In his own time it kindled the enthusiasm of Muslim intellectuals for the values of Islam and rallied the Muslim community once again to the banner of their faith. For this reason Iqbal is looked upon today as the spiritual founder of Pakistan.

Muhammad Iqbal (1873–1938) was born at Sialkot in the Punjab in the year 1873. His parents, devout and pious Muslims, inculcated in him the teachings of Islam. Eventually Iqbal was sent to the Government College at Lahore where he graduated in 1899 and was appointed a lecturer in philosophy. After studying philosophy at Cambridge and in Germany, and having also qualified as a barrister-at-law, he came back to his teaching at Lahore in 1908. Two years later, in order to free himself from service to a foreign government, he gave up teaching and started the private practice of law. Still, his heart was not in the legal profession, and he undertook only enough work to keep himself in modest comfort. For the most part, his time was spent in study and writing. It was not long before he came to be recognized as a thinker of importance and the greatest Urdu poet of his time.

While in Europe, Iqbal had come into contact with the leading schools of Western philosophy and was particularly influenced by Nietzsche and Bergson. These influences are evident in his thought, and yet the main source of Iqbal's ideas is the Islamic tradition itself. His knowledge of Islamic thought and literature, especially of the Persian classics, was profound. Above all he was indebted to the great mystic thinker of Turkey, Jalāl-uʾd-dīn Rūmī, whom he quotes again and again with deep appreciation. Iqbal had an aversion, however, for those Sufis who tended toward a mystical quietism. He held their philosophy of inaction responsible for the decadence of Islam. Action is life and inaction is death, he taught. In strife with evil, not in the peace of the grave, lies the true meaning of human life. Iqbal had a burning conviction that Islam provided the remedy for many of the world's ills. The division of humanity into national and racial groups, according to him, was the greatest curse of the day. Injustice in any form was abhorrent and had to be fought. The evils of colonialism, the tyranny of the landlord over the unprotected tenant, the cupidity of capitalism, and the exploitation of the resources of a weaker people by a stronger nation, were all hateful in his eyes. The real remedy lay, according to him, in the cultivation of the innate greatness of the human self, so that realizing its real qualities, it would become incapable of meaner tendencies like greed, injustice, and fear. Such development of the self, he insisted, is possible only through a true understanding of the relationship between God and man. Even God does not demand the destruction of the self; He is desirous that the self should be developed to its fullest capacity. The self, however, finds its fullest meaning only through identification with the life of the community, and for that purpose the community should be organized on a righteous basis. Such a community is the community of Islam, because its sole foundation is the acceptance of God and the Law, which is the criterion of righteousness. As Islam recognizes no superiority of birth or rank or wealth within its bosom and judges excellence by righteousness alone, the fullest cultivation of the self is possible within its fold. This community, moreover, is not limited by time or space, according to the Islamic doctrine that all truth from God revealed anywhere at any time is Islam, Muhammad being the final recipient of this truth in its most perfect form. Such a community was not meant to be fragmented into nations. The means by which the self can develop to its full height is love, which is the Sufi word for the ecstatic devotion to God. Whereas human reason is limited by time and space, love is not; it is therefore capable of creating immutable qualities in the self. Iqbal thinks that real time is not the linear time of which we have a feeling, nor the limited time of the scientist, because he must think in terms of transient and limited space, but that it is higher and everlasting. It is infinite and eternal, indeed an attribute of God himself. It is in this time that the self finds its ultimate fulfillment.

Realizing the importance of his message to the whole Islamic world, Iqbal began to write in Persian, which is more widely understood and read in the Muslim world than Urdu. In Urdu, he ranks high as a philosophic poet and is considered next only to Ghalib (1796–1869) in charm, depth, and richness of ideas. Unfortunately Iqbal's poetry is difficult to translate; even in the excellent translations reproduced below, they lose much of the charm and force of the original.

Iqbal's interest in politics grew out of his concern for the future of his community. He was elected to the Punjab provincial legislature in 1926 and took part in its debates but made no great mark as a legislator. Tempermentally, he was not suited to politics, and his real contributions in this field were made in the realm of ideas. Although his thoughts on the creation of a separate state within India for Muslims aroused no immediate response, this was the first time they had been put forward from the platform of a political party.

Toward the end of his life Iqbal became convinced that the Muslims in India were threatened with extermination. He called the endless succession of Hindu-Muslim riots a virtual civil war, which he foresaw would develop in magnitude as time progressed. Feeling that the Muslims were unprepared for a final showdown, ill-organized and without a leader, he singled out Jinnah as the one person capable of serving the Muslims.

Iqbal died in 1938, deeply mourned by Hindus as well as Muslims in India and by Muslims in other lands as well. Rabindranath Tagore, his closest counterpart as both poet and philosopher anxious to revitalize his own cultural heritage, paid this tribute: "The death of Sir Muhammad Iqbal creates a void in our literature that, like a mortal wound, will take a very long time to heal. India, whose place to-day in the world is too narrow, can ill afford to miss a poet whose poetry had such universal value." Today Pakistan honors Muhammad Iqbal as its national poet.

Freedom, the Self, and Desire

In order to stir Muslims from their lethargy and despair, Iqbal extols a positive, active attitude to the world, in contrast to the world-negating quietism preached by certain Sufis. And yet some of his verse suggests the mystical identity of the consciousness of the individual with that of God.

[From Iqbal, *Poems from Iqbal*, trans. by V.G. Kiernan, p. 90, and Iqbal, *The Secrets of the Self*, pp. 16, 18–19, 23, 25–27]

FREEDOM

The freeman's veins are firm as veins of granite;
The bondman's weak as tendrils of the vine,
And his heart too despairing and repining—
The free heart has life's tingling breath to fan it.
Quick pulse, clear vision, are the freeman's treasure;
The unfree, to kindness and affection dead,
Has no more wealth than tears of his own shedding
And those glib words he has in such good measure.

Bondman and free can never come to accord:
One is the heavens' lackey, one their lord.

THE SELF

The form of existence is an effect of the Self,
Whatsoever thou seest is a secret of the Self,
When the Self awoke to consciousness,
It revealed the universe of Thought.
A hundred worlds are hidden in its essence:
Self-affirmation brings Not-self to light.

. . . .

Subject, object, means, and causes—
All these are forms which it assumes for the purpose of action.
The Self rises, kindles, falls, glows, breathes,
Burns, shines, walks, and flies.
The spaciousness of time is its arena,
Heaven is a billow of the dust on its road.
From its rose-planting the world abounds in roses;
Night is born of its sleep, day springs from its waking.

DESIRE

Life is preserved by purpose:
Because of the goal its caravan-bell tinkles.
Life is latent in seeking,
Its origin is hidden in desire.
Keep desire alive in thy heart,
Lest thy little dust become a tomb.

. . . .

'Tis desire that enriches life,
And the mind is a child of its womb.
What are social organization, customs, and laws?
What is the secret of the novelties of science?
A desire which realized itself by its own strength
And burst forth from the heart and took shape.

. . . .

Rise intoxicated with the wine of an ideal,
An ideal shining as the dawn
A blazing fire to all that is other than God,
An ideal higher than Heaven—
Winning, captivating, enchanting men's hearts;
A destroyer of ancient falsehood,
Fraught with turmoil, an embodiment of the Last Day.
We live by forming ideals,
We glow with the sunbeams of desire!

Love

Iqbal writes of love as the ecstatic love of God, not in a quietist, passive sense, but as the source of the highest inspiration for true knowledge and effective, righteous action.

[From Iqbal, *The Secrets of the Self*, pp. 28–29]

The luminous point whose name is the Self
Is the life-spark beneath our dust.
By love it is made more lasting,
More living, more burning, more glowing.
From love proceeds the radiance of its being
And the development of its unknown possibilities.
Its nature gathers fire from love,
Love instructs it to illumine the world.
Love fears neither sword nor dagger,
Love is not born of water and air and earth.
Love makes peace and war in the world,
Love is the fountain of life, love is the flashing sword of death.
The hardest rocks are shivered by love's glance:
Love of God at last becomes wholly God.

Time

Iqbal believed that the conception of time as finite and limited induced a passive attitude toward life; if time itself is limited, nothing that exists in time can be of everlasting value and all that is achieved by human action must perish. To combat this tendency toward passivity Iqbal held that time is eternal, and, therefore, human action has a lasting importance. This idea militated against both inaction and mere expediency.

[From Iqbal, *The Secrets of the Self*, pp. 137–38]

The cause of time is not the revolution of the sun:
Time is everlasting, but the sun does not last forever.
Time is joy and sorrow, festival and fast;
Time is the secret of moonlight and sunlight.
Thou hast extended time, like space,
And distinguished yesterday from tomorrow.
Thou hast fled, like a scent, from thine own garden;
Thou hast made thy prison with thine own hand.
Our time which has neither beginning nor end,
Blossoms from the flower bed of our mind.
To know its root quickens the living with new life:
Its being is more splendid than the dawn.
Life is of time, and time is of life.

Muslims Are One in Soul

In the following passages from his *Mysteries of Selflessness*, Iqbal attempts to correct the overindividualistic effect of his previous work, *The Secrets of the Self*, by empha-sizing the Muslim community. Reflecting the concern of Muslims at that time over the fate of the Ottoman Empire and other Muslim lands conquered or threatened by European powers, Iqbal propagates pan-Islamism based on the doctrine of an indivisible Muslim community. The Muslims are united throughout space and time by a common faith and a common history.

[From Iqbal, *The Mysteries of Selflessness*, pp. 20, 29, 32, 36–37, 60–62]

A common aim shared by the multitude
Is unity which, when it is mature,
Forms the Community; the many live
Only by virtue of the single bond.
The Muslim's unity from natural faith
Derives, and this the Prophet taught us,
So that we lit a lantern on truth's way.

This pearl was fished from his unfathomed sea,
And of his bounty we are one in soul.
Let not this unity go from our hands,
And we endure to all eternity.

MUSLIMS PROFESS NO FATHERLAND

Our Essence is not bound to any place;
The vigor of our wine is not contained
In any bowl; Chinese and Indian
Alike the shard that constitutes our jar,
Turkish and Syrian alike the clay
Forming our body; neither is our heart
Of India, or Syria, or Rum,[7]
Nor any fatherland do we profess
Except Islam.

THE CONCEPT OF COUNTRY DIVIDES HUMANITY

Now brotherhood has been so cut to shreds
That in the stead of community
The country has been given pride of place
In men's allegiance and constructive work;
The country is the darling of their hearts,
And wide humanity is whittled down
Into dismembered tribes. . . .
Vanished is humankind; there but abide
The disunited nations. Politics
Dethroned religion. . . .

THE MUSLIM COMMUNITY IS UNBOUNDED IN TIME

          . . . When the burning brands
Of time's great revolution ring our mead,
Then Spring returns. The mighty power of Rome,
Conqueror and ruler of the world entire,
Sank into small account; the golden glass
Of the Sassanians was drowned in blood;
Broken the brilliant genius of Greece;
Egypt too failed in the great test of time,

Her bones lie buried neath the pyramids.
Yet still the voice of the muezzin rings
Throughout the earth, still the Community
Of World-Islam maintains its ancient forms.
Love is the universal law of life,
Mingling the fragmentary elements
Of a disordered world. Through our hearts' glow
Love lives, irradiated by the spark
There is no god but God.

THE IMPORTANCE OF HISTORY

Like to a child is a community
Newborn, an infant in its mother's arms;
All unaware of Self. . . .
But when with energy it falls upon
The world's great labor, stable then becomes
This new-won consciousness; it raises up
A thousand images, and casts them down;
So it createth its own history. . . .
The record of the past illuminates
The conscience of a people; memory
Of past achievements makes it Self-aware;
But if that memory fades, and is forgot,
The folk again is lost in nothingness. . . .
What thing is history, O Self-unaware?
A fable? Or a legendary tale?
Nay, 'tis the thing that maketh thee aware
Of thy true Self, alert unto the task,
A seasoned traveler; this is the source
Of the soul's ardor, this the nerves that knit
The body of the whole community.
This whets thee like a dagger on its sheath,
To dash thee in the face of all the world. . . .
If thou desirest everlasting life,
Break not the thread between the past and now
And the far future. What is Life? A wave
Of consciousness of continuity,
A gurgling wine that flames the revelers.

The Need for Understanding Islam in the Light of Modern Knowledge

[From Iqbal, *The Reconstruction of Religious Thought in Islam*, pp. 7–8, 97]

During the last five hundred years religious thought in Islam has been practically stationary. There was a time when European thought received inspiration from the world of Islam. The most remarkable phenomenon of modern history, however, is the enormous rapidity with which the world of
Islam is spiritually moving towards the West. There is nothing wrong in
this movement, for European culture, on its intellectual side, is only a further development of some of the most important phases of the culture of
Islam. Our only fear is that the dazzling exterior of European culture may
arrest our movement and we may fail to reach the true inwardness of that
culture. During all the centuries of our intellectual stupor Europe has been
seriously thinking on the great problems in which the philosophers and
scientists of Islam were so keenly interested. Since the Middle Ages, when
the schools of Muslim theology were completed, infinite advance has taken
place in the domain of human thought and experience. The extension of
man's power over nature has given him a new faith and a fresh sense of
superiority over the forces that constitute his environment. New points of
view have been suggested, old problems have been restated in the light of
fresh experience, and new problems have arisen. It seems as if the intellect
of man is outgrowing its own most fundamental categories—time, space,
and causality. With the advance of scientific thought even our concept of
intelligibility is undergoing a change. The theory of Einstein has brought a
new vision of the universe and suggests new ways of looking at the problems
common to both religion and philosophy. No wonder then that the younger
generation of Islam in Asia and Africa demand a fresh orientation of their
faith. With the reawakening of Islam, therefore, it is necessary to examine,
in an independent spirit, what Europe has thought and how far the conclusions reached by her can help us in the revision and, if necessary, reconstruction, of theological thought in Islam. Besides this it is not possible to
ignore the generally antireligious and especially anti-Islamic propaganda in
Central Asia which has already crossed the Indian frontier.

The task before the modern Muslim is, therefore, immense. He has to
rethink the whole system of Islam without completely breaking with the
past. . . . The only course open to us is to approach modern knowledge
with a respectful but independent attitude and to appreciate the teachings

of Islam in the light of that knowledge, even though we may be led to differ from those who have gone before us.

The Facts of Religious Experience and the Revolutionary Effects of Prayer

In his major work on the philosophy of religion, Iqbal suggested how modern man could rediscover, and learn from, the reality of religious experience.

[Iqbal, *The Reconstruction of Religious Thought in Islam*, pp. 16–17, 23, 25–26, 92–94, 173–74]

The facts of religious experience are facts among other facts of human experience and, in the capacity of yielding knowledge by interpretation, one fact is as good as another. Nor is there anything irreverent in critically examining this region of human experience. The Prophet of Islam was the first critical observer of psychic phenomena. Bukhari and other traditionists have given us a full account of his observation of the psychic Jewish youth, Ibn-i-Sayyad, whose ecstatic moods attracted the Prophet's notice. He tested him, questioned him, and examined him in his various moods. Once he hid himself behind the stem of a tree to listen to his mutterings. The boy's mother, however, warned him of the approach of the Prophet. Thereupon the boy immediately shook off his mood and the Prophet remarked: "If she had let him alone the thing would have been cleared up." . . .

For the purpose of knowledge, then, the region of mystic experience is as real as any other region of human experience and cannot be ignored merely because it cannot be traced back to sense-perception. . . .

Religion is not physics or chemistry seeking an explanation of nature in terms of causation; it really aims at interpreting a totally different region of human experience—religious experience—the data of which cannot be reduced to the data of any other science. In fact, it must be said in justice to religion that it insisted on the necessity of concrete experience in religious life long before science learned to do so [in its sphere]. The conflict between the two is due not to the fact that the one is, and the other is not, based on concrete experience. Both seek concrete experience as a point of departure. Their conflict is due to the misapprehension that both interpret the same data of experience. We forget that religion aims at reaching the real significance of a special variety of human experience. . . .

The truth is that in a state of religious passion we know a factual reality in some sense outside the narrow circuit of our personality. . . . In all knowledge there is an element of passion, and the object of knowledge gains or loses in objectivity with the rise and fall of the intensity of passion. That is most real to us which stirs up the entire fabric of our personality.

Prayer, then, whether individual or associative, is an expression of man's inner yearning for a response in the awful silence of the universe. It is a unique process of discovery whereby the searching ego affirms itself in the very moment of self-negation, and thus discovers its own worth and justification as a dynamic factor in the life of the universe. True to the psychology of mental attitude in prayer, the form of worship in Islam symbolizes both affirmation and negation. Yet, in view of the fact borne out by the experience of the race that prayer, as an inner act, has found expression in a variety of forms, the Quran says: "To every people have We appointed ways of worship which they observe. Therefore let them not dispute this matter with thee, but bid them to thy Lord for thou art on the right way; but if they debate with thee, then say: God best knoweth what ye do! He will judge between you on the Day of Resurrection, to the matters wherein ye differ." [22:67–69] . . . Yet we cannot ignore the important consideration that the posture of the body is a real factor in determining the attitude of mind. The choice of one particular direction in Islamic worship is meant to secure the unity of feeling in the congregation, and its form in general creates and fosters the sense of social equality inasmuch as it tends to destroy the feeling of rank or race-superiority in the worshippers. What a tremendous spiritual revolution will take place, practically in no time, if the proud aristocratic Brahman of South India is daily made to stand shoulder to shoulder with the untouchable! From the unity of the all-inclusive Ego who creates and sustains all egos follows the essential unity of all mankind. The division of mankind into races, nations, and tribes, according to the Quran, is for purposes of identification only. The Islamic form of association in prayer, besides its cognitive value, is further indicative of the aspiration to realize this essential unity of mankind as a fact in life by demolishing all barriers which stand between man and man.

From Prophecy to Individual Judgment of One's Inner and Outer Experience

The creed of Islam states that "There is no god but God and Muhammad is His prophet." The second half of the statement is taken by Muslims to mean that Muhammad was the last of the prophets. Iqbal here interprets the closing of the age of prophecy as opening a new age in which individuals may explore for themselves the realm of inner, mystical experience, while maintaining the spirit of critical, independent judgment about it.

[From Iqbal, *The Reconstruction of Religious Thought in Islam*, pp. 125–27]

Now during the minority of mankind psychic energy develops what I call prophetic consciousness—a mode of economizing individual thought and choice by providing ready-made judgments, choices, and ways of action. With the birth of reason and critical faculty, however, life, in its own interest, inhibits the formation and growth of non-rational modes of consciousness through which psychic energy flowed at an earlier stage of human evolution. Man is primarily governed by passion and instinct. Inductive reason, which alone makes man master of his environment, is an achievement; and when once born it must be reinforced by inhibiting the growth of other modes of knowledge. There is no doubt that the ancient world produced some great systems of philosophy at a time when man was comparatively primitive and governed more or less by suggestion. But we must not forget that this system-building in the ancient world was the work of abstract thought which cannot go beyond the systematization of vague religious beliefs and traditions, and gives us no hold on the concrete situations of life.

Looking at the matter from this point of view, then, the Prophet of Islam seems to stand between the ancient and the modern world. In so far as the source of his revelation is concerned he belongs to the ancient world; in so far as the spirit of his revelation is concerned he belongs to the modern world. In him life discovers other sources of knowledge suitable to its new direction. The birth of Islam, as I hope to be able presently to prove to your satisfaction, is the birth of inductive intellect. In Islam prophecy reaches its perfection in discovering the need of its own abolition. This involves the keen perception that life cannot forever be kept in leading strings; that in order to achieve full self-consciousness man must finally be thrown back on his own resources. The abolition of priesthood and hereditary kingship in Islam, the constant appeal to reason and experience in the Quran, and the emphasis that it lays on Nature and History as sources of human knowledge, are all different aspects of the same idea of finality. The idea, however, does not mean that mystic experience, which qualitatively does not differ from the experience of the prophet, has now ceased to exist. . . .

God reveals His signs in inner as well as outer experience, and it is the duty of man to judge the knowledge-yielding capacity of all aspects of experience. The idea of finality, therefore, [the belief that Muhammad was the final prophet] should not be taken to suggest that the ultimate fate of life is complete displacement of emotion by reason. Such a thing is neither possible nor desirable. The intellectual value of the idea is that it tends to create an independent critical attitude towards mystic experience by generating the belief that all personal authority, claiming a supernatural origin, has come to an end in the history of man. . . . The function of the idea is to open up fresh vistas of knowledge in the domain of man's inner experience, just as the first half of the formula of Islam ["There is no god but God"] has created and fostered the spirit of a critical observation of man's outer experience by divesting the forces of nature of that divine character with which earlier culture had clothed them. Mystical experience, then, however unusual and abnormal, must now be regarded by a Muslim as a perfectly natural experience, open to critical scrutiny like other aspects of human experience. This is clear from the Prophet's own attitude towards Ibn-i-Sayyad's psychic experiences.

Muslim Legislatures as the Means for the Evolution of Islamic Law

[From Iqbal, *The Reconstruction of Religious Thought in Islam,* pp. 173-74]

The third source of Mohammedan [i.e., Islamic] Law is Ijma, [consensus][8] which is in my opinion perhaps the most important legal notion in Islam. It is, however, strange that this important notion, while invoking great academic discussions in early Islam, remained practically a mere idea, and rarely assumed the form of a permanent institution of any Mohammedan country. Possibly its transformation into a permanent legislative institution was contrary to the political interests of absolute monarchy that grew up in Islam. . . . It is, however, extremely satisfactory to note that the pressure of new world forces and the political experience of European nations are impressing on the mind of modern Islam the value and possibilities of the idea of Ijma. The growth of republican spirit, and the gradual formation of legislative assemblies in Muslim lands constitutes a great step in advance. The transfer of the power of Ijtihad[9] from individual representatives of schools to a Muslim legislative assembly which, in view of the growth of opposing sects, is the only possible form Ijma can take in modern times, will secure contributions to legal discussion from laymen who happen to possess a keen insight into affairs. In this way alone we can stir into activity the dormant spirit of life in our legal system, and give it an evolutionary outlook. In India, however, difficulties are likely to arise; for it is doubtful whether a non-Muslim legislative assembly can exercise the power of Ijtihad.

A Separate State for Muslims Within India

Iqbal's presidential address before the All-India Muslim League in Allahabad on December 29, 1930, is his most important political statement in relation to the later establishment of a separate state for the Muslims of India in those areas where they were in the majority. His argument is that a polity that makes religion a purely private matter, as in European states, dooms religion. Islam, on the other hand, is organically connected with the social order and in India needs an autonomous area for its full expression and development. In 1937 he went further, asking in a letter to Jinnah: "Why should not the Muslims of North-West India and Bengal be considered as nations entitled to self-determination just as other nations in India and outside India are?"—thus anticipating not only the creation of Pakistan in 1947 but also the emergence of Bangladesh in 1971.

[From Iqbal, *Speeches and Statements*, "Presidential Address," pp. 3-6, 8-13, 15, 34-36]

It cannot be denied that Islam, regarded as an ethical ideal plus a certain kind of polity—by which expression I mean a social structure regulated by a legal system and animated by a specific ethical ideal—has been the chief formative factor in the life-history of the Muslims of India. It has furnished those basic emotions and loyalties which gradually unify scattered individuals and groups and finally transform them into a well-defined people. Indeed it is no exaggeration to say that India is perhaps the only country in the world where Islam, as a people-building force, has worked at its best. In India, as elsewhere, the structure of Islam as a society is almost entirely due to the working of Islam as a culture inspired by a specific ethical ideal. What I mean to say is that Muslim society, with its remarkable homogeneity and inner unity, has grown to be what it is under the pressure of the laws and institutions associated with the culture of Islam. The ideas set free by European thinking, however, are now rapidly changing the outlook of the present generation of Muslims both in India and outside India. Our younger men, inspired by these ideas, are anxious to see them as living forces in their own countries without any critical appreciation of the facts which have determined their evolution in Europe. . . .

The conclusion to which Europe is . . . driven is that religion is a private affair of the individual and has nothing to do with what is called man's temporal life. Islam does not bifurcate the unity of man into an irreconcilable duality of spirit and matter. In Islam, God and the universe, spirit and matter, church and state, are organic to each other. Man is not the citizen of a profane world to be renounced in the interest of a world of spirit situated elsewhere. To Islam matter is spirit realising itself in space and time. . . . In the world of Islam we have a universal polity whose fundamentals are believed to have been revealed, but whose structure, owing to our legists' want of contact with [the] modern world, stands today in need of renewed power by fresh adjustments. I do not know what will be the final fate of the national idea in the world of Islam. Whether Islam will assimilate and transform it, as it has assimilated and transformed before many ideas expressive of different spirits, or allow a radical transformation of its own structure by the force of this idea, is hard to predict. . . .

What, then, is the problem and its implications? Is religion a private affair? Would you like to see Islam, as a moral and political ideal, meeting the same fate in the world of Islam as Christianity has already met in Europe? Is it possible to retain Islam as an ethical ideal and to reject it as a polity in favor of national politics, in which a religious attitude is not permitted to play any part? This question becomes of special importance in India where the Muslims happen to be in a minority. The proposition that religion is a private individual experience is not surprising on the lips of a European. In Europe the conception of Christianity as a monastic order, renouncing the world of matter and fixing its gaze entirely on the world of spirit led, by a logical process of thought, to the view embodied in this proposition. The nature of the Prophet's religious experience, as disclosed in the Qurʾān, however, is wholly different. It is not mere experience in the sense of a purely biological event, happening inside the experient and necessitating no reactions on his social environment. It is individual experience creative of a social order. Its immediate outcome is the fundamentals of a polity with implicit legal concepts whose civic significance cannot be belittled merely because their origin is revelational. The religious ideal of Islam, therefore, is organically related to the social order which it has created. The rejection of the one will eventually involve the rejection of the other. Therefore the construction of a polity on national lines, if it means a displacement of the Islamic principle of solidarity, is simply unthinkable to a Muslim. This is a matter which at the present moment directly concerns the Muslims of India. . . . The unity of an Indian nation, therefore, must be sought, not in the negation but in the mutual harmony and cooperation of the many. True statesmanship cannot ignore facts, however unpleasant they may be. The only practical course is not to assume the existence of a state of things which does not exist, but to recognize facts as they are, and to exploit them to our greatest advantage. . . .

Events seem to be tending in the direction of some sort of internal harmony. And as far as I have been able to read the Muslim mind, I have no hesitation in declaring that if the principle that the Indian Muslim is entitled to full and free development on the lines of his own culture and tradition in his own Indian home-lands is recognised as the basis of a permanent communal settlement, he will be ready to stake his all for the freedom of India. The principle that each group is entitled to free development on its own lines is not inspired by any feeling of narrow communalism. There are communalisms and communalisms. A community which is inspired by feelings of ill-will toward other communities is low and ignoble. I entertain the highest respect for the customs, laws, religions, and social institutions of other communities. Nay, it is my duty according to the teaching of the Qur'ān, even to defend their places of worship, if need be. Yet I love the communal group which is the source of my life and behavior and which has formed me what I am by giving me its religion, its literature, its thought, its culture and thereby recreating its whole past as a living factor in my present consciousness. . . .

Communalism in its higher aspect, then, is indispensable to the formation of a harmonious whole in a country like India. The units of Indian society are not territorial as in European countries. India is a continent of human groups belonging to different races, speaking different languages and professing different religions. Their behavior is not at all determined by a common race-consciousness. Even the Hindus do not form a homogeneous group. The principle of European democracy cannot be applied to India without recognizing the fact of communal groups. The Muslim demand for the creation of a Muslim India within India is, therefore, perfectly justified. The [1929] resolution of the All-Parties Muslim Conference at Delhi, is, to my mind, wholly inspired by this noble ideal of a harmonious whole which, instead of stifling the respective individualities of its component wholes, affords them chances of fully working out the possibilities that may be latent in them. And I have no doubt that this House will emphatically endorse the Muslim demands embodied in this resolution. Personally, I would go further than the demands embodied in it. I would like to see the Punjab, North-West Frontier Province, Sind and Baluchistan amalgamated into a single State. Self-government within the British empire or without the British empire, the formation of a consolidated North-West Indian Muslim State appears to me to be the final destiny of the Muslims, at least of North-West India. . . .

The idea need not alarm the Hindus or the British. India is the greatest Muslim country in the world. The life of Islam, as a cultural force, in this country very largely depends on its centralisation in a specified territory. This centralisation of the most living portion of the Muslims of India, whose military and police service has, notwithstanding unfair treatment from the British, made the British rule possible in this country, will eventually solve the problem of India as well as of Asia. It will intensify their sense of responsibility and deepen their patriotic feeling. Thus possessing full opportunity of development within the body politic of India, the North-West India Muslims will prove the best defenders of India against a foreign invasion, be the invasion one of ideas or of bayonets. . . .

I therefore demand the formation of a consolidated Muslim State in the best interests of India and Islam. For India it means security and peace resulting from an internal balance of power; for Islam an opportunity to rid itself of the stamp that Arabian imperialism was forced to give it, to mobilize its law, its education, its culture, and to bring them into closer contact with its own original spirit and with the spirit of modern times.

Thus it is clear that in view of India's infinite variety in climates, races, languages, creeds and social systems, the creation of autonomous States based on the unity of language, race, history, religion and identity of economic interests, is the only possible way to secure a stable constitutional structure in India. . . .

In conclusion I cannot but impress upon you that the present crisis in the history of India demands complete organization and unity of will and purpose in the Muslim community, both in your own interest as a community, and in the interest of India as a whole. . . .

Our disorganized condition has already confused political issues vital to the life of the community. I am not hopeless of an intercommunal understanding, but I cannot conceal from you the feeling that in the near future our community may be called upon to adopt an independent line of action to cope with the present crisis. And an independent line of political action, in such a crisis, is possible only to a determined people, possessing a will focalized by a single purpose. Is it possible for you to achieve the organic wholeness of a unified will? Yes, it is. Rise above sectional interests and private ambitions, and learn to determine the value of your individual and collective action, however directed on material ends, in the light of the ideal which you are supposed to represent. Pass from matter to spirit. Matter is diversity; spirit is light, life and unity. One lesson I have learnt from the history of Muslims. At critical moments in their history it is Islam that has saved Muslims and not vice versa. If today you focus your vision on Islam and see inspiration from the ever-vitalizing idea embodied in it, you will be only reassembling your scattered forces, regaining your lost integrity, and thereby saving yourself from total destruction. One of the profoundest verses in the Holy Qur'ān teaches us that the birth and rebirth of the whole of humanity is like the birth of a single individual. Why cannot you who, as a people, can well claim to be the first practical exponents of this superb conception of humanity, live and move and have your being as a single individual? . . . In the words of the Qur'ān: "Hold fast to yourself; no one who erreth can hurt you, provided you are well guided." [5:104]

MUHAMMED ALI JINNAH: FOUNDER OF PAKISTAN (PART 1)

The long and eventful life of Muhammed Ali Jinnah (1875-1948) began and ended in the city of Karachi in a predominantly Muslim area on the Arabian Sea.[10] His parents had moved there from the Kathiawar peninsula of Gujarat to the southeast, and so their eldest son shared with his chief political rival, M. K. Gandhi, a common heritage of ancestral life in that highly political peninsula. Jinnah's father was a restless and ambitious man. Trade drew him to Karachi and enabled him to become one of that city's leading businessmen. He sent his son Muhammed Ali to a Muslim-managed school with classes in English, had him married, then sent him to England for further education at the age of sixteen. Young Jinnah arrived in London to start his studies the year after Gandhi finished his and left for home.

Jinnah's legal studies in London developed his keen mind, and the parliamentary elections of 1892 aroused his fighting instincts. Dadabhai Naoroji, the elder statesman of the Congress, ran for Parliament that year in a workingman's district in London on the Liberal ticket. When the Tory prime minister, Lord Salisbury, insulted him with a racial slur, Jinnah joined other Indian students in working for his campaign, which was victorious. Meanwhile, Jinnah's mother and wife had died, and when he returned to Karachi in 1896 he found his father deep in business troubles. Rather than go into practice there, where his family had numerous friends, the young lawyer insisted on enrolling as a barrister at the Bombay High Court, where he could work his way up on his own resources. After three lean years, Jinnah's abilities began to receive favorable attention from British officials: first the acting advocate-general, then the head of the judicial administration, and in 1903 the president of the Bombay municipality, who hired him as its attorney. Nattily dressed after the latest English fashion, he gradually became an independent, wealthy, and highly respected member of the Bombay bar.

Jinnah's upright character and forthright manner made a lasting impression on the legal community in this sophisticated city. The sharpness of his wit and repartee are encapsulated in the story told of his encounter with a judge who evidently resented his tone of speaking. "Mr. Jinnah," the judge said, "remember that you are not addressing a third-class magistrate." "My Lord," answered Jinnah, "allow me to warn you that you are not addressing a third-class pleader."[11]

Once established in his chosen profession, Jinnah began to take interest in political matters. He joined the Moderate wing of the Congress, attended its annual sessions, and in 1906 acted as the personal secretary of Dadabhai Naoroji, Congress president for that year. In 1909 the Bombay Presidency's Muslim constituency elected him to the Imperial Legislative Council at Calcutta, where his ability and independence soon won him recognition. He now came into close contact with his fellow legislator from Bombay, G. K. Gokhale, and a warm friendship grew up between the two men. Both were dedicated to gradually improving the lot of the Indian people through constitutional means. Each admired the other: Jinnah aspired to become "the Muslim Gokhale," and Gokhale called Jinnah "the best ambassador of Hindu-Muslim unity."[12]

Jinnah did in fact serve as such an ambassador during the second decade of the twentieth century by joining the Muslim League in 1913 (at the suggestion of Mohamed Ali), and working in both Congress and League to bring the two bodies to agree in 1916 to a common national demand for India's self-government within the British Empire. This represented a great change for the Muslim League, and to bring it about Jinnah persuaded

Tilak, then president of the Congress, to accept the League's principle that Muslims should continue to be protected from Hindu domination by the three major constitutional safeguards created in 1909 by the British Parliament. These were separate seats in the provincial and central legislatures, reserved for Muslim legislators only; a somewhat greater proportion of seats than the percentage of Muslims in the total electorate; and the election of Muslim legislators by Muslims alone. This so-called "communal electorate" was subsequently attacked by Hindus who feared being underrepresented in the legislatures, and it remained a source of bitter controversy for the next thirty years. Jinnah's argument for it resembled Lincoln's defense of majority rule in his First Inaugural Address: for a democracy to function, there should be no permanent majority, but always the possibility that the minority could attract enough support to become a majority.

Jinnah's masterful debating powers were described by Britain's cabinet officer, Secretary of State for India Edwin Montagu, after their 1917 meeting: "They were followed by Jinnah, young, perfectly mannered, impressive looking, armed to the teeth with dialectics. . . . I was rather tired and I funked him. Chelmsford [the viceroy] tried to argue with him, and was tied up into knots. Jinnah is a very clever man, and it is, of course, an outrage that such a man should have no chance of running the affairs of his own country."[13]

The years after the end of the First World War saw the rise of Gandhi as the leader of the national movement. Jinnah, however, had no use for the new techniques of noncooperation and civil disobedience, nor had he much liking for the defense of the prewar status of the Ottoman caliph, which Gandhi and Mohamed Ali were making the basis for Hindu-Muslim unity. The unrealistic aims of this movement, the unqualified acceptance of Gandhi's leadership, and the confidence that the mere withdrawal of the British would enable Hindus and Muslims to settle their differences struck Jinnah as dangerous for the future of the country.

Gandhi's movement for achieving brotherhood between India's two major religious communities through popular antigovernment agitation did prove unrealistic. Nevertheless it ousted Jinnah from his role as mediator between the Congress and the League. Jinnah tried again in 1927 to forge an agreement on a constitutional demand, proposing that the Muslims give up their right to a separate electorate if the Congress would grant them 33 percent of the seats in the national legislature. (At that time they formed 26 percent of the inhabitants of the British-ruled provinces.) Gandhi opposed the plan and wrote, "no special legislation without a change of heart can possibly bring about organic unity,"[14] and the Muslim League split over the issue, leaving Jinnah in political limbo. To add to his troubles, his second wife, a beautiful young Parsi, died after a painful separation.

In 1931 Jinnah decided to withdraw completely from India's problems and settled down to a lucrative law practice in London. Two years later Liaquat Ali Khan (later Pakistan's first prime minister) urged him to return to India to lead the Muslims and the Muslim League. Jinnah waited for evidence of greater support; when it was forthcoming, he sold his house in London and in 1935 moved back to Bombay. Parliament's enactment of a new constitution for the governing of India in that year accelerated the tempo of political life, for it enlarged the suffrage from 4 to 10 percent and made the provinces virtually self-governing. The Muslim League fared badly in the elections, however, whereas the Congress, led by Nehru, captured majorities in six of British India's eleven provinces. At this point Muhammad Iqbal, whose life was nearing its end, wrote Jinnah advising him to turn the League into a body representing the Muslim masses, and to demand the creation of "a free Muslim state or states"[15] in order to ensure the survival and development of Islamic culture and law.

From 1936 to 1946 Jinnah worked tirelessly in province after province to recruit Muslims into the League so that it could become what it claimed to be: their sole representative. He accused the Congress of anti-Muslim activities and declared it was a "day of deliverance" for Muslims when the Congress provincial governments resigned in 1939 (in protest against not being consulted when the viceroy declared India at war with Germany). Not until 1940 did he embrace Iqbal's idea of a separate Muslim polity. He then had the League adopt as its goal the establishment of "independent states" in the northwestern and eastern parts of India, where Muslims formed the majority of the population.

While the entire Congress cadre remained in jail from 1942 to 1945, Jinnah continued to build and organize the Muslim League. As a result, in the central and provincial elections of 1945-1946 it won 460 out of the 533 seats reserved for Muslims. Jinnah's case for Pakistan was now very strong, although the British, the Congress, and some Muslim religious groups remained reluctant to grant it. He now took the momentous step in mid-August 1946 of calling for Muslims to resort to "direct action" to gain their hoped-for national homeland. "This day we bid good-bye to constitutional methods," he declared.[16] His opponents accused him of unleashing a tide of blood as killings—of Hindus by Muslims, of Muslims by Hindus, of Sikhs and Muslims by each other—spread across the plains of eastern, northern, and northwestern India. To stop this violence the new viceroy, Lord Mountbatten, persuaded the Congress, League, Sikh, and princely leaders to agree that India should undergo a surgical operation—partition into Hindu- and Muslim-majority areas—as soon as possible.

Muhammed Ali Jinnah assumed power at Karachi as governor-general of Pakistan on August 14, 1947. Already ill, he wore himself out trying to meet the new nation's most pressing problems: a shortage of administrative personnel; an influx of millions of refugees into West Pakistan; a war with India over Kashmir; hunger, disease, and poverty. Amidst all these trials, the task of framing a constitution receded into the background. Unfortunately for the land he had worked so hard to see established, and for those Muslims who had hailed him as their *quaid-i-āzam* ("supreme leader"), he died in September 1948. Had he and his successor Liaquat Ali Khan lived longer, they might have established more stable procedures for solving Pakistan's political problems than were resorted to in the years that followed. Selections from their speeches and writings after the creation of Pakistan are given in chapter 9.

"We Have to Live Together. . .We Have to Work Together. . . ."

At the 1928 All Parties National Convention in Calcutta, Jinnah made a strong plea for constitutional guarantees to protect the Muslim minority. At the time he was clearly hoping for unity between Hindus and Muslims, but after all but one of the resolutions he introduced on behalf of the Muslim League were voted down by large majorities, he left the Convention. As he boarded the train for Delhi, with tearful eyes he said to a Parsi friend, "This is the parting of the ways."[17]

[From *The Proceedings of the All Parties National Convention*, pp. 78-79, 92-95]

The Report of the Committee which you appointed has already been read out and placed before you. I am exceedingly sorry that the Report of the Committee is neither helpful nor fruitful in any way whatsoever. I am sure, gentlemen, that you all realize that the present moment is very critical and vital to the interest not only of the Musalmans, but to the whole of India. I think it will be recognized that it is absolutely essential to our progress that Hindu-Muslim Settlement should be reached, and that all communities should live in a friendly and harmonious spirit in this vast country of ours. . . . I am sure you will, therefore, consider the present situation in which we are working and struggling for freedom and record your vote in favour of [the] modifications proposed, which, I have said before, are fair and reasonable and thus enable us to triumph in our cause.

. . . Every country struggling for freedom and desirous of establishing a democratic system of Government has had to face the problem of minorities wherever they existed and no constitution, however idealistic it may be, and however perfect from [a] theoretical point of view it may seem will ever receive the support of the minorities unless they can feel that they, as an entity, are secured under the proposed constitution and government and whether a constitution will succeed or not must necessarily depend as a matter of acid test [on] whether the minorities are in fact secure. Otherwise no proper constitution will last but result in a revolution and a civil war. . . .

We are here, as I understand, for the purpose of entering into [a] solemn contract and all parties who enter into it will have to work for it and fight for it together. What we want is that Hindus and Musalmans should march together until our object is obtained. . . . Do you want or do you not want Muslim India to go along with you? You must remember [that] the two major communities in India—I say this without the slightest disrespect to the other communities like Sikhs, Christians, and Parsis—are the Hindus and Musalmans and naturally therefore these two communities have got to be reconciled and united and made to feel that their interests are common and they are marching together for a common goal. . . . I am asking for this adjustment [giving Muslims one-third of the seats in the national legislature, keeping residuary powers in the provinces rather than in the central government, along with other safeguards] because I think it is the best and fair to the Musalmans. Look at the constitutional history of Canada and Egypt. The minorities are always afraid of majorities. The majorities are apt to be tyrannical and oppressive, particularly religious majorities, and the minorities therefore have a right to be absolutely secured. Was the adjustment between French Canadians and British [Canadians] arrived at on [a] population basis or on the ground of pure equity? Was the adjustment between the Coptic Christians and Musalmans in Egypt regulated by such considerations? . . .

If you do not settle this question today, we shall have to settle it tomorrow, but in the meantime our national interests are bound to suffer. We are all sons of this land. We have to live together. We have to work together and whatever our differences may be let us at any rate not create more bad blood. If we cannot agree, let us at any rate agree to differ but let us part as friends. I once more repeat. Believe me there is no progress for India until the Musalmans and Hindus are united and let no logic, philosophy or squabble stand in the way of our coming to a compromise and nothing will make me more happy than to see the Hindu Muslim Union.

Hindus and Muslims: Two Separate Nations

The following selection is taken from Jinnah's most famous speech, his presidential address to the annual meeting of the Muslim League at Lahore in March 1940. It is the clearest statement of "the two-nation theory," that is, that Hindus and Muslims were more than two religions; they were two nations. At the conclusion of this speech the great gathering passed what became known as the Lahore Resolution. It stated that "no constitutional plan would be workable in this country or acceptable to the Muslims" unless it was recognized that "the areas in which the Muslims are numerically in a majority . . . should be grouped to constitute 'Independent States' in which the constituent units shall be autonomous and sovereign."

[From Jinnah, *Recent Speeches and Writings*, I:174-80]

The British government and Parliament, and more so the British nation, have been for many decades past brought up and nurtured with settled notions about India's future, based on developments in their own country which has built up the British constitution, functioning now through the Houses of Parliament and the system of cabinet. Their concept of party government functioning on political planes has become the ideal with them as the best form of government for every country, and the one-sided and powerful propaganda, which naturally appeals to the British, has led them into a serious blunder, in producing the constitution envisaged in the Government of India Act of 1935. We find that the most leading statesmen of Great Britain, saturated with these notions, have in their pronouncements seriously asserted and expressed a hope that the passage of time will harmonize the inconsistent elements of India.

A leading journal like the London *Times*, commenting on the Government of India Act of 1935, wrote: "Undoubtedly the differences between the Hindus and Muslims are not of religion in the strict sense of the word but also of law and culture, that they may be said, indeed, to represent two entirely distinct and separate civilizations. However, in the course of time, the superstition will die out and India will be molded into a single nation." So, according to the London *Times*, the only difficulties are superstitions. These fundamental and deep-rooted differences, spiritual, economic, cultural, social, and political, have been euphemized as mere "superstitions." But surely it is a flagrant disregard of the past history of the subcontinent of India as well as the fundamental Islamic conception of society vis-à-vis that of Hinduism to characterize them as mere "superstitions." Notwithstanding a thousand years of close contact, nationalities, which are as divergent today as ever, cannot at any time be expected to transform themselves into one nation merely by means of subjecting them to a democratic constitution and holding them forcibly together by unnatural and artificial methods of British parliamentary statute. What the unitary government of India for one hundred fifty years had failed to achieve cannot be realized by the imposition of a central federal government. It is inconceivable that the fiat or the writ of a government so constituted can ever command a willing and loyal obedience throughout the subcontinent by various nationalities except by means of armed force behind it.

The problem in India is not of an intercommunal character but manifestly of an international one, and it must be treated as such. So long as this basic and fundamental truth is not realized, any constitution that may be built will result in disaster and will prove destructive and harmful not only to the Mussalmans but to the British and Hindus also. If the British government are really in earnest and sincere to secure [the] peace and happiness of the people of this subcontinent, the only course open to us all is to allow the major nations separate homelands by dividing India into "autonomous national states." There is no reason why these states should be antagonistic to each other. On the other hand, the rivalry and the natural desire and efforts on the part of one to dominate the social order and establish political supremacy over the other in the government of the country will disappear. It will lead more towards natural good will by international pacts between them, and they can live in complete harmony with their neighbors. This will lead further to a friendly settlement all the more easily with regard to minorities by reciprocal arrangements and adjustments between Muslim India and Hindu India, which will far more adequately and effectively safeguard the rights and interests of Muslims and various other minorities.

It is extremely difficult to appreciate why our Hindu friends fail to understand the real nature of Islam and Hinduism. They are not religions in the strict sense of the word, but are, in fact, different and distinct social orders, and it is a dream that the Hindus and Muslims can ever evolve a common nationality, and this misconception of one Indian nation has gone far beyond the limits and is the cause of most of your troubles and will lead India to destruction if we fail to revise our notions in time. The Hindus and Muslims belong to two different religious philosophies, social customs, literatures. They neither intermarry nor interdine together and, indeed, they belong to two different civilizations which are based mainly on conflicting ideas and conceptions. Their aspects on life and of life are different. It is quite clear that Hindus and Mussalmans derive their inspiration from different sources of history. They have different epics, different heroes, and different episodes. Very often the hero of one is a foe of the other and, likewise, their victories and defeats overlap. To yoke together two such nations under a single state, one as a numerical minority and the other as a majority, must lead to growing discontent and final destruction of any fabric that may be so built up for the government of such a state.

. . . History has also shown us many geographical tracts, much smaller than the subcontinent of India, which otherwise might have been called one country, but which have been divided into as many states as there are nations inhabiting them. [The] Balkan Peninsula comprises as many as seven or eight sovereign states. Likewise, the Portuguese and the Spanish stand divided in the Iberian Peninsula. Whereas under the plea of the unity of India and one nation, which does not exist, it is sought to pursue here the line of one central government, we know that the history of the last twelve hundred years has failed to achieve unity and has witnessed, during the ages, India always divided into Hindu India and Muslim India. The present artificial unity of India dates back only to the British conquest and is maintained by the British bayonet, but termination of the British regime, which is implicit in the recent declaration of His Majesty's government, will be the herald of the entire break-up with worse disaster than has ever taken place during the last one thousand years under Muslims. Surely that is not the legacy which Britain would bequeath to India after one hundred fifty years of her rule, nor would Hindu and Muslim India risk such a sure catastrophe.

Muslim India cannot accept any constitution which must necessarily result in a Hindu majority government. Hindus and Muslims brought together under a democratic system forced upon the minorities can only mean Hindu rāj [rule]. Democracy of the kind with which the Congress High Command is enamored would mean the complete destruction of what is most precious in Islam. We have had ample experience of the working of the provincial constitutions during the last two and a half years and any repetition of such a government must lead to civil war and raising of private armies as recommended by Mr. Gandhi to [the] Hindus of Sukkur when he said that they must defend themselves violently or nonviolently, blow for blow, and if they could not, they must emigrate.

Mussalmans are not a minority as it is commonly known and understood. One has only got to look round. Even today, according to the British map of India, four out of eleven provinces, where the Muslims dominate more or less, are functioning notwithstanding the decision of the Hindu Congress High Command to noncooperate and prepare for civil disobedience. Mussalmans are a nation according to any definition of a nation, and they must have their homelands, their territory, and their state. We wish to live in peace and harmony with our neighbors as a free and independent people. We wish our people to develop to the fullest our spiritual, cultural, economic, social, and political life in a way that we think best and in consonance with our own ideals and according to the genius of our people. Honesty demands and the vital interests of millions of our people impose a sacred duty upon us to find an honorable and peaceful solution, which would be just and fair to all. But at the same time we cannot be moved or diverted from our purpose and objective by threats or intimidations. We must be prepared to face all difficulties and consequences, make all the sacrifices that may be required of us to achieve the goal we have set in front of us.

The Thrust Toward a New Muslim Nation

In 1943, Jinnah voiced his confidence that India's Muslims would turn the idea of Pakistan into a reality and, inspired by Islam's ideals, would then create their own constitutional democracy. His attack on "landlords and capitalists" won the greatest applause, perhaps because Hindus were generally wealthier than Muslims.

[From Jinnah, *Speeches and Writings*, 1:470-71, 506-8]

The progress that Mussalmans, as a nation, have made, during these three years, is a remarkable fact. Never before in the history of the world has a nation rallied around a common platform and a common ideal in such a short time as the Muslims have done in this vast subcontinent. Never before has a nation, miscalled a minority, asserted itself so quickly, and so effectively. Never before has the mental outlook of a nation been unified so suddenly. Never before has the solidarity of millions of population been established and demonstrated in so limited a time and under such peculiar circumstances as are prevalent in India. Three years ago Pakistan was a resolution. Today it is an article of faith, a matter of life and death with Muslim India. . . .

We have created a solidarity of opinion, a union of mind and thought. Let us concentrate on the uplift of our people for their educational, political, economic, social and moral well-being. Let us cooperate with and give all help to our leaders to work for our collective good. Let us make our organization stronger and put it on a thorough[ly] efficient footing. In all this, the final sanction and censure rests with and upon the verdict of our people. We, the Muslims, must rely mainly upon our own inherent qualities, our own natural potentialities, our own international solidarity and our own united will to face the future.

I particularly appeal to our intelligentsia and Muslim students to come forward and rise to the occasion. Train yourselves, equip yourselves for the task that lies before us. The final victory depends upon you and is within our grasp. You have performed wonders in the past. You are still capable of repeating the history. You are not lacking in the great qualities and virtues in comparison with the other nations. Only you have to be fully conscious of that fact and act with courage, faith and unity. . . .

I have no doubt in my mind that a large body of us visualize Pakistan as people's government. Either you seize it by force or get it by agreement. But until you get it, whether it is from a foreign nation or whether it is our own government, the question as to the constitution and the form and system of a government does not arise. . . . You will elect your representatives to the constitution-making body. You may not know your power, you may not know how to use it. This would be your fault. But I am sure that democracy is in our blood. It is in our marrows. Only centuries of adverse circumstances have made the circulation of that blood cold. It has got frozen and your arteries have not been functioning. But, thank God, the blood is circulating again, thanks to the Muslim League efforts. It will be a people's government. Here I should like to give a warning to the landlords and capitalists who have flourished at our expense by a system which is so vicious, which is so wicked and which makes them so selfish that it is difficult to reason with them. [Tremendous applause.] The exploitation of the masses has gone into their blood. They have forgotten the lessons of Islam. Greed and selfishness have made these people subordinate others to their interests in order to fatten themselves. It is true we are not in power today. You go anywhere to the countryside. I have visited villages. There are millions and millions of our people who hardly get one meal a day. Is this civilization? Is this the aim of Pakistan? [Cries of no, no.] Do you visualize that millions have been exploited and cannot get one meal a day? If that is the idea of Pakistan I would not have it. [Cheers.] If they are wise they will have to adjust themselves to the new modern conditions of life. If they don't, God help them. [Hear, hear, renewed cheers and applause.] Therefore let us have faith in ourselves. Let us not falter or hesitate. That is our goal. We are going to achieve it. [Cheers.] The constitution of Pakistan can only be framed by the Millat [the Muslim community or nation] and the people. Prepare yourselves and see that you frame a constitution which is to your heart's desire. There is a lot of misunderstanding. A lot of mischief is created. Is it going to be an Islamic government? Is it not begging the question? Is it not a question of passing a vote of censure on yourself? The constitution and the government will be what the people will decide. The only question is that of minorities.

The minorities are entitled to get a definite assurance and ask: "Where do we stand in the Pakistan that you visualize?" That is an issue of giving a definite and clear assurance to the minorities. We have done it. We have passed a resolution that the minorities must be protected and safeguarded to the fullest extent and as I said before any civilized government will do it and ought to do it. So far as we are concerned our own history, our Prophet, have given the clearest proof that non-Muslims have been treated not only justly and fairly but generously. [Cheers and applause.]

RAHMAT ALI: GIVING A NAME TO PAKISTAN

There has been considerable controversy over the origin and meaning of the word "Pakistan." It was first widely used after the Lahore Resolution of 1940 (see above) when newspapers hostile to Jinnah began saying that he wanted to divide the country into "India" and "Pakistan." Jinnah commented that neither he nor the Muslim League had invented the word, but that it had been foisted upon them by the Hindus and the British. He went on to say that he was grateful that they had done so, for he had wanted a word to cover what was being asked for in the Lahore Resolution. As he pointed out, "Some young fellows in London, who wanted a particular part of the northwest to be separated from the rest of India, coined a name, started the idea, and called a zone Pakistan."[18] One of the "young fellows" was Choudhary Rahmat Ali, a student at Cambridge who, with a group of friends, issued a manifesto in 1933 on behalf of the Muslim population of Punjab, the Northwest Frontier Province, Kashmir, Sind, and Baluchistan in what they called a "grim and fateful struggle against political crucifixion and annihilation" by the Hindu majority.[19] Rahmat Ali's account given here of how the name was chosen was written some years later.

[Choudhary Rahmat Ali, *Pakistan,* quoted in Pirzada, *Evolution of Pakistan,* pp. 28-32]

In my early youth three fundamental truths became clear to me about the future of our people and our lands.

First, that such old names of our "Indian" homelands as the Sindh Valley, the Indus Valley, and North-Western India, were anachronistic and dangerous. They were anachronistic because they were the relics both of a mythology which we exploded in the 7th century A.D. [sic] and of a hegemony which we annihilated in the 8th; and they were dangerous because they made out our "Indian" homelands Hindoolands and our people Indian—which they had ceased to be at least twelve centuries ago. So, to my mind, these names were our worst enemies; for through them the ghosts of dead ages and of defunct hegemonies were still ruling us and ruining our nationhood in our own country.

Second, that in the modern world the recognition of our nationhood was impossible without a national name for our people and our "Indian" homelands—a name which would equally serve and suit after the reintegration of our "Indian" and "Asian" homelands a reintegration which in my judgment was both vital and inevitable; that the absence of such a name, in the past, had proved harmful to our interests, but, in the future, would prove fatal to our existence. For, more than anything else, it would encourage the Caste Hindoos—and others—to repeat "Spain" on us,[20] and to suck into the orbit of Indianism not only our "Indian" homelands but also our "Asian" homelands—Iran, Afghanistan, and Tukharistan.

Third, that unless and until we all in our "Indian" and "Asian" homelands, now separated by the twists and turns of history and exploited by our enemies, reintegrate ourselves into one nation under a new fraternal name, none of us whether living in the "Indian" or in the "Asian" homelands could survive and thrive in the world.

The realization of these truths created in me a solemn, surging urge to invent such a name as would reflect the soul and spirit of us all, symbolize the history and hopes of us all, strengthen the national bonds of us all, and ensure the realization of the destiny of us all. That is, a name that would detach those of us who are living in our "Indian" homelands from Indian Nationalism and re-attach us to Islamic nationalism; that would sever our artificial, national and territorial bonds with India and cement our Islamic, national and territorial ties with Iran, Afghanistan, and Tukharistan; and that would meet the challenge of Indianism and British Imperialism both to us in our Indian homelands and to our brethren in Iran, Afghanistan and Tukharistan.

It had therefore to be a name born of all the elements of our life— spiritual and fraternal, moral and ethnical, historical and geographical, supra-regional and supra-national. In other words, it had to be charged with an irresistible, eternal appeal to the heart and head of all our people, and possessed of elemental power to seize on our being and make us all go out crusading for the Millat's Mission.[21] For nothing short of that could generate those mighty forces which alone could ensure the liberation of us all, the transformation of some of the most important parts of India and Asia, and the fulfilment of our Millat's Mission in India and its Islands.

In view of that none could have realized more than myself that this was a herculean task; but it was also a holy task, a task of destiny, a task that had to be attempted. I undertook it years ago, and gave to it all that was in me. Neglecting my studies and renouncing every idea of a career or home, I made it the be-all and end-all of my life, and devoted to it every spark of the fire and fervour of my faith, and every particle of what knowledge and enlightenment I possessed. I observed *chillahs*[22] and prayed for Allah's guidance. I did everything that could help the accomplishment of the task, and never lost faith in Divine guidance. I carried on till, at last, in His dispensation Allah showed me the light, and led me to the name "Pakistan" and to the Pak Plan, both of which are now animating the lives of our people.

So much for the invention of the name Pakistan. Now a word about its composition.

"Pakistan" is both a Persian and an Urdu word. It is composed of letters taken from the names of all our homelands—"Indian" and "Asian." That is, Punjab, Afghania (North-West Frontier Province), Kashmir, Iran, Sindh (including Kachch and Kathiawar), Tukharistan, Afghanistan, and Balochistan. It means the land of the Paks—the spiritually pure and clean. It symbolizes the religious beliefs and the ethnical stocks of our people; and it stands for all the territorial constituents of our original Fatherland. It has no other origin and no other meaning; and it does not admit of any other interpretation. Those writers who have tried to interpret it in more than one way have done so either through love of casuistry, or through ignorance of its inspiration, origin, and composition.

ABUL KALAM AZAD: MUSLIM NATIONALIST

There were many Muslims who rejected the two-nation theory of Jinnah and the Muslim League. They were convinced that the best hope for the future of the Muslim population of the subcontinent was in a united India, and they supported the Indian National Congress. Among them was Maulana Abul Kalam Azad (1888-1958), a distinguished scholar and writer who was president of the Congress during the difficult period from 1940 to 1946. Born in Mecca of an Indian father and an Arabian mother, he received a traditional Islamic education in Calcutta, but he was persuaded by the writings of Syed Ahmed Khan to study the historical and philosophical heritage of Europe through the medium of English. "The ideas I had acquired from my family and early training could no longer satisfy me," he wrote. "I felt that I must find the truth for myself. Almost instinctively I began to move out of my family orbit and seek my own path."[23] He adopted the pen name of Azad ("free") to indicate this change in outlook and joined an all-Hindu revolutionary group (partly through the influence of Aurobindo Ghose). In 1912 he founded the Urdu journal *al-Hilāl* ("the crescent moon," symbolic of the Islamic community, which follows the lunar calendar). Like Mohamed Ali, he was kept in detention during World War I and later joined the pro-caliphate noncooperation movement under Gandhi's leadership. Unlike Mohamed Ali, Jinnah, and others, he remained within the Congress, believing the Muslims and Hindus could share citizenship in an independent India without compromising their religious beliefs. He became the Union of India's minister of education from its birth until his death. His great work of scholarship was his commentary on the Qur'ān in Urdu, in which he stressed the benevolent guidance of God to mankind.

The Muslims of India and the Future of India

The following selection is taken from the speech Maulana Azad gave as president of the Indian National Congress in 1940, and it is one of the most searching attempts by a Congress leader to deal with the treatment of minorities in general and of the Muslims in particular. He asserted that the Congress had two basic principles with regard to minorities. One was that, when a new constitution was adopted for India, the rights of the minorities would be fully guaranteed; the other was that the minorities, not the majority, would decide what safeguards were necessary.

[Sankar Ghose, ed., *Congress Presidential Speeches*, pp. 356-63]

We have considered the problem of the minorities of India. But are the Muslims such a minority as to have the least doubt or fear about their future? A small minority may legitimately have fears and apprehensions, but can the Muslims allow themselves to be disturbed by them? I do not know how many of you are familiar with my writings, twenty-eight years ago, in the "Al Hilal". If there are any such here, I would request them to refresh their memories. Even then I gave expression to my conviction, and I repeat this to-day, that in the texture of Indian politics, nothing is further removed from the truth than to say that Indian Muslims occupy the position of a political minority. It is equally absurd for them to be apprehensive about their rights and interests in a democratic India. This fundamental mistake has opened the door to countless misunderstandings. False arguments were built up on wrong premises. This error, on the one hand, brought confusion into the minds of Musalmans about their own true position, and, on the other hand, it involved the world in misunderstandings, so that the picture of India could not be seen in right perspective.

If time had permitted, I would have told you in detail, how during the last sixty years, this artificial and untrue picture of India was made, and whose hands traced it. In effect, this was the result of the same policy of divide and rule which took particular shape in the minds of British Officialdom in India after the Congress launched the national movement. The object of this was to prepare the Musalmans for use against the new political awakening. In this plan, prominence was given to two points. First, that India was inhabited by two different communities, the Hindus and the Musalmans, and for this reason no demand could be made in the name of a united nation. Second: that numerically the Musalmans were far less than the Hindus, and because of this, the necessary consequence of the establish-

238 Islamic Revival, Reform, and Nationalism

ment of democratic institutions in India would be to establish the rule of the Hindu majority and to jeopardise the existence of the Muslims.

Thus were sown the seeds of disunity by British Imperialism on Indian soil. The plant grew and was nurtured and spread its nettles, and even though fifty years have passed since then, the roots are still there.

Politically speaking, the word minority does not mean just a group that is so small in number and so lacking in other qualities that give strength, that it has no confidence in its own capacity to protect itself from the much larger group that surrounds it. It is not enough that the group should be relatively the smaller, but that it should be absolutely so small as to be incapable of protecting its interests. Thus this is not merely a question of numbers; other factors count also. If a country has two major groups nu' 1-bering a million and two millions respectively, it does not necessarily follow that because one is half the other, therefore it must call itself politically a minority and consider itself weak.

If this is the right test, let us apply it to the position of the Muslims in India. You will see at a glance a vast concourse, spreading out all over the country; they stand erect, and to imagine that they exist helplessly as a "minority" is to delude oneself.

The Muslims in India number between eighty and ninety millions. The same type of social or racial divisions, which affect other communities, do not divide them. The powerful bonds of Islamic brotherhood and equality have protected them to a large extent from the weakness that flows from social divisions. It is true that they number only one-fourth of the total population; but the question is not one of population ratio, but of the large numbers and the strength behind them. Can such a vast mass of humanity have any legitimate reason for apprehension that in a free and democratic India, it might be unable to protect its rights and interest?

These numbers are not confined to any particular area but spread out unevenly over different parts of the country. In four provinces out of eleven in India there is a Muslim majority, the other religious groups being minorities. If British Baluchistan is added, there are five provinces with Muslim majority. Even if we are compelled at present to consider this question on a basis of religious groupings, the position of the Muslims is not that of a minority only. If they are in a minority in seven provinces, they are in a majority in five. This being so, there is absolutely no reason why they should be oppressed by the feeling of being a minority.

Whatever may be the details of the future constitution of India, we know that it will be an all-India federation which is, in the fullest sense, democratic, and every unit of which will have autonomy in regard to internal affairs. The federal centre will be concerned only with all-India matters of common concern, such as, foreign relations, defence, customs, etc. Under these circumstances, can any one who has any conception of the actual working of a democratic constitution, allow himself to be led astray by this false issue of majority and minority? I cannot believe for an instant that there can be any room whatever for these misgivings in the picture of India's future. These apprehensions are arising because, in the words of a British statesman regarding Ireland, we are yet standing on the banks of the river and, though wishing to swim, are unwilling to enter the water. There is only one remedy: we should take the plunge fearlessly. No sooner is this done we shall realise that all our apprehensions were without foundation. . . .

Do we, Indian Musalmans, view the free India of the future with suspicion and distrust or with courage and confidence? If we view it with fear and suspicion, then undoubtedly we have to follow a different path. No present declaration, no promise for the future, no constitutional safeguards, can be a remedy for our doubts and fears. We are then forced to tolerate the existence of a third power. This third power is already entrenched here and has no intention of withdrawing and, if we follow this path of fear, we must need look forward to its continuance. But if we are convinced that for us fear and doubt have no place, and that we must view the future with courage and confidence in ourselves, then our course of action becomes absolutely clear. We find ourselves in a new world, which is free from the dark shadows of doubt, vacillation, inaction and apathy, and where the light of faith and determination, action and enthusiasm never fails. The confusions of the times, the ups and downs that come our way, the difficulties that beset our thorny path, cannot change the direction of our steps. It becomes our bounden duty then to march with assured steps to India's national goal. . . .

I am a Musalman and am proud of that fact. Islam's splendid traditions of thirteen hundred years are my inheritance. I am unwilling to lose even the smallest part of this inheritance. The teaching and history of Islam, its arts and letters and civilisation are my wealth and my fortune. It is my duty to protect them.

As a Musalman I have a special interest in Islamic religion and culture and I cannot tolerate any interference with them. But in addition to these sentiments, I have others also which the realities and conditions of my life have forced upon me. The spirit of Islam does not come in the way of these sentiments; it guides and helps me forward. I am proud of being an Indian. I am a part of the indivisible unity that is Indian nationality. I am indispensable to this noble edifice and without me this splendid structure of India is incomplete. I am an essential element which has gone to build India. I can never surrender this claim.

It was India's historic destiny that many human races and cultures and religions should flow to her, finding a home in her hospitable soil, and that many a caravan should find rest here. Even before the dawn of history, these caravans trekked into India and wave after wave of newcomers followed. This vast and fertile land gave welcome to all and took them to her bosom. One of the last of these caravans, following the footsteps of its predecessors, was that of the followers of Islam. This came here and settled here for good. This led to a meeting of the culture-currents of two different races. Like the Ganga and Jumna, they flowed for a while through separate courses, but nature's immutable law brought them together and joined them in a sangam.[24] This fusion was a notable event in history. Since then, destiny, in her own hidden way, began to fashion a new India in place of the old. We brought our treasures with us, and India too was full of the riches of her own precious heritage. We gave our wealth to her and she unlocked the doors of her own treasures to us. We gave her, what she needed most, the most precious of gifts from Islam's treasury, the message of democracy and human equality.

Full eleven centuries have passed by since then. Islam has now as great a claim on the soil of India as Hinduism. If Hinduism has been the religion of the people here for several thousands of years, Islam also has been their religion for a thousand years. Just as a Hindu can say with pride that he is an Indian and follows Hinduism, so also we can say with equal pride that we are Indians and follow Islam. I shall enlarge this orbit still further. The Indian Christian is equally entitled to say with pride that he is an Indian and is following a religion of India, namely Christianity.

Eleven hundred years of common history have enriched India with our common achievement. Our languages, our poetry, our literature, our culture, our art, our dress, our manners and customs, the innumerable happenings of our daily life, everything bears the stamp of our joint endeavour. There is indeed no aspect of our life which has escaped this stamp. Our languages were different, but we grew to use a common language; our manners and customs were dissimilar, but they acted and reacted on each other and thus produced a new synthesis. Our old dress may be seen only in ancient pictures of by-gone days; no one wears it to-day. This joint wealth is the heritage of our common nationality and we do not want to leave it and go back to the times when this joint life had not begun. If there are any Hindus amongst us who desire to bring back the Hindu life of a thousand years ago and more, they dream, and such dreams are vain fantasies. So also if there are any Muslims who wish to revive their past civilization and culture, which they brought a thousand years ago from Iran and Central Asia, they dream also and the sooner they wake up the better. These are unnatural fancies which cannot take root in the soil of reality. I am one of those who believe that revival may be a necessity in a religion but in social matters it is a denial of progress.

This thousand years of our joint life has moulded us into a common nationality. This cannot be done artificially. Nature does her fashioning through her hidden processes in the course of centuries. The cast has now been moulded and destiny has set her seal upon it. Whether we like it or not, we have now become an Indian nation, united and indivisible. No fantasy or artificial scheming to separate and divide can break this unity. We must accept the logic of fact and history and engage ourselves in the fashioning of our future destiny.

I shall not take any more of your time. My address must end now. But before I do so, permit me to remind you that our success depends upon three factors: unity, discipline and full confidence in Mahatma Gandhi's leadership. The glorious past record of our movement was due to his great leadership, and it is only under his leadership that we can look forward to a future of successful achievement.

The time of our trial is upon us. We have already focussed the world's attention. Let us endeavour to prove ourselves worthy.

NOTES

1. Sayeed, *Pakistan: The Formative Phase*, p. 78.
2. At that time, "Hindustan" referred to the land between Bihar and the Punjab, not to all of India.
3. "Great hero," an epithet of Vishnu, as well as the name of Jainism's founder.
4. Land from the cultivators of which he collects taxes for the government, keeping a share for himself.

5. A leatherworker, considered polluting by those at higher levels of Hindu society.
6. Mohamed Ali, *My Life: A Fragment*, p. 35.
7. Rome, or Europe generally.
8. *Ijmāᶜ*, the consensus arrived at by Muslims who have exercised *ijtihād*. (The first two sources referred to here are the Qurᵓān and the actions and sayings of the Prophet Muhammad, i.e., the Hadīth.
9. *Ijtihād*, the strong mental effort required to form an original judgment on a question of Islamic law.
10. According to some records, he was born in 1876.
11. Bolitho, *Jinnah*, p. 17. In English law, a pleader is a trial lawyer.
12. Allana, *Quaid-e-azam Jinnah*, p. 62.
13. Montagu, *An Indian Diary*, pp. 57-58.
14. M. K. Gandhi, *Collected Works*, 34:175.
15. Iqbal, *Letters to Jinnah*, p. 16.
16. Jinnah, *Speeches and Writings*, 2:314.
17. Bolitho, *Jinnah*, p. 95.
18. Pirzada, *Evolution of Pakistan*, pp. 31-32.
19. *Ibid.*, p. 27.
20. The reference is to the expulsion of Muslims from Spain.
21. The Muslim community.
22. Meditation.
23. Azad, *India Wins Freedom*, p. 3.
24. The confluence of the two rivers.

Chapter 6

MAHATMA GANDHI: NATIONALIST INDIA'S "GREAT SOUL"

Mohandas Karamchand Gandhi (1869–1948) dominated the Indian National Congress from the time of Tilak's death in 1920 until the eve of independence in 1947. A deeply moral man, he believed he had a mission to keep the national movement from degenerating into anti-British violence and internecine warfare. Like the early Moderate leaders (among whom he most admired Gokhale), he worked for greater social and economic reforms as well as for political progress toward national self-government. His spiritual strength, austere life-style, and dedicated service to the poorest and most humiliated of his countrymen won him the popular title of mahātmā (great soul). His powerful leadership of mass movements, great common sense, and courageous firmness in opposing and negotiating with India's British rulers made him his countrymen's chief guide during the final decades of foreign rule.

Gandhi's homeland of Gujarat was one of the country's most prosperous regions, its many rivers welcoming merchant ships from ports along the Arabian Sea. When British forces entered Gujarat in the early nineteenth century, they left most of this remote and turbulent peninsula under the control of its many warring chieftains but froze their warfare with one another by forcing them to sign treaties placing themselves under British protection. The Gandhi family, many of whom were merchants, thrived under this new peace. Gandhi's father's father, a skilled customs collector and diplomat, rose to the office of dewan (chief minister) to the Rajput king of the tiny coastal state of Porbandar. Gandhi's father inherited the post in turn, although he passed it on to his younger brother after he received a better dewanship at Rajkot, an inland principality the British were using as the center of their post-1857 efforts to improve the lot and enlighten the minds of the people in this rugged frontier area.

Mohandas was seven when his family moved to Rajkot, and he at once began what would be eleven years of study in the school system created by the Bombay Department of Public Instruction. At first all his classes were conducted in his mother tongue, Gujarati; then English was added; and in high school everything except Gujarati literature was taught in the language of India's rulers from overseas. But the education that made the deepest impression on him emanated from his parents. He was their youngest child, and their favorite. A lot of his father's character seems to have entered into Gandhi's own: the stubborn persistence in doing what he believed was right, regardless of the consequences; the ability to manage the work of hundreds of men and women; and the occasional loss of temper, quickly brought under control. From both his mother and his father he imbibed the love of devotional worship of a protecting God—usually but not exclusively conceived of as Rāma. His mother influenced him most by her example of saintly self-denial and her readiness to serve others, including the sick and the poor. Western secular influences were weak and Jain nonviolence strong among the merchant castes of peninsular Gujarat, and, although young Gandhi tried secretly eating meat in his early teens, he discontinued the experiment because he knew how horrified his parents would have been had they known of this breach of nonviolence to living creatures.

When Mohandas was sixteen his father died, having named him as heir to the position of dewan, saying: "This Manu [Mohandas] will uphold my reputation. He will make the lineage a distinguished one."[1] Six months later the British deposed Porbandar's king for misgoverning, took over the management of the kingdom, and purged many members of the Gandhi extended family from the administration. A wise brahman friend of the family suggested they send young Mohandas to London to earn a law degree (which at that time could be done without having gone to college). In this way they could satisfy the British requirement that only well-educated men be appointed to high office in India's semiautonomous kingdoms. At first young Gandhi's mother refused to let him go, fearing that English habits would corrupt her dearest child. She agreed only when he took a triple vow, suggested and administered by a learned Jain monk of their same caste. Mohandas vowed not to touch meat, wine, or women. Although in Rajkot his adventurous voyage was approved by his caste fellows, at Bombay the caste's headman declared him outcaste for making this supposedly polluting voyage across the ocean.

London made a twofold impact on this impressionable lad from one of India's most tradition-bound regions. One effect was to anglicize his appearance, speech, and social conduct, turning him into a nattily dressed barrister-at-law. Another was to bring him into close touch with English men and women holding ideas similar to those of his parents on subjects such as vegetarianism, reincarnation, the law of karma, and the immortality of the soul. Gandhi also sought out Christian churches in order to hear some of the best preachers of the day. After nearly three years in the capital of Britain's empire he was admitted to the bar and boarded a steamship for home, feeling "deep regret" at leaving "dear London."[2]

Now twenty-one, Gandhi found it difficult to re-enter his own society and culture after his English experiences. First he found that his beloved mother had died a few months earlier. "Most of my childhood hopes were shattered," he recalled.[3] Next he failed in his attempt to set up a law practice in Bombay, India's most Westernized city, and was forced to join his eldest brother in doing petty legal work in their hometown. Deracinated from the culture of his family (he insisted that his wife and child wear shoes and socks and eat oatmeal), he was also treated as socially inferior by the English, whose company he had enjoyed in London. His restlessness increased after he clashed with the chief British official in the region, on whom his hopes for a more prestigious job depended. He decided to leave India again, this time for South Africa, where his brother had found him a job with a Muslim trading firm from Gujarat.

A series of racist actions by white South Africans impressed Gandhi with the need for the 40,000 Indian settlers there to do something to defend their rights as human beings. Within a month of landing he was shoved out of a first-class train compartment, beaten on a stagecoach for not giving up his seat to a white man, and kicked off the sidewalk—all because of the color of his skin. In response, he used British methods of political agitation: writing letters to the newspapers, leading a petition drive, founding a political organization with membership drives, carefully kept accounts, a small library, and regular meetings for lectures, debates, and group decisions. With this organization's support, he then wrote two pamphlets to describe the injustices his countrymen were suffering and to appeal for redress. "All this activity resulted in winning the Indians numerous friends in South Africa and in obtaining the active sympathy of all parties in India. It also opened up and placed before the South African Indians a definite line of action."[4]

Thus, at twenty-four was born Gandhi the political leader—the de facto dewan of a community about the same size as the ones his father had served.

At twenty-seven he toured India to enlist further support for the cause; he met Banerjea, Ranade, Tilak, and Gokhale, and adopted Gokhale as his "political guru." He was nearly killed by a white mob when he returned to South Africa but refused to press charges and cheerfully volunteered to form and lead an ambulance corps two years later (in 1899) when war broke out between the Dutch-descended Boers of the interior and the coastally based British who coveted the former's gold- and diamond-rich territory. Gandhi believed then, and up until 1920, that India was benefiting from being governed under the British constitution, and he repeatedly pointed out that arbitrary and racist legislation violated the principles and spirit of that constitution. When in 1906 a law was passed requiring every Indian to carry an identification pass, he led the community in a mass refusal to obey it. Shortly before his first jail term in 1908 he and a cousin coined the term *"satyāgraha"* ("holding firmly to *satya*," that is, to the moral and spiritual reality in the soul) to indicate the nature of this nonviolent fight against unjust laws, waged primarily by disobeying them and suffering the hardships of imprisonment. By 1914 this expanding movement, supported finally by the Government of India, produced the repeal of some repressive laws, and Gandhi felt free to return to India after laboring twenty years for justice and human dignity in South Africa.

Paralleling and reinforcing his growing experience in serving his community, Gandhi evolved in these years his own system of spiritual ideals and moral practices. Its roots lay in his childhood training in Vaishnava devotional prayer, Jain nonviolence and self-denial, and in the service his parents had required of him, especially during his father's illness. Christian friends in London and South Africa had acquainted him with Jesus' teachings on nonretaliation, forgiveness, faith in God, and the need to love and serve others. Tolstoy's expression of these ideals in a nondoctrinal perspective had also impressed him greatly, as did his continuing study of the *Gītā* and of other religious writings sent to him by friends in India and England. The deeper his involvement in serving others became, the more he felt the need to simplify his life and to give up sexual relations with his wife. Letters and books sent from Bombay by his Jain friend Raychand (Rajachandra) strengthened his resolve to adopt these self-restraints so as to hasten his soul's liberation from further rebirths. Thus the two paths of service and progress toward *mokṣa* began to converge, with the path to liberation the higher one, giving meaning and motivation to the path of service.

Gandhi was forty-five when he returned to India to spend his remaining thirty-three years there, years of continuing growth both in the scope of his public work and in the intensity of his religious life. The two paths tended increasingly to merge as the difficulties he faced drove him more and more to prayer, and as his efforts to help the downtrodden in his society convinced him that it was only through identifying with and serving his fellow men that he could come closer to God. The villagers of India were his first love, for he believed that the "curse" of modern materialism was spreading outward from the coastal cities, contaminating India's great heritage of spiritual striving and simple living. He quickly responded to opportunities to lead villagers in opposing excessive taxes, but he also helped city workers in their 1918 strike against a wage reduction.

After forming an alliance with Mohamed Ali and other Muslim leaders anxious to defend the postwar powers of the defeated caliph of Turkey, and convinced that all-India grievances could be solved by the same means he had used in South Africa, Gandhi persuaded the Congress in 1920 to start a movement of noncooperation with British rule and commerce. He hoped that by bringing together national and Islamic issues the resultant Hindu-Muslim unity would hasten the end of British rule. The secularist Muslim leader Mohammed Ali Jinnah—who with Tilak had worked out in 1916 a united constitutional demand for India's self-government—condemned Gandhi for his "extreme programme" which "struck the imagination mostly of the inexperienced youth and the ignorant and the illiterate." "All this means complete disorganization and chaos."[5] Gandhi nevertheless persisted in his plan and insisted on strict discipline and nonviolence within the "Non-Co-Operation Movement" (as it was then called). When in 1922 villagers attacked and killed a group of twenty-one policemen and rural watchmen, he held himself personally responsible, called an immediate halt to the movement, and fasted for five days as penance for his failure to control it.

Although his dramatic program had won widespread support, awakened national pride, and checked the growth of terrorist methods, his plan to unify Hindus and Muslims collapsed with the noncooperation movement. A rising tide of riots and killings between the two communities followed in the mid- and late 1920s, despite Gandhi's 1924 twenty-one-day fast for Hindu-Muslim unity. By 1930 the Congress, with Gandhi at its head, was ready to launch another nationwide movement of nonviolent noncooperation and civil disobedience. Muslim support was less this time, but women were considerably more active. The Government of India moved quickly to arrest the Congress workers and some 60,000 filled the jails to overcrowding. A truce resulted in face-to-face talks between Gandhi and the British viceroy. The Conservative M. P. Winston Churchill called it a "nauseating and humiliating spectacle" that this "seditious fakir" should go "striding half-naked up the steps of the Viceroy's palace, there to negotiate and parley on equal terms with the representative of the King-Emperor."[6]

Nine months later a new and harsher viceroy jailed the Congress activists again, but Gandhi once more showed the moral power of suffering for a just cause by declaring he would fast to death in prison rather than accept the British plan to separate the voters and candidates of the lowest castes (the Untouchables) from the rest of the Hindus in future elections (as the Muslims had been separated since 1909). The news stirred sympathy throughout India and around the world and moved some higher caste Hindus to drop some of the barriers they had held up to guard themselves against the supposedly polluting contact with the lowest castes. On the fifth day the British gave in and accepted a compromise worked out between Gandhi and the Untouchable leader Dr. B. R. Ambedkar.

All through these years Gandhi was writing articles, letters (sometimes fifty a day), and delivering speeches on tours to every part of India, in a ceaseless effort to educate his countrymen on how to cure their social, economic, political, and moral-spiritual ills. Like Rammohun Roy and Syed Ahmed Khan, he cherished and made good use of the printing press and its freedom from censorship that Britain had brought to India; he founded, raised funds for, and was the main contributor to, one weekly newspaper in South Africa (from 1903 to 1915) and four in India (from 1919 to 1948, with interruptions)—two in English and two in the Gujarati language.

Despite this outpouring of words—most of them now available in the *Collected Works of Mahatma Gandhi*—Gandhi's favorite word remains a mysterious one to Western readers. That word is "Truth." Gandhi did not mean by it knowledge that could be embodied in statements based on evidence available to the senses and to the mind. "Truth" for Gandhi was the goal of his soul; it was his word for the Supreme Being toward which every thought, word, and deed should be directed. "The pursuit of Truth is true *bhakti*, devotion. It is the path that leads to God."[7] Like many Hindus and Jains, Gandhi believed that his soul had gone through countless incarnations and could only be liberated from endless future ones by emancipating itself from pride, anger, lust, fear, and all impure activities. More in the manner of Christian than Indian teachers, he insisted that it was only through a pure life of selfless service and suffering for others that he could attain

Come again, Buddah beat Christ to this one

that liberation. Perhaps this conviction stemmed from the examples and teachings of his father and mother and from his belief that his soul had been born into a family whose primary duty was to serve the public.

The 1930s and 1940s are the best-documented years of Gandhi's life, and they show him striving for perfection in the midst of growing turmoil, yet preserving his faith in human nature, his sense of humor, and his determination to keep the movement for independence free of hatred and violence. In 1939, Bengal's Subhas Chandra Bose tried to steer the Congress away from Gandhi's nonviolent path; in 1940 Jinnah called for separate states for those areas where Muslims were in the majority; in 1942 Gandhi's chief secretary and closest friend Mahadev Desai died, just after the British again jailed the entire Congress leadership (which had planned to mount another civil disobedience movement while Japan seemed about to invade India); in 1944 his faithful wife Kasturba died in prison; and from 1944 to 1947 he tried and failed to halt Jinnah's drive to divide British-ruled India into two independent nations. Worst of all, in 1946 and 1947 he saw his lifelong dream of peace and harmony between Hindus and Muslims drown in blood as killings between the two religious communities mounted all across northern India.

On August 15, 1947, the day a truncated India became free, he refused to join the ceremonies in New Delhi, remaining instead in Calcutta to continue his efforts to persuade the Muslims and Hindus there to live peacefully together. Two weeks later, as mob violence revived, an angry Hindu mob smashed its way into the Muslim house where he was staying; Gandhi started fasting the next day, saying "either there will be peace or I shall be dead."[8] Peace came in three days. In January 1948, he started fasting again in New Delhi to stop Hindu attacks on Muslims there; again pledges of peace by leaders of all groups enabled him to end his fast. But on January 30, as he was walking to begin his evening prayer meeting, he was shot by a fanatic Hindu who believed him too lenient with India's Muslims.

"The light has gone out of our lives," said Nehru to the nation. Sarojini Naidu, the poetess who had worked with and for Gandhi since 1914, and who had served as president of the Indian National Congress, reacted somewhat differently. When she saw people weeping in Delhi the day Gandhi was cremated there, she cried: "What is all this snivelling about? Would you rather he died of decrepit old age or indigestion? This was the only death great enough for him." Later she reminisced, "Every speaker that spoke about him said, 'May his spirit rest in peace.' I said: 'O my father, do not curse him. Do not let his spirit rest in peace. Let every ash from the funeral pyre be dynamic and create in us a power to fulfill his orders with vigour and follow his example.' "[9]

On Himself and His Inner Voice

[From M. K. Gandhi, *Collected Works,* unless otherwise attributed]

I am but a poor struggling soul yearning to be wholly good—wholly truthful and wholly non-violent in thought, word and deed, but ever failing to reach the ideal which I know to be true. . . . It is a painful climb, but the pain of it is a positive pleasure to me. Each step upward makes me feel stronger and fit for the next. [26:491]

I am not built for academic writings. Action is my domain. What I understand, according to my lights, to be my duty and what comes my way I do. All my action is actuated by the spirit of service. . . . The world does not hunger for *shastras* [treatises]. What it craves and will always crave is sincere action. [83:180]

Quite selfishly, as I wish to live in peace in the midst of a bellowing storm howling around me, I have been experimenting with myself and my friends by introducing religion into politics. Let me explain what I mean by religion. It is not the Hindu religion, which I certainly prize above all religions, but the religion which transcends Hinduism, which changes one's very nature, which binds one indissolubly to the truth within and which ever purifies. It is the permanent element in human nature which counts no cost too great in order to find full expression and which leaves the soul utterly restless until it has found itself, known its Maker and appreciated the true correspondence between the Maker and itself. [17:406]

The fact is, I have no desire for prestige anywhere. It is furniture required in courts of kings. I am a servant of Mussalmans [Muslims], Christians, Parsis and Jews, as I am of Hindus. And a servant is in need of love, not prestige. That is assured to me so long as I remain a faithful servant. [26:415]

I have not conceived my mission to be that of a knight-errant wandering everywhere to deliver people from difficult situations. My humble occupation has been to show people how they can solve their own difficulties. [76:231]

I ask nobody to follow me. Everyone should follow his or her own inner voice. If he or she has no ears to listen to it, he or she should do the best he or she can. In no case should he or she imitate others sheep-like. [*Harijan* (1947), p. 209]

The inner voice is something which cannot be described in words. But sometimes we have a positive feeling that something in us prompts us to do a certain thing. The time when I learnt to recognize this voice was, I may say, the time when I started praying regularly. [50:326]

Individual worship cannot be described in words. It goes on continuously and even unconsciously. There is not a moment when I do not feel the presence of a witness whose eye misses nothing and with whom I strive to keep in tune. I do not pray as Christian friends do. Not because I think there is anything wrong in it, but because words won't come to me. I suppose it is a matter of habit. [68:207]

Prayer is to the God within. It does not provoke God to change his will; but it enables us to know His will which is everything. [44:325]

When I think of the horizon about us, my heart becomes sick and weary. And when I listen to the still small voice within, I derive hope and smile in spite of the conflagration raging round me. [28:437–38]

I do want growth, I do want self-determination, I do want freedom, but I want all these for the soul. I doubt if the steel age is an advance upon the flint age. I am indifferent. It is the evolution of the soul to which the intellect and all our faculties have to be devoted. [21:289]

Nonviolence (Ahimsā): [10] *The Force of Love, of the Soul, and of God*

[From M. K. Gandhi, *Collected Works*, unless otherwise attributed]

Scientists tell us that without the presence of the cohesive force amongst the atoms that comprise this globe of ours, it would crumble to pieces and we would cease to exist; and even as there is cohesive force in blind matter, so must there be in all things animate, and the name for that cohesive force among animate things is Love. We notice it between father and son, between brother and sister, friend and friend. But we have to learn to use that force among all that lives, and in the use of it consists our knowledge of God. [17:326]

My field of labour is clearly defined and it pleases me. I am fascinated by the law of love. It is the philosopher's stone for me. I know ahimsa alone can provide a remedy for our ills. In my view the path of non-violence is not the path of the timid or the unmanly. Ahimsa is the height of the Kshatriya dharma[11] as it represents the climax of fearlessness. In it there is no scope for flight or for defeat. Being a quality of the soul it is not difficult of attainment. It comes easily to a person who feels the presence of the soul within. I believe that no other path but that of non-violence will suit India. [25:563]

Consciously or unconsciously we are acting non-violently towards one another in daily life. All well-ordered societies are based on the law of non-violence. I have found that life persists in the midst of destruction and, therefore, there must be a higher law than that of destruction. Only under that law would a well-ordered society be intelligible and life worth living. And if that is the law of life, we have to work it out in daily life. Wherever there are jars, wherever you are confronted with an opponent, conquer him with love. In a crude manner I have worked it out in my life. That does not mean that all my difficulties are solved. I have found, however, that this law of love has answered as the law of destruction has never done. In India we have had an ocular demonstration of the operation of this law on the widest scale possible. I do not claim that non-violence has penetrated the three hundred millions, but I do claim that it has penetrated deeper than any other message, and in an incredibly short time. We have not been all uniformly non-violent; and with the vast majority, non-violence has been a matter of policy. Even so, I want you to find out if the country has not made phenomenal progress under the protecting power of non-violence. . . .

The law of love will work, just as the law of gravitation will work, whether we accept it or not. Just as a scientist will work wonders out of various applications of the laws of nature, even so a man who applies the law of love with scientific precision can work greater wonders. For the force of non-violence is infinitely more wonderful and subtle than the material forces of nature, like, for instance, electricity. The men who discovered for us the law of love were greater scientists than any of our modern scientists. Only our explorations have not gone far enough and so it is not possible for everyone to see all its working. Such, at any rate, is the hallucination, if it is one, under which I am labouring. The more I work at this law the more I feel delight in life, delight in the scheme of this universe. It gives me a peace and a meaning of the mysteries of nature that I have no power to describe. [*Young India*, October 1, 1931]

All society is held together by non-violence, even as the earth is held in her position by gravitation. But when the law of gravitation was discovered the discovery yielded results of which our ancestors had no knowledge. Even so when society is deliberately constructed in accordance with the law of non-violence, its structure will be different in material particulars from what it is today. . . . What is happening today is disregard of the law of non-violence and enthronement of violence as if it were an eternal law. [68:389]

Non-violence is a matter of the heart. It does not come to us through any intellectual feat. Everyone has faith in God though everyone does not know it. For, everyone has faith in himself and that multiplied to the nth degree is God. The sum total of all that lives is God. We may not be God but we are of God—even as a little drop of water is of the ocean. [69:88]

Non-violence is an active force of the highest order. It is soul force or the power of the godhead within us. Imperfect man cannot grasp the whole of that Essence—he would not be able to bear its full blaze—but even an infinitesimal fraction of it, when it becomes active within us, can work wonders. The sun in the heavens fills the whole universe with its life-giving warmth. But if one went too near it, it would consume him to ashes. Even so is it with godhead. We become godlike to the extent we realize non-violence; but we can never become wholly God. . . .

The soul persists even after death, its existence does not depend on the physical body. Similarly, non-violence or soul force too, does not need physical aids for its propagation or effect. It acts independently of them. It transcends time and space. [68:29]

Man and his deed are two distinct things. Whereas a good deed should call forth approbation and a wicked deed disapprobation, the doer of the deed, whether good or wicked, always deserves respect or pity as the case may be. 'Hate the sin and not the sinner' is a precept which, though easy enough to understand, is rarely practised, and that is why the poison of hatred spreads in the world. . . .

It is quite proper to resist and attack a system, but to resist and attack its author is tantamount to resisting and attacking oneself. For we are all tarred with the same brush, and are children of one and the same Creator, and as such the divine powers within us are infinite. To slight a human being is to slight those divine powers, and thus to harm not only that being but with him the whole world. [39:220–21]

Having flung aside the sword, there is nothing except the cup of love which I can offer to those who oppose me. It is by offering that cup that I expect to draw them close to me. I cannot think of permanent enmity between man and man and, believing as I do in the theory of rebirth, I live in the hope that if not in this birth, in some other birth, I shall be able to hug all humanity in a friendly embrace. [45:349]

It is no non-violence if we merely love those that love us. It is non-violence only when we love those that hate us. I know how difficult it is to follow this grand law of love. But are not all great and good things difficult to do? Love of the hater is the most difficult of all. [N. K. Bose, *Selections from Gandhi*, p. 17]

Life to me would lose all its interest if I felt that I *could* not attain perfect love on earth. After all, what matters is that our capacity for loving ever expands. It is a slow process. How shall you love the men who thwart you even in well-doing? And yet that is the time of supreme test. [14:146]

Love is the strongest force the world possesses and yet it is the humblest imaginable. [28:30]

Methods of violence are not consistent with human dignity. It is no an-swer to say that all Europe today is saturated with strong belief in brute force. True *paurusha*, true bravery, consists in driving out the brute in us and then only can we give freest play to our conscience. [Desai, *Day-to-day with Gandhi*, 1:318]

I do believe that where there is only a choice between cowardice and violence I would advise violence. Thus when my eldest son asked me what he should have done, had he been present when I was almost fatally assaulted in 1908, whether he should have run away and seen me killed or whether he should have used his physical force which he could and wanted to use, and defended me, I told him that it was his duty to defend me even by using violence. Hence it was that I took part in the Boer War, the so-called Zulu rebellion and the late War.[12] Hence also do I advocate training in arms for those who believe in the method of violence. I would rather have India resort to arms in order to defend her honour than that she should in a cowardly manner become or remain a helpless witness to her own dishonour.

[margin note: action over cowardice => violence over cowardice and inaction]

But I believe that non-violence is infinitely superior to violence, forgiveness is more manly than punishment. . . . Let me not be misunderstood. Strength does not come from physical capacity. It comes from an indomitable will. [18:132–33]

My creed of non-violence is an extremely active force. It has no room for cowardice or even weakness. There is hope for a violent man to be some day non-violent, but there is none for a coward. [34:3]

Non-violence is a weapon of the strong. With the weak it might easily be hypocrisy. Fear and love are contradictory terms. Love is reckless in giving away, oblivious as to what it gets in return. Love wrestles with the world as with the self and ultimately gains a mastery over all other feelings. [M. K. Gandhi, *The Nation's Voice*, p. 110]

Non-violence presupposes ability to strike. It is a conscious, deliberate restraint put upon one's desire for vengeance. But vengeance is anyday superior to passive, effeminate and helpless submission. Forgiveness is higher still. . . . A man who fears no one on earth would consider it troublesome even to summon up anger against one who is vainly trying to injury him. [31:292–93]

I have learnt through bitter experience the one supreme lesson to con-serve my anger and as heat conserved is transmuted into energy, even so our anger controlled can be transmuted into a power which can move the world. [18:246]

The moral to be legitimately drawn from the supreme tragedy of the atom bomb is that it will not be destroyed by counter-bombs, even as violence cannot be by counter-violence. Mankind has to get out of violence only through non-violence. Hatred can be overcome only by love. Counter-hatred only increases the surface, as well as the depth of hatred. [84:394]

Nonviolent Democracy: Control by the People of Themselves and Their Government

[From M. K. Gandhi, *Collected Works*, unless otherwise attributed]

Independence must begin at the bottom. Thus, every village will be a re-public or *panchayat*[13] having full powers. It follows, therefore, that every village has to be self-sustained and capable of managing its affairs even to the extent of defending itself against the whole world. . . . Ultimately, it is the individual who is the unit. . . .

In this structure composed of innumerable villages, there will be ever widening, never ascending circles. Life will not be a pyramid with the apex sustained by the bottom. But it will be an oceanic circle whose centre will be the individual always ready to perish for the village, the latter ready to perish for the circle of villagers, till at last the whole becomes one life composed of individuals, never aggressive in their arrogance but ever hum-ble, sharing the majesty of the oceanic circle of which they are integral units.

Therefore, the outermost circumference [i.e., the national government] will not wield power to crush the inner circle but will give strength to all within and derive its own strength from it. [85:32–33]

The end to be sought is human happiness combined with full mental and moral development. I use the adjective moral as synonymous with spiritual. This end can be achieved under decentralisation. Centralisation as a system is inconsistent with [the] non-violent structure of society. [75:216]

The average individual's soul-force is any day the most important thing. The political form is but a concrete expression of that soul-force. I do not conceive the average individual's soul-force as distinguished and existing apart from the political form of government. Hence I believe that after all a people has the government which it deserves. In other words self-government can only come through self-effort. [28:190]

Self-government depends entirely upon our own internal strength, upon our ability to fight against the heaviest odds. Indeed, self-government which does not require that continuous striving to attain it and to sustain it is not worth the name. I have therefore endeavoured to show both in word and in deed that political self-government, that is, self-government for a large number of men and women, is no better than individual self-government [or self-control], and therefore it is to be attained by precisely the same means that are required for individual self-government or self-rule, and so as you know also, I have striven to place this ideal before the people, in season and out of season, very often much to the disgust of those who are merely politically minded. [35:294]

(SELF-RULE)

Swaraj[14] of a people means the sum-total of the swaraj of individuals. And such swaraj comes only from performance by individuals of their duty as citizens. In it no one thinks of his rights. They come, when they are needed, for better performance of duty. [69:52]

A born democrat is a born disciplinarian. Democracy comes naturally to him who is habituated normally to yield willing obedience to all laws, human or divine. [69:258]

A popular State can never act in advance of public opinion. If it goes against it, it will be destroyed. Democracy disciplined and enlightened is the finest thing in the world. A democracy prejudiced, ignorant, superstitious will land itself in chaos and may be self-destroyed. [47:235–36]

Swaraj for me means freedom for the meanest of our countrymen. . . . I am not interested in freeing India merely from the English yoke. I am bent upon freeing India from any yoke whatsoever. . . . Hence for me the movement of swaraj is a movement for self-purification. [24:227]

Swaraj does consist in the change of government and its real control by the people, but that would be merely the form. The substance that I am hankering after is a definite acceptance of the means and therefore a real change of heart on the part of the people. I am certain that it does not require ages for Hindus to discard the error of untouchability, for Hindus and Mussalmans to shed enmity and accept heart-friendship as an eternal factor of national life, for all to adopt the charkha [spinning wheel] as the only universal means of attaining India's economic salvation and finally for all to believe that India's freedom lies only through non-violence and no other method. Definite, intelligent and free adoption by the nation of this programme I hold as the attainment of the substance. The symbol, the transfer of power, is sure to follow, even as the seed truly laid must develop into a tree. [21:458]

They say "means are after all means." I would say "means are after all everything". As the means so the end. Violent means will give violent swaraj. That would be a menace to the world and to India herself. . . . There is no wall of separation between means and end. Indeed, the Creator has given us control (and that too very limited) over means, none over the end. Realization of the goal is in exact proportion to that of the means. This is a proposition that admits of no exception. Holding such a belief, I have been endeavouring to keep the country to means that are purely "peaceful and legitimate." [24:396]

Let nobody be misled by the Russian parallel. . . . A non-violent revolution is not a programme of 'seizure of power'. It is a programme of transformation of relationships ending in a peaceful transfer of power. . . . It will never use coercion. Even those who might hold contrary views will receive a full measure of security under it. [82:78]

True democracy or the swaraj of the masses can never come through untruthful and violent means, for the simple reason that the natural corollary to their use would be to remove all opposition through the suppression or extermination of the antagonists. That does not make for individual freedom. Individual freedom can have the fullest play only under a regime of unadulterated *ahiṁsā*. [69:50]

If we wish to achieve swaraj through truth and non-violence, gradual but steady building up from the bottom upwards by constructive effort is the only way. This rules out the deliberate creation of an anarchical state for the overthrow of the established order in the hope of throwing up from within a dictator who would rule with a rod of iron and produce order out of disorder. [75:213]

There must be no impatience, no barbarity, no insolence, no undue pressure. If we want to cultivate a true spirit of democracy, we cannot afford to be intolerant. Intolerance betrays want of faith in one's cause. [19:313]

To me political power is not an end but one of the means of enabling people to better their condition in every department of life. Political power means capacity to regulate national life through national representatives. If national life becomes so perfect as to become self-regulated, no representation becomes necessary. There is then a state of enlightened anarchy. In such a state every one is his own ruler. He rules himself in such a manner that he is never a hindrance to his neighbour. In the ideal State, therefore, there is no political power because there is no State. But the ideal is never fully realized in life. Hence the classical statement of Thoreau that that government is best which governs the least. [47:91]

. . . Real swaraj will come not by the acquisition of authority by a few but by the acquisition of the capacity by all to resist authority when it is abused. In other words, swaraj is to be attained by educating the masses to a sense of their capacity to regulate and control authority. [26:52]

Mere withdrawal of the English is not independence. It [independence] means the consciousness in the average villager that he is the maker of his own destiny, he is his own legislator through his chosen representatives. [42:469]

I would be deeply distressed, if on every conceivable occasion every one of us were to be a law unto oneself and to scrutinize in golden scales every action of our future national assembly. I would surrender my judgment in most matters to national representatives, taking particular care in making my choice of such representatives. I know that in no other manner would a democratic government be possible for one single day. [21:438]

Having our own government means a government never strong enough to override by force of arms the wishes of the majority, in other words, a government responsible to public opinion. . . . Self-government means continuous effort to be independent of government control, whether it is foreign government or whether it is national. Swaraj government will be a sorry affair if people look up to it for the regulation of every detail of life. [28:33–34]

The rule of majority has a narrow application, i.e., one should yield to the majority in matters of detail. But it is slavery to be amenable to the majority no matter what its decisions are. . . . Democracy is not a state in which people act like sheep. Under democracy individual liberty of opinion and action is jealously guarded. [22:485]

I have often said that if one takes care of the means, the end will take care of itself. Non-violence is the means, the end for every nation is complete independence. There will be an international League only when all the nations, big or small, composing it are fully independent. The nature of that independence will correspond to the extent of non-violence assimilated by the nations concerned. One thing is certain. In a society based on non-violence, the smallest nation will feel as tall as the tallest. The idea of superiority and inferiority will be wholly obliterated. [68:390]

Mutual love enables Nature to persist. Man does not live by destruction. Self-love compels regard for others. Nations cohere because there is mutual regard among the individuals composing them. Some day we must extend the national law to the universe, even as we have extended the family law to form nations—a larger family. [22:489]

Toward a Purer Social and Economic Life for All

[From M. K. Gandhi, *Collected Works*, unless otherwise attributed]

It is idle to talk of swaraj so long as we do not protect the weak and the helpless, or so long as it is possible for a single swarajist to injure the feelings of any individual. Swaraj means that not a single Hindu or Muslim shall for a moment arrogantly think that he can crush with impunity meek Hindus or Muslims. Unless this condition is fulfilled we will gain swaraj only to lose it the next moment. We are no better than the brutes until we have purged ourselves of the sins we have committed against our weaker brethren.

But I have faith in me still. In the course of my peregrinations in India I have realized that the spirit of kindness of which the poet Tulsidas sings so eloquently, which forms the cornerstone of the Jain and Vaishnava religions, which is the quintessence of the *Bhagavat*[15] and which every verse of the *Gita* is saturated with—this kindness, this love, this charity, is slowly but steadily gaining ground in the hearts of the masses of this country. [19:572]

It has always been a mystery to me how men can feel themselves honoured by the humiliation of their fellow-beings. [39:127]

I do want to attain *moksha.* I do not want to be reborn. But if I have to be reborn, I should be born an untouchable, so that I may share their sorrows, sufferings, and the affronts levelled at them, in order that I may endeavour to free myself and them from that miserable condition. [19:573]

It is wrong, it is sinful, to consider some people lower than ourselves. On God's earth nobody is low and nobody is high. We are all His creatures; and just as in the eyes of parents all their children are absolutely equal, so also in God's eyes all His creatures must be equal. . . . There is no sanction in religion for untouchability. I would, therefore, ask you to give a place in your hearts to all Harijans[16] around you. [56:409]

Everyone, whatever his caste, should have the qualities of all the four castes. The distinctive quality of one's own may predominate in one, but a person altogether devoid of the qualities associated with castes other than his own is no man. The mother who knows how to die for the sake of her child is a Kshatriya [warrior class] woman and the husband who gives up his life to save his wife is a Kshatriya. [21:426]

The idea of superiority and inferiority has to be demolished. The four divisions are not a vertical section, but a horizontal plane on which all stand on a footing of equality, doing the same services respectively assigned to them. . . . In the book of God the same number of marks are assigned to the Brahman that has done his task well as to the bhangi [sweeper of floors or streets] who has done his likewise. [M. E. Jones, *Gandhi Lives*, p. 65]

. . . I do not believe that multiplication of wants and machinery con-trived to supply them is taking the world a single step nearer its goal. . . . I whole-heartedly detest this mad desire to destroy distance and time, to increase animal appetites and go to the ends of the earth in search of their satisfaction. If modern civilization stands for all this, and I have understood it to do so, I call it satanic and with it the present system of Government, its best exponent. . . . The movement of 1920 was designed to show that we could not reform the soulless system by violent means, thus becoming soulless ourselves, but we could do so only by not becoming victims of the system, i.e., by non-co-operation, by saying an emphatic 'No' to every ad-vance made to entrap us into the nets spread by satan. [33:164–65]

Civilization in the real sense of the term, consists not in the multiplica-tion, but in the deliberate and voluntary reduction of wants. [44:103]

The rich have a superfluous store of things which they do not need, and which are therefore neglected and wasted; while millions are starved to death for want of sustenance. If each retained possession only of what he needed, no one would be in want, and all would live in contentment. As it is, the rich are discontented no less than the poor. The poor man would fain become a millionaire, and the millionaire a multi-millionaire. . . . The rich should take the initiative in dispossession with a view to universal diffusion of the spirit of contentment. If only they keep their own property within moderate limits, the starving will be easily fed and will learn the lesson of contentment along with the rich. [44:103]

I do not regard capital to be the enemy of labour. I hold their co-opera-tion to be perfectly possible. . . . My ideal is equal distribution, but so far as I can see, it is not to be realized. I therefore work for equitable distribu-tion. [33:167]

Those who own money now are asked to behave like the trustees holding their riches on behalf of the poor. You may say that trusteeship is a legal fiction. But, if people meditate over it constantly and try to act up to it, then life on earth would be governed far more by love than it is at present.

Absolute trusteeship is an abstraction like Euclid's definition of a point, and is equally unattainable. But if we strive for it, we shall be able to go further in realizing a state of equality on earth than by any other method. . . .

What I would personally prefer would be not a centralization of power in the hands of the State, but an extension of the sense of trusteeship, as, in my opinion, the violence of private ownership is less injurious than the violence of the State. However, if it is unavoidable, I would support a minimum of State ownership. . . .

I look upon an increase of the power of the State with the greatest fear, because, although while apparently doing good by minimizing exploitation, it does the greatest harm to mankind by destroying individuality which lies at the root of all progress. [59:318–19]

I cannot accept benevolent or any other dictatorship. Neither will the rich vanish nor will the poor be protected. Some rich men will certainly be killed out and some poor men will be spoon-fed. As a class the rich will remain, and the poor also, in spite of dictatorship labelled benevolent. The real remedy is non-violent democracy, otherwise spelt true education of all. The rich should be taught the doctrine of stewardship and the poor that of self-help. [72:136]

I have claimed that I was a socialist long before those I know in India had avowed their creed. But my socialism was natural to me and not adopted from any books. It came out of my unshakable belief in non-violence. No man could be actively non-violent and not rise against social injustice, no matter where it occurred. . . . I have always held that social justice, even unto the least and the lowliest, is impossible of attainment by force. I have further believed that it is possible by proper training of the lowliest by non-violent means to secure redress of the wrongs suffered by them. That means is non-violent non-co-operation. [71:424]

Q. What is the difference between your technique and that of the Communists or Socialists for realizing the goal of economic equality?

A. The Socialists and Communists say they can do nothing to bring about economic equality today. They will just carry on propaganda in its favour and to that end they believe in generating and accentuating hatred. They say, "When they get control over the State they will enforce equality." Under my plan the State will be there to carry out the will of the people, not to dictate to them or force them to do its will. I shall bring about economic equality through non-violence, by converting the people to my point of view by harnessing the forces of love as against hatred. I will not wait till I have converted the whole society to my view but will straightaway make a beginning with myself. [83:27]

[To cotton mill workers he had helped to organize:] . . . What though your wages were quadrupled and you had to work only a quarter of the time you are doing now if, notwithstanding, you did not know the value of true speech, if the *rakshasa* [demon] in you injured others and gave the reins to your passions. We must have more wages, we must have less work because we want clean houses, clean bodies, clean minds and a clean soul, and we strive for better wages and less work in the belief that both are essential for this fourfold cleanliness. But if that be not the object to be achieved, it would be a sin to attempt and get better wages and reduce the hours of labour. [17:327]

I claim that even now, though the social structure is not based on a conscious acceptance of non-violence, all the world over mankind lives and men retain their possessions on the sufferance of one another. If they had not done so, only the fewest and the most ferocious would have survived. But such is not the case. Families are bound together by ties of love, and so are groups in the so-called civilised society called nations. Only they do not recognise the supremacy of the law of non-violence. It follows, therefore, that they have not investigated its vast possibilities. . . . I have been pleading for the past fifty years for a conscious acceptance of the law and its zealous practice even in the face of failures. Fifty years' work has shown marvellous results and strengthened my faith. I do claim that by constant practice we shall come to a state of things when lawful possession will command universal and voluntary respect. No doubt such possession will not be tainted. It will not be an insolent demonstration of the inequalities that surround us everywhere. [75:300–1]

In serving those who suffer, one serves God. Discretion should be exercised in this service. There is no reason to believe that one is doing nothing but service by giving grains to the hungry. It is a sin to provide food for an idle person who makes no effort and depends on others for food. It is a meritorious act to provide him with an occupation and, if he refuses to work, to let him starve is to render service to him. [28:384–85]

Q. What is your goal in education when India obtains self-rule?
A. Character-building. I would try to develop courage, strength, virtue, the ability to forget oneself in working towards great aims. This is more important than literacy, academic learning is only a means to this greater end. [Washburne, *Remakers of Mankind*, pp. 104–5]

Satyagraha: Transforming Unjust Relationships Through the Power of the Soul

[From M. K. Gandhi, *Collected Works*, unless otherwise attributed]

Satyagraha[17] is pure soul-force. Truth [*satya*] is the very substance of the soul. That is why this force is called satyagraha. The soul is informed with knowledge. In it burns the flame of love. If someone gives us pain through ignorance, we shall win him through love. . . . Non-violence is a dormant state. In the waking state, it is love. Ruled by love, the world goes on. . . . We are alive solely because of love. We are all ourselves the proof of this. Deluded by modern western civilization, we have forgotten our ancient civilization and worship the might of arms. [13:521]

Non-violence in its dynamic condition means conscious suffering. It does not mean meek submission to the will of the evil-doer, but it means the putting of one's whole soul against the will of the tyrant. Working under this law of our being, it is possible for a single individual to defy the whole might of an unjust empire to save his honour, his religion, his soul and lay the foundation for that empire's fall or its regeneration. [18:133]

Satyagraha has been conceived as a weapon of the strongest and excludes the use of violence in any shape or form. . . . Its root meaning is holding on to truth, hence truth-force. I have also called it love-force or soul-force. In the application of satyagraha, I discovered in the earliest stages that pursuit of truth did not admit of violence being inflicted on one's opponent but that he must be weaned from error by patience and sympathy. For what appears to be truth to the one may appear to be error to the other. And

CONFLICT RESOLUTION

patience means self-suffering. So the doctrine came to mean vindication of truth, not by infliction of suffering on the opponent, but on one's self.

But on the political field, the struggle on behalf of the people mostly consists in opposing error in the shape of unjust laws. When you have failed to bring the error home to the law-giver by way of petitions and the like, the only remedy open to you, if you do not wish to submit to error, is to compel him by physical force to yield to you, or by suffering in your own person by inviting the penalty for the breach of the law. Hence satyagraha largely appears to the public as civil disobedience or civil resistance. It is civil in the sense that it is not criminal. [16:368–69]

Before one can be fit for the practice of civil disobedience one must have rendered a willing and respectful obedience to the State laws. . . . A sa-tyagrahi obeys the laws of society intelligently and of his own free will, because he considers it to be his sacred duty to do so. It is only when a person has thus obeyed the laws of society scrupulously that he is in a position to judge as to which particular rules are good and just and which unjust and iniquitous. Only then does the right accrue to him of the civil disobedience of certain laws in well-defined circumstances. [39:374]

Up to the year 1906 I simply relied on appeal to reason. I was a very industrious reformer. I was a good draftsman, as I always had a close grip of facts which in its turn was the necessary result of my meticulous regard for truth. But I found that reason failed to produce an impression when the critical moment arrived in South Africa. My people were excited—even a worm will and does sometimes turn—and there was talk of wreaking vengeance. I had then to choose between allying myself to violence or finding out some other method of meeting the crisis and stopping the rot, and it came to me that we should refuse to obey legislation that was degrading and let them put us in jail if they liked. Thus came into being the moral equivalent of war. I was then a loyalist, because I implicitly believed that the sum total of the activities of the British Empire was good for India and for humanity. Arriving in England soon after the outbreak of the war, I plunged into it and later when I was forced to go to India as a result of the pleurisy that I had developed, I led a recruiting campaign at the risk of my life, and to the horror of some of my friends. The disillusionment came in 1919 after the passage of the Black Rowlatt Act[18] and the refusal of the Government to give the simple elementary redress of proved wrongs that we had asked for. And so, in 1920, I became a rebel. Since then the conviction has been growing upon me that things of fundamental importance to the people are not secured by reason alone but have to be purchased with their suffering. Suffering is the law of human beings; war is the law of the jungle. But suffering is infinitely more powerful than the law of the jungle for converting the opponent and opening his ears, which are otherwise shut, to the voice of reason. Nobody has probably drawn up more petitions or espoused more forlorn causes than I, and I have come to this fundamental conclusion that if you want something really important to be done you must not merely satisfy the reason, you must move the heart also. The appeal of reason is more to the head but the penetration of the heart comes from suffering. It opens up the inner understanding in man. Suffering is the badge of the human race, not the sword. [48:188–89]

Suffering injury in one's own person is . . . of the essence of non-violence and is the chosen substitute for violence to others. It is not because I value life low that I countenance with joy thousands voluntarily losing their lives for satyagraha, but because I know that it results in the long run in the least loss of life, and what is more, it ennobles those who lose their lives and morally enriches the world for their sacrifice. . . .

I do justify entire non-violence and consider it possible in relations between man and man and nations and nations, but it is not "a resignation from all real fighting against wickedness." On the contrary, the non-violence of my conception is a more active and more real fighting against wickedness than retaliation whose very nature is to increase wickedness. I contemplate a mental and, therefore, a moral opposition to immoralities. I seek entirely to blunt the edge of the tyrant's sword, not by putting up against it a sharper-edged weapon, but by disappointing his expectation that I would be offering physical resistance. The resistance of the soul that I should offer instead would elude him. It would at first dazzle him and at last compel recognition from him which recognition would not humiliate him but would uplift him. [28:305–6]

Satyagraha presupposes self-discipline, self-control, self-purification, and a recognized social status in the person offering it. A satyagrahi must never forget the distinction between evil and the evil-doer. He must not harbour ill will or bitterness against the latter. He may not even employ needlessly offensive language against the evil person, however unrelieved his evil might be. For it should be an article of faith with every satyagrahi that there is none so fallen in this world but can be converted by love. A satyagrahi will always try to overcome evil by good, anger by love, untruth by truth, himsa[19] by ahimsa. There is no other way of purging the world of evil. Therefore a person who claims to be a satyagrahi always tries by close and prayerful self-introspection and self-analysis to find out whether he is himself completely free from the taint of anger, ill will and such other human infirmities, whether he is not himself capable of those very evils against which he is out to lead a crusade. In self-purification and penance lies half the victory of a satyagrahi. A satyagrahi has faith that the silent and undemonstrative action of truth and love produces far more permanent and abiding results than speeches or such other showy performances.

But although satyagraha can operate silently, it requires a certain amount of action on the part of a satyagrahi. A satyagrahi, for instance, must first mobilize public opinion against the evil which he is out to eradicate, by means of a wide and intensive agitation. When public opinion is sufficiently roused against a social abuse even the tallest will not dare to practise or openly to lend support to it. An awakened and intelligent public opinion is the most potent weapon of a satyagrahi. [41:203–4]

Since satyagraha is one of the most powerful methods of direct action, a satyagrahi exhausts all other means before he resorts to satyagraha. He will therefore constantly and continually approach the constituted authority, he will appeal to public opinion, educate public opinion, state his case calmly and coolly before everybody who wants to listen to him, and only after he has exhausted all these avenues will he resort to satyagraha. But when he has found the impelling call of the inner voice within him and launches out upon satyagraha he has burnt his boats and there is no receding. [35:100]

Disobedience to be civil must be sincere, respectful, restrained, never defiant, must be based upon some well-understood principle, must not be capricious and, above all, must have no ill-will or hatred behind it. [17:114]

A satyagrahi bids good-bye to fear. He is, therefore, never afraid of trusting the opponent. Even if the opponent plays him false twenty times, the satyagrahi is ready to trust him the twenty-first time, for an implicit trust in human nature is the very essence of his creed. [29:130]

A satyagrahi never misses, can never miss, a chance of compromise on honourable terms, it being always assumed that, in the event of failure, he is ever ready to offer battle. He needs no previous preparation [to negotiate], his cards are always on the table. [46:7]

The essence of non-violent technique is that it seeks to liquidate antagonisms but not the antagonists themselves. In a non-violent fight you have to a certain measure to conform to the traditions and conventions of the system you are pitted against. Avoidance of all relationship with the opposing power, therefore, can never be a satyagrahi's object, but transformation or purification of that relationship. [69:41]

. . . Immediately we begin to think of things as our opponents think of them we shall be able to do them full justice. I know that this requires a detached state of mind, and is a state very difficult to reach. Nevertheless, for a satyagrahi it is absolutely essential. Three-fourths of all the miseries and misunderstandings in the world will disappear, if we step into the shoes of our adversaries and understand their viewpoint. We will then agree with our adversaries quickly or think of them charitably. [26:271]

. . . It is often forgotten that it is never the intention of a satyagrahi to embarrass the wrong-doer. The appeal is never to his fear; it is, must be, always to his heart. The satyagrahi's object is to convert, not to coerce, the wrong-doer. He should avoid artificiality in all his doings. He acts naturally and from inward conviction. [69:69]

If you want to convert your opponent you must present to him his better and nobler side. Work on, round, upon that side. Do not dangle his faults before him. [Mira, *Gleanings Gathered at Bapu's Feet*, p. 17]

The aim of a satyagrahi . . . always is to put the brute in everyone to sleep. [69:31]

Even a handful of true satyagrahis, well organized and disciplined through selfless service of the masses, can win independence for India, because behind them will be the power of the silent millions. Satyagraha is soul-force. It is subtle and universal in its action. Once it is set in motion it goes

forward with gathering momentum and speed till it bursts through all physical barriers and overspreads the whole world. [69:8]

There is certainty of victory if firmness is combined with gentleness. The
cause is doomed if anger, hatred, ill will, recklessness and finally violence
are to reign supreme. I shall resist them with my life even if I should stand
alone. My goal is friendship with the world and I can combine the greatest
love with the greatest opposition to wrong. [17:76]

Life as a Search for God or Truth

[From M. K. Gandhi, *Collected Works*, unless otherwise attributed]

What I want to achieve—what I have been striving and pining to achieve
these thirty years [since his mid-twenties]—is self-realization, to see God
face to face, to attain *moksha*.[20] I live and move and have my being in
pursuit of this goal. All that I do by way of speaking and writings, and all
my ventures in the political field, are directed to this same end. [39.3]

Seeing God means realization of the fact that God abides in one's heart.
The yearning must persist until one has attained this realization, and will
vanish upon realization. It is with this end in view that we keep observances, and engage ourselves in spiritual endeavour at the Ashram. Realization is the final fruit of constant effort. [50:211]

God is not a person. To affirm that He descends to earth every now and
again in the form of a human being is a partial truth which merely signifies
that such a person lives nearer to God. Inasmuch as God is omnipresent,
He dwells within every human being and all may, therefore, be said to be
incarnations of Him. . . .
   The truth is that God is the force. He is the essence of life. He is pure
and undefiled consciousness. He is eternal. And yet, strangely enough, all
are not able to derive either benefit from or shelter in the all-pervading
living presence.
   Electricity is a powerful force. Not all can benefit from it. It can only be
produced by following certain laws. It is a lifeless force. Man can utilize it
if he labours hard enough to acquire the knowledge of its laws.
   The living force which we call God can similarly be found if we know

and follow His law leading to the discovery of Him in us. But it is self-evident that to find out God's law requires far harder labour. [88:148–49]

He is no God who merely satisfies the intellect, if He ever does. God to be God must rule the heart and transform it. He must express Himself in even the smallest act of His votary. This can only be done through a definite realization more real than the five senses can produce. . . . Where there is realization . . . . it is proved not by extraneous evidence but in the transformed conduct and character of those who have felt the real presence of God within. Such testimony is to be found in the experiences of an unbroken line of prophets and sages in all countries and climes. [37:349]

God is not a Power residing in the clouds. God is an unseen Power residing within us and nearer to us than finger-nails to the flesh. There are many powers lying hidden within us and we discover them by constant struggle. Even so may we find this Supreme Power if we make diligent search with the fixed determination to find Him. One such way is the way of Ahimsa. It is so very necessary because God is in every one of us and, therefore, we have to identify ourselves with every human being without exception. This is called cohesion or attraction in scientific language. In the popular language it is called love. It binds us to one another and to God. [N. K. Bose, Selections from Gandhi, p. 7]

I am endeavouring to see God through service of humanity, for I know that God is neither in heaven, nor down below, but in every one. . . . [Young India, August 4, 1927]

I believe in the immortality of the soul. I would like to give you the analogy of the ocean. The ocean is composed of drops of water; each drop is an entity and yet it is part of the whole, 'the one and the many'. In this ocean of life, we are little drops. My doctrine means that I must identify myself with life, with everything that lives, that I must share the majesty of life in the presence of God. The sum-total of this life is God. [48:180]

We are all sparks of Truth. The sum total of these sparks is [the] indestructible, as-yet-Unknown Truth, which is God. I am being daily led nearer to it by constant prayer. [60:106]

True humility means most strenuous and constant endeavour entirely directed towards the service of humanity. God is continuously in action without resting for a single moment. If we would serve Him or become one with Him, our activity must be as unwearied as His. There may be momentary rest in store for the drop which is separated from the ocean, but not for the drop in the ocean, which knows no rest. The same is the case with ourselves. As soon as we become one with the ocean in the shape of God, there is no more rest for us, nor indeed do we need rest any longer. Our very sleep is action. For we sleep with the thought of God in our hearts. This restlessness constitutes true rest. This never-ceasing agitation holds the key to peace ineffable. [44:206]

God demands nothing less than complete self-surrender as the price for the only real freedom that is worth having. And when a man thus loses himself, he immediately finds himself in the service of all that lives. It becomes his delight and his recreation. He is a new man, never weary of spending himself in the service of God's creation. [38:248]

The world *satya* is derived from *sat*, which means that which is. *Satya* means a state of being. Nothing is or exists in reality except Truth. That is why *sat* or *satya* is the right name for God. In fact it is more correct to say that Truth is God than to say that God is Truth. But as we cannot do without a ruler or general, the name God is and will remain more current. On deeper thinking, however, it will be realized that *sat* or *satya* is the only correct and fully significant name for God. . . .

Devotion to this Truth is the sole justification for our existence. All our activities should be centred in truth. Truth should be the very breath of our life. . . . Generally speaking, [observance of the law of] Truth is understood merely to mean that we must speak the truth. But we in the Ashram should understand the word *satya* or Truth in a much wider sense. There should be Truth in thought, Truth in speech and Truth in action. . . . If we once learn how to apply this never-failing test of Truth, we shall at once be able to find out what is worth doing, what is worth seeing, what is worth reading. [44:40–41]

It is not given to man to know the whole Truth. His duty lies in living up to the truth as he sees it, and, in doing so, to resort to the purest means, i.e., to non-violence. . . . But truth is not to be found in books. Truth resides in every human heart, and one has to search for it there, and to be guided by truth as one sees it. But no one has a right to coerce others to act according to his own view of truth. [56:216]

I am but a humble seeker after Truth and bent upon finding It. I count no sacrifice too great for the sake of seeing God face to face. The whole of my activity, whether it may be called social, political, humanitarian or ethical, is directed to that end. And as I know that God is found more often in the lowliest of His creatures than in the high and mighty, I am struggling to reach the status of these. I cannot do so without their service. Hence my passion for the service of the suppressed classes. And as I cannot render this service without entering politics, I find myself in them. Thus I am no master. I am but a struggling, erring, humble servant of India and therethrough of humanity. [25:117]

Truth, which is God, is ever present, ever working in all beings. Therefore, one should simply live one's life amongst them and serve them according to their needs. . . . It is not for me to interfere with the working of the Spirit. When I am face to face with the [a] man, in proportion as I have God's spirit in me will it go out to him. My purpose is not to give him my religion. My purpose is to let him see God through me if I have Him and express Him in reality in my daily doings. [77:102; and Mira, *Gleanings Gathered at Bapu's Feet,* pp. 20–21]

As I am nearing the end of my earthly life, I can say that purity of life is the highest and truest art. The art of producing good music from a cultivated voice can be achieved by many, but the art of producing that music from the harmony of a pure life is achieved very rarely. [66:357]

NOTES

1. Translated from Prabhudas Gandhi, *Jīvannu parodh,* p. 23.
2. M. K. Gandhi, *Collected Works* (2d ed.), 1:51.
3. *Ibid.,* 39:74.
4. *Ibid.,* 39:125.
5. Bolitho, *Jinnah, Creator of Pakistan,* p. 84.
6. Fischer, *Gandhi, His Life and Message,* p. 103.
7. M. K. Gandhi, *Collected Works,* 44:41.

8. Pyarelal, *Mahatma Gandhi—The Last Phase*, 2:409.
9. Sengupta, *Sarojini Naidu*, p. 328.
10. *Ahiṁsā:* not harming, or intending to harm, any living being. Gandhi expanded the meaning of this ancient concept of nonviolence by adding to it the path of selfless love and service to others.
11. The warrior's path of duty.
12. World War I.
13. Assembly headed by a committee of elected elders, ideally five in number.
14. *Svarāj:* literally, "self-rule." To this term, popularized by Tilak and meaning national self-government, Gandhi gave the additional meaning of individual self-control.
15. The *Bhāgavata Purāṇa.*
16. "The people of God"—the name Gandhi gave to the Untouchables of India.
17. Gandhi coined this word from two Sanskrit ones: *satya* ("the Real," "the Genuine"), which he translated into English as Truth or God; and *agraha* ("holding firmly"). A person who practices *satyāgraha* is a *satyāgrahī*—one who holds firmly to, and aligns every thought, word, and deed with the moral and spiritual Reality that is the soul's essence. Sustained by the power of this Reality, the *satyāgrahī* seeks to awaken others to its presence in themselves, especially when they are acting unjustly or immorally.
18. Enacted by the Government of India to continue its wartime powers to imprison suspected persons without trial or release on bond.
19. *Hiṁsa:* doing or wishing injury or harm to another living being.
20. *Mokṣa:* liberation of the soul from further incarnations. See vol. 1, chapter 11.

Chapter 7

OTHER NATIONALIST LEADERS IN THE DECADES BEFORE INDEPENDENCE

Although Gandhi became the leader who was first in the hearts of his countrymen, other leaders and thinkers won the support of growing numbers of Indians in the decades preceding independence. The spread of education in English, foreign travel, and the growth of newspaper, magazine, and book publishing brought closer the world outside India. Muslims became highly interested in events in the rest of the Islamic world and, to protest the treatment of the sultan of the defeated Ottoman Empire, joined the non-cooperation movement under Gandhi's leadership. The collapse of that alliance left them politically adrift and divided. Young Hindu leaders as well, freshly returned from higher education and travel in Europe, infused a variety of new ideals into the discussion of India's future. As the new blended with the old, and the foreign with the indigenous, the political pot grew steadily hotter. It became increasingly important to decide what group, and what philosophy of government, should succeed to the imperial power and its authoritarian rule when India became once more independent of foreign domination.

This chapter presents the views of six thinkers—five of whom were also active political leaders—from three major provinces of preindependent India: Rabindranath Tagore and Subhas Chandra Bose from Bengal, Vinayak Savarkar and B. R. Ambedkar from Maharashtra, Jawaharlal Nehru from the United Provinces (later renamed Uttar Pradesh), and Manabendra Nath Roy, an expatriate Bengali. None of them totally agreed with Gandhi: Tagore and Nehru most appreciated his virtues; Savarkar and Roy attacked him most bitterly; Bose openly challenged his leadership of the Congress; and a disciple of Savarkar assassinated him. All were of one accord in wanting the British to leave India to govern itself, and all assumed that when that happened India would remain united.

Like Gandhi, all six men were fluent in English and absorbed ways and ideas from Western sources that reinforced various Indian traditions, or that promised to help solve India's problems. With Tagore, the synthesis begun with his father, Debendranath, and the Brahmo Samaj, was deepened both with studies of ancient and medieval Indian philosophy and literature and with numerous trips to Europe, America, and East Asia. Savarkar grew up steeped in the martial traditions of the Maratha regions and the militant nationalism of Tilak to which he added the skills in bomb-making and assassination learned in London from Russian and Irish revolutionaries. Roy found in Marxist-Leninist ideas and methods a more impressive path to revolution than the terrorist methods he had been using in Bengal, though he later rejected those ideas in favor of a more humane and open-minded philosophy consistent with materialist thought in India. Bose admired, and finally sought support from, the authoritarian governments of Italy, Germany, and Japan in his impatience to achieve independence for India. And Nehru fervently believed democratic socialism would be the cure for India's economic and political ills.

The sixth leader in this chapter spoke from a very different point of view on India's future as an independent nation. He was Dr. B. R. Ambedkar, a distinguished lawyer who was a member of one of the low-status groups often referred to as "Untouchables." Ambedkar wanted to give these groups, which were both economically and socially oppressed, a political role separate from that of the Hindu majority. He did not, as did some of his Muslim contemporaries, advocate a separate nation for his people.

As in Ireland under British rule and Poland under Russian, in India during its last three decades under foreign rule, most of the leading spokesmen for political, social, and economic aspirations were drawn from the elites of earlier times. Four of the six leaders quoted here were brāhmans (in 1921, brāhmans represented 6 percent of the population of the British-ruled provinces), and another belonged to a caste nearly as high in social standing. In addition to excellent education (all but Tagore and Roy held college degrees and spent some years studying in England), they enjoyed greater leisure than have their counterparts since independence. (It generally takes less time to oppose a government than to administer one.) Savarkar, Roy, Bose, and Nehru all spent years in jail, time they used well to examine and to express their views. The thoughts these six men articulated, and the active lives they led, left models for later generations to consider, and to emulate or reject.

RABINDRANATH TAGORE: POET, EDUCATOR, AND INDIA'S AMBASSADOR TO THE WORLD

The fourteenth of Maharshi Debendranath Tagore's fifteen children, Rabindranath Tagore (1861–1941) grew to manhood in a highly cultured family environment. A number of his brothers and sisters were artistically inclined—one composed music, another staged amateur theatricals, and several contributed to the literary magazine edited by their eldest brother, who was also a philosopher. The venerable Debendranath gave special attention to his youngest son's education and, after investing him with the brahmanical sacred thread, took him on an extended pilgrimage to Amritsar and the Himalayas. Rabindranath's religious views were decisively shaped by his father's influence.

A steady income from the family's landed estates freed Rabindranath of the necessity of earning his own livelihood, and he was allowed to give up formal studies at the age of thirteen. Living at home, he began to experiment with writing verse. Encouraged by his older siblings, he went on to win renown at twenty with his first volume of Bengali poems—Bankim Chandra Chatterjee himself hailing their appearance. Year after year his writing matured in style and grew richer in content. Translating into English from the devotional poems written after the death of his wife and three of his five children, he published in 1912 the collection entitled Gītāñjali (Song Offerings). A year later the world was startled to hear that he had been awarded the Nobel Prize for Literature. Educated India went wild with excitement, sensing that Rabindranath had vindicated Indian culture in the eyes of the West. As for the poet, he is said to have cried, "I shall never have any peace again."[1]

Although his prediction proved correct, the ceaseless activity in which he spent the rest of his life was mostly of his own making. He had already founded a school at Shantiniketan, the rural retreat where his father used to pass days in meditation. He now began to develop there a center of Indian culture, where all the creative and performing arts could thrive in a new birth. In 1921, as a crowning step in his educational work, Tagore opened his Vishva-Bharati[2] University at Shantiniketan, dedicating it to his ideal of world brotherhood and cultural interchange.

Like his father, Rabindranath loved to travel, and he seldom refused the many invitations that came to him from all parts of the world. In addition to many tours within India, he lectured on five occasions in the United States, five times in Europe, three times in Japan, and once each in China, South America, Soviet Russia, and Southeast Asia. He made good use of his opportunities to address important audiences by denouncing—especially after the First World War—the evils of nationalism and materialism. Mankind could only save itself from destruction, he declared, by a return to the spiritual values that permeate all religions. Asia, the home of the world's great faiths, lay under a special obligation to lead this religious revival, and to India, the home of both Hinduism and Buddhism, belonged the mission of reawakening herself, Asia, and the world. Although this message, like that of Vivekananda, stressed India's role as spiritual teacher to mankind, Tagore never tired of reminding his countrymen that they also needed to learn from the West's vitality and dedicated search for truth.

Through an irony of fate, this preacher of the complementary relationship between Asian and Western cultures returned from a triumphant European tour in 1921 to find Gandhi leading a mass movement of noncooperation with every aspect of British influence in India, including the prevailing form of English education. Rabindranath publicly opposed the Mahatma and was accordingly accused of taking an "unpatriotic" position. He had already been virtually ostracized for his withdrawal in 1908 from Bengal politics in disgust at the extremist violence of the antipartition agitation. On both occasions he bore his isolation stoically and without yielding his ground, much like the great Bengali he considered his spiritual kinsman—Rammohun Roy. Although the intellectual gulf between Tagore and Gandhi was never bridged, the two remained friends and visited one another—most dramatically in 1932 when Tagore sat by the bedside of Gandhi as the latter ended his fast against separating the Untouchables from the main body of the Hindu electorate. When he visited Shantiniketan after the poet's death, Gandhi remarked, "I started with a disposition to detect a conflict between Gurudev [the godlike teacher, as Tagore's disciples called him] and myself, but ended with the glorious discovery that there was none."[3]

Jawaharlal Nehru, who admired both men greatly (perhaps because they served as models for the two sides of his own personality) once wrote: "Tagore was primarily the man of thought, Gandhi of concentrated and ceaseless activity. Both, in their different ways, had a world outlook, and both were at the same time wholly India. They seemed to represent different but harmonious aspects of India and to complement one another.[4]

Shy and aloof, Tagore was able to look more dispassionately on the events of his time than those who hurled themselves into the struggle against British rule. Reversing Tilak's dictum that social reform diverted and divided the movement for independence, Tagore held (as did Gandhi) that the clamor for political rights distracted men from more fundamental tasks such as erasing caste barriers, reconciling Hindus and Muslims, uplifting the poor and helpless villagers, and liberating men's minds and bodies from a host of self-made but unnecessary burdens.

Right down to his eightieth year, Tagore never lost his childlike wonderment at the variety and beauty of the creation and he expressed his delight with life in a ceaseless outpouring of poetry, prose, drama, and song. By making the speech of the common people the medium for his masterly style, he revolutionized and revitalized Bengali literature. His interests, although basically aesthetic, were truly universal; in his seventies he wrote a textbook on elementary science that explained the theory of relativity and the working of the solar system. In an age of growing xenophobia he sought to keep India's windows open on the world. For his creativity, his breadth of vision, and his zeal in championing man's freedom from arbitrary restraints—whether social, political or religious—Tagore deserves comparison with the great artists and thinkers of Renaissance Europe.

To The Supreme Leader of the Minds of All People

In 1912, indignant at the request that he contribute a song honoring King George V on his visit to India for his coronation as the country's "King-Emperor," Tagore composed a hymn in praise of God, as India's real Lord. After independence, the hymn's first verse was adopted as India's national anthem, "Jana, Gana, Mana." In 1971, another of his songs, "Amār sonar Banglā" ("Our Golden Bengal") became the national anthem of the new nation of Bangladesh.

[From "Bhāratavidhātā," in *Sanchayitā*, p. 727, trans. by Stephen Hay and Sanjit K. Mitra, after Tagore, *Collected Poems and Plays*, p. 68]

Supreme Leader of the minds of all people, glory to thee,
    Ruler of India's destiny!
Punjab, Sind, Gujarat, Maharashtra, Dravida, Orissa, Bengal,

The Vindyas, Himalayas, Jamuna, and Ganga,
    The waves of the swelling ocean,
All awaken sounding thy auspicious name,
    Praying for thy fruitful blessing,
    And singing of thy glory.
Giver of the people's good fortune, glory to thee,
    Ruler of India's destiny!
Glory to thee, glory to thee, glory to thee,
    Glory, glory, glory, glory to thee.

Where the Mind Is Without Fear

In one of the hundred-odd poems that comprise his 1912 volume *Gītāñjali,* Tagore listed in a rising crescendo his ambitions for his native land. As with all English translations of his poetry (including those he did himself) much of the beauty of the original Bengali is lost here.

[From Tagore, *Collected Poems and Plays,* p. 16]

Where the mind is without fear and the head is held high;
Where knowledge is free;
Where the world has not been broken up into fragments by narrow do-
    mestic walls;
Where words come out from the depth of truth;
Where tireless striving stretches its arms towards perfection;
Where the clear stream of reason has not lost its way into the dreary
    desert sand of dead habit;
Where the mind is led forward by thee into everwidening thought and
    action—
Into that heaven of freedom, my Father, let my country awake.

The Renunciation of Renunciation

Tagore renounced the ancient yogic traditions of gradual withdrawal from the delights (and pains) of the senses and urged his countrymen to abandon the correlative
theory that the world our senses gives us knowledge of is *māyā* (illusion).

[From Tagore, *Gitāñjalī,* trans. in Chakravarty, ed., *A Tagore Reader,* p.
305, and Tagore, *Sonār Tarī* (The Golden Boat), trans. in Kripalani,
Rabindranath Tagore, p. 164]

Deliverance is not for me in renunciation. I feel the embrace of freedom
in a thousands bonds of delight.
Thou ever pourest for me the fresh draught of thy wine of various colors
and fragrance, filling this earthen vessel to the brim.
My world will light its hundred different lamps with thy flame and place
them before the altar of thy temple.
No, I will never shut the doors of my senses. The delights of sight and
hearing and touch will bear thy delight.
Yes, all my illusions will burn into illumination of joy, and all my desires
ripen into fruits of love.

.   .   .   .

Alas, my cheerless country, dressed in worn-out rags, loaded with decrepit
wisdom, you pride yourself on your subtlety in having seen through the
fraud of creation. Sitting idly in your corner, all you do is to sharpen the
edge of your metaphysical mumbo jumbo and dismiss as unreal this boundless, star-studded sky and this great, big earth whose lap has nurtured myriad forms of life, age after age. Millions of living beings make up the vast
fair of this world and you, unbelieving dotard, ignore it all as a child's play.

Thoughts on the Future of Humanity

In a lecture delivered during a tour of the United States in the autumn of 1916,
Tagore noted the opportunities for transcending the barriers raised by nation-states,
as well as the dangers of greed, hatred, armaments, and pollution.

[From Tagore, *Nationalism*, pp. 98–99, 100–2, 109–10]

This problem of race unity which we [in India] have been trying to solve
for so many years has likewise to be faced by you here in America. Many
people in this country ask me what is happening as to the caste distinctions
in India. But when this question is asked me, it is usually done with a
superior air. And I feel tempted to put the same question to our American
critics with a slight modification, "What have you done with the Red Indian and the Negro?" For you have not got over your attitude of caste
toward them. . . .

In finding the solution of our problems we shall have helped to solve the
world problem as well. What India has been [in its disunity], the whole

world is now. The whole world is becoming one country through scientific facility. And the moment is arriving when you also must find a basis of unity which is not political. If India can offer to the world her solution, it will be a contribution to humanity. There is only one history—the history of man. All national histories are merely chapters in the larger one. And we are content in India to suffer for such a great cause. . . .

The most important fact of the present age is that all the different races of men have come close together. And again we are confronted with two alternatives. The problem is whether the different groups of peoples shall go on fighting with one another or find out some true basis of reconciliation and mutual help; whether it will be interminable competition or co-operation.

I have no hesitation in saying that those who are gifted with the moral power of love and vision of spiritual unity, who have the least feeling of enmity against aliens, and the sympathetic insight to place themselves in the position of others, will be the fittest to take their permanent place in the age that is lying before us, and those who are constantly developing their instinct of fight and intolerance of aliens will be eliminated. . . .

The first impulse of this change of circumstances has been the churning up of man's baser passions of greed and cruel hatred. If this persists indefinitely, and armaments go on exaggerating themselves to unimaginable absurdities, and machines and storehouses envelop this fair earth with their dirt and smoke and ugliness, then it will end in a conflagration of suicide. Therefore man will have to exert all his power of love and clarity of vision to make another great moral adjustment which will comprehend the whole world of men and not merely the fractional groups of nationality. The call has come to every individual in the present age to prepare himself and his surroundings for this dawn of a new era, when man shall discover his soul in the spiritual unity of all human beings.

If it is given at all to the West to struggle out of these tangles of the lower slopes to the spiritual summit of humanity then I cannot but think that it is the special mission of America to fulfill this hope of God and man. . . .

I have great faith in human nature, and I think the West will find its true mission. I speak bitterly of Western civilization when I am conscious that it is betraying its trust and thwarting its own purpose. The West must not make herself a curse to the world by using her power for her own selfish needs, but, by teaching the ignorant and helping the weak, she should save herself from the worst danger that the strong is liable to incur by making the feeble acquire power enough to resist her intrusion. And also she must not make her materialism to be the final thing, but must realize that she is doing a service in freeing the spiritual being from the tyranny of matter.

Gandhi versus Truth

On his return from a lecture tour in Europe and the United States in 1921, Tagore found many parts of India aflame with the Gandhi-led movement of noncooperation with British institutions. Much as he admired Gandhi and his ideals, he became alarmed by the narrowness of his vision of the path to swaraj (national independence). After a personal talk between the two at Tagore's Calcutta house failed to resolve their differences, Tagore publicly criticized Gandhi's call for all to spin, burn foreign-made clothing, and to turn away from the life of the mind.

[From Tagore, "The Call of Truth," in *Modern Review* 30(4):429–32]

The Mahatma has won the heart of India with his love; for that we have all acknowledged his sovereignty. He has given us a vision of the shakti[5] of truth; for that our gratitude to him is unbounded. We read about truth in books: we talk about it: but it is indeed a red-letter day, when we see it face to face. Rare is the moment, in many a long year, when such good fortune happens. We can make and break Congresses every other day. It is at any time possible for us to stump the country preaching politics in English. But the golden rod which can awaken our country in Truth and Love is not a thing which can be manufactured by the nearest goldsmith. To the wielder of that rod our profound salutation! But if, having seen truth, our belief in it is not confirmed, what is the good of it all? Our mind must acknowledge the truth of the intellect, just as our heart does the truth of love. No Congress or other outside institution succeeded in touching the heart of India. It was roused only by the touch of love. Having had such a clear vision of this wonderful power of Truth, are we to cease to believe in it, just where the attainment of *Swaraj* is concerned? Has the truth, which was needed in the process of awakenment, to be got rid of in the process of achievement? . . .

From our master, the Mahatma—may our devotion to him never grow less!—we must learn the truth of love in all its purity, but the science and art of building up *swaraj* is a vast subject. Its pathways are difficult to traverse and take time. For this task, aspiration and emotion must be there, but no less must study and thought be there likewise. For it, the economist must think, the mechanic must labor, the educationist and statesman must teach and contrive. In a word, the mind of the country must exert itself in all directions. Above all, the spirit of inquiry throughout the whole country must be kept intact and untrammelled, its mind not made timid or inactive by compulsion, open or secret.

We know from past experience that it is not any and every call to which the country responds. It is because no one has yet been able to unite in Yoga all the forces of the country in the work of its creation, that so much time has been lost over and over again. And we have been kept waiting and waiting for him who has the right and the power to make the call upon us. In the old forests of India, our gurus, in the fullness of their vision of the Truth had sent forth such a call saying: "As the rivers flow on their downward course, as the months flow on to the year, so let all seekers after truth come from all sides." The initiation into Truth of that day has borne fruit, undying to this day, and the voice of its message still rings in the ears of the world.

Why should not our Guru of today, who would lead us on the paths of Karma, send forth such a call? Why should he not say: "Come ye from all sides and be welcome. Let all the forces of the land be brought into action, for then alone shall the country awake. Freedom is in complete awakening, in full self-expression." God has given the Mahatma the voice that can call, for in him there is the Truth. Why should this not be our long-awaited opportunity?

But his call came to one narrow field alone. To one and all he simply says: Spin and weave, spin and weave. Is this the call: "Let all seekers after truth come from all sides"? Is this the call of the New Age to new creation? When nature called to the bee to take refuge in the narrow life of the hive, millions of bees responded to it for the sake of efficiency, and accepted the loss of sex in consequence. But this sacrifice by way of self-atrophy led to the opposite of freedom. Any country, the people of which can agree to become neuters for the sake of some temptation, or command, carries within itself its own prison-house. To spin is easy, therefore for all men it is an imposition hard to bear. The call to the ease of mere efficiency is well enough for the Bee. The wealth of power that is Man's can only become manifest when his utmost is claimed.

Sparta tried to gain strength by narrowing herself down to a particular purpose, but she did not win. Athens sought to attain perfection by opening herself out in all her fullness—and she did win. Her flag of victory still flies at the masthead of man's civilization. It is admitted that European military camps and factories are stunting man, that their greed is cutting man down to the measure of their own narrow purpose, that for these reasons joylessness darkly lowers over the West. But if man be stunted by big machines, the danger of his being stunted by small machines must not be lost sight of. The charkha[6] in its proper place can do no harm, but will rather do much good. But where, by reason of failure to acknowledge the differences in man's temperament, it is in the wrong place, there thread can only be spun at the cost of a great deal of the mind itself. Mind is no less valuable than cotton thread. . . .

The command to burn our foreign clothes has been laid on us. I, for one, am unable to obey it. Firstly, because I conceive it to be my very first duty to put up a valiant fight against this terrible habit of blindly obeying orders, and this fight can never be carried on by our people being driven from one injunction to another. Secondly, I feel that the clothes to be burnt are not mine, but belong to those who most sorely need them. If those who are going naked should have given us the mandate to burn, it would, at least, have been a case of self-immolation and the crime of incendiarism would not lie at our door. But how can we expiate the sin of the forcible destruction of clothes which might have gone to women whose nakedness is actually keeping them prisoners, unable to stir out of the privacy of their homes?

I have said repeatedly and must repeat once more that we cannot afford to lose our mind for the sake of any external gain. Where Mahatma Gandhi has declared war against the tyranny of the machine which is oppressing the whole world, we are all enrolled under his banner. But we must refuse to accept as our ally the illusion-haunted, magic-ridden, slave-mentality that is at the root of all the poverty and insult under which our country groans. Here is the enemy itself, on whose defeat alone *Swaraj* within and without can come to us.

The time, moreover, has arrived when we must think of one thing more, and that is this. The awakening of India is a part of the awakening of the world. The door of the New Age has been flung open at the trumpet blast of a great war. We have read in the *Mahābhārata* how the day of self-revelation had to be preceded by a year of retirement. The same has happened in the world today. Nations had attained nearness to each other without being aware of it, that is to say, the outside fact was there, but it had not penetrated into the mind. At the shock of the war, the truth of it stood revealed to mankind. The foundation of modern, that is Western, civilization was shaken; and it has become evident that the convulsion is neither local nor temporary, but has traversed the whole earth and will last until the shocks between man and man, which have extended from continent to continent, can be brought to rest, and a harmony be established.

From now onward, any nation which takes an isolated view of its own country will run counter to the spirit of the New Age, and know no peace. From now onward, the anxiety that each country has for its own safety must embrace the welfare of the world.

Gandhi: "The Best of Men" in the New Age

As the years passed, Tagore became a firm supporter of the man he had been one of the first to call *mahātmā*. In his 1937 tribute, he interpreted Gandhi as a true follower of the teachings of Jesus.

[From Tagore, "Mahatma Gandhi," in his *Boundless Sky*, pp. 330–31]

As before, the genius of India has taken from her aggressors the most spiritually significant principle of their culture and fashioned of it a new message of hope for mankind. There is in Christianity the great doctrine that God became man in order to save humanity by taking the burden of its sin and suffering on Himself, here in this very world, not waiting for the next. That the starving must be fed, the ragged clad, has been emphasized by Christianity as no other religion has done. Charity, benevolence, and the like, no doubt have an important place in the religions of our country as well, but there they are in practice circumscribed within much narrower limits, and are only partially inspired by love of man. To our great good fortune, Gandhiji was able to receive this teaching of Christ in a living way. It was fortunate that he . . . should have found in Tolstoy a teacher who realized the value of non-violence through the multifarious experience of his own life's struggles. For it was this great gift from Europe that our country had all along been awaiting.

In the Middle Ages also we had received gifts from Muslim sources. Dadu, Kabir and other saints had proclaimed that purity and liberation are not for being hoarded up in any temple, but are wealth to which all humanity is entitled. We should have no hesitation in admitting freely that this message was inspired by contact with Islam. The best of men always accept the best of teaching, whenever and wherever it may be found, in religion, moral culture, or in the lives of individuals. But the Middle Ages are past, and we have stepped into a New Age. And now the best of men, Mahatma Gandhi, has come to us with this best of gifts from the West.

But though Christ declared that the meek shall inherit the earth, Christians now aver that victory is to the strong, the aggressive. And no wonder. For the doctrine seemed on the face of it absurd and contrary to the principles of Natural History as interpreted by Western scientists. It needed another prophet to vindicate the truth of this paradox and interpret 'meekness' as the positive force of love and righteousness, as *satyāgraha*. This meekness is not submission, or mere passive endurance of wrong or injustice: such submission would be cowardly and would imply co-operation, even though involuntary, with the power of tyranny. But Gandhiji has made of this meekness or *ahimsā*, the highest form of bravery, a perpetual challenge to the insolence of the strong.

Symphony

In this poem, written in his eightieth year, Tagore acknowledged that his love of nature and the fame he had won had kept him from giving voice to the experiences of the peasant, the weaver, and the fisherman. (The original Bengali poem is composed of rhymed couplets of various meters.)

["Oikatān," trans. by Amalendu Das Gupta in Tagore, *One Hundred and One Poems*, pp. 172–73, and slightly amended here]

How little I know of this great big world.
Of towns and cities in diverse lands, of man's varied deeds, of rivers and
seas, deserts and mountains, of strange animals and unfamiliar trees—
so much has remained beyond my ken.
Amid the world's immensity, my mind occupies but a tiny corner. Stung
by this awareness, I collect with ceaseless ardour words and images
from tales of travel, and try to fill up the store of my meagre knowledge with riches I have begged from others.

I am a poet of the earth. I strive that all its sounds shall seek expression
in my flute, and yet there are many gaps. Many notes have failed to
find their way to this music making.
The earth's great symphony has often in silent moments filled my life
through images and hints.

The unheard song that inaccessible snowy mountains sing to the silent blue of the heavens has again and again moved my heart. The unknown star over the South Pole that keeps its long vigil in utter loneliness has at midnight hours touched my sleepless eyes with ineffable light. The violent, surging waterfall has sent from afar its voice to the depth of my mind.

Poets from many lands pour their songs into Nature's symphonic stream. I have this link with all of them: I enjoy their company, partake of their joy, receive the blessing of the Muse and a taste of the music of the universe.

Most inaccessible of all is man, hidden behind his own self, and with no measure in time and space. He has an inner life that is revealed only through a communion of minds. Barred by the fences I have raised, I do not always find an entry into that secret world.

The peasant tills the field, the weaver works his loom, the fisherman casts his net—their varied work extends far and wide and the world moves on their support.

I live in a small corner in the perpetual exile of prestige, seated by a narrow window of society's high platform. Sometimes I have ventured near their homes but have lacked the courage to enter.

Without a meeting of lives the store of songs can collect only false merchandise. So I accept the blame and admit the incompleteness of my tunes. I know that my poetry, though it has wandered on many paths, has yet not found its way everywhere.

I wait for the message of the poet who is close to the soil, who shares the peasant's life and becomes his kin through word and action.

Forever do I look for what I myself cannot give to poetry's joyful feast. But let the gift be real and not merely tempting to the eye. It is not good to steal a literary badge, to acquire a name without paying the price. False, false, is such fashionable love for the labourer.

Come, poet of mute, obscure men, give voice to their hidden sorrow, fill with life and joy this dry, songless land, release the spring hidden in its heart.

Let there be honour also for those who in the court of the Muse play one-stringed harps in the orchestra. Let us listen to those who are wordless in sorrow and joy, who stand silent and humble before the world, who live near us and yet remain unknown.

If you be their kin, let your renown make them known! I shall offer you salutations again and again.

VINAYAK DAMODAR SAVARKAR:
HINDU NATIONALIST

The tradition of extremist Hindu nationalism begun by Tilak, Aurobindo, and Lajpat Rai was continued and given a more virulent, anti-Muslim form by Vinayak Damodar Savarkar (1883–1966). Born a Chitpāvan brāhman like his fellow-Maharashtrians Ranade, Gokhale, and Tilak, Savarkar was the second son of a landowner known for both his Sanskrit scholarship and his Western-style education. Two incidents from his youth presaged his lifelong antipathy to those he considered Hinduism's foes. At the age of ten, hearing of bloody Hindu-Muslim riots in the United Provinces, he led a gang of his schoolmates in a stone-throwing attack on the village mosque. At sixteen, his anger at the hanging of two Maharashtrian terrorists made him vow to devote his life to driving the British out of India.

On entering Fergusson College at Poona, Savarkar quickly organized a patriotic society among his fellow students. Through poems, articles, and speeches, he reminded them of India's glorious past and the need to regain her freedom. In 1905 he arranged for a huge bonfire of foreign cloth and persuaded Tilak to speak to the crowd gathered around it. For this he was rusticated from his college. With Tilak's help, however, he secured from an Indian patriot in London a scholarship to study there, on the understanding that he would never enter government service.

From 1906 to 1910, in the guise of a student of law, the young Savarkar bearded the British lion in its den. His "New India" group learned the art of bomb-making from a Russian revolutionary in Paris and planned the assassination of the hated Lord Curzon. One member of the group electrified London when he shot and killed an important official of the India Office and then went proudly to the gallows. Savarkar himself was arrested a few months later, but by this time he had already published his nationalistic interpretation of the 1857–1858 rebellion, entitling it *The First Indian War of Independence of 1857.*

When the ship carrying him back to India for trial stopped at Marseilles, Savarkar created an international incident by swimming ashore and claiming asylum on French soil. The Hague International Tribunal ultimately judged his recapture by the British authorities irregular but justifiable, but by this time he had already been twice sentenced to life-imprisonment. In 1911 Savarkar was transported to the Andaman Islands (India's "Devil's

Island" in the tropical Bay of Bengal) where he found his elder brother, a renowned terrorist, already there before him.

Agitation in India secured his release from confinement in 1924, but until 1937 his movements were restricted and he was forbidden to take part in politics. Nehru, Bose, and Roy all sent him congratulatory messages on his final return to the political arena, and the Hindu Mahasabha (Great Assembly of Hindus, founded in 1919 and the largest Hindu communal party), elected him as their president for seven consecutive years, until failing health forced him to resign.

Intending to unite and strengthen all Hindudom, Savarkar advocated the removal of intercaste barriers, the entry of Untouchables into orthodox temples, and the reconversion of Hindus who had become Muslims or Christians. During the Second World War he propagated the slogan: "Hinduize all politics and militarize Hindudom," and urged Hindus to enlist in the armed forces in order to learn the arts of war.

Savarkar and Gandhi had disagreed from the time of their discussions in London in 1909 (discussions that may have helped to provoke the latter to write his famous *Hind Swarāj*, a pamphlet denouncing the evils of modern civilization). Savarkar now made no bones about his conviction that Gandhi's doctrine of nonviolence was "absolutely sinful."[7] As the fateful hour of independence from British rule drew near, Savarkar and the Mahasabha strenuously opposed the Muslim League's demand for Pakistan. Gandhi's apparent vacillation on this issue and his postpartition fasts for the protection of India's Muslims and for goodwill toward Pakistan infuriated many of Savarkar's followers. Early in 1948 one of them, to avenge what he felt was Gandhi's betrayal of the Hindu cause, felled him with three pistol shots.

The assassin, N. V. Godse, although no longer a member of the Mahasabha, was still known as a devoted lieutenant of Savarkar, who consequently had to stand trial with him. Acquitted because of lack of evidence linking him to the crime itself, but too ill to lead an active life, Savarkar returned under a cloud to his home in Bombay. In the 1950s he made speeches urging military preparedness and other causes, and until the last year of his life he issued statements and wrote books and articles.

The theory of Hindu national solidarity and political dominance Savarkar evolved continued after independence to animate such organizations as the Rashtriya Swayamsevak Sangh ("National Assembly of Volunteers") and the Bharatiya Jan Sangh ("All-India People's League"). Although greatly overshadowed by the Congress Party, their appeal to patriotic, moral, and religious sentiments has given them considerable influence on the Indian political scene.

The Glories of the Hindu Nation

Deprived of writing materials during his days of imprisonment, Savarkar scratched on the whitewashed walls of his cell and then committed to memory the notes for his treatise on *Hindutva* ("Hindu-ness"). In the final portion of this work, published in 1923, he exultantly cited the geographical, racial, cultural, numerical, and religious ways in which the Hindu nation is superior to all other polities.

[From Savarkar, *Hindutva*, pp. 108–16]

So far we have not allowed any consideration of utility to prejudice our inquiry. But having come to its end it will not be out of place to see how far the attributes, which we found to be the essentials of *Hindutva*, contribute toward [the] strength, cohesion, and progress of our people. Do these essentials constitute a foundation so broad, so deep, so strong, that basing upon it the Hindu people can build a future which can face and repel the attacks of all the adverse winds that blow; or does the Hindu race stand on feet of clay?

Some of the ancient nations raised huge walls so as to convert a whole country into a fortified castle. Today their walls are trodden to dust or are but scarcely discernible by a few scattered mounds here and there; while the people they were meant to protect are not discernible at all! Our ancient neighbors, the Chinese, labored from generation to generation and raised a rampart, embracing the limits of an empire—so wide, so high, so strong—a wonder of human world. That too, as all human wonders must, sank under its own weight. But behold the ramparts of Nature! Have they not, these Himalayas, been standing there as one whose desires are satisfied—so they seemed to the Vedic bard—so they seem to us today. These are *our* ramparts that have converted this vast continent into a cosy castle.

You take up buckets and fill your trenches with water and call it [a] moat. Behold, Varuna[8] himself, with his one hand pushing continents aside, fills the gap by pouring seas on seas with the other! This Indian ocean, with its bays and gulfs, is *our* moat.

These are our frontier lines bringing within our reach the advantages of an inland as well as an insular country.

She is the richly endowed daughter of God—this our Motherland. Her rivers are deep and perennial. Her land is yielding to the plow and her fields are loaded with golden harvests. Her necessaries of life are few and a genial nature yields them all almost for the asking. Rich in her fauna, rich in her flora, she knows she owes it all to the immediate source of light and heat— the sun. She covets not the icy lands; blessed be they and their frozen latitudes. If heat is at times "enervating" here, cold is at times benumbing there. If cold induces manual labor, heat removes much of its very necessity. She takes more delight in quenched thirst than in the parched throat. Those who have not, let them delight in exerting to have. But those who have—may be allowed to derive pleasure from the very fact of having. Father Thames is free to work at feverish speed, wrapped in his icy sheets. She loves to visit her ghats and watch her boats gliding down the Ganges, on her moonlit waters. With the plow, the peacocks, the lotus, the elephant, and the *Gītā*, she is willing to forego, if that must be, whatever advantage the colder latitudes enjoy. She knows she cannot have all her own way. Her gardens are green and shady, her granaries well stocked, her waters crystal, her flowers scented, her fruits juicy, and her herbs healing. Her brush is dipped in the colors of dawn and her flute resonant with the music of Gokul.[9] Verily Hind is the richly endowed daughter of God.

Neither the English nor the French—with the exception of [the] Chinese and perhaps the Americans, no people are gifted with a land that can equal in natural strength and richness the land of *Sindhustān*.[10] A country, a common home, is the first important essential of stable strong nationality; and as of all countries in the world our country can hardly be surpassed by any in its capacity to afford a soil so specially fitted for the growth of a great nation; we Hindus, whose very first article of faith is the love we bear to the common Fatherland, have in that love the strongest talismanic tie that can bind close and keep a nation firm and enthuse and enable it to accomplish things greater than ever.

The second essential of *Hindutva* puts the estimate of our latent powers of national cohesion and greatness yet higher. No country in the world, with the exception of China again, is peopled by a race so homogenous, yet so ancient and yet so strong both numerically and vitally. The Americans, too, whom we found equally fortunate with us so far as the gift of an excellent geographical basis of nationality is concerned, are decidedly left behind. Mohammedans are no race nor are the Christians. They are a religious unit, yet neither a racial nor a national one. But we Hindus, if possible, are all the three put together and live under our ancient and common roof. The numerical strength of our race is an asset that cannot be too highly prized.

And culture? The English and the Americans feel they are kith and kin because they possess a Shakespeare in common. But not only a Kalidas or a Bhas, but Oh Hindus! ye possess a Ramayan and a Mahabharat in common—and the Vedas! One of the national songs the American children are taught to sing attempts to rouse their sense of eternal self-importance by pointing out to the hundred years twice told that stand behind their history. The Hindu counts his years not by centuries but by cycles—the *Yug* and the *Kalpa*[11]—and amazed asks: "O Lord of the line of Raghu [Rama], where has the kingdom of Ayodhya gone? O Lord of the line of Yadu [Krishna], where has Mathura gone!!" He does not attempt to rouse the sense of self-importance so much as the sense of proportion, which is Truth. And that has perhaps made him last longer than Ramses and Nebuchadnezzar. If a people that had no past have no future, then a people that had produced an unending galaxy of heroes and heroworshipers and who are conscious of having fought with and vanquished the forces whose might struck Greece and Rome, the Pharaohs and the Incas, dead, have in their history a guarantee of their future greatness more assuring than any other people on earth yet possess.

But besides culture the tie of common holyland has at times proved stronger than the chains of a Motherland. Look at the Mohamedans. Mecca to them is a sterner reality than Delhi or Agra. Some of them do not make any secret of being bound to sacrifice all India if that be to the glory of Islam or [if it] could save the city of their prophet. Look at the Jews. Neither centuries of prosperity nor sense of gratitude for the shelter they found can make them more attached or even equally attached to the several countries they inhabit. Their love is, and must necessarily be, divided between the land of their birth and the land of their prophets. If the Zionists' dreams are ever realized—if Palestine becomes a Jewish state and it will gladden us almost as much as our Jewish friends—they, like the Mohamedans, would naturally set the interests of their holyland above those of their Motherlands in America and Europe, and, in case of war between their adopted country and the Jewish state, would naturally sympathize with the latter, if indeed they do not bodily go over to it. History is too full of examples of such desertions to cite particulars. The Crusades again, attest to the wonderful influence that a common holyland exercises over peoples widely separated in race, nationality, and language, to bind and hold them together.

The ideal conditions, therefore, under which a nation can attain perfect solidarity and cohesion would, other things being equal, be found in the case of those people who inhabit the land they adore, the land of whose forefathers is also the land of their Gods and Angels, of Seers and Prophets; the scenes of whose history are also the scenes of their mythology.

The Hindus are about the only people who are blessed with these ideal conditions that are at the same time incentive to national solidarity, cohesion, and greatness. Not even the Chinese are blessed thus. Only Arabia and Palestine—if ever the Jews can succeed in founding their state there—can be said to possess this unique advantage. But Arabia is incomparably poorer in the natural, cultural, historical, and numerical essentials of a great people; and even if the dreams of the Zionists are ever realized into a Palestine state still they too must be equally lacking in these.

England, France, Germany, Italy, Turkey proper, Persia, Japan, Afghanistan, [the] Egypt of today (for the old descendants of "Punto" and their Egypt is dead long since)—and other African states, Mexico, Peru, Chilly [Chile] (not to mention states and nations lesser than all these)—though racially more or less homogeneous, are yet less advantageously situated than we are in geographical, cultural, historical, and numerical essentials, besides lacking the unique gift of a sanctified Motherland. Of the remaining nations Russia in Europe, and the United States in America, though geographically equally well-gifted with us, are yet poorer, in almost every other requisite of nationality. China alone of the present comity of nations is almost as richly gifted with the geographical, racial, cultural, and numerical essentials as the Hindus are. Only in the possession of a common, a sacred, and a perfect language, the Sanskrit, and a sanctified Motherland, we are so far [as] the essentials that contribute to national solidarity are concerned more fortunate.

Thus the actual essentials of *Hindutva* are, as this running sketch reveals, also the ideal essentials of nationality. If we would we can build on this foundation of *Hindutva,* a future greater than what any other people on earth can dream of—greater even than our own past; provided we are able to utilize our opportunities! For let our people remember that great combinations are the order of the day. The leagues of nations, the alliances of powers, Pan-Islamism, Pan-Slavism, Pan-Ethiopism—all little beings are seeking to get themselves incorporated into greater wholes, so as to be better fitted for the struggle for existence and power. Those who are not naturally and historically blessed with numerical or geographical or racial advantages are seeking to share them with others. Woe to those who have them already as their birthright and know them not; or worse, despise them! The nations of the world are desperately trying to find a place in this or that combination for aggression:—can any one of you, Oh Hindus! whether Jain or Samāji[12] or Sanātani[13] or Sīkh or any other subsection, afford to cut yourselves off or fall out and destroy the ancient, the natural, and the organic combination that already exists?—a combination that is bound not by any scraps of paper nor by the ties of exigencies alone, but by the ties of blood and birth and culture? Strengthen them if you can; pull down the barriers that have survived their utility, of castes and customs, of sects and sections. What of interdining? But intermarriages between provinces and provinces, castes and castes, be encouraged where they do not exist. But where they already exist as between the Sīkhs and Sanātanies, Jains and Vaishnavas, Lingayats[14] and Non-Lingayats—suicidal be the hand that tries to cut the nuptial tie. Let the minorities remember they would be cutting the very branch on which they stand. Strengthen every tie that binds you to the main organism, whether of blood or language or common festivals and feasts or culture love you bear to the common Motherland. Let this ancient and noble stream of Hindu blood flow from vein to vein . . . till at last the Hindu people get fused and welded into an indivisible whole, till our race gets consolidated and strong and sharp as steel. . . .

Thirty crores of people, with India for their basis of operation, for their Fatherland and for their Holyland, with such a history behind them, bound together by ties of a common blood and common culture can dictate their terms to the whole world. A day will come when mankind will have to face the force.

Equally certain it is that whenever the Hindus come to hold such a position whence they could dictate terms to the whole world—those terms cannot be very different from the terms which [the] Gītā dictates or the Buddha lays down. A Hindu most intensely so, when he ceases to be a Hindu; and with a Kabir claims the whole earth for a Benares . . . or with a Tukaram exclaims: "My country? Oh brothers, the limits of the Universe—there the frontiers of my country lie."

MANABENDRA NATH ROY: FROM INTERNATIONAL COMMUNIST TO RADICAL HUMANIST

Perhaps the most potent of the political ideologies that entered India in the twentieth century arrived, not from Western Europe, but from Russia—a country with which Indians had previously had very little direct contact. Vladimir I. Lenin had long seen the nationalist movements in Asia as useful adjuncts to the revolution he expected to sweep Europe. Immediately on seizing power in Russia in 1917, his Bolshevik Party championed the right of colonial peoples to complete independence of foreign rule. Although British restrictions prevented Communist literature from entering the Indian Empire openly and in quantity, the news that Bolshevik Russia stood ready to help their cause gave new hope to the numerous Indians in exile all over the world.

One of these was Narendranath Bhattacharya (1887–1954), who had slipped out of India in 1915 to make contact in Java with German agents bringing arms for an Indian insurrection. This plot having failed, he continued eastward to the United States and settled in Mexico under the name of Manabendra Nath Roy. When news of the Bolshevik Revolution reached him, he first helped found the Mexican Communist Party and then hurried to Moscow. There he made such a favorable impression on Lenin that he was put on the Executive Committee of the newly founded Communist International. For a time Roy was busy in Tashkent, Central Asia, training for revolutionary work Indians who had come to Russia via Afghanistan. His career as an international Communist leader extended through the 1920s, but, after his unsuccessful mission to China in 1927 and the victory of Stalin over Trotsky, he fell from favor and left Russia for Germany.

Expelled by Stalin from the Comintern in 1929, Roy returned incognito to India, but was arrested by the British authorities and imprisoned for six years. On his release he attempted to organize a Marxist party within the Indian National Congress. During the Second World War he opposed Gandhi and Nehru, whom he called the tools of Indian Fascism, and supported the Allied cause. After the war, disenchanted with Communism, he sought in the rational and secular humanism of Europe the basis for a new social order.

Notwithstanding his disillusionment with Communism, M. N. Roy remained an internationalist to the end of his life, and the Radical Humanist group that he founded has ties with similar groups in the Western world.

Significantly, he also retained from his Communist period a belief in materialism and a deep suspicion of the religious outlook on life, which has played such a dominant role throughout the history of Indian culture. It was precisely what many considered "changeless" in India that he wanted most to change.

The Anti-Imperialist Struggle in India

Roy's article with this title, written in 1924, is a typical expression of his hopes for an Indian revolution, whose momentum was to come from the hitherto unorganized energies of the workers and peasants.

[From M. N. Roy, "Anti-Imperialist Struggle in India," in *The Communist International* (1924), no. 6, pp. 83, 92–93]

Slowly but surely British domination in India is being undermined. It is true that this historic process is not so speedy as many expected or even prophesied. Nevertheless, the process is going on unceasingly. The depression that followed the sudden collapse of the great noncooperation movement lasted rather long, only to be enlivened, not by an intensified revolutionary activity, but by a concerted effort on the part of the bourgeoisie to challenge the absolute position of imperialism on constitutional lines. The development of this new stage has been during the last twelve months. It has culminated in a political deadlock which has not only nonplussed the nationalist bourgeoisie, but has also placed the British government in a somewhat uncomfortable position. Some decisive action must be taken from one side or the other to break this deadlock. For the nationalists, it is necessary either to compromise with imperialism or to go a few steps further towards revolution. Imperialism, on the other hand, is faced with the alternatives: to placate the nationalist bourgeoisie with concessions or to adopt openly the policy of blood and iron.

It is obvious what should be the nature of our activities. While supporting the nationalist bourgeoisie in every act of resistance to imperialism, we should mobilize the revolutionary mass energy which the nationalist bourgeoisie is afraid of touching. The rapid crystallization of bourgeois nationalism around a reformist program has left the field clear. For the first time in the history of the Indian national movement, there will come into existence a political party demanding separation from the empire. Nationalist elements, which up till now followed the bourgeoisie, will enter this party; because the program of reformism advocated by the bourgeoisie neglects their interests altogether. To aid the organization of this party of revolutionary nationalism is our immediate task. The objective situation is quite ripe, although there are enormous subjective difficulties. The masses are very restive. The peasantry is a veritable inflammable material, while the city proletariat demonstrates its revolutionary zeal whenever there is an opportunity. The process of uniting all these revolutionary elements into an anti-imperialist army is going on steadily. The collapse of bourgeois nationalism, as expressed by the present Parliamentary deadlock, will only accentuate this process. The people will see that the reformist program of the bourgeoisie does not lead anywhere. The center of gravity of the nationalist movement will be shifted back to its proper place—namely, mass action. As soon as the rank and file of the nationalist forces are freed from the reformist leadership of the bourgeoisie, they will begin to follow the standard of revolution, because in that case, they will be convinced that the anti-imperialist struggle cannot be conducted successfully in a different way. There is every indication that things are moving in that direction, and that the next stage of the Indian movement will be a great advance towards revolution.

Revolution—Necessary and Inevitable

Believing in the inevitability of the proletarian revolution, M. N. Roy declared himself simply a servant of the historical process. Not he, but the British were to blame for refusing to cooperate with the inevitable, he asserted in the statement he intended (but was not allowed) to make at his trial for conspiracy in 1931.

[From M. N. Roy, *I Accuse*, pp. 26–27, 28–29]

The evidence proves that I pointed out the inevitability of a revolutionary change in the social and political conditions of India and that the welfare of the toiling masses was dependent upon the revolution. I have been working for the welfare of the Indian masses and have urged the elimination of all obstacles in the way to that goal. I tried to organize a working class party because it is necessary for the liberation of the masses from political slavery, economic exploitation, and social degradation. The party is a historic necessity and has a historically revolutionary mission. It is neither a conspiracy nor a weapon in any conspiracy. The British king, as well as any other power that stands in the way of the progress and prosperity of the Indian masses, must go.

Of course, our attempt to organize a party of the workers and peasants would be a quixotic venture had the condition of the masses been really what the public prosecutor imagines it to be. In his opening address he told the assessors that the Indian peasants were happy in their misery and that I was trying to disturb their happiness for some sinister purpose of mine. I have already given a few facts and figures to show that "happy peasants" live only in the imagination of the public prosecutor, unless the gentleman would venture to advance a theory that the less one eats and the more one toils the happier he is.

In reality, the government is against the most harmless economic program, for its enforcement would mean loss to imperialism and its Indian allies, the princes, big landlords, and capitalists. Therefore, the realization of the program will necessarily mean violation of the laws of the imperialist government. The function of the laws is to hold the masses on the starvation level so that foreign imperialism and its native allies can grow rich, and to suppress the attempts of the masses to rise above the present conditions.

I have not preached violent revolution. I have maintained that revolution is a historic necessity. From time to time, surging forces of social progress reach the period of a violent outburst. This is caused by the resistance of the old to the new. An impending revolution produces its pioneers who force events and herald the maturing of the conflict. The task of the revolutionary vanguard is to expedite the historical process caused by objective necessity. They consciously organize the forces of the revolution and lead them to victory. I have acted as a pioneer of the Indian revolution; but the revolution itself is not my invention. It grows out of the historical conditions of the country. I have simply been one who perceived it earlier than others.

I do not make a secret of my determination of helping the organization of the great revolution which must take place in order to open up before the Indian masses the road to liberty, progress, and prosperity. The impending revolution is an historic necessity. Conditions for it are maturing rapidly. Colonial exploitation of the country creates those conditions. So, I am not responsible for the revolution, nor is the Communist International. Imperialism is responsible for it. My punishment, therefore, will not stop the revolution. Imperialism has created its own grave-digger, namely, the forces of national revolution. These will continue operating till their historic task is accomplished. No law, however ruthless may be the sanction behind it, can suppress them.

India's Message to the World

In one of his most pungent essays, M. N. Roy sought to debunk the popular notion that Indian spirituality in general, and "Gandhism" in particular, held an important message for the world.

[From M. N. Roy, *India's Message (Fragments of a Prisoner's Diary)*, 2:190–91, 209–11, 217]

The preachers of India's "world mission" . . . take their stand on the dogmatic assertion that Indian philosophy is different from Western idealism. The basic principles of idealist philosophy, together with the survey of its medieval and pre-Christian background, prove that this assertion is utterly groundless. While the emotional aspect of Indian speculation is well matched, if not surpassed, by Christian mysticism, intellectually it can hardly claim superiority to Western idealism, either modern or ancient. As regards transcendental fantasies, the Western mind has been no less fertile. The great Sage of Athens, the seers of Alexandria, the saints of early Christianity, the monks of the Middle Ages—that is a record which can proudly meet any competition. On the question of moral doctrines, Christianity stands unbeaten on the solid ground of the Jewish, Socratic, and Stoic traditions. Should the modern West be accused of not having lived up to those noble principles, could India conscientiously be absolved of a similar charge? The claim that the Indian people as a whole are morally less corrupt, emotionally purer, idealistically less worldly, in short, spiritually more elevated, than the bulk of the Western society, is based upon a wanton disregard for reality. . . .

The most commonly agreed form of India's world message is Gandhism. Not only does it dominate the nationalist ideology: it has found some echo outside of India. It is as the moralizing mysticism of Gandhi that Indian thought makes any appeal to the Western mind. Therefore, an analysis of Gandhism will give a correct idea of the real nature of India's message to the world.

But Gandhism is not a coordinated system of thought. There is little of philosophy in it. In the midst of a mass of platitudes and hopeless self-contradictions, it harps on one constant note—a conception of morality based upon dogmatic faith. But what Gandhi preaches is primarily a religion: the faith in God is the only reliable guide in life. The fact that even in the twentieth century India is swayed by the naive doctrines of Gandhi speaks for the cultural backwardness of the masses of her people. The subtlety of the Hindu philosophy is not the measure of the intellectual level of the Indian people as a whole. It was the brain-child of a pampered intellectual elite sharing power and privileges with the temporal ruling class. It still remains confined to the comparatively small circle of intellectuals who try to put on a thin veneer of modernism, and represents nothing more than a nostalgia. The popularity of Gandhi and the uncritical acceptance of his antics as the highest of human wisdom knock the bottom off the doctrine that the Indian people as a whole are morally and spiritually superior to the Western. The fact is that the great bulk of the Indian people are steeped in religious superstitions. Otherwise, Gandhism would have no social background and [would] disappear before long. They have neither any understanding of philosophical problems nor are they concerned with metaphysical speculations in preference to material questions. As normal human beings, they are engrossed with the problems of worldly life, and being culturally backward, necessarily think in terms of religion, conceive their earthly ideals, their egoistic aspirations, in religious forms. Faith is the mainstay of their existence; prejudice the trusted guide of life; and superstition their only philosophy.

Gandhism is the ideological reflex of this social background. It sways the mass mind, not as a moral philosophy, but as a religion. It is neither a philosopher nor a moralist who has become the idol of the Indian people. The masses pay their homage to a Mahātmā—a source of revealed wisdom and agency of supernatural power. The social basis of Gandhism is cultural backwardness; its intellectual mainstay, superstition. . . .

The Gandhist utopia thus is a static society—a state of absolute social stagnation. It is an utopia because it can never be realized. Absolute stagnation is identical with death. To begin with, all resistance to the established [social and economic] order must cease. That would offer absolute guarantee to the *status quo*. The ruling classes would refrain from using force simply because it would not be necessary. Their power and privilege, being completely undisputed, would require no active defense. But this idyllic picture can be drawn only by the cold hand of death. Life expresses itself as a movement—individually, in space, and collectively, in time. And movement implies overwhelming of obstacles on the way. Disappearance of all resistance to the established order would mean extinction of social life. Perfect peace reigns only in the grave.

Radical Humanism

In August 1947, M. N. Roy presented a summary of his new political ideals, which were founded, not on dogma or Machiavellianism, but on human reason and morality, enriched by scientific knowledge and centuries of social experience.

[From M. N. Roy, *New Humanism: A Manifesto*, pp. 34–47]

The question of all questions is: Can politics be rationalized? An affirmative answer to this controversial question would not take us very far unless rationalism was differentiated from the metaphysical concept of reason. To replace the teleology of Marxist materialism by an appeal to the mystical category of reason would not be an advance.

The cognate question is about the relation of politics and morality: Must revolutionary political practice be guided by the Jesuitic dictum—the end justifies the means? The final sanction of revolution being its moral appeal—the appeal for social justice—logically, the answer to the latter question must be in the negative. It is very doubtful if a moral object can ever be attained by immoral means. In critical moments, when larger issues are involved and greater things are at stake, some temporary compromise in behavior may be permissible. But when practices repugnant to ethical principles and traditional human values are stabilized as the permanent features of the revolutionary regime, the means defeat the end. Therefore Communist political practice has not taken the world, not even the working class, anywhere near a new order of freedom and social justice. On the contrary, it has plunged the army of revolution—proletarian as well as nonproletarian—in an intellectual confusion, spiritual chaos, emotional frustration, and a general demoralization.

To overcome this crisis, the fighters for a new world order must turn to the traditions of Humanism and moral Radicalism. The inspiration for a new philosophy of revolution must be drawn from those sources. The nineteenth-century Radicals, actuated by the humanist principle of individualism, realized the possibility of a secular rationalism and a rationalist ethics. They applied to the study of man and society the principles and methods of the physical sciences. Positive knowledge of nature—living as well as inanimate—being so much greater today than a hundred years ago, the Radical scientific approach to the problem of man's life and interrelations is bound to be more successful. Today we can begin with the conviction that it is long since man emerged from the jungle of "pre-history," that social relations can be rationally harmonized, and that therefore appreciation of moral values can be reconciled with efforts for replacing the corrupt and corrosive *status quo* by a new order of democratic freedom. A moral order will result from a rationally organized society, because, viewed in the context of his rise out of the background of a harmonious physical universe, man is essentially rational and therefore moral. Morality emanates from the rational desire for harmonious and mutually beneficial social relations.

Man did not appear on the earth out of nowhere. He rose out of the background of the physical universe, through the long process of biological evolution. The umbilical cord was never broken: man, with his mind, intelligence, will, remains an integral part of the physical universe. The latter is a cosmos—a law-governed system. Therefore, man's being and becoming, his emotions, will, ideas are also determined: man is essentially rational. The reason in man is an echo of the harmony of the universe. Morality must be referred back to man's innate rationality. Only then, man can be moral, spontaneously and voluntarily. Reason is only sanction for morality, which is an appeal to conscience, and conscience, in its turn, is the instinctive awareness of, and reaction to, environments. In the last analysis, conscience is nothing mystic or mysterious. It is a biological function, as such mechanistic, on the level of consciousness. The innate rationality of man is the only guarantee of a harmonious order, which will also be a moral order, because morality is a rational function. Therefore, the purpose of all social endeavor should be to make man increasingly conscious of his innate rationality.

Any effort for a reorganization of society must begin from the unit of society—from the root, so to say. Such an effort to develop a new philosophy of revolution, on the basis of the entire stock of human heritage, and then to elaborate the theory and formulate the principles of the practice of political action and economic reconstruction, therefore, can be called Radicalism.

Radicalism thinks in terms neither of nation nor of class; its concern is man; it conceives freedom as freedom of the individual. Therefore, it can also be called New Humanism, new, because it is Humanism enriched, reinforced and elaborated by scientific knowledge and social experience gained during the centuries of modern civilization.

Humanism is cosmopolitan. It does not run after the utopia of internationalism, which presupposes the existence of autonomous national states. The one makes of the other a pious desire or wishful thinking. A cosmopolitan commonwealth of free men and women is a possibility. It will be a spiritual community, not limited by the boundaries of national states—capitalist, fascist, communist or of any other kind—which will gradually disappear under the impact of cosmopolitan Humanism. That is the Radical perspective of the future of mankind.

SUBHAS CHANDRA BOSE: MILITARY-MINDED MODERNIST

"The earliest recollection I have of myself is that I used to feel like a thoroughly insignificant being."[15] So wrote the man who rose to become one of twentieth-century India's most popular, and most controversial, national leaders. The ninth of fourteen children, Subhas Chandra Bose (1897–1945) grew up in Cuttack, Orissa, where his father was a successful Bengali lawyer. From his youth, Subhas showed a burning desire to excel. Throughout his scholastic career he generally stood at the top of his class. His first seven school years were spent at a Baptist mission school, but his parents insisted on his studying Sanskrit at the same time. At twelve he joined a higher school, and at fifteen he discovered in the writings of Vivekananda the ideals of self-purification and social service. Then Ramakrishna's example and precepts captured his imagination, and he organized a group of friends interested in studying and practicing the teachings of both Ramakrishna and Vivekananda. Entering the prestigious Presidency College of Calcutta University at sixteen, Subhas soon fell under the influence of Aurobindo's writings on yoga and speeches on religious devotion to India's emancipation.

Subhas grew to manhood during the First World War and found military life so appealing that he joined the Calcutta University unit of the India Defense Force. After finishing his B.A. in 1919, he was sent by his father to Cambridge to prepare for the Indian Civil Service. He succeeded in passing the rigorous I.C.S. examination but a few months later resigned / from the service and returned to India to join the noncooperation move-\/ ment, which was then at its height.

Subhas Chandra Bose's career both paralleled and rivaled that of his contemporary Jawaharlal Nehru. Each got his start under the wing of an outstanding Congress statesman—Bose under the Bengali lawyer Chittaranjan Das, and Nehru under his father, Motilal Nehru, who was a very close friend of Das. Both Subhas and Jawaharlal agitated for Congress to adopt the goal of complete independence (as opposed to dominion status) in the late 1920s; both were interested in spreading socialist ideas and in bringing the youth of the country into the nationalist movement; and both suffered numerous imprisonments for their active roles in that movement.

With his emergence as the spokesman for Bengal in the 1930s, Bose grew increasingly impatient with Gandhi's leadership and methods. Finally, in 1939, he openly challenged Gandhi by running for a second term as Congress president and proposing a renewal of civil disobedience under his own direction. Although re-elected, Bose was so hampered by Gandhi's noncooperation with his program that he resigned within a few months and founded his own leftist party, the Forward Bloc.

From 1933 to 1936 and again in 1937 Bose lived and traveled in Europe and was much impressed by the new Fascist form of government (although not with the ideologies) prevailing in Italy and Germany. Closer to the ideal for India, he thought, was the modernizing dictatorship of Turkey's Mustapha Kemal Pasha, lauded as Atatürk ("the father of the Turks") for both his military and his civilian careers in the service of his country. With such ideas in his restless mind, Subhas Bose in 1940 began a civil disobedience movement and was soon jailed. In 1941 he made a dramatic escape from house arrest and made his way secretly via Kabul and Moscow to Berlin. He called on Foreign Minister Ribbentrop and then on Hitler and secured their backing in forming an Indian armed force made up of captured Indian soldiers and officers. In 1943 a German submarine carried him to southern African waters, a Japanese submarine to Indonesia, then a Japanese plane to Tokyo. General Tojo welcomed his collaboration, and soon he was back in Southeast Asia organizing the Indian National Army (the I.N.A.), again from prisoners of war and also from civilian volunteers from the Indian communities there. As a military venture, the I.N.A. had little effect, however heroic its campaign on India's eastern border in 1944. But its psychological effect on Indian public opinion after the war was considerable, and it did help to create in the British grave doubts about the future loyalty of their Indian troops.

Bose died of burns received in a plane crash on Taiwan in August 1945. Had he lived, his independent and highly active personality would have greatly complicated the negotiations that led up to the independence and partition decisions of 1947. Short as his life had been, he had added to the Extremist tradition the glamor of military discipline and sacrifice under a determined and charismatic leader.

A Philosophy of Activism and Modernism

Speaking as chairman of the All-India Youth Congress in 1928, Bose warned its members against the theories both of Aurobindo (then at Pondichéry in South India) and of Gandhi (then at Sabarmati in Gujarat). As against what he called their passivism and antimodernism, he proposed his own philosophy of pragmatic activism and modernism.

[From *The Indian Quarterly Register* (1928) 2:446–47]

As I look around me today, I am struck by two movements or two schools of thought about which, however, small and insignificant I may be, it is my duty to speak out openly and fearlessly. I am referring to the two schools of thought, which have their centers at Sabarmati and Pondichéry. I am not considering the fundamental philosophy underlying those two schools of thought. This is not the time for metaphysical speculation. I shall talk to you today as a pragmatist, as one who will judge the intrinsic value of a school of thought not from a metaphysical point of view, but from experience of its actual effects and consequences.

The actual effect of the propaganda carried on by the Sabarmati School of thought is to create a feeling and an impression that modernism is bad, large scale production is an evil, wants should not be increased, and the standard of living should not be raised, that we must endeavour to the best of our ability to go back to the days of the bullock-cart and that the soul is so important that physical culture and military training can well be ignored.

The actual effect of the propaganda carried on by the Pondichéry school of thought is to create a feeling and an impression that there is nothing higher or nobler than peaceful contemplation, that Yoga means Pranayama[16] and Dhyana,[17] that while action may be tolerated as good, this particular brand of Yoga is something higher and better. This propaganda has led many a man to forget that spiritual progress under the present-day conditions is possible only by ceaseless and unselfish action, that the best way to conquer nature is to fight her and that it is weakness to seek refuge in contemplation when we are hemmed in on all sides by dangers and difficulties.

It is the passivism, not philosophic but actual, inculcated by these schools of thought against which I protest. In this holy land of ours, Ashramas[18] are not new institutions and ascetics and Yogis are not novel phenomena. They have held and they will continue to hold an honored place in society. But it is not their lead we shall have to follow if we are to create a new India at once free, happy, and great.

Friends, you will pardon me if in a fit of outspokenness I have trod on your sentiments. As I have just said I do not for one moment consider the fundamental philosophy underlying the two schools of thought but the actual consequences from a pragmatic point of view. In India we want today a philosophy of activism. We must be inspired by robust optimism. We have to live in the present and to adapt ourselves to modern conditions. We can no longer live in an isolated corner of the world. When India is free, she will have to fight her modern enemies with modern methods, both in the economic and in the political spheres. The days of the bullock-cart are gone and are gone for ever. Free India must prepare herself for any eventuality as long as the whole world does not accept wholeheartedly the policy of disarmament.

I am not one of those who in their zeal for modernism forget the glories of the past. We must take our stand on our past. India has a culture of her own which she must continue to develop along her own distinctive channels. In philosophy, literature, art, science, we have something new to give to the world which the world eagerly awaits. In a word, we must arrive at a synthesis between our ancient culture and modern science. Some of our best thinkers and workers are already engaged in the important task. We must resist the cry of "Back to the Vedas" on the one side, and on the other the meaningless craze for fashion and change of modern Europe. It is difficult to restrict a living movement within proper bounds, but I believe that if the pioneers and leaders of the movement are on the whole on the right track, things will take their proper shape in due time.

Reality As Unfolding Love

Bose concluded his brief autobiography (1936) with a statement of his personal philosophy. It suggests the influence on him of his earlier exposure to Christianity, Aurobindo, European philosophy, and Gandhi and dates from the time of his secret marriage in Vienna to an Austrian woman.

[From Subhas Chandra Bose, *Netaji's Life and Writings. Part One: An Indian Pilgrim*, pp. 140–44]

Reality is, for me, Spirit working with a conscious purpose through time and space. This conception does not, of course, represent the Absolute Truth which is beyond description for all time and which for me is also beyond comprehension at the present moment. It is therefore a relative truth and is liable to change along with the changes in my mind. Nevertheless, it is a conception which represents my utmost effort to comprehend reality and which offers a basis on which to build my life.

Why do I believe in Spirit? Because it is a pragmatic necessity. My nature demands it. I see purpose and design in nature; I discern an 'increasing purpose' in my own life. I feel that I am not a mere conglomeration of atoms. I perceive, too, that reality is not a fortuitous combination of molecules. Moreover, no other theory can explain reality (as I understand it) so well. This theory is in short an intellectual and moral necessity, a necessity of my very life, so far as I am concerned. . . .

What then is the nature of this Spirit which is reality? One is reminded of the parable of Ramakrishna about a number of blind men trying to describe an elephant—each giving a description in accordance with the organ he touched and therefore violently disagreeing with the rest. My own view is that most of the conceptions of reality are true, though partially, and the main question is which conception represents the maximum truth. For me, the essential nature of reality is LOVE. LOVE is the essence of the Universe and is the essential principle in human life. . . .

This statement may be challenged when one can see so much in life that is opposed to love; but the paradox can be easily explained. The 'essential principle' is not fully manifest yet; it is unfolding itself in space and time. Love, like reality of which it is the essence, is dynamic.

What, now, is the nature of the process of unfolding: Firstly, is it a movement forward or not? Secondly, is there any law underlying this movement?

The unfolding process is progressive in character. This assertion is not quite dogmatic. Observation and study of nature point to the conclusion that everywhere there is progress. This progress may not be unilinear; there may be periodic set-backs—but on the whole, i.e., considered from a long period point of view, there is progress. Apart from this rational consideration there is the intuitive experience that we are moving ahead with the lapse of time. And last but not least, there is the necessity, both biological and moral, to have faith in progress.

Bose then summarizes various efforts "to comprehend the law of progress"—Sankhya philosophy, Spencer, von Hartmann, Bergson, and Hegel.

Hegel . . . would dogmatise that the nature of the evolutionary process, whether in the thought world or in reality outside, is dialectic. We progress through conflicts and their solutions. Every thesis provokes an antithesis. This conflict is solved by a synthesis, which in its turn, provokes a new antithesis—and so on.

All these theories have undoubtedly an element of truth. Each of the above thinkers has endeavoured to reveal the truth as he has perceived it. But undoubtedly Hegel's theory is the nearest approximation to truth. It explains the facts more satisfactorily than any other theory. At the same time, it cannot be regarded as the whole truth since all the facts, as we know them, do not accord with it. Reality is, after all, too big for our frail understanding to fully comprehend. Nevertheless, we have to build our life on the theory which contains the maximum truth. We cannot sit still because we cannot, or do not, know the Absolute Truth.

Reality, therefore, is Spirit, the essence of which is Love, gradually unfolding itself in an eternal play of conflicting forces and their solutions.

A Program for Reconstructing "Post-War" India

In 1938, in his first presidential address to the Congress, Subhas Bose proposed a comprehensive program of reconstruction for India after what he hinted would be a war against the British Empire—nonviolent in India and violent abroad. Even though he did not survive that war, most of his proposals (except for the use of roman script and the total socialization of agriculture and industry) have been adopted as goals in independent India.

[From Subhas Chandra Bose, *Selected Speeches*, pp. 79–83]

I know that there are friends who think that after freedom is won the Congress Party, having achieved its objective, should wither away. Such a conception is entirely erroneous. The party that wins freedom for India should be also the party that will put into effect the entire programme of post-war reconstruction. Only those who have won power can handle it properly. If other people are pitchforked into seats of power which they were not responsible for capturing, they will lack that strength, confidence and idealism which is indispensable for revolutionary reconstruction. It is this which accounts for the difference in the record of the Congress and non-Congress Ministries even in the very narrow sphere of provincial autonomy.

No, there can be no question of the Congress Party withering away after political freedom has been won. On the contrary, the party will have to take over power, assume responsibility for administration and put through its programme of reconstruction. Only then will it fulfil its role. If it were forcibly to liquidate itself, chaos would follow. Looking at . . . Europe, we find that only in those countries has there been orderly and continuous progress where the party which seized power undertook the work of reconstruction.

I know that it will be argued that the continuance of a party in such circumstances, standing behind the State, will convert that State into a totalitarian one; but I cannot admit the charge. The State will possibly become a totalitarian one if there be only one party as in countries like Russia, Germany and Italy. But there is no reason why other parties should be banned. Moreover, the party itself will have a democratic basis, unlike, for instance, the Nazi Party which is based on the "leader principle". The existence of more than one party and the democratic basis of the Congress Party will prevent the future Indian State becoming a totalitarian one. Further, the democratic basis of the party will ensure that leaders are not thrust upon the people from above, but are elected from below.

Though it may be somewhat premature to give a detailed plan of reconstruction, we might as well consider some of the principles according to which our future social reconstruction should take place. I have no doubt in my mind that our chief national problems relating to the eradication of poverty, illiteracy and disease, and to scientific production and distribution, can be effectively tackled only along socialistic lines. The very first thing which our future national government will have to do would be to set up a commission for drawing up a comprehensive plan of reconstruction. This plan will have two parts—an immediate programme and a long-period programme. In drawing up the first part, the immediate objectives which will have to be kept in view will be three-fold: firstly, to prepare the country for self-sacrifice; secondly, to unify India; and, thirdly, to give scope for local and cultural autonomy. The second and third objectives may appear to be contradictory, but they are not really so. Whatever political talent or genius we may possess as a people will have to be used in reconciling these two objectives. We shall have to unify the country so that we may be able to hold India against any foreign invasion. While unifying the country through a strong Central Government, we shall have to put all the minority communities as well as the provinces at their ease, by allowing them a large measure of autonomy in cultural as well as governmental affairs. Special efforts will be needed to keep our people together when the load of foreign domination is removed, because alien rule has demoralized and disorganized us to a degree. To promote national unity we shall have to develop our *lingua franca* and a common script. Further, with the help of such modern scientific contrivances as aeroplanes, telephone, radio, films, television, etc., we shall have to bring the different parts of India closer to one another and through a common educational policy we shall have to foster a common spirit among the entire population.

So far as our *lingua franca* is concerned, I am inclined to think that the distinction between Hindi and Urdu is an artificial one. The most natural *lingua franca* would be a mixture of the two, such as is spoken in daily life in large portions of the country, and this common language may be written in either of the two scripts, Nagri[19] or Urdu.[20] I am aware that there are people in India who strongly favour either of the two scripts to the exclusion of the other. Our policy, however, should not be one of exclusion. We should allow the fullest latitude to use either script. At the same time, I am inclined to think that the ultimate solution and the best solution would be the adoption of a script that would bring us into line with the rest of the world. Perhaps, some of our countrymen will gape with horror when they hear of the adoption of the Roman script, but I would beg them to consider this problem from the scientific and historical point of view. If we do that, we shall realize at once that there is nothing sacrosanct in a script. The Nagri script, as we know it today, has passed through several phases of evolution. Besides, most of the major provinces of India have their own script and there is the Urdu script which is used largely by the Urdu-speaking public in India and by both Muslims and Hindus in provinces like the Punjab and Sind. In view of such diversity, the choice of a uniform script for the whole of India should be made in a thoroughly scientific and impartial spirit, free from bias of every kind. I confess that there was a time when I felt that it would be anti-national to adopt a foreign script. But my visit to Turkey in 1934 was responsible for converting me.[21] I then realized for the first time what a great advantage it was to have the same script as the rest of the world. So far as our masses are concerned, since more than 90 per cent are illiterate and are not familiar with any script, it will not matter to them which script we introduce when they are educated. The Roman script will, moreover, facilitate their learning a European language. I am quite aware how unpopular the immediate adoption of the Roman script would be in our country. Nevertheless, I would beg my countrymen to consider what would be the wisest solution in the long run.

With regard to the long-period programme for a free India, the first problem to tackle is that of our increasing population. I do not desire to go into the theoretical question as to whether India is over-populated or not. I simply want to point out that where poverty, starvation and disease are stalking the land, we cannot afford to have our population mounting up by thirty millions during a single decade. If the population goes up by leaps and bounds, as it has done in the recent past, our plans are likely to fall through. It will, therefore, be desirable to restrict our population until we are able to feed, clothe and educate those who already exist. It is not necessary at this stage to prescribe the methods that should be adopted to prevent a further increase in population, but I would urge that public attention be drawn to this question.

Regarding reconstruction, our principal problem will be how to eradicate poverty from our country. That will require radical reform of our land system, including the abolition of landlordism. Agricultural indebtedness will have to be liquidated and provision made for cheap credit for the rural population. An extension of the co-operative movement will be necessary for the benefit of both producers and consumers. Agriculture will have to be put on a scientific basis with a view to increasing the yield from the land.

To solve the economic problem, agricultural improvement will not be enough. A comprehensive scheme of industrial development under State ownership and State control will be indispensable. A new industrial system will have to be built up in place of the old one, which has collapsed as a result of mass production abroad and alien rule at home. The Planning Commission will have to consider carefully and decide which of the home industries could be revived despite the competition of modern factories, and in which sphere large-scale production should be encouraged. However much we may dislike modern industrialism and condemn the evils which follow in its train, we cannot go back to the pre-industrial era, even if we desire to do so. It is well, therefore, that we should reconcile ourselves to industrialization and devise means to minimize its evils and at the same time explore the possibilities of reviving cottage industries where there is a possibility of their surviving the inevitable competition of factories. In a country like India there will be plenty of room for cottage industries, especially in the case of industries, including hand-spinning and hand-weaving, allied to agriculture.

Last but not the least, the State, on the advice of a Planning Commission, will have to adopt a comprehensive scheme for gradually socializing our entire agricultural and industrial system in the spheres of both production and distribution. Extra capital will have to be procured for this, whether through internal or external loans or through inflation.

India Needs a Dictator

Bose's private thoughts about his role in independent India were revealed in the following chance remark in Kabul, Afghanistan—his first stop on his secret trip to Berlin in 1941. His plan was a logical one, given the persistence of Hindu-Muslim communal conflicts and Bose's rejection of both Gandhi's nonviolent methods and Jinnah's demand for a separate Muslim-majority nation.

[From Toye, *Subhas Chandra Bose*, p. 60].

So long as there is a third party in the country, that is, the British, these [Hindu-Muslim] dissensions will not end. They will go on growing. They will disappear only when an iron dictatorship rules India for twenty years. For a few years at least after the end of British rule in India there must be a dictatorship. No other constitution can flourish in the country. And it is to India's good that she should be ruled by a dictator to begin with. None but a dictator can wipe out such dissensions. India does not suffer from one ailment. She suffers from so many political ills that only a ruthless dictator can cure her. . . . India needs a Kemal Pasha.

On to Delhi!

In July 1943, Subhas Bose arrived in Singapore to greet the small force of Indian military men captured by the Japanese in their swift conquest of Southeast Asia. Here he announced his plan to build, train, and command an army (which later included Indian women) to drive the British out of India. As a practical matter, his plan's success depended on Japan's military might, which proved insufficient to penetrate more than a few miles into eastern India.

[From Subhas Chandra Bose, *On to Delhi*, pp. 54–58]

Soldiers of India's Army of Liberation! Today is the proudest day of my life. Today it has pleased Providence to give me the unique privilege and honour of announcing to the whole world that India's Army of Liberation has come into being. This army has now been drawn up in military formation on the battlefield of Singapore—which was once the bulwark of the British Empire. This is not only the Army that will emancipate India from the British yoke, it is also the Army that will hereafter, create the future national army of Free India. Every Indian must feel proud that this Army—his own Army—has been organised entirely under Indian leadership and that when the historic moment arrives, under Indian leadership it will go to battle.

There are people who thought at one time that the Empire on which the sun is not set, was an everlasting Empire. No such thought ever troubled me. History had taught me that every empire has its inevitable decline and collapse. Moreover, I had seen with my own eyes, cities and fortresses that were once the bulwarks, but which became the grave yards, of by-gone Empires. But standing today on the graveyard of the British Empire, even a child is convinced that the almighty British Empire is already a thing of the past.

When France declared war on Germany in 1939 and the campaign began, there was but one cry which rose from the lips of German soldiers— "To Paris, To Paris!". When the brave soldiers of Nippon set out on their march in December, 1941, there was but one cry which rose from their lips—"To Singapore, to Singapore!" Comrades! my soldiers! Let your battle-cry be—"To Delhi, To Delhi!". How many of us will individually survive this war of Freedom, I do not know. But I do know this, that we shall ultimately win and our task will not end until our surviving heroes hold the victory-parade on another graveyard of the British Empire—the Lal Kila or Red Fortress of ancient Delhi. . . .

Comrades! You have voluntarily accepted a mission that is the noblest that the human mind can conceive of. For the fulfillment of such a mission no sacrifice is too great—not even the sacrifice of one's life. You are today the custodians of India's national honour and the embodiment of India's hopes and aspirations. So conduct yourself that your countrymen may bless you and posterity may be proud of you.

I have said that today is the proudest day of my life. For an enslaved people, there can be no greater pride, no higher honour, than to be the first soldier in the army of liberation. But this honour carries with it a corresponding responsibility and I am deeply conscious of it. I assure you that I shall be with you in darkness and in sunshine, in sorrow and in joy, in suffering and in victory. For the present, I can offer you nothing except hunger, thirst, privation, forced marches and death. But if you follow me in life and in death as I am confident you will—I shall lead you to victory and freedom. It does not matter who among us will live to see India free. It is enough that India shall be free and that we shall give our all to make her free. May god now bless our Army and grant us victory in the coming fight!

INQUILAB ZINDABAD(!)

AZAD HIND ZINDABAD(!)[22]

JAWAHARLAL NEHRU: DEMOCRATIC SOCIALIST (PART 1)

Descended from a proud line of Kashmiri brahmans, Jawaharlal Nehru (1889–1964) was born in Allahabad, where the Ganges and Jumna rivers converge. His ancestors had settled in Delhi and served at the court of the Mughal emperors, but his father, Motilal Nehru, had moved on to Allahabad to become a successful and wealthy lawyer at the high court there. As Jawaharlal wrote of his childhood, "An only son of prosperous parents is apt to be spoilt, especially so in India."[23] The apple of his father's eye, he studied at home under a series of English governesses and tutors. When he was fifteen, his father sent him to Harrow; at seventeen he entered Cambridge University; and at twenty he went down to London to take his law degree at the Inns of Court, where Gandhi had studied some two decades earlier. After seven formative years in England, Jawaharlal returned to India in 1912 to practice law with his father.

Motilal Nehru possessed a powerful personality and a patrician bearing, and his son admired him tremendously. Jawaharlal would no doubt have been drawn to politics of his own accord, but his father's position as leading Moderate in the Indian National Congress made the attraction an irresistible one. He joined the Congress and began to speak at its sessions, but it was not until 1920, when Gandhi launched his great noncooperation movement against British rule, that Jawaharlal found full expression for his energies. He made tours in remote village areas (discovering the hard lot of the peasantry), organized volunteer workers, and delivered speeches to large patriotic gatherings. "I experienced [then] the thrill of mass-feeling, the power of influencing the mass,"[24] he tells us, and this power has been one of the keys to his success as a national leader. The climax of his activities came when, for the first of many times in his career, he went gladly to jail as a political prisoner.

Jawaharlal was disappointed by Gandhi's sudden suspension of the movement in 1922 after an outbreak of violence, and in the following years he felt himself groping for a clearer analysis of, and a more predictable solution to, India's problems than those provided by the Mahatma's intuitive and moralistic mind. A trip to Europe for his wife's health in 1926–1927 gave him a new perspective on the conflict between Indian nationalism and British rule. Conversations with Socialists and Communists in Europe—especially at the Congress of the League of Oppressed Peoples at Brussels—convinced him that the principal international conflict was between capitalist imperialism and anticapitalist socialism. A week's visit to Moscow, where he talked with M. N. Roy, impressed him with the achievements of the Soviet system, and with the common interest of Russia and India in opposing British imperialism.[25]

Back in India once more, Jawaharlal threw himself with renewed vigor into the national struggle, for he now saw it as part of a worldwide movement to liberate mankind from every kind of oppression and exploitation. He demanded that the Congress declare its ultimate goal to be, not dominion status (as his father wished), but complete independence. Jawaharlal was joined by Subhas Chandra Bose and others, and Gandhi wisely yielded to their demand in order to keep the nationalist movement from again splitting into Moderate and Extremist wings, as it had in 1907. Gandhi went on to persuade the Congress to accept Jawaharlal as its president on the eve of the second nationwide campaign of civil disobedience, which lasted from 1930 to 1934. After repeated imprisonments during and after that movement, Jawaharlal flew to Switzerland to be with his wife, who was dying of tuberculosis. There he learned of his election to a second term as Congress president. In 1937 he was honored with re-election to a third one-year term.

From this time onward Nehru came increasingly to be regarded as Gandhi's heir apparent and was so designated by Gandhi in 1942. Devotion to the cause of India's freedom and compassion for the lot of their nation's poor created between the two men an indissoluble bond. In their attitudes toward other questions, however, Nehru and Gandhi were poles apart. Religion held no meaning for Nehru, but for his guru it was all-important. Gandhi held nonviolence and simple living to be ends in themselves, but Nehru considered them merely as practical expedients in the political struggle. Gandhi's ideal India was a decentralized family of self-sufficient villages; Nehru's ideal India was a centralized modern state with a planned industrial economy. Despite their intellectual differences, however, Nehru found in Gandhi a faithful friend and a wise counselor. At one time he telegraphed him, "I feel lost in a strange country where you are the only familiar landmark. . . ."[26] and after Gandhi's assassination he mourned, "the light has gone out of our lives and there is darkness everywhere."[27]

The selections that follow come from Nehru's speeches and writings before 1947. Some of his thoughts after India achieved independence appear in chapter 8.

The Socialist Creed

In his 1936 address to the Congress as its newly elected president, Nehru urged its conversion to what he had been persuaded was the civilization of the future, the Soviet form of socialism.

[From Nehru, *Selected Works*, 7:180–82]

I am convinced that the only key to the solution of the world's problems and of India's problems lies in socialism, and when I use this word I do so not in a vague humanitarian way but in the scientific economic sense. Socialism is, however, something even more than an economic doctrine; it is a philosophy of life and as such also it appeals to me. I see no way of ending the poverty, the vast unemployment, the degradation and the subjection of the Indian people except through socialism. That involves vast and revolutionary changes in our political and social structure, the ending of vested interests in land and industry, as well as the feudal and autocratic Indian states system. That means the ending of private property, except in a restricted sense, and the replacement of the present profit system by a higher ideal of cooperative service. It means ultimately a change in our instincts and habits and desires. In short, it means a new civilization, radically different from the present capitalist order. Some glimpse we can have of this new civilization in the territories of the U.S.S.R. Much has happened there which has pained me greatly and with which I disagree, but I look upon that great and fascinating unfolding of a new order and a new civilization as the most promising feature of our dismal age. If the future is full of hope it is largely because of Soviet Russia and what it has done, and I am convinced that, if some world catastrophe does not intervene, this new civilization will spread to other lands and put an end to the wars and conflicts which capitalism feeds.

I do not know how or when this new order will come to India. I imagine that every country will fashion it after its own way and fit it in with its national genius. But the essential basis of that order must remain and be a link in the world order that will emerge out of the present chaos.

Socialism is thus for me not merely an economic doctrine which I favor; it is a vital creed which I hold with all my head and heart. I work for Indian independence because the nationalist in me cannot tolerate an alien domination; I work for it even more because for me it is the inevitable step to social and economic change. I should like the Congress to become a socialist organization and to join hands with the other forces that in the world are working for the new civilization. But I realize that the majority in the Congress, as it is constituted today, may not be prepared to go thus far. We are a nationalist organization and we think and work on the nationalist plane. It is evident enough now that this is too narrow even for the limited objective of political independence, and so we talk of the masses and their economic needs. But still most of us hesitate, because of our nationalist backgrounds, to take a step which might frighten away some vested interests. Most of those interests are already ranged against us and we can expect little from them except opposition even in the political struggle.

Much as I wish for the advancement of socialism in this country, I have no desire to force the issue on the Congress and thereby create difficulties in the way of our struggle for independence. I shall cooperate gladly and with all the strength in me with all those who work for independence even though they do not agree with the socialist solution. But I shall do so stating my position frankly and hoping in course of time to convert the Congress and the country to it, for only thus can I see it achieving independence.

Between Gandhi and Marx—And Beyond Them

Eight years later, writing a history of India while in jail, Nehru reflected on his basic beliefs.

[From Nehru, *The Discovery of India*, pp. 10, 13–15]

Six or seven years ago an American publisher asked me to write an essay on my philosophy of life for a symposium he was preparing. I was attracted to the idea but I hesitated, and the more I thought over it, the more reluctant I grew. Ultimately, I did not write that essay.

What was my philosophy of life? I did not know. Some years earlier I would not have been so hesitant. There was a definiteness about my thinking and objectives then which has faded away since. The events of the past few years in India, China, Europe, and all over the world have been confusing, upsetting and distressing, and the future has become vague and shadowy and has lost that clearness of outline which it once possessed in my mind. . . .

Some kind of ethical approach to life has a strong appeal for me, though it would be difficult for me to justify it logically. I have been attracted by Gandhiji's stress on right means and I think one of his greatest contributions to our public life has been this emphasis. The idea is by no means new, but this application of an ethical doctrine to large-scale public activity was certainly novel. It is full of difficulty, and perhaps ends and means are not really separable but form together one organic whole. . . .

A study of Marx and Lenin produced a powerful effect on my mind and helped me to see history and current affairs in a new light. The long chain of history and of social development appeared to have some meaning, some sequence, and the future lost some of its obscurity. The practical achievements of the Soviet Union were also tremendously impressive. . . .

Much in the Marxist philosophical outlook I could accept without difficulty: its monism and non-duality of mind and matter, the dynamics of matter and the dialectic of continuous change by evolution as well as leap, through action and interaction, cause and effect, thesis, antithesis and synthesis. It did not satisfy me completely, nor did it answer all the questions in my mind, and, almost unawares, a vague idealist approach would creep into my mind, something rather akin to the Vedanta approach. It was not a difference between mind and matter, but rather of something that lay beyond the mind. Also there was the background of ethics. I realised that the moral approach is a changing one and depends upon the growing mind and an advancing civilization; it is conditioned by the mental climate of the age. Yet there was something more to it than that, certain basic urges which had greater permanence. I did not like the frequent divorce in communist, as in other, practice between action and these basic urges or principles. So there was an odd mixture in my mind which I could not rationally explain or resolve. There was a general tendency not to think too much of those fundamental questions which appear to be beyond reach, but rather to concentrate on the problems of life—to understand in the narrower and more immediate sense what should be done and how. Whatever ultimate reality may be, and whether we can ever grasp it in whole or in part, there certainly appear to be vast possibilities of increasing human knowledge, even though this may be partly or largely subjective, and of applying this to the advancement and betterment of human living and social organization. . . .

And so while I accepted the fundamentals of the socialist theory, I did not trouble myself about its numerous inner controversies. I had little patience with leftist groups in India, spending much of their energy in mutual conflict and recrimination over fine points of doctrine which did not interest me at all. Life is too complicated and, as far as we can understand it in our present state of knowledge, too illogical, for it to be confined within the four corners of a fixed doctrine.

The real problems for me remain problems of individual and social life, of harmonious living, of a proper balancing of an individual's inner and outer life, of an adjustment of the relations between individuals and groups, of a continuous becoming something better and higher, of social development, of the ceaseless adventure of man. In the solution of these problems the way of observation and precise knowledge and deliberate reasoning, according to the method of science, must be followed.

On Gandhi

Although not a follower of Gandhi in the fullest sense, Nehru was deeply influenced by his leader in the Congress. He wrote the first of the following statements in 1934 and made the second at the beginning of his broadcast to the nation a few hours after Gandhi's assassination.

[From Nehru, *Toward Freedom*, pp. 110, 240, and *Independence and After*, p. 42]

It was clear that this little man of poor physique had something of steel in him, something rocklike which did not yield to physical powers, however great they might be. And in spite of his unimpressive features, his loincloth and bare body, there was a royalty and a kingliness in him which compelled a willing obeisance from others. Consciously and deliberately meek and humble, yet he was full of power and authority, and he knew it, and at times he was imperious enough, issuing commands which had to be obeyed. His calm, deep eyes would hold one and gently probe into the depths; his voice, clear and limpid, would purr its way into the heart and evoke an emotional response. Whether his audience consisted of one person or a thousand, the charm and magnetism of the man passed on to it, and each one had a feeling of communion with the speaker. This feeling had little to do with the mind, though the appeal to the mind was not wholly ignored. But mind and reason definitely had second place. This process of "spellbinding" was not brought about by oratory or the hypnotism of silken phrases. The language was always simple and to the point, and seldom was an unnecessary word used. It was the utter sincerity of the man and his personality that gripped; he gave the impress of tremendous inner reserves of power. Perhaps also it was a tradition that had grown up about him which helped in creating a suitable atmosphere. A stranger, ignorant of this tradition and not in harmony with the surroundings, would probably not have been touched by that spell, or, at any rate, not to the same extent. And yet one of the most remarkable things about Gandhiji was, and is, his capacity to win over, or at least to disarm, his opponents.

. . . Gandhiji did not encourage others to think; his insistence was only on purity and sacrifice. I felt that I was drifting further and further away from him mentally, in spite of my strong emotional attachment to him.

Often enough he was guided in his political activities by an unerring instinct. He had the flair for action, but was the way of faith the right way to train a nation? It might pay for a short while, but in the long run?

. . . .

Friends and comrades, the light has gone out of our lives and there is darkness everywhere. I do not know what to tell you and how to say it. Our beloved leader, Bapu as we called him, the Father of the Nation, is no more. Perhaps I am wrong to say that. Nevertheless, we will not see him again as we have seen him for these many years. We will not run to him for advice and seek solace from him, and that is a terrible blow, not to me only but to millions and millions in this country. And it is a little difficult to soften the blow by any other advice that I or anyone else can give you.

The light has gone out, I said, and yet I was wrong. For the light that shone in this country was no ordinary light. The light that has illumined this country for these many many years will illumine this country for many more years, and a thousand years later, that light will still be seen in this country and the world will see it and it will give solace to innumerable hearts. For that light represented something more than the immediate present; it represented the living, the eternal truths, reminding us of the right path, drawing us from error, taking this ancient country to freedom.

On the Threshold of a New Era

More than most modern Indians, Nehru possessed and cultivated a deep and sometimes romantic awareness of his country's past. This sense of history stands out in his speech to the Constituent Assembly in 1946 as it prepared to adopt its basic "Declaration of Objectives." Note, however, that the three examples he cited as models of constituent assemblies are all taken, not from Indian, but from Western history.

[From Nehru, *Independence and After*, pp. 346–48]

As I stand here, Sir, I feel the weight of all manner of things crowding upon me. We are at the end of an era and possibly very soon we shall embark upon a new age; and my mind goes back to the great past of India, to the 5,000 years of India's history, from the very dawn of that history which might be considered almost the dawn of human history, till today.

All that past crowds upon me and exhilarates me and, at the same time, somewhat oppresses me. Am I worthy of that past? When I think also of the future, the greater future I hope, standing on this sword's edge of the present between the mighty past and the mightier future, I tremble a little and feel overwhelmed by this mighty task. We have come here at a strange moment in India's history. I do not know, but I do feel, that there is some magic in this moment of transition from the old to the new, something of that magic which one sees when the night turns into day and even though the day may be a cloudy one, it is day after all, for when the clouds move away, we can see the sun again. Because of all this I find a little difficulty in addressing this House and putting all my ideas before it and I feel also that in this long succession of thousands of years, I see the mighty figures that have come and gone and I see also the long succession of our comrades who have labored for the freedom of India. And now we stand on the verge of this passing age, trying, laboring, to usher in the new. I am sure the House will feel the solemnity of this moment and will endeavor to treat this Resolution which it is my proud privilege to place before it in a correspondingly solemn manner.

I think also of the various constituent assemblies that have gone before and of what took place at the making of the great American nation when the fathers of that nation met and fashioned a constitution which has stood the test for so many years, more than a century and a half, and of the great nation that has resulted, which has been built up on the basis of that constitution. My mind goes back to that mighty revolution which took place also over one hundred fifty years ago and the constituent assembly that met in that gracious and lovely city of Paris which has fought so many battles for freedom. My mind goes back to the difficulties that that constituent assembly had to face from the king and other authorities, and still it continued. The House will remember that when these difficulties came and even the room for a meeting was denied to that constituent assembly, they betook themselves to an open tennis court and met there and took the oath, which is called the Oath of the Tennis Court. They continued meeting in spite of kings, in spite of the others, and did not disperse till they had finished the task they had undertaken. Well, I trust that it is in that solemn spirit that we too are meeting here and that we too whether we meet in this chamber or in other chambers, or in the fields or in the market place, will go on meeting and continue our work till we have finished it.

Then my mind goes back to a more recent revolution which gave rise to a new type of state, the revolution that took place in Russia and out of which has arisen the Union of the Soviet Socialist Republics, another mighty country which is playing a tremendous part in the world, not only a mighty country, but for us in India, a neighboring country.

So our mind goes back to these great examples and we seek to learn from their success and to avoid their failures. Perhaps we may not be able to avoid failures, because some measure of failure is inherent in human effort. Nevertheless, we shall advance, I am certain, in spite of obstructions and difficulties, and achieve and realize the dream that we have dreamt so long.

BHIM RAO AMBEDKAR: SPOKESMAN FOR THE UNTOUCHABLES (PART 1)

One of the most unusual thinkers, statesmen, and reformers of twentieth-century India, Dr. B. R. Ambedkar (1891–1956) was born into the un-touchable Mahar caste of Maharashtra. The key to his rise was education. At a time when less then 1 percent of his caste was literate, Ambedkar secured a B.A. in Bombay, an M.A. and Ph.D. from Columbia University in New York, a D.Sc. from London University, and passed the bar from Grey's Inn, London. This extraordinary education, added to his lifelong commitment to improve the lives of Untouchables and to his great faith in parliamentary democracy, enabled him not only to stamp his mark on his own caste but also to improve the status of all of India's lowest castes in the Constitution and legal system of his country.

Ambedkar's father had left the traditional low-status work of the Mahars (untouchable village servants) to join the British army. The birth of Bhim Rao, his fourteenth child, coincided with a time when a number of Mahars had freed themselves from the village structure and begun to protest the limitations of their status. Ambedkar, pushed by his family and aided by caste Hindu reformers, secured the education that enabled him to organize and dominate this burgeoning movement. The direction was set in the early 1920s: organization for social and political activity, attempts to secure civil and religious rights, and the building of pride and self-respect. In his thirty-five years as leader of the movement, Ambedkar's activities paralleled those of black leaders in the United States: the scholarship and literary interests of W.E.B. DuBois, the charisma and innovative methods of Martin Luther King, and the outspoken and bitter rhetoric of H. Rap Brown.

His earliest efforts involved a newspaper, an organization of all "Depressed Classes" in Bombay to present grievances to government, the opening of a hostel to facilitate the education of Untouchables, testimony to government commissions investigating political conditions and education, and the holding of conferences for the Depressed Classes all over the Marathi-speaking area. Not until the 1930s did Ambedkar become an all-India personage. He was selected by the British as a delegate to the London Round Table Conferences (1930–1933), and there, confronted with demands for separate electorates by all the minorities of India, he stated his case for the Untouchables as a minority entitled to its own electorate.

The granting of special electorates for the Untouchables was unacceptable to M. K. Gandhi, who began a fast in 1932 against their separation from the Hindu body politic. Faced with the possibility of causing Gandhi's death, Ambedkar capitulated and accepted Gandhi's offer of separate electorates during primary elections and an increased number of reserved seats for Untouchables. This involved drawing up a schedule of those castes needing special representation, and "Scheduled Castes" became thereafter the governmental name for Untouchables.

From this time on, Gandhi and Ambedkar went separate ways—Gandhi to give the name "Harijan" (people of God) to Untouchables and to plead with caste Hindus to abolish untouchability; Ambedkar to plan a political party. Ambedkar first attempted to secure temple entry and religious rights for Untouchables. When that failed, he rejected Hinduism and continued the thrust toward education. Ambedkar's Independent Labour Party won fourteen seats in the Bombay Legislative Assembly in 1937; those elected under its banner included eleven Scheduled Caste members. The party attempted to abolish hereditary discrimination in village economic structures, to ban the use of the term "Harijan," and to secure family-planning measures. Because it was a small minority party, it was unsuccessful, and, although Ambedkar never lost faith in the party system, he never found the key to political power for a group that was, by definition, a permanent minority.

More conferences, including one to discuss conversion to another religion, broadened the movement during the 1930s, but Ambedkar also concerned himself with other issues. As Member for Labour in the Viceroy's Executive Council, he worked on labor laws and dam projects. He taught at the Government Law College in Bombay. He wrote on the need to reform and liberalize the university system and on the hypocrisy of the Congress and Gandhi. In 1945 he founded the People's Education Society and a year later opened Siddharth College in Bombay. But as India drew near to independence, he again stressed separatism from the other Hindu groups as the way to empower the Scheduled Castes in the battle to gain equality and integration. He was now known all over India as Babasaheb ("respected master") Ambedkar, the champion of the Untouchables.

Change Your Religion

In 1935, at a small town near the pilgrimage city of Nasik (now in Maharashtra), where Untouchables had for five years conducted a fruitless *satyāgraha* for the right to enter Hindu temples, Ambedkar proclaimed, "I was born a Hindu, but I will not die a Hindu." In the following year he called a conference of all the Mahars in the province of Bombay (where they formed 9 percent of the population) and proposed that they change to a different religion rather than prolong their efforts to secure religious rights as Hindus. The following translation of Ambedkar's speech to the conference is printed, as it was in Marathi, as a poem.

[From Ambedkar, *Mukti kon pathe?* (Which Path to Liberation?), front end paper, trans. by Eleanor Zelliot, Rekha Damle, and Jayant Karve]

If you want to gain self-respect, change your religion.
If you want to create a cooperating society, change your religion.
If you want power, change your religion.
If you want equality, change your religion.
If you want independence, change your religion.
If you want to make the world in which you live happy, change your religion.

Why should you remain in a religion that does not value your manhood?
Why should you remain in a religion that does not let you enter its temples?
Why should you remain in a religion that does not let you get water to drink? [28]
Why should you remain in a religion that does not let you become educated?
Why should you remain in a religion that bars you from good jobs?
Why should you remain in a religion that dishonors you at every step?

That religion which forbids humanitarian behavior between men is not a
religion but a reckless penalty.

That religion which regards the recognition of human dignity as sin is
not a religion but a sickness.

That religion which allows one to touch a foul animal but not a man is
not a religion but a madness.

That religion which says one class may not gain knowledge, may not
acquire wealth, may not take up arms, is not a religion but a mockery of man's life.

That religion which teaches that the unlearned should remain unlearned,
that the poor should remain poor, is not a religion but a punishment. . . .

Those who say God exists in all beings and yet treat men as animals are
hypocrites. Don't associate with them.

Those who feed ants with sugar and let men go without water are hypocrites. Don't associate with them.

Those who embrace foreigners and keep their own countrymen from them
are traitors to society. Don't associate with them.

Partition India into Hindustan and Pakistan

In an astute analysis of the Muslim League's 1940 demand, written six years before
the actual partition of British-ruled India, Ambedkar articulated more clearly than
any other statesman of the time the potential advantages of the separation.

[From Ambedkar, *Thoughts on Pakistan*, pp. 341–44]

Summing up the whole discussion it appears that an integral India is incom-
patible with an independent India or even with India as a dominion. On
the footing that India is to be one integral whole there is a frustration of
all her hopes of freedom writ large on her future. There is frustration if the
national destiny is conceived in terms of independence, because the Hindus
will not follow that path. They have reasons not to follow it. They fear
that that way lies the establishment of the domination of the Muslims over
the Hindus. The Hindus see that the Muslim move for independence is not
innocent. It is strategy. It is to be used only to bring the Hindus out of the
protecting shield of the British Empire in the open and then by alliance

with the neighbouring Muslim countries and by their aid subjugate them. For the Muslims independence is not the end. It is only a means to establish Muslim Raj. There is frustration if the national destiny is conceived of in terms of Dominion Status because the Muslims will not agree to abide by it. They fear that under Dominion Status the Hindus will establish Hindu Raj over them by taking benefit of the principle of one man one vote and one vote one value and that however much the benefit of the principle is curtailed by weightage to Muslims the result cannot fail to be a Government of the Hindus, by the Hindus and therefore for the Hindus. Complete frustration of her destiny therefore seems to be the fate of India if it is insisted that India shall remain as one integral whole.

It is a question to be considered whether integral India is an ideal worth fighting for. In the first place even if India remained as one integral whole it will never be an organic whole. India may in name be continued to be known as one country but in reality it will be two separate countries— Pakistan and Hindustan—joined together by a forced and artificial union. This will be specially so under the stress of the two-nation theory [of Mr. Jinnah]. As it is, the idea of unity has had little hold on the Indian world of fact and reality, little charm for the common Indian, Hindu or Muslim, whose vision is bounded by the valley in which he lives. But it did appeal to the imaginative and unsophisticated minds on both sides. The two-nation theory will not leave room even for the growth of that sentimental desire for unity. The spread of that virus of dualism in the body politic must some day create a mentality which is sure to call for a life and death struggle for the dissolution of this forced union. If by reason of some superior force the dissolution does not take place, one thing is sure to happen to India— namely that this continued union will go on sapping her vitality, loosening its cohesion, weakening its hold on the love and faith of her people and preventing the use, if not retarding the growth, of its moral and material resources. India will be an anæmic and sickly state, ineffective, a living corpse, dead though not buried. . . .

Ambedkar next predicted that a forced union of Hindus and Muslims would both retard their progress and result in "a federation of mutually suspicious and unfriendly states," which would then have to appeal to a third party to enforce peace among them.

All this of course means the frustration of the political destiny which both Hindus and Muslims profess to cherish and the early consumation of which they so devoutly wish. What else, however, can be expected if two warring nations are locked in the bosom of one Country and one Constitution?

Compare with this dark vista, the vista that opens out if India is divided into Pakistan and Hindustan. The partition opens the way to a fulfilment of the destiny each may fix for itself. Muslims will be free to choose for their Pakistan independence or dominion status, whatever they think good for themselves. Hindus will be free to choose for their Hindustan independence or dominion status, whatever they may think wise for their condition. The Muslims will be freed from the nightmare of Hindu Raj and Hindus will save themselves from the hazard of a Muslim Raj. Thus the path of political progress becomes smooth for both. The fear of the object being frustrated gives place to the hope of its fulfilment. . . . Communal Settlement must remain a necessary condition precedent, if India, as one integral whole, desires to make any political advance. But Pakistan and Hindustan are free from the rigourous trammels of such a condition precedent and even if a communal settlement with minorities remained to be a condition precedent it will not be difficult of fulfilment. The path of each is cleared of this obstacle. There is another advantage of Pakistan which must be mentioned. It is generally admitted that there does exist a kind of antagonism between Hindus and Muslims which if not dissolved will prove ruinous to the peace and progress of India. But it is not realized that the mischief is caused not so much by the existence of mutual antagonism as by the existence of a common theatre for its display. It is the common theatre which calls this antagonism in action. It cannot but be so. When the two are called to participate in acts of common concern what else can happen except a display of that antagonism which is inherent in them. Now this scheme of Pakistan has this advantage, namely, that it leaves no theatre for the play of that social antagonism which is the cause of disaffection among Hindus and Muslims. There is no fear of Hindustan and Pakistan suffering from that disturbance of peace and tranquility which has torn and shattered India for so many years. Last, but by no means least, is the elimination of the necessity of a third party to maintain peace. Freed from the trammels which one imposes upon the other by reason of this forced union—Pakistan and Hindustan can each grow into a strong stable State with no fear of disruption from within. As two separate entities, they can reach respective destinies which as parts of one whole they never can.

A Denunciation of Mr. Gandhi

In 1945, the differences between Gandhi and Ambedkar—between the man who called himself an Untouchable by choice and the man who was one by birth—brought forth Ambedkar's bitterest rhetoric. Although Gandhi had made the removal of untouchability one of his major concerns, he upheld the traditional arrangement of India's thousands of castes into four major groups, or *varnas*. He proposed that none of these groups—the priest, warrior, merchant, and manual worker—be treated as inferior to any of the others, and he supposed that the Untouchables could be fitted into the manual worker group. Ambedkar regarded this as impossible. He considered the name *harijan* (people of God), which Gandhi bestowed on the Untouchables, patronizing, and he renewed his criticism of Gandhi's opposition to the demand for separate untouchable electorates. Gandhi wanted to change men's hearts; Ambedkar's experience encouraged him to rely on legal safeguards and political opportunities for minority groups in danger of being tyrannized by a permanent majority.

The harsh tone of Ambedkar's attack has prototypes in the Marathi writings of the nineteenth-century nonbrāhman reformer Jotirao Phule and of B. G. Tilak.

[From Ambedkar, *What Gandhi and Congress Have Done to the Untouchables*, pp. 307–8]

What is there in Gandhism which is not to be found in orthodox Hinduism? There is caste in Hinduism, there is caste in Gandhism. Hinduism believes in the law of hereditary profession, so does Gandhism. Hinduism enjoins cow-worship. So does Gandhism. Hinduism upholds the law of *karma*, predestination of man's condition in this world, so does Gandhism. Hinduism accepts the authority of the Shastras. So does Gandhism. Hinduism believes in *avatars* or incarnations of God. So does Gandhism. Hinduism believes in idols. So does Gandhism.[29] All that Gandhism has done is to find a philosophic justification for Hinduism and its dogmas. Hinduism is bald in the sense that it is just a set of rules which bear on their face the appearance of a crude and cruel system. Gandhism supplies the philosophy which smoothens its surface and gives it the appearance of decency and respectability and so alters it and embellishes it as to make it even attractive. What philosophy does Gandhism propound to cover the nudity of Hinduism? This philosophy can be put in a nutshell. It is a philosophy which says: "All that is in Hinduism is well, all that is in Hinduism is necessary for public good." Those who are familiar with Voltaire's *Candide* will recognize that it is the philosophy of Master Pangloss and recall the mockery Voltaire made of it. The Hindus are of course pleased with it. No doubt it suits them and accords with their interest. Prof. Radhakrishnan[30]— whether out of genuine feeling or out of sycophancy we need not stop to inquire—has gone to the length of describing Mr. Gandhi as 'God on earth.' What do the Untouchables understand this to mean? To them it means: "This God by name Gandhi came to console an afflicted race: He saw India and changed it not saying all is well and will be, if the Hindus will only fulfil the law of caste. He told the afflicted race, 'I have come to fulfil the law of caste.' Not a tittle, not a jot shall I allow to abate from it."

What hope can Gandhism offer to the Untouchables? To the Untouchables, Hinduism is a veritable chamber of horrors. The sanctity and infallibility of the Vedas, Smritis and Shastras, the iron law of caste, the heartless law of karma and the senseless law of status by birth are to the Untouchables veritable instruments of torture which Hinduism has forged against the Untouchables. These very instruments which have mutilated, blasted and blighted the life of the Untouchables are to be found intact and untarnished in the bosom of Gandhism. How can the Untouchables say that Gandhism is a heaven and not a chamber of horrors as Hinduism has been? The only reaction and a very natural reaction of the Untouchables would be to run away from Gandhism.

Gandhists may say that what I have stated applies to the old type of Gandhism. There is a new Gandhism, Gandhism without caste. This has reference to the recent statement[31] of Mr. Gandhi that caste is an anachronism. Reformers were naturally gladdened by this declaration of Mr. Gandhi. And who would not be glad to see that a man like Mr. Gandhi having such terrible influence over the Hindus, after having played the most mischievous part of a social reactionary, after having stood out as the protagonist of the caste system, after having beguiled and befooled the unthinking Hindus with arguments which made no distinction between what is fair and foul should have come out with this recantation? But is this really a matter for jubilation? Does it change the nature of Gandhism? Does it make Gandhism a new and a better 'ism' than it was before. Those who are carried away by this recantation of Mr. Gandhi, forget two things. In the first place, all that Mr. Gandhi has said is that caste is an anachronism. He does not say it is an evil. He does not say it is anathema. Mr. Gandhi may be taken to be not in favour of caste. But Mr. Gandhi does not say that he is against the *varna* system. And what is Mr. Gandhi's *varna* system? It is simply a new name for the caste system and retains all the worst features of the caste system.

The declaration of Mr. Gandhi cannot be taken to mean any fundamental change in Gandhism. It cannot make Gandhism acceptable to the Untouchables. The Untouchables will still have ground to say: "Good God! Is this man Gandhi our Saviour?"

NOTES

1. Thompson, *Rabindranath Tagore: His Life and Work*, p. 44.
2. Translatable as "universal learning," as "all-India," or as "the world and India."
3. Chattopadhyaya, "Mahatma Gandhi at Rabindranath's Santiniketan," in *Visva-Bharati Quarterly (special issue, 1949)*, p. 336.
4. Nehru, *The Discovery of India*, pp. 342-43.
5. Divine creative power.
6. The hand-operated spinning wheel, traditionally plied by women and people of low status.
7. Keer, *Savarkar and His Times*, p. 219.
8. God of the Waters.
9. The village near Mathura where Krishna is said to have spent his boyhood.
10. "Land of the Rivers." *Sindhu* (river) is presumably the earlier form from which *Hindu* derives.
11. The age and the eon.
12. A member of the Brahmo, Prarthana, or Arya Samajes.
13. Orthodox Hindu.
14. A Shaivite sect.
15. S. C. Bose, *Netaji's Life and Writings. Part One: An Indian Pilgrim; or, Autobiography of Subhas Chandra Bose, 1897–1920*, p. 3.
16. *Prāṇāyāma*: breath-control.
17. *Dhyāna*: meditation.
18. Hermitages; communities engaged in spiritual effort and abstinence from the pleasures of the senses.
19. Short for *devanāgarī*, "of the city of the gods," the script in which Sanskrit, Hindi, and Marathi are written.
20. *Urdū*, "the language of the army camp," developed under Muslim rule into the language of high culture of both Muslims and Hindus, but especially the former. It is written in a modified Arabic script.
21. In 1928 President Mustafa Kemal had ordered that the Roman script, instead of the Arabic, be used as the common script in Turkey.
22. "Long live the revolution! Long live free India!"

23. Nehru: *An Autobiography*, p. 1.
24. *Ibid.*, p. 77.
25. Nehru: *Soviet Russia, Some Random Sketches and Impressions*.
26. Singh, *Nehru, the Rising Star of India*, p. 143.
27. Nehru, *Independence and After*, p. 17.
28. Untouchables are forbidden by custom to take water from a source used by caste Hindus, lest their presence there pollute it.
29. "Mr. Gandhi's articles of faith have been outlined by him in *Young India* of 6th October 1921." [Ambedkar's note.]
30. Sarvepalli Radhakrishnan (1888–1975), exponent of Indian philosophy and president of India, 1962–1967.
31. *Hindustan Times*, April 15, 1945.

Chapter 8

PUBLIC POLICIES FOR
INDEPENDENT INDIA

The coming of independence and the passing of Gandhi ushered in a new era for the diverse peoples of India. Along with the natural euphoria produced by the departure of their former rulers, Indians had to deal with the new problems of armed conflict with Pakistan over Kashmir, a huge influx of refugees, the integration of the semi-autonomous kingdoms, and the redrawing of the old provincial boundaries so as to form one state for each major regional language area. A new constitution was set in place, dedicated to the high goals of justice, liberty, equality, and fraternity, and providing orderly procedures for moving toward these goals. Meanwhile the old, less manageable problems of massive and widespread poverty, malnutrition, ill-health, and illiteracy persisted.

As time went on, spokesmen for different philosophies of governmental, economic, and social reform sought to attract public support for their solutions to the country's problems. The dominant school of thought in the ruling Congress Party may be described as pragmatic, progressive, and in direct continuity with the philosophy and methods of the earlier Moderates and their program of social reform, education, and strengthening of civil liberties. From 1947 to 1964 under Nehru, and from 1966 to 1977 and 1980 to 1984 under his daughter Indira Gandhi, the Congress provided a centralizing force in a country well-supplied with competing groups, whether political, religious, social, economic, linguistic, or regional.

Among the numerous parties and political philosophies that have competed with the Congress and that have survived the elections held usually at five-year intervals, three major schools of thought are represented in this chapter. At polar opposites are the Marxist-Leninist (or Communist) and the Hinducentric nationalist viewpoints. Closer to the Congress, but more idealistic, is the liberal Socialist school. All these schools have emerged as political parties and have competed for the support of the voters under the broad umbrella of India's democratic constitution.

THE CONSTITUTION OF INDIA

The legal framework for all public life in India since 1950 has been the Constitution. In its original form, it emerged from the collective wisdom of certain civil servants and the members elected to the Central Legislative Assembly in 1946 under the procedures of the 1935 Government of India Act. In many respects the political system it produced grew out of that Act and the institution that fathered it—the British Parliament. Amended forty-four times by 1979, the Constitution contained at that time 395 articles grouped into twenty-two parts, with further provisions appended under nine "schedules." It resembled the U.S. federal system in assuring each state considerable autonomy from the central government (except in times of "emergency"), but the executive branch at both levels was formed in a fashion like that of the British Parliament (the chief ministers and prime minister being chosen by whichever party or coalition could hold the majority in the elected state and central legislatures).

Although this document's many intricately worded articles may seem to justify the saying that it was written *by* lawyers, *for* lawyers, in spirit and structure it embodies and protects the yearning for greater liberty and justice under law that had animated the members of the Indian National Congress since its inception in 1885. To this political aspiration the drafters of the Constitution added steps for achieving stronger national unity and greater social and economic equality—insofar as these could be mandated by law. Perhaps at a deeper, more emotional level, this charter for India's future resonated to the age-old Indian feeling that there is an order in creation, be that *dīn* or *dharma*, with which human actions, if they are to succeed, must be aligned.

The Preamble

[From *Constitution of India* (1979), p. 1]

WE, THE PEOPLE OF INDIA, having solemnly resolved to constitute India into a SOVEREIGN SOCIALIST SECULAR DEMOCRATIC REPUBLIC[1] and to secure to all its citizens:

JUSTICE, social, economic and political;

LIBERTY of thought, expression, belief, faith and worship;

EQUALITY of status and of opportunity; and to promote among them all

FRATERNITY assuring the dignity of the individual and the unity and integrity of the nation;

IN OUR CONSTITUENT ASSEMBLY this twenty-sixth day of November, 1949, do HEREBY ADOPT, ENACT AND GIVE TO OUR-SELVES THIS CONSTITUTION.

Part III: Fundamental Rights

Except for a complicated article concerning arrest without trial, the passages quoted here delineate the major civil liberties set forth in this part of the Constitution. For clarity, in article 19 the "reasonable restrictions" for each freedom have here been placed immediately following it, instead of after the whole list, as in the Constitution itself.

[From *Constitution of India* (1979), pp. 6–10]

14. The State [the Government of India] shall not deny to any person equality before the law or the equal protection of the laws within the territory of India.

15. (1) The State shall not discriminate against any citizen on grounds only of religion, race, sex, place of birth or any of them. . . .

16. There shall be equality of opportunity for all citizens in matters relating to employment or appointment to any office under the State. . . .

17. "Untouchability" is abolished and its practice in any form is forbidden. . . .

19. (1) All citizens shall have the right—

  (a) to freedom of speech and expression . . . [except that] reasonable restrictions on the exercise of the right conferred . . . [may be imposed by the State] in the interests of the sovereignty and integrity of India, the security of the State, friendly relations with foreign States, public order, decency or morality or in relation to contempt of court, defamation or incitement to an offence. . . .

  (b) to assemble peaceably and without arms . . . [except when] the interests of the sovereignty and integrity of India or public order [justify] reasonable restrictions on the exercise of the right conferred. . . .

(c) to form associations or unions . . . [except when] the interests of the sovereignty and integrity of India or public order or morality [justify] reasonable restrictions on the exercise of the right conferred. . . .

(d) to move freely throughout the territory of India . . . [except that] reasonable restrictions [may be imposed by the State] . . . either in the interests of the general public or for the protection of the interests of any Scheduled Tribe.[2]

(e) to reside and settle in any part of the territory of India . . . [except as in (d)]. . . .

(g) to practise any profession, or to carry on any occupation, trade or business . . . [except when the State imposes] in the interests of the general public, reasonable restrictions on the exercise of the right conferred. . . .[3]

Part IV: Directive Principles of State Policy

Part III of the Constitution of India spelled out the individual's rights; Part IV the State's duties, especially in making improvements in the social and economic spheres. As in Part III, the most important articles come at the beginning.

[From *Constitution of India* (1979), pp. 15–16]

38. (1) The State shall strive to promote the welfare of the people by securing and protecting as effectively as it may a social order in which justice, social, economic and political, shall inform all the institutions of the national life.

(2) The State shall, in particular, strive to minimise the inequalities in income, and endeavour to eliminate inequalities in status, facilities and opportunities, not only amongst individuals but also amongst groups of people residing in different areas or engaged in different vocations.

39. The State shall, in particular, direct its policy towards securing—

(a) that the citizens, men and women equally, have the right to an adequate means to livelihood;

(b) that the ownership and control of the material resources of the community are so distributed as best to subserve the common good;

(c) that the operation of the economic system does not result in the concentration of wealth and means of production to the common detriment;

(d) that there is equal pay for equal work for both men and women;

(e) that the health and strength of workers, men and women, and the tender age of children are not abused and that citizens are not forced by economic necessity to enter avocations unsuited to their age or strength;

(f) that children are given opportunities and facilities to develop in a healthy manner and in conditions of freedom and dignity and that childhood and youth are protected against exploitation and against moral and material abandonment. . . .

Part IVA: Fundamental Duties

During the 1975–1977 "Emergency," the constitution was considerably amended to increase the powers of the central government over the state governments and over individuals. One of the few changes that was left untouched by the Janata government—when in 1978 it passed the Forty-Fourth Amendment—was the 1976 introduction of the "fundamental duties" of citizens.

[From *Constitution of India* (1979), p. 18]

51A. It shall be the duty of every citizen of India—

(a) to abide by the Constitution and respect its ideals and institutions, the National Flag and the National Anthem;

(b) to cherish and follow the noble ideals which inspired our national struggle for freedom;

(c) to uphold and protect the sovereignty, unity and integrity of India;

(d) to defend the country and render national service when called upon to do so;

(e) to promote harmony and the spirit of common brotherhood amongst all the people of India transcending religious, linguistic and regional or sectarian diversities; to renounce practices derogatory to the dignity of women;

(f) to value and preserve the rich heritage of our composite culture;

(g) to protect and improve the natural environment including forests, lakes, rivers and wild life, and to have compassion for living creatures;

(h) to develop the scientific temper, humanism and the spirit of in-quiry and reform;

(i) to safeguard public property and to abjure violence;

(j) to strive towards excellence in all spheres of individual and col-lective activity, so that the nation constantly rises to higher lev-els of endeavour and achievement.

AMBEDKAR: UNTOUCHABLE STATESMAN (PART 2)

In the euphoria of independence, B. R. Ambedkar, champion of the Un-touchables and major critic of the Congress and Gandhi, entered into a four-year period of creative cooperation with the Congress government. On August 3, 1947, he was named to the first Nehru cabinet as Minister for Law. On August 29, 1947, the Drafting Committee for the Constitution was set up with Ambedkar as its chairman. In this capacity, he served ably and objectively, bending his efforts toward securing as effective a constitu-tion as possible for all India in the light of the Constituent Assembly mem-bers' combined wisdom. His earlier demands for separate untouchable elec-torates and villages were dropped, but the new Government of India committed itself to the abolition of untouchability and to a wide range of benefits for depressed minorities.

By 1951, Ambedkar was dissatisfied with India's progress. He resigned as law minister in protest over the withdrawal of support by Nehru's cabinet for the Hindu Code Bill.[4] He was also in disagreement with Nehru's foreign policy of nonalignment, since he felt India's best friends were the democ-racies, and he charged that the interests of the Scheduled Castes were not given prime importance by the government. But in spite of his disillusion-ment and increasing ill health, he continued to break new ground. He established Milind College in Aurangabad in 1951, deliberately choosing the most backward and neglected area in Marathi-speaking territory. He visited Buddhist countries, wrote about Buddhism, and, on October 14, 1956, converted to Buddhism in a massive ceremony in Nagpur. In the following years, over four million Indians, chiefly from the Scheduled Castes, declared themselves Buddhists. Ambedkar also set in motion the framework for a new political party, the Republican Party, which, like the Buddhist movement, was intended to serve not only the Scheduled Castes but all the dispossessed of India.

Ambedkar's death on December 6, 1956, only two months after his conversion, did not bring an end to his movement. The Republican Party was to have little more success than the earlier Scheduled Castes Federation, but the dynamics of the movement continued to flow in other channels. Educational institutions sprang up over the Marathi-speaking area. The psychological freedom induced by the Buddhist conversion and the ability brought about by the stress on education produced a literary movement that now flourishes as one of the most important and creative schools of writing in Marathi. Urban-educated young Buddhists began the Dalit Panther movement, taking their name from the Marathi word for "downtrodden" and the American Black Panther movement. The Scheduled Castes who had secured government jobs under the reservation scheme organized in a nonpolitical but socially effective group. Former Untouchables who had migrated to the U.S. and Canada created groups to press, in Ambedkar's name, for better conditions for their brothers in India. A spate of biographies, political studies, and university lectures on Ambedkar and his thought appeared in various parts of India.

A backlash against the reservations, and in villages against the visible progress of the former Untouchables, has appeared in several regions of India, the most telling incident being the anti-Buddhist riots in 1968 in Marathawada, the very area in which Ambedkar established higher education. The issue was the renaming of Marathawada University as Ambedkar University. Ambedkar's name as a symbol of the greatness that could be achieved by the lowly and as a symbol of the oppression still suffered continues to be the most important rallying cry of India's former Untouchables.

Debating the Draft Constitution

On November 4, 1948, Ambedkar, as chairman of the drafting committee, moved that the first draft of the constitution be considered by the Constituent Assembly. Answering the criticism of Gandhians as to why the constitution was not based on the villages of India, he denounced the iniquities of village life. He then proposed a logical way to end the governmental safeguards previously accorded to minority communities.

[From *Constituent Assembly Debates*, 7:38–39]

Another criticism against the Draft Constitution is that no part of it represents the ancient polity of India. It is said that the new Constitution should have been drafted on the ancient Hindu model of a State and that instead of incorporating Western theories the new Constitution should have been raised and built upon village panchayats and District Panchayats. There are others who have taken a more extreme view. They do not want any Central or Provincial Governments. They just want India to contain so many village Governments. The love of the intellectual Indians for the village community is of course infinite if not pathetic *(laughter)*. It is largely due to the fulsome praise bestowed upon it by Metcalfe[5] who described them as little republics having nearly everything that they want within themselves, and almost independent of any foreign relations. The existence of these village communities each one forming a separate little State in itself has according to Metcalfe contributed more than any other cause to the preservation of the people of India, through all the revolutions and changes which they have suffered, and is in a high degree conducive to their happiness and to the enjoyment of a great portion of the freedom and independence. No doubt the village communities have lasted where nothing else lasts. But those who take pride in the village communities do not care to consider what little part they have played in the affairs and the destiny of the country; and why? Their part in the destiny of the country has been well described by Metcalfe himself who says:

"Dynasty after dynasty tumbles down. Revolution succeeds to revolution. Hindoo, Pathan, Mogul, Maharatha, Sikh, English, are all masters in turn but the village communities remain the same. In times of trouble they arm and fortify themselves. A hostile army passes through the country. The village communities collect their little cattle within their walls and let the enemy pass unprovoked."

Such is the part the village communities have played in the history of their country. Knowing this, what pride can one feel in them? That they have survived through all viscisitudes may be a fact. But mere survival has no value. The question is on what plane they have survived. Surely on a low, on a selfish level. I hold that these village republics have been the ruination of India. I am therefore surprised that those who condemn Provincialism and communalism should come forward as champions of the village. What is the village but a sink of localism, a den of ignorance, narrowmindedness and communalism? I am glad that the Draft Constitution has discarded the village and adopted the individual as its unit.

The Draft Constitution is also criticised because of the safeguards it provides for minorities. In this, the Drafting Committee has no responsibility. It follows the decisions of the Constituent Assembly. Speaking for myself,

I have no doubt that the Constituent Assembly has done wisely in providing such safeguards for minorities as it has done. In this country both the minorities and the majorities have followed a wrong path. It is wrong for the majority to deny the existence of minorities. It is equally wrong for the minorities to perpetuate themselves. A solution must be found which will serve a double purpose. It must recognize the existence of the minorities to start with. It must also be such that it will enable majorities and minorities to merge someday into one. The solution proposed by the Constituent Assembly is to be welcomed because it is a solution which serves this twofold purpose. To diehards who have developed a kind of fanaticism against minority protection I would like to say two things. One is that minorities are an explosive force which, if it erupts, can blow up the whole fabric of the State. The history of Europe bears ample and appalling testimony to this fact. The other is that the minorities in India have agreed to place their existence in the hands of the majority. In the history of negotiations for preventing the partition of Ireland, Redmond said to Carson "ask for any safeguard you like for the Protestant minority but let us have a United Ireland." Carson's reply was "Damn your safeguards, we don't want to be ruled by you." No minority in India has taken this stand. They have loyally accepted the rule of the majority which is basically a communal majority and not a political majority. It is for the majority to realize its duty not to discriminate against minorities. Whether the minorities will continue or will vanish must depend upon this habit of the majority. The moment the majority loses the habit of discriminating against the minority, the minorities can have no ground to exist. They will vanish.

Looking to the Future

At the third and final reading of the bill to enact the new constitution into law (in November 1949), Ambedkar warned the Constituent Assembly of the dangers both to India's independence and to her democratic constitution. As remedies, he advised devotion to the country, an end to civil disobedience, avoidance of hero-worship, the fostering of social and economic equality, and adherence to constitutional methods of self-government.

[From *Constituent Assembly Debates*, 11:977–81]

On 26th January 1950, India will be an independent country (*Cheers*). What would happen to her independence? Will she maintain her independence or will she lose it again? This is the first thought that comes to my mind. It is not that India was never an independent country. The point is that she once lost the independence she had. Will she lose it a second time? It is this thought which makes me most anxious for the future. What perturbs me greatly is the fact that not only India has once before lost her independence, but she lost it by the infidelity and treachery of some of her own people. In the invasion of Sind by Mahommed-Bin-Kasim, the military commanders of King Dahar accepted bribes from the agents of Mahommend-Bin-Kasim and refused to fight on the side of their King. It was Jaichand who invited Mahommed Ghori to invade India and fight against Prithvi Raj and promised him the help of himself and the Solanki kings. When Shivaji was fighting for the liberation of Hindus, the other Maratha noblemen and the Rajput Kings were fighting the battle on the side of Moghul Emperors. When the British were trying to destroy the Sikh Rulers, Gulab Singh, their principal commander sat silent and did not help to save the Sikh kingdom. In 1857, when a large part of India had declared a war of independence against the British, the Sikhs stood and watched the event as silent spectators.

Will history repeat itself? It is this thought which fills me with anxiety. This anxiety is deepened by the realization of the fact that in addition to our old enemies in the form of castes and creeds we are going to have many political parties with diverse and opposing political creeds. Will Indians place the country above their creed or will they place creed above country? I do not know. But this much is certain that if the parties place creed above country, our independence will be put in jeopardy a second time and probably be lost for ever. This eventuality we must all resolutely guard against. We must be determined to defend our independence with the last drop of our blood. (*Cheers.*)

On the 26th of January 1950, India would be a democratic country in the sense that India from that day would have a government of the people, by the people, and for the people. The same thought comes to my mind. What would happen to her democratic Constitution? Will she be able to maintain it or will she lose it again. This is the second thought that comes to my mind and makes me as anxious as the first.

It is not that India did not know what is Democracy. There was a time when India was studded with republics, and even where there were monarchies, they were either elected or limited. They were never absolute. It is not that India did not know Parliaments or Parliamentary Procedure. A study of the Buddhist Bhikshu Sanghas [monastic orders] discloses that not only there were Parliaments—for the Sanghas were nothing but Parliaments—but the Sanghas knew and observed all the rules of Parliamentary Procedure known to modern times. They had rules regarding seating arrangements, rules regarding Motions, Resolutions, Quorum, Whip, Counting of Votes, Voting by Ballot, Censure Motion, Regularization, *Res Judicata*, etc. Although these rules of Parliamentary Procedure were applied by the Buddha to the meetings of the Sanghas, he must have borrowed them from the rules of the Political Assemblies functioning in the country in his time.

This democratic system India lost. Will she lose it a second time? I do not know. But it is quite possible in a country like India—where democracy from its long disuse must be regarded as something quite new—there is danger of democracy giving place to dictatorship. It is quite possible for this new born democracy to retain its form but give place to dictatorship in fact. If there is a landslide, the danger of the second possibility becoming actuality is much greater.

If we wish to maintain democracy not merely in form, but also in fact, what must we do? The first thing in my judgment we must do is to hold fast to constitutional methods of achieving our social and economic objectives. It means we must abandon the bloody methods of revolution. It means that we must abandon the method of civil disobedience, non-cooperation and satyagraha. When there was no way left for constitutional methods for achieving economic and social objectives, there was a great deal of justification for unconstitutional methods. But where constitutional methods are open, there can be no justification for these unconstitutional methods. These methods are nothing but the Grammar of Anarchy and the sooner they are abandoned, the better for us.

The second thing we must do is to observe the caution which John Stuart Mill has given to all who are interested in the maintenance of democracy, namely, not "to lay their liberties at the feet of even a great man, or to trust him with powers which enable him to subvert their institutions". There is nothing wrong in being grateful to great men who have rendered life-long services to the country. But there are limits to gratefulness. As has been well said by the Irish Patriot Daniel O'Connell, no man can be grateful at the cost of his honour, no woman can be grateful at the cost of her chastity and no nation can be grateful at the cost of its liberty. This caution is far more necessary in the case of India than in the case of any other country. For in India, Bhakti or what may be called the path of devotion or hero-worship, plays a part in its politics unequalled in magnitude by the part it plays in the politics of any other country in the world. Bhakti in religion may be a road to the salvation of the soul. But in politics, Bhakti or hero-worship is a sure road to degradation and to eventual dictatorship.

The third thing we must do is not to be content with mere political democracy. We must make our political democracy a social democracy as well. Political democracy cannot last unless there lies at the base of it social democracy. What does social democracy mean? It means a way of life which recognizes liberty, equality and fraternity as the principles of life. These principles of liberty, equality and fraternity are not to be treated as separate items in a trinity. They form a union of trinity in the sense that to divorce one from the other is to defeat the very purpose of democracy. Liberty cannot be divorced from equality, equality cannot be divorced from liberty. Nor can liberty and equality be divorced from fraternity. Without equality, liberty would produce the supremacy of the few over the many. Equality without liberty would kill individual initiative. Without fraternity, liberty and equality could not become a natural course of things. It would require a constable to enforce them.

We must begin by acknowledging the fact that there is complete absence of two things in Indian Society. One of these is equality. On the social plane, we have in India a society based on the principle of graded inequality which means elevation for some and degradation for others. On the economic plane, we have a society in which there are some who have immense wealth as against many who live in abject poverty. On the 26th of January 1950, we are going to enter into a life of contradictions. In politics we will have equality and in social and economic life we will have inequality. In politics we will be recognizing the principle of one man one vote and one vote one value. In our social and economic life, we shall, by reason of our social and economic structure, continue to deny the principle of one man one value. How long shall we continue to live this life of contradictions? How long shall we continue to deny equality in our social and economic life? If we continue to deny it for long, we will do so only by putting our political democracy in peril. We must remove this contradiction at the earliest possible moment or else those who suffer from inequality will blow up the structure of political democracy which this Assembly has so laboriously built up.

The second thing we are wanting in is recognition of the principle of fraternity. What does fraternity mean? Fraternity means a sense of common brotherhood of all Indians—of Indians being one people. It is the principle which gives unity and solidarity to social life. It is a difficult thing to achieve. . . .

I am of [the] opinion that in believing that we are a nation, we are cherishing a great delusion. How can people divided into several thousands of castes be a nation? The sooner we realize that we are not as yet a nation in the social and psychological sense of the word, the better for us. For then only we shall realize the necessity of becoming a nation and seriously think of ways and means of realizing the goal. The realization of this goal is going to be very difficult—far more difficult than it has been in the United States. The United States has no caste problem. In India there are castes. The castes are anti-national. In the first place because they bring about separation in social life. They are anti-national also because they generate jealousy and antipathy between caste and caste. But we must overcome all these difficulties if we wish to become a nation in reality. For fraternity can be a fact only when there is a nation. Without fraternity equality and liberty will be no deeper than coats of paint.

These are my reflections about the tasks that lie ahead of us. They may not be very pleasant to some. But there can be no gainsaying that political power in this country has too long been the monopoly of a few and the many are not only beasts of burden, but also beasts of prey. This monopoly has not merely deprived them of their chance of betterment, it has sapped them of what may be called the significance of life. These down-trodden classes are tired of being governed. They are impatient to govern themselves. This urge for self-realization in the down-trodden classes must not be allowed to devolve into class struggle or class war. It would lead to a division of the House. That would indeed be a day of disaster. For, as has been well said by Abraham Lincoln, a House divided against itself cannot stand very long. Therefore the sooner room is made for the realization of their aspiration, the better for the few, the better for the country, the better for the maintenance of its independence and the better for the continuance of its democratic structure. This can only be done by the establishment of equality and fraternity in all spheres of life. That is why I have laid so much stress on them.

I do not wish to weary the House any further. Independence is no doubt a matter of joy. But let us not forget that this independence has thrown on us great responsibilities. By independence, we have lost the excuse of blaming the British for anything going wrong. If hereafter things go wrong, we will have nobody to blame except ourselves. There is great danger of things going wrong. Times are fast changing. People including our own are being moved by new ideologies. They are getting tired of Government by the people. They are prepared to have Government for the people and are indifferent whether it is Government of the people and by the people. If we wish to preserve the Constitution in which we have sought to enshrine the principle of Government of the people, for the people and by the people, let us resolve not to be so tardy in the recognition of the evils that lie across our path and which induce people to prefer Government for the people to Government by the people, nor to be weak in our initiative to remove them. This is the only way to serve the country. I know of no better.

Why Accept Buddhism?

Although Ambedkar's interest in Buddhism began in the 1920s, his conversion to it (immediately followed by a mass conversion of Untouchables to Buddhism) did not take place until October of 1956. The oldest Buddhist monk in India initiated him, and then Ambedkar administered the three refuges, the five vows, and twenty-four oaths of his own devising to an assembled multitude that may have numbered half a million people. He had been ill for several years and was to die within two months. The day after the conversion ceremony he spoke in simple, colorful Marathi to the other converts. He spoke not as a lawyer or statesman, but as a weary fighter, wanting to leave his followers with a religion he felt was moral, egalitarian, and respected—a religion that they should honor and practice in the best possible way, thus "saving themselves and their country."

[From *Prabuddha Bhārat* (Awakened India), October 27, 1956, trans. by Eleanor Zelliot and Rekha Damle]

Much discussion has been going on everywhere, but not even one man has asked me, "Why did you accept Buddhism?" . . . In any movement to change religion, this is the main question. . . . "Even though I was born in the Hindu religion, I will not die in the Hindu religion"—this oath I made earlier. Yesterday I proved it true. I am happy; I am ecstatic; I have left hell—this is how I feel. I do not want any blind followers. Those who come into the Buddhist religion should come with understanding; they should consciously accept that religion.

Religion is a very necessary thing for the progress of mankind. I know that a sect has appeared because of the writings of Karl Marx. According to their creed, religion means nothing at all. Religion is not important to them. They get a breakfast in the morning of bread, cream, butter, chicken legs, etc.; they get undisturbed sleep; they get to see movies; and that's all there is. This is their philosophy. I am not of that opinion. My father was poor and therefore we did not get comforts of that kind. . . . How hard a man's life can be without happiness and comforts, that I know. I agree that an economic elevation movement is necessary. . . .

In this country, the situation is such that we can be kept in a hopeless state for a thousand years. As long as such conditions prevail, it is not possible to begin to produce ambition to progress. . . . It is written in the *Manusmriti* that Shudras should do only menial service. Why should they have education? . . . There is no equality in the Hindu religion. . . .

In the Buddhist religion, seventy-five percent of the monks were Brahman; twenty-five percent were Shudra and others. But Lord Buddha said: "O monks, you have come from different countries and castes. Rivers flow separately in their own countries, but do not remain distinct when they meet in the sea. They become one and the same. The Buddhist brotherhood of monks is like the sea. In this sangha [religious order] all are equal. It is impossible to know Ganga water from Mahanadi water after both have merged in the sea. In that way, after coming into the Buddhist sangha your caste goes, and all people are equal."

Only one great man spoke of equality, and that great man is the Lord Buddha. . . .

We will go by our path; others should go by their path. We have found a new way. This is a day of hope. This is a way of success, of prosperity. . . . No one can say that Buddhist principles are for this time only. Even today, 2500 years afterwards, all the world respects the principles of Buddhism. . . . Buddhist principles are immortal. Nevertheless the Buddha did not make the claim that this religion is from God. The Buddha said, "My father was a common man, my mother was a common woman. If you want a religion, then you should take this religion. If this religion suits your mind, then accept it."

JAWAHARLAL NEHRU: DEMOCRATIC SOCIALIST (PART 2)

Independent India was fortunate during her first seventeen years to have Jawaharlal Nehru as both her prime minister and minister for external (i.e., foreign) affairs. Nehru provided the dynamic leadership essential for preserving national unity, fostering democratic procedures, and accelerating economic progress. He enhanced India's position in the world by his frequent trips abroad and by his organization of a "third force" of nonaligned nations. Yet, although he worked for world peace, he failed to settle the quarrel over Kashmir that had festered between India and Pakistan since 1947. And his hopes for lasting friendship with China were dashed by the war in 1962 over territory claimed by both countries on India's northern and northeastern frontiers.

Nehru's greatest legacy to succeeding prime ministers—who have included his daughter, Indira Gandhi and his grandson, Rajiv—was his firm commitment to both parliamentary democracy with full civil liberties, and to the creation of what he called in 1954 "a socialist pattern of society which is classless, casteless."[6] Within the framework of these two systems—one political, the other economic and social—he envisaged a world in which each individual would be assured of "full opportunities to develop," with opportunities to meet not only material needs, but also moral and spiritual ones. And in regard to ways of meeting these higher needs, he told an interviewer, "Whatever raises a person above his normal level is good, however he approaches that—provided he does not sit on somebody and force *him* to do it."[7]

To Peace Through Nonalignment and Freedom from Fear

In a speech at Columbia University in 1949, Nehru explained his government's policy of not choosing sides in the cold war.

[From Nehru, *Speeches, 1949–1953*, pp. 400–2]

India is a very old country with a great past. But she is a new country also, with new urges and desires. Since August 1947, she has been in a position to pursue a foreign policy of her own. She was limited by the realities of the situation which we could not ignore or overcome. But even so, she could not forget the lesson of her great leader. She has tried to adapt, however imperfectly, theory to reality in so far as she could. . . . India came into the family of nations with no prejudices or enmities, ready to welcome and be welcomed. Inevitably, she had to consider her foreign policy in terms of enlightened self-interest but at the same time she brought to it a touch of her idealism. Thus, she has tried to combine idealism with national interest. The main objectives of that policy are: the pursuit of peace, not through alignment with any major power or group of powers but through an independent approach to each controversial or disputed issue, the liberation of subject peoples, the maintenance of freedom, both national and individual, the elimination of racial discrimination and the elimination of want, disease and ignorance, which afflict the greater part of the world's population. I am asked frequently why India does not align herself with a particular nation or a group of nations and told that because we have refrained from doing so we are sitting on the fence. The question and the comment are easily understood, because in times of crisis it is not unnatural for those who are involved in it deeply to regard calm objectivity in others as irrational, short-sighted, negative, unreal or even unmanly. But I should like to make it clear that the policy India has sought to pursue is not a negative and neutral policy. It is a positive and a vital policy that flows from our struggle for freedom and from the teaching of Mahatma Gandhi. Peace is not only an absolute necessity for us in India in order to progress and develop but is also of paramount importance to the world. How can that peace be preserved? Not by surrendering to aggression, not by compromising with evil or injustice but also not by talking and preparing for war! Aggression has to be met, for it endangers peace. At the same time, the lesson of the last two wars has to be remembered and it seems to me astonishing that, in spite of that lesson, we go the same way. The very process of marshalling the world into two hostile camps precipitates the conflict which it has sought to avoid. It produces a sense of terrible fear and that fear darkens men's minds and leads them into wrong courses. There is perhaps nothing so bad and so dangerous in life as fear. As a great President of the United States said, there is nothing really to fear except fear itself.

Full Progress in a Full Democracy

In the closing years of his life, Nehru stressed the basic problems that future generations in India and elsewhere have had to confront in order to achieve a better life for all.

[From Nehru, *Speeches*, 1963–1964, as indicated]

You will remember that when the Industrial Revolution came to England and Western Europe, they did not have democracy, except in a very very limited way. In a sense, that smoothened the process of change there, although it brought a good deal of suffering to those people at that time.

But we have to function in the context of full democracy, a full realization by people of their political and economic demands. That comes in the way of a smooth change-over to industrialization as it happened in Europe in the early days of the Industrial Revolution. So, functioning in this context, we have had to carry on an experiment, a tremendous experiment of maintaining our democratic structure and at the same time of planning for as rapid a progress, industrial and scientific, as was feasible for us. In what measure we have succeeded is a matter for you to judge and for the world to judge.

I believe that in spite of many difficulties and errors of commission and omission, we have made considerable progress. Progress does not ultimately consist of merely industrial enterprises. That is only a symbol of it. Progress ultimately has to be measured by the quality of human beings—how they are improving, how their lot is improving, and how they are adapting themselves to modern ways and yet keep their feet firmly planted on their soil.

It is difficult to judge this by statistics, although statistics help greatly. But I think it may be said, on the whole, that we have been laying sound foundations for our progress. [pp. 42–43]

As I look back . . . over the last 50 years of my life, it is amazing how changes have occurred all over the world, including India, of course. The pace of change is becoming greater every year. We read about them now and then and do not get much excited about it. We read about cosmonauts and astronauts going round and round the planet, or somebody aiming at the moon or Mars. We take these things in our stride. The way most extraordinary developments become commonplace shows how we adapt ourselves to changing conditions. The whole point is that the world is changing very rapidly and that affects us, too.

In India, there is another aspect to the problem, an important aspect that we have to bear in mind, namely, the growth of population. This is having lasting effects on us. There is the possibility that this growth of population may overwhelm us and upset all our calculations. We have to be aware of this danger. When all these big things are happening around us, one has to fit them into the chart of progress which we make for the country.

Obviously, everybody will agree, almost everybody, that we have to provide a good life to all our citizens. We may argue about what a good life is. But essentially a good life means certain basic material things that everybody should have, like enough food and clothing, a house to live in, education, health services and work. These are the natural things that everyone should have. How do we do that? We can only do that by producing the wherewithal to provide these good things. We do not go about giving them by loans or doles, but by the wealth we produce. We can produce them only by applying modern methods of science, technology, etc. There is no other way of doing it. [pp. 65–66]

What is the place of small industries? We have big plans and all that. I am all in favour of machinery. I like the feel of machinery, the look of it, but more and more, I have felt that from the point of view of balanced development, we have to lay greater stress on many small industries in our villages, make them slightly urbanized, lessen the gap between them and the urban areas and increase the facilities available to the people who live there, instead of concentrating on the towns and cities and drawing out people from the villages, thus creating problems in the cities. [pp. 101–2]

We have always to consider that we work for the vast mass of people in India. India is not merely a land of mountains and rivers and forests and cities and towns; it is a mass of human beings, many of them struggling for a bare pittance. The real test is how we make the life of those people better. If we think only of our individual betterment and profits, we lose grip of the real problem, and all perspective. . . . Therefore, everything that we aim at should keep in view this mass of people, for whose security we work and for whose betterment we labour. [p. 49]

E. M. S. NAMBOODIRIPAD: MARXIST-LENINIST

Over the centuries, India's thinkers and leaders have assimilated ideas and methods originating in other parts of the world. This traditional receptivity has not abated in the twentieth century. The ideas of Marx and Lenin, first accepted then rejected by Manabendra Nath Roy, won, after independence, the enthusiasm of growing numbers of well-educated young men and women.

Many of them came from families of high social and economic status and felt keenly the gap between their wealth and the poverty of so many others. In addition, the religious beliefs and practices of their elders often seemed inconsistent with the secular knowledge they were acquiring in college, and Marx's dictum that "religion is the opiate of the people" appeared to explain why the poorest people also seemed the most superstitious. The sweeping solutions offered by Marx and Lenin also attracted ardent young minds as yet unfamiliar with the complexities of India's economic and political life, and with realistic ways of improving it.

One convert to Marxist ideas was E. M. S. Namboodiripad (1909–   ), scion of a South Indian brāhman family of the highest social rank. Namboodiripad's father died when he was a small child, and his mother took charge of his education by having him trained to memorize and recite the *Rig Veda* from the age of eight. He did this for several years, then acquired through his own efforts a knowledge of English and secular learning. At seventeen he entered high school at an advanced level and from there attended colleges in his home region of Cochin (now part of the state of Kerala).

"As a mere boy of 11 or 12, I was fascinated by the whirlwind campaign of non-cooperation" started by Gandhi in 1920–21, Namboodiripad states.[8] He imposed on himself some of the disciplines that Gandhi demanded of his followers. Then Nehru's leftist ideas attracted him. Through a relative on his mother's side, Namboodiripad became involved in active political life and soon was editing the weekly newspaper of the revolutionary wing of his community's social reform movement. In 1932, at twenty-three, he left college to join the national movement of civil disobedience, was arrested, and spent a year and a half in jail. There he met both eminent Gandhians and revolutionaries from other parts of India, and there he was converted to Marx's and Lenin's faith in an inevitable future revolution by the poor against the rich.

From 1934 to 1940, young Namboodiripad took an active part in the work of the Congress Socialist Party and served as one of its joint secretaries. He also helped in Congress Party work in his home region and in 1937 was elected one of its members in the Madras provincial legislature. But it was socialism in the Marxist-Leninist sense rather than Gandhi's gradualism that he was engaged in spreading. He broke with the Congress in 1940 and led the Congress Socialist Party in his native Cochin in joining the Communist Party of India (CPI). He was elected to the latter's central committee in 1943 and later became a member of its politburo. From 1953 to 1964 he served several times as the party's acting general secretary.

But Namboodiripad achieved his greatest success at the state rather than the national level. After the 1957 elections, he was able to form the first democratically elected Communist government in history, in his own state of Kerala. Opposition to the Communist Party ministry within Kerala (accelerated by the Congress Party, of which Indira Gandhi was then president) gave the central government in New Delhi an excuse to intervene and replace Namboodiripad in 1959. He then led the parliamentary opposition after the next state election, and at the national level acted as the CPI's general secretary and editor of its magazine, *New Age*.

Tensions within the party on matters of policy and personality produced a split in 1964. Namboodiripad and the Bengali leader Jyoti Basu called on the party to repudiate its "reformist" and pro-Congress line, staged a walk-out, were expelled, and formed a new party, the Communist Party of India (Marxist). Returning to Kerala, Namboodiripad became chief minister again after the 1967 elections, but the coalition of parties supporting him broke apart in 1969. Since then he has continued to guide the CPI(M) as its chief theorist. With the precision of a Vedic pandit, he has vigorously criticized deviations from the teachings of Marx and Lenin, and in 1978 he had his party denounce both the Soviet Union's "revisionism" and Mao's theory of the "three worlds" (the superpowers, the developed countries, and the developing "third world"). But in tactical matters, he has been alternately willing to work with the parliamentary system, and to "break the Constitution from within."[9]

Gandhi and India's "Bourgeoisie"

From Namboodiripad's Marxist-Leninist perspective, M. K. Gandhi's ideas and methods led the nationalist movement to success only because they enabled India's wealthier class (the "bourgeoisie") to seize power and thereby tighten their domination over the country's workers and peasants.

[From Namboodiripad, *The Mahatma and the Ism*, p. xii]

Summing up, . . . we come to the conclusion that Gandhiji's idealism had its strong and weak points. His strong points may be summed up in his

ability to rouse the masses and organise them in the struggle against imperialism and feudalism; his weak points may be summed up in his insistence
on a scrupulous adherence to what is called non-violence, which, in effect,
served to restrain the mass of the workers and peasants who want to shake
off the triple yoke of imperialism, feudalism and capitalism. This, incidentally, is precisely what the interests of the bourgeoisie demanded. They
wanted the mass of our people to be roused and organised against imperialism and feudalism; they, however, wanted these masses to be severely restrained in their actions and struggles. It was this coincidence of what the
interests of the bourgeoisie required and the totality of the results of Gandhiji's leadership that is meant when I say that Gandhiji's approach to life
and history is a bourgeois-democratic approach.

Either to the Left, or to the Right

Namboodiripad believed that Marx's view of history as a succession of struggles
between exploited and exploiting classes fitted well India's postindependence economic and social picture, although he expanded Marx's term "working class" to
include agricultural as well as industrial laborers. In the following passage, Namboodiripad uses certain phrases in a specifically Marxist sense. For example, "capitalist
society" means a society selfishly exploited by its wealthier members, the ruling
"bourgeoisie"; "Left democracy" or "the path of democracy and socialism" means
moving toward the "democratic centralism" of Lenin whereby the Communist Party
controls and remodels the entire society, its economy, and its political and military
systems.

[From Namboodiripad, *Economics and Politics*, pp. vii, 409–12]

What exactly are the economic and political implications of the 'socialist
pattern of society', the objective that the Indian National Congress set before itself at its Avadi session in 1955?[10] The question is of particular interest to the Left in India, both communist and non-communist, and it is
only natural that the subject should have generated some discussion among
them.

No one suggested, of course, that the Congress leaders, at any rate the
majority of them, were either sincere in their acceptance of the new objective or were keen to take such steps as would take the country in the direc-

tion of socialism. On the contrary, there was general agreement that the dominant section of the Congress leadership consisted of confirmed enemies of socialism and that their acceptance of the socialist pattern, whatever it may mean, was simply a political manoeuvre.

It was, however, realised that there were elements inside the Congress—not only in its ranks but in its leadership, too—who were as opposed to the rabidly anti-socialist sections of the leadership as are the Left outside the Congress. It was the pressure of these elements that forced even the rabidly anti-socialist sections to pay lip service to the newly-declared objective of socialism.

The Left and communist circles, however, were by no means agreed on the extent to which those elements inside the Congress, who are genuinely opposed to the anti-socialist leadership, can be mobilised to put up an effective fight for socialism, thereby transforming the Congress itself into an organisation fighting for socialism. A section of the Left thought that this was possible, while the others held the contrary view.

All this shows the importance of an objective analysis of the factors which made the Congress adopt the socialist objective; the limitations and weaknesses of the socialist objective as defined by the Congress; the economic and political consequences of Congress rule before and after the acceptance of the socialist objective, etc. It was this that prompted me to write this book. . . .

In the opening pages of this book, we quoted the late Prime Minister Jawaharlal Nehru who on 15 August 1947 asked: 'Whither do we go and what shall be our endeavour?' We also quoted from the official pronouncements of President Radhakrishnan and from the resolutions of the Congress to point out what claims were being made on behalf of the government and the ruling party. Now that we have completed a rapid survey of the most important aspects of national development, we may try to sum up the conclusions we have arrived at, to find out how far the reality conforms to the claims made by the ruling circles.

The first thing that becomes obvious is that, far from building a socialist society as is claimed, the ruling party is building a capitalist society. The two classes of capitalist society—owners of means of production and the proletarians—are growing from year to year. Even within the class of capitalist owners, the richer and bigger sections are becoming still richer and bigger. As for the proletarians, they are unable not only to get a living wage and decent conditions of work, but even regular and guaranteed employment. The ever-increasing numbers of the unemployed and the under-employed cry aloud that here is a social system in which those who have no property have no means of honest living.

Developing as it does a capitalist society, free India has undoubtedly built new industries which could not have been dreamt of in the days of British rule. This, however, touches only a narrow sector of the national economy. Over the vast sector of the still undeveloped economy may be seen the antiquated methods and techniques of production. The same thing applies to the agricultural sector where a small number of prosperous farms owned by landlords and rich peasants and using modern techniques coexist with the bulk of dwarf farms cultivated by poor owner peasants, tenant cultivators or share-croppers, and employing antiquated techniques.

As regards relations of production in the rural areas, the old forms of exploitation carried on by feudal landlords, usurers, etc., are being given new, modernised forms. In place of the old feudal lords who combined rent with other forms of feudal exploitation and social oppression are emerging a new class of the rural gentry who combine semi-feudal and capitalist forms of exploitation, supplemented by political domination arising out of their hold on the politics and administration of the country. The mass of agricultural labourers, artisans, poor peasants and rural intelligentsia have to bear the burdens of new forms of rent and crop-sharing exploitation together with ever-increasing tax burdens, heavy interest rates, unequal exchange between rural and urban produce, inequitable allocation of developmental finance as between urban and rural areas, etc.

The bulk of the working people are thus subjected to various forms of capitalist exploitation which goes hand-in-hand with the innumerable remnants of pre-capitalist exploitation. At the same time, the bulk of entrepreneural sections of society—traders, industrialists, organisers of transport and other categories of middlemen who do not own big capital—are subjected to various disabilities and discriminations because the institutions of finance and other media of economic activity are controlled by big businessmen and top bureaucrats who act in concert with the big businessmen. Most of them find it difficult to carry on their business while many even go bankrupt.

These small and medium scale businessmen, as well as sections of big businessmen, feel the pinch of the pressure exerted by foreign monopolists who, acting in collaboration with a section of Indian monopolists and with the blessings of the government, have launched a fierce attack on the Indian entrepreneur.

Thus far about the economic consequences of building capitalist society under the garb of socialist slogans. What about the political developments?

Ours has been declared a democratic political setup. The ruling party has, however, made it clear that it has no use for democracy if it results in the Party being replaced by other parties, particularly if the party that replaces it happens to be one wedded to Left democracy and genuine socialism (like the Communist Party). It has also become clear that some of the most fundamental principles of democracy like the formation of linguistic states, equality of all Indian languages, absolute prohibition of the interference of religious institutions in the affairs of the state and of the state in the affairs of the religious community, and so on, have been grossly violated. Civil liberties and democratic rights, like freedom of speech, expression and assembly, freedom from arbitrary arrests and detentions, etc., are also violated without compunction.

These features of the economic and political developments in the country—the growth of monopoly capitalism, its alliance with the exploiting classes of pre-capitalist society, the consequent failure to modernise the economic life of the entire country, the monopoly of power enjoyed by the ruling party, its refusal to observe the canons of parliamentary democracy when some other party happens to secure the allegiance of the majority of the electorate, the shameless violation of civil liberties and democratic rights, etc.—have accentuated all the social conflicts which have been handed down by the pre-capitalist to the newly-emerging capitalist society. Conflicts of castes, religious communities, linguistic and cultural groups, tribes, states and regions break out in unprecedentedly acute forms. Behind them, of course, are hidden the conflicts and competitions between sections of the ruling classes who rally the masses belonging to their respective social groups in order to beat their rivals. In other words, far from uniting the nation on a democratic socialist basis, the ruling classes are actually dividing and disrupting the nation.

These realities of the economic, political, social and cultural life of the nation have raised and accentuated, the danger that the freedom and democracy, established over 16 years ago, may be subverted. Forces of reaction who have no use for a free and sovereign nation with a genuinely democratic political system are acting in concert with the reactionary monopolist circles abroad. Launching violent attacks on the policies of independent development, protection of the country's sovereignty, radical socio-economic reforms, etc., they are trying to divert the nation from the path of democracy and socialism to that of military dictatorship and monopoly capitalism. On the other hand, the ruling party is itself laying the basis for the growth of these reactionary forces by its economic, political and socio-cultural policies. We may, therefore conclude this review with the following observation made [in 1962] by the late Ajoy Ghosh at the Sixth Congress of the Communist Party:

It is necessary today to shed all complacency. It is necessary to realise that sharp alternatives face our nation. *Either* the democratic forces unite, isolate and defeat the forces of right reaction, arrest the shift of the government to the right and bring about a shift to the left, i.e., towards democratic advance. *Or* forces of reaction, pressing on with the offensive and aided by their allies in the Congress and the government bring about an all-sided shift to the Right.[11]

BALRAJ MADHOK: SPOKESMAN FOR HINDUCENTRIC NATIONALISM

India's Constitution guarantees voting rights for all adult citizens, with state and federal elections every five years or less. With hundreds of millions of eligible voters, the world's largest democracy has offered fertile soil for the emergence of new political parties and the rebirth of old ones in new forms. Although the Congress Party dominated the first five general elections, it was never able to capture a majority of the votes; these were divided among the many smaller parties and independent candidates. Only in 1977 did enough of these group together with ex-Congress members to defeat the Congress. One of these smaller parties was the Jana Sangh ("the assembly of the people"), founded in 1951 ostensibly as a noncommunal nationalistic party. But from its inception the Jana Sangh served as the political arm of an older Hindu paramilitary society, the national volunteer corps known as the Rashtriya Swayamsevak Sangh (RSS).

Balraj Madhok, born in Ladakh in 1920, joined the RSS at 18 while still a student. He earned his B.A. and M.A. at Lahore, then joined the faculty at the Arya Samaj's Dayananda Anglo-Vedic (D.A.V.) College in Srinagar, capital of the princely state of Kashmir. When the Pakistan-based invasion of Kashmir began in 1947, he helped organize the civilian defense effort. From 1949 he wrote in the RSS magazine urging the organization to enter politics, and in 1951 he collaborated in founding the Jana Sangh. As the party's general secretary, first for the Punjab (the land of his ancestors), and then at a national level, he wrote, spoke, and recruited for the new party.

He also continued his career as a teacher of history, eventually becoming the head of his department at the D.A.V. College in Delhi.

Madhok's career as an elected member of the Lok Sabha ("house of the people," equivalent to Britain's House of Commons) began in 1961 with his stunning defeat of the Congress candidate in a New Delhi by-election. He was elected president of the Jana Sangh in 1966 and 1967 and was re-elected to the Lok Sabha in 1967. In those same years, however, his efforts to build up a combined opposition to the Congress Party through alliances with the even more conservative Swatantra Party and discontented Congress members isolated him from the rest of his own party. He continued to work for such alliances in 1970–1971, but the young RSS workers who formed the backbone of the party's campaign organization were moving in a different direction, toward greater identification with the peasantry, landless laborers, industrial workers, and women. A showdown came in 1973, and Madhok was expelled from the party for three years. During the "Emergency" of 1975–1977, he was imprisoned without trial. Then in 1977 his strategy of coalition-building was finally vindicated in the two-month-long electoral campaign: the conservative combination he had worked for coalesced and joined with other parties and independents to win the election. Madhok emerged as president of the All-India Janata ("people's") Front. After those exciting days, he retired from political activity.

In some ways, the policies Madhok advocated resemble those of conservative party leaders in other countries: strengthen the nation's defense, increase patriotism and national unity, lower taxes, allow the market economy more freedom from government control, and oppose communism at home and abroad. In other ways he voiced the anxieties of Hindi-speaking Hindus in north and central India—particularly those influenced by the reforms initiated by Swami Dayananda and continued by the Arya Samaj movement. (For example, he was jailed briefly in 1966 for his part in a massive New Delhi demonstration to protest the slaughter of cows in that city.) But unlike the older Hindu Mahasabha (which contested the general elections with little success), the Jana Sangh and Madhok favored the inclusion of non-Hindus in their party and in public offices.

Having entered political life as a militant Hindu, Madhok gradually moved to a more inclusive nationalism carefully balanced between attachment to ancient Indian culture and modern (but not necessarily Western) ways. With his prolific writings and speeches in both English and Hindi he succeeded in rallying increasing support in the 1950s and 1960s for the Hinducentric party. He ceased to play a significant role in Indian politics, but his views illustrate an important undercurrent in Indian social and political thought.

Indianize the Consciousness of the Indian People

From the viewpoint of a staunch nationalist who was also a Hindu from North India, the political, economic, social, and cultural scene in 1969 seemed crowded with dangers to the strength of his country and his own community. In his book of that year, Madhok put much of the blame on the Congress Party (as led by Nehru and Indira Gandhi) and on the divisive forces of linguistic regionalism, "casteism," Communism, and Muslim communalism.

[From Madhok, *Indianisation*, pp. 32, 39–41, 44–46, 58, 61–68, 71, 74, 121–22]

The call for Indianisation both as a concept and as a programme of action has evoked mixed reaction in the country. While most nationalist and patriotic Indians who have been worried by the growing strength of fissiparous and disruptive forces and tendencies in the country have welcomed it as the need of the time, the Communists, their fellow travellers and communalists with extra-territorial loyalties, who are mentally afraid of Indian nationalism, are upset by the popular response to this call. . . .

[After the reorganization of state boundaries on linguistic lines] the sense of glory of India began to be subordinated to the glory and greatness of respective linguistic States which began to take the place of Bharat Mata [Mother India] in the hearts and minds of the people. . . . In short regional consciousness began to take the better of national consciousness. . . .

The net result of this is that most Indians today are Punjabis or Bengalis or Malayalis first and Indians only next or never. . . . That is one compelling reason for taking to Indianisation of our people in right earnestness before it becomes too late. . . .

It was clear to the leaders of modern Indian renaissance right from Maharishi Daya Nand [Dayananda Saraswati] and Raja Ram Mohan Rai [Rammohun Roy] that antipathies and conflicts within the Indian society based on caste had been a major cause of Indian failure before foreign invaders in spite of dauntless courage and prowess of Indian soldiers, man to man, compared to most of the invading hordes. They, therefore, started a campaign against it. . . . Eradication of untouchability has been one of the major planks in all the reform and political movements in India during the last hundred years. Mahatma Gandhi made the work of uplift of Harijans and removal of caste barriers as a passion of his life. . . .

But it is a painful fact that casteism has become more pronounced rather than getting weakened during the twenty-two years of freedom. There are many reasons for it. The most important of them is the exploitation of caste for political purposes by the political leadership and parties. . . . As a result casteism is tending to become as great if not greater danger to Indian unity as regionalism. Today most Indians are either Jats, or Brahmins or Rajputs or Harijans first and Indians afterwards.

The reservations [of government jobs and seats in legislatures] given to Scheduled Castes [Untouchables] and Scheduled Tribes in the Constitution have created vested interests in the perpetuation of caste system. Before such reservations came, there was going on an imperceptible process of change of castes. The people belonging to lower castes tried to upgrade their social status with the improvement of their economic and educational condition. . . . Now the process has been reversed. Some people born in higher castes go about seeking false certificates to the intent that they belong to lower castes so that they may get a job or other benefits out of the reserved share of Scheduled Castes and Tribes. . . .

Lack of a strong sense of nationalism is not only reflected in the growing strength of the divisive forces of linguism [demanding political safeguards for various languages], regionalism, casteism and communalism but it has also resulted in intensification of mental slavery which came with foreign rule. This is particularly true of the intellectual elite and the upper classes of the society which dominate and control the apparatus of power in the name of the people. In the name of modernism, progressivism, socialism, and secularism everything Indian has come under a cloud. . . . But the mental slavery of Indian leadership which looks upon everything with American or Russian eyes has stood in the way of reorientation of our economic thinking and policies. Indianisation in the economic field therefore also is a need of the hour. . . .

It is well-known that laws and jurisprudence of a country reflect its values, civilisation and socio-economic thinking. It is therefore essential that legal education and legal system be Indianised.

In the field of medicine, allopathy has come to occupy the seat of power to the utter neglect of Indian systems of medicine. . . . Why should not an Indian medical graduate not swear by Charak [an ancient Indian medical authority] or Dhanwantri [a legendary physician to the Hindu gods] instead of Hippocrates and why should some grounding in Ayurveda [the traditional Hindu system of medicine] not form an essential part of medical studies in India? . . .

But Indianisation of certain sections of our society is more urgent in view of the immediate dangers to the unity and integrity of the country. The first in the order of priority of such elements come the Communists. . . . According to the Communist ideology the workers of the world are one and class struggle is the basis of all human progress. It is like a monolithic religion with a book and a dogma but without God. It is as intolerant and exclusive as any other monolithic religion ever was. . . . It goes to the credit of Communists that they have never concealed their extra-territorial loyalties and their intention to wreck the Indian Constitution and establish a totalitarian regime in India. The only basic difference between them [i.e., among the three Communist parties in India] is that while CPI [the Communist Party of India] would like a Red India to be a satellite of Soviet Union, the other factions would like it to be a part of the expanding empire of Mao-tse-tung.

It is, therefore, obvious that the need for Indianisation of the Communists is the greatest and most urgent if this country is not to lose its freedom and identity as a nation.

It is a pity that Indian political leaders and intellectuals are generally ignorant of Communist ideology and methodology. In their misplaced liberalism and emotional antipathy for the USA and erstwhile colonial powers of the West, they have developed notions about Communist countries and communism which have no relation with facts. It is wrong to call Communists as progressive. A progressive mind is one which is open and which is prepared to judge things on merit without any dogmatic inhibitions. The mind of Communists is closed. It is bound hand and foot to the four walls of Marxist dogma and philosophy. That explains the double standards of Communists regarding all national and international issues. If Communist China and its allies occupy Tibet or South Vietnam and commit genocide there, it is liberation. But if a non-Communist country goes to the help of any country to save it from being overrun by the foreign Communist armies, it becomes aggression.

Nor are the Communist countries a heaven for the common man. Their socialism which means state control of all means of production and distribution is a step towards statism and establishment of totalitarian regimes and not towards welfare of the people. . . .

Therefore, Communists are not only a danger to national unity and dem-ocratic liberties of the people, they pose the greatest threat to the economic health of the country as well. In their blind adoration of Soviet Union and China they have mortgaged their bodies and souls to them. Therefore, their re-education and redemption through Indianisation has become an impera-tive necessity.

Then there are those Communalists who place their loyalty to their reli-gious group above everything else. They are no less dangerous than the Communists and need to be Indianised on a priority basis. Most notorious and dangerous of such communalists is that section of the Muslim commu-nity which fought for the partition of the Motherland before 1947 and which continues to look towards Pakistan for guidance and inspiration even twenty-two years after freedom.

As explained earlier, there are a number of reasons for the wayward be-haviour and extra-territorial loyalties of this section of Muslims. Stress of Islam on renouncing and rejecting non-Muslims ancestors and heritage after a man is converted to Islam and its antipathy to the concept of territorial nationalism in which respect for past heroes and heritage plays a significant part is one reason for it. . . .

Instead of creating respect for the Indian inheritance and bringing Mus-lims into the national mainstream, systematic efforts are being made at Ali-garh and elsewhere to completely insulate the Muslim mind from Indian life and thought, cultural tradition and other influences that could remove the canker of two-nation theory from their minds.

. . . Their Indianisation [is] a vital necessity for the peace, security and integrity of India. . . .

[There must be] honesty of purpose and determination to place the coun-try above the party, sect, caste or region which is possible only if the poli-ticians get Indianised. The heart and mind of the Indian people is still sound. But to get the right response one must touch the right chord and create the right type of motivation. The way Indian nationalism asserted and acquitted itself at the time of the Chinese invasion of 1962 and Paki-stani invasion of 1965 creates the hope that everything is not lost and that embers of nationalism can still be transformed into a burning flame. There must be leaders who can do that. The present leadership has failed and is failing the country. It does not have the flame of patriotism in it. So it cannot light that flame in others. . . . Mother India has still enough treasure of men that can make India great and strong. They have to be found out and given opportunity to lead the country. Maybe the situation itself will throw them up, and blow away the chaff that has masqueraded too long as the grain.

Let all patriotic Indians strive to that end. Let Indianisation triumph so that the dreams of those who are striving for another partition of the Motherland be smashed once for all.

JAYAPRAKASH NARAYAN: EX-MARXIST
GANDHIAN SOCIALIST

Jayaprakash Narayan (1902–1979), India's most popular postindependence political figure next to Nehru, left the ruling Congress Party in 1948, then in 1954 abandoned politics altogether in favor of Gandhian "constructive work" (*sarvodaya*) at the village level. His urge to spur sweeping political reforms resurfaced in the mid-1970s, and he played a major role both in precipitating Indira Gandhi's "Emergency" of 1975 to 1977 and in leading the coalition that defeated her party in 1977. Jayaprakash (or "J. P.," as he was affectionately known), died of kidney and heart failure in 1979 after the coalition broke apart. His contributions to political thought, although utopian in many ways, won him a worldwide audience and continue today to influence those who envision the economic, social, and political life of the future infused with greater equality, justice, and respect for the individual and his local community.

Jayaprakash ("the light of victory") Nayaran was born in a village in eastern India now in the state of Bihar. His father, an official superintending the operation of irrigation canals, was required by his work to move from place to place. Probably for health reasons (his eldest son died of cholera and his eldest daughter succumbed to the plague), he left young Jayaprakash in his native village with the boy's step-grandmother while the rest of the family moved away. At six, Jayaprakash started his education in the village primary school. When he was nine, his father sent him to the Collegiate School at Patna, Bihar's major city. The shy and dutiful son worked diligently and won a merit scholarship to Patna College at the age of sixteen. He had considered himself a political extremist since he was fourteen, and at nineteen, when Gandhi's noncooperation movement arrived in Patna, Jayaprakash threw away his schoolbooks and prepared to join it. His father wanted him to continue studying and had him enrolled in a nationalist school, the newly founded Bihar Vidyapith.

In the following year, 1922, Gandhi suspended the noncooperation movement, and Jayaprakash was deeply disillusioned. In addition, he was finding his new school ill equipped with the apparatus for experiments he needed to carry on his studies in the natural sciences. A friend wrote him from the University of Iowa urging him to complete his higher education in the U.S.A. Other young men had sought higher degrees in England— among them Banerjea, Tagore, Aurobindo, Gandhi, Jinnah, Iqbal, Mohamed Ali, Savarkar, Nehru, and Subhas Bose. Ambedkar had earned his M.A. and Ph.D. at Columbia University, but for Jayaprakash to seek an American B.A. was to venture into relatively new pastures. He finally secured his mother's permission and some funds from his father, but his wife refused to join him. (They had been married two years earlier, by arrangement of their parents, and soon after the marriage her father had sent her to live in Gandhi's ashram near Ahmedabad; she was then sixteen.)

Jayaprakash spent seven years in the United States, combining study with work at odd jobs in California, Iowa, Chicago, Wisconsin, and Ohio. He picked grapes and peaches, packed fruit and jam, worked in restaurants, a pottery factory, a foundry, a garage, and a meat packing plant, and sold hair straightener. He nearly died of malnutrition and a throat infection during a cold Chicago winter. He experienced both racial discrimination and greater social equality than he had known before.

In 1924 at the University of Wisconsin he discovered the writings of Marx and was especially influenced by Marx's claim to have found the "inevitable" solution to the problem of poverty. Jayaprakash soon became a regular reader of M. N. Roy's *New Masses* magazine and the U.S. Communist Party's *Daily Worker*. He switched from natural science to sociology and from Wisconsin to Ohio State, where he took his B.A. in 1928 and M.A. in 1929. He wanted to go on for a Ph.D., but his mother was critically ill, and so he returned home.

At once he was drawn into the mainstream of nationalist politics: his wife took him to meet Gandhi; he met Nehru, the next Congress president, and the two became friends. Nehru invited him and his wife to live in Allahabad and help with the work of the Congress, and in 1932, when most other leaders of the Congress were in jail, he served as its general secretary until he, too, was arrested, tried, and imprisoned. In 1934 he and other leftists founded a group within the Congress which they named the

Congress Socialist Party; Jayaprakash became its chief organizer and traveled all over India to recruit and teach new members. From 1936 he encouraged the newly legalized Communists to enroll as Congress Socialists,
but by 1940 he was fed up with their maneuvering for power and sudden
changes in policy in obedience to dictates from the Soviet Union. At the
same time he was impatient with the Congress under Gandhi's moderating
influence and courted and received two successive prison sentences from
1940 to 1942 for his fiery speeches urging factory workers to start a general
strike, stop paying taxes, and set up their own police, courts, and government.

Jayaprakash became a national hero in 1942 when he and five other prisoners climbed over the seventeen-foot high wall of their jail on the night
of Diwali (the festival of lights) and escaped capture. Undetected, he visited the major cities of India to instruct guerrilla fighters and issue procla-
mations urging struggle against British rule. Within a year he was arrested
at Lahore and subjected to prolonged torture in a vain attempt to make him
talk about his activities. Although he was released only in 1946, a year
after most of the Congress leaders, he remained determined to oust the
British by a massive uprising of the people.

Thirteen years younger than Nehru, and tall, handsome, intellectual,
and idealistic, Jayaprakash could easily have become Nehru's right-hand
man and ultimately his successor as India's prime minister. But there was
something in him that rebelled against the actual exercise of political power
(he was never a candidate for public office). In 1948 he led his socialist
followers out of the Congress and from then on steadily lost interest in
political activity. Instead, he gravitated toward Gandhian work at the village level, beginning with the *bhūdān* (land-gift) movement begun by Gandhi's disciple Vinoba Bhave.[12] In 1954 he founded his own ashram in a
rural part of Bihar to try to apply Gandhi's methods of village economic
improvement, and by the 1960s he was sending workers to train in Israel
and Japan in order to adapt modern technology to villagers' needs.

Jayaprakash never ceased to reflect and speak on his ideals for India's
future. At the core of his vision lay a blend of Marx's and Gandhi's dreams:
unselfish and altruistic individuals living in self-supporting communities undisturbed by a powerful government, hostile neighbors, or rich industrialists. Greed, falsehood, and competition for wealth or power would be ban-
ished by the common ethic of self-restraint and the moral force of the people.
He repeatedly refused opportunities to serve in the government, but his

restless nature moved him to try to solve or mediate problems in one area after another—Kashmir, Nagaland, and throughout his home state of Bihar. He played the role of gadfly to both state and central governments and attracted huge crowds of youthful sympathizers when he called for an end to corruption, police terrorism, and the misuse of power. The size of these crowds and his vague but catchy call for "total revolution" in 1975 provoked an extreme clampdown by Indira Gandhi and her government that left a scar on India's record as a liberal-democratic polity. Jayaprakash died a frustrated man, but his ideals remain for future generations to contemplate, and perhaps selectively apply.

A Plan for India's Future

Starting from a Marxist-Leninist perspective, Jayaprakash moved gradually toward a secular interpretation of Gandhi's ideas. In 1940 he submitted to Gandhi the following draft of a resolution he hoped the Congress would adopt. Gandhi approved all of his proposals except the one concerning the rajas and nawabs of "the Indian States," who were legally independent of the rest of India until they had to join either India or Pakistan in 1947.

[From Narayan, *Towards Struggle*, pp. 240–42; also in *Harijan*, 1940, pp. 96–97]

The Congress and the country are on the eve of a great national upheaval. The final battle for freedom is soon to be fought. This will happen when the whole world is being shaken by mighty forces of change. Out of the catastrophe of the European War, thoughtful minds everywhere are anxious to create a new world—a world based on the co-operative goodwill of nations and men. At such a time the Congress considers it necessary to state definitely the ideal of freedom for which it stands and for which it is soon to invite the Indian people to undergo the uttermost sufferings.

The free Indian nation shall work for peace between nations and total rejection of armaments and for the method of peaceful settlement of national disputes through some international authority freely established. It will endeavour particularly to live on the friendliest terms with its neighbours, whether they be great powers or small nations, and shall covet no foreign territory.

The law of the land will be based on the will of the people freely expressed by them. The ultimate basis of maintenance of order shall be the sanction and concurrence of the people.

The free Indian State shall guarantee full individual and civil liberty and cultural and religious freedom, provided that there shall be no freedom to overthrow by violence the constitution framed by the Indian people through a Constituent Assembly.

The State shall not discriminate in any manner between citizens of the nation. Every citizen shall be guaranteed equal rights. All distinctions of birth and privilege shall be abolished. There shall be no titles emanating either from inherited social status or the State.

The political and economic organisation of the State shall be based on principles of social justice and economic freedom. While this organisation shall conduce to the satisfaction of the national requirements of every member of society, material satisfaction shall not be its sole objective. It shall aim at healthy living and the moral and intellectual development of the individual. To this end [and] to secure social justice, the State shall endeavour to promote small-scale production carried on by individual or co-operative effort for the equal benefit of all concerned. All large-scale collective production [in private hands] shall be eventually brought under collective ownership and control, and in this behalf the State shall begin by nationalising heavy transport, shipping, mining and the heavy industries. The textile industry shall be progressively decentralised.

The life of the villages shall be reorganised and the villages shall be made self-governing units, self-sufficient in as large a measure as possible. The land laws of the country shall be drastically reformed on the principle that land shall belong to the actual cultivator alone, and that no cultivator shall have more land than is necessary to support his family on a fair standard of living. This will end the various systems of landlordism on the one hand and farm bondage [share-cropping] on the other.

The State shall protect the interests of the [upper and middle] classes, but when these impinge upon the interests of those who have been poor and downtrodden it shall defend the latter and thus restore the balance of social justice.

In all State-owned and State-managed enterprises, the workers shall be represented in the management through their elected representatives and shall have an equal share in it with the representatives of the Government.

In the Indian [princely] States, there shall be complete democratic government established and in accordance with the principles of abolition of social distinction and equality between citizens, there shall not be any titular heads of the States in the persons of Rajas and Nawabs.

This is the order which the Congress envisages and which it shall work to establish. The Congress firmly believes that this order shall bring happiness, prosperity and freedom to the people of all races and religions in India who together shall build on these foundations a great and glorious nation.

A Plea for a Communitarian Polity and Economy

In his longest piece of theoretical writing, entitled "A Plea for the Reconstruction of Indian Polity," Jayaprakash set forth in 1959 his plan for the radical decentralization of his country's government and economy. Although it draws heavily on Gandhi's dream for independent India, the plan omits the religious or spiritual incentives that have provided the "glue" holding together successful communitarian experiments of the past. It does, however, stress the values of "ancient India," which many understood to mean the values of Hinduism, such as the concept of *dharma*. Its ban on political parties and national leaders, and absence of checks on the seizure and abuse of power by a small minority, also give it a utopian flavor. Jayaprakash's ideas and influence nevertheless encouraged the healthy emphasis of the 1960s on village self-government and rural economic development. (An excellent critique of Jayaprakash's ideal scheme may be found in W. H. Morris-Jones, *Politics, Mainly Indian*, pp. 97–106.)

[From Narayan, *Socialism, Sarvodaya and Democracy*, pp. 192–93, 196–99, 206–7, 211–14, 219–21, 224–25, and 236]

I propose in this paper to describe the main outline of the polity which to my mind is not only most suited for us, but is also most rational and scientific, with a brief statement of the reasons for my views.

I have pleaded for our present political institutions to be based on the principles that had been enunciated and practised in the ancient Indian polity, because (a) I believe that would be in line with the natural course of social evolution and (b) those principles are more valid from the point of view of social science than any others. . . . My search here has been for the forms of social life, particularly of political life, that would assure the preservation of human values about which there is hardly any dispute in the world today; and my approach has been non-partisan and non-sectarian. . . .

First of all, let it be pointed out that the problem of democracy is basically, and above all, a moral problem. Constitutions, systems of government, parties, elections—all these are relevant to the business of democracy. But unless the moral and spiritual qualities of the people are appropriate, the best of constitutions and political systems will not make democracy work. The moral qualities and mental attitudes most needed for democracy are: (1) concern for truth; (2) aversion to violence; (3) love of liberty and courage to resist oppression and tyranny; (4) spirit of co-operation; (5) preparedness to adjust self-interest to the larger interest; (6) respect for other's opinions and tolerance; (7) readiness to take responsibility; (8) belief in the fundamental equality of man; (9) faith in the educability of human nature.

These qualities and attitudes are not inborn in man. But he can be educated in them and trained to acquire and practise them. This task, let it be emphasised, is beyond the scope of the State. The quality of the life of society should itself be such that it inculcates these values in its members. The prevailing social ethics, the family, the religious and educational authorities and institutions, the example that the *elite* set in their own lives, the organs of public opinion—all these have to combine to create the necessary moral climate for democracy to thrive. Thus, it should be clear that the task of preparing the soil in which the plant of democracy may take root and grow is not a political but an educative task. . . .

When there is liberty it leads to abuse and necessitates State interference, and when there is State interference it leads to curtailment of liberty. How then to preserve liberty and prevent its abuse? There are no political means by which the dilemma can be resolved, there are only moral means. The obverse side of the medal of liberty is responsibility. If the individual is not prepared to take social responsibility, if he uses liberty for self-aggrandisement and neglects or hurts the interests of others, some form of state-ism becomes inevitable. It is here that the pertinence and wisdom of Gandhiji's concept of trusteeship becomes evident. The only democratic answer to state-ism and totalitarianism is trusteeship. But trusteeship cannot be practised without voluntary limitation of wants. An individual cannot function as a trustee unless he is prepared to share his possessions with his fellowmen; this he cannot do unless he has learned to curtail his wants. Thus voluntary limitation of wants, in other words, the rejection of materialism or the unlimited pursuit of material satisfactions, is essential for the achievement and preservation of democracy. . . .

It should be remembered that democracy does not consist merely in its formal institutions. It lives really and truly in the life of the people; it is a way of life. It is not only through the representative assemblies and elected governments that democracy works, but in an equally true sense through the voluntary associations and actions of the citizens which they carry on and establish to deal with their problems, promote their interests and manage their affairs. Professor Harold Laski, when asked how he would judge the worth of a democracy, replied that he would do so by the amount of voluntary activity within it. Democracy has worked best among peoples that have shown initiative and enterprise.

Democracy is not merely a question of political rights and people's part in government. Particularly since the First World War, democracy has come to mean more and more social and economic justice, equal opportunity, industrial democracy. The old distinction between political and economic democracy has been given up and the two concepts have been merged into one to mean full democracy. This is not to suggest that democracy is bound up with any such politico-economic ideologies as socialism or communism. It is true that these ideologies had promised full democracy in the sense used above. But experience has shown that in the case of communism there has been not enlargement but a severe curtailment of democracy—both political and economic. The old belief that State ownership and management of the means of production, distribution and exchange will lead to economic self-government, elimination of exploitation and equitable distribution of the products of labour, a stateless order of society, has not been confirmed by experience. It is the very opposite that has actually happened.

In the case of socialism the position is somewhat better, because socialism preserves the institutions of political democracy. But it is questionable—and this has been recognised by socialists themselves—if concentration of economic power in the hands of a central State, even under democratic conditions, works for economic democracy; and, further, if it does not result even in the thwarting and limiting of political democracy itself.

It should, however, be pointed out, as it has been indicated above, that the fault is not so much with socialism, as with (a) the centralised State and (b) large-scale industrialisation.

In a centralised, unitary State the people are barred from participation in the government, even though they retain and exercise the right of choosing and dismissing it. This latter right too is substantially restricted by the operation of the party system, because it limits the choice of the people.

As for large-scale industrialisation, there is a very large measure of agreement among social thinkers that it inevitably leads to shrinkage of democracy.

But whatever the experience of the working of socialism or communism the fact remains that the concept of democracy does include social and economic justice, equal opportunity, industrial democracy together with all that is meant by political democracy. And if communism and socialism have failed so far to lead human society to these goals, the endeavour to reach them must continue to form part of the quest for democracy. It has been indicated above that the answer is moral rather than political or economic. . . .

A word that figures boldly on the ancient sign-post is *dharma*.[13] Indian polity held that the State was subject to the *dharma*, which it was its duty to uphold and protect.

The concept of *dharma* was of great importance in ancient Indian society and it prescribed and regulated individual and group behaviour in all walks of life.

This concept of *dharma* and its role in Indian polity and the wider life of society is another example of that synthetic, organic, communal organisation of Indian society which has been discussed above. . . . Unless life in India is again organised on the basis of self-determining and mutually co-ordinating and integrating communities, that organic self-regulation of society which the concept of *dharma* represented will not be possible. To that extent democracy will remain distantly removed from the life of the people. . . . [If] the village becomes a community . . . only then will it be possible for the village to adopt as its *dharma* the welfare of all the villagers, so that none goes without food, clothing, a roof over his head, work to do; no child goes without the benefit of a knowledge of the three R's; none goes without the benefit of a minimum health service. . . .

If man decided that instead of being herded together in large cities it was better to live in small communities, instead of being automatons it was better to be conscious human beings, instead of being a grain in the sand-heap it was better to be a member of a community, it should not be difficult for scientists to evolve the appropriate [small-scale industrial] technology.

Thus the society we are visualising here will be neither "urban" nor "rural," it will be, if a name has to be given to it, communitarian. In other words, it will truly be society. Development of science has made it possible for the distinction between urban and rural to be abolished. The communities of the future will have a balance of agriculture and industry; they will be agro-industrial; they will make full use of science and technology so as to serve the ends of their life and no more. Owing to geographical and historical conditions agriculture may predominate in one and industry in another, but a balance between them will be the ideal of all. The present monstrosities, the big cities, will have to be decentralised as far as possible to relieve congestion and create healthy conditions of life; and for the rest, they will have to be so re-organised as to be made federations of smaller sized communities. To the extent this is not possible, the big cities will have to be endured, care being taken to see that they do not become bigger, and no new big cities come up. . . .

We have so far discussed the local or primary community and shown how it is a creation of man's social nature and the unit with which the structure of society has to be built. . . . Just as in the primary community a number of families come together and cooperate to build a common life, so in order that there may be society, the primary communities must come together and cooperate with other primary communities so as to tackle common problems and promote common aims. . . . The next step in the building up of an integrated society is for a number of neighbouring primary communities to come together and cooperate amongst themselves to build, let us say, a regional community. . . . Thus the regional community comes into existence by an organic process of growth. The circle of community is widened. . . . The regional community, however, is not a superior or higher body that can control, or interfere with, the internal administration of the primary communities. Each in its sphere is equally sovereign.

The regional community in its turn will do all that is within its competence. But again, there will be many things which will be beyond its competence, such as running a techno-agricultural college, a major irrigation project, production of electricity, manufacture of machines, etc. In order that these tasks be tackled a number of regional communities will have to come together to form a still larger community—the district community, let us say. The district community too will be an integrated community and its relationship with the regional communities be of a pattern similar to that of the latter with the primary communities.

In this manner the district communities in their turn would federate together to form the provincial community. The provincial communities would come together to form the National Community. A day might come when the national communities might federate together to form the World Community. . . .

However, a treatment of the polity would be incomplete without a brief description of the economy that would underlie it. Society is a complex whole, as man himself is; and, therefore, social and human reconstruction requires an all-sided approach.

The aim of the community's economy is the welfare of the community and each of its members. Its aim cannot be individual profit, exclusive of the welfare of other individuals in the community. The community's economy is neither exploitative, nor competitive: it is co-operative and co-sharing. . . .

The community is an enlarged family, and like the family it represents the eternal flow of life. Just as the family is interested not only in its present members but even in those who are unborn, so the community thinks of future generations. Its economy, therefore, is not wasteful. It is particularly careful about the non-renewable resources of nature which are being wasted at such a criminal rate by the so-called advanced nations of the world. A balanced economy concerned with future generations of men, that is, with life rather than death, would try to do its best to return to nature what it takes from it. It will, therefore, try to restrict consumption as far as possible to renewable resources and use as little as possible of the resources it cannot put back. The economy of the community is in co-operative harmony with nature, while present-day economy both of the West and East is at perpetual and destructive war with nature. . . .

The economic life of the communitarian society would be so organised that human needs are satisfied as near at home as possible: first, in the primary community, then in the regional, district, provincial, national and international community—in that ascending order. This means that each expanding area of community would be as self-sufficient as possible. Incidentally, this would save much of the unnecessary energy and time devoted today to the business of commerce, advertisement, etc. . . .

A word about private enterprise. Private enterprise, in the sense of *purushartha*, the individual's spirit of enterprise, would have fullest scope in the community. But in the community the individual would be imbued with the spirit of community. Therefore, private enterprise in a communitarian society would also partake of that spirit and work for private as well as communal good. Further, private enterprise would also be subject to the principles of self-government and responsibility to, and integration with, the community. . . .

It is time now to gather all the threads of the argument and tie them together. Ancient Indian thought and tradition; social nature of man; social science; ethical and spiritual goals of civilization; the demand of democracy that the citizen should participate in the ordering and running of his life; the need of saving man from alienation from himself and from the fate of robotism; the requirement that the State and other institutions of society be reduced to a human scale; the ideal, above all, that man should become the centre of civilization—all these point in the same direction: a communal or communitarian way of life; communitarian ethics and education; communitarian social, economic and political organization. In this paper I have been mainly interested in the political aspect of the matter: the shape of the political organization, or polity, most desirable for our country.

The foundation of this polity, as I have pointed out, must necessarily be self-governing, self-sufficient, agro-industrial, urbo-rural, local communities. The existing villages and townships provide the physical base for such reconstruction. . . .

In the light of the above, it might be useful to turn for a moment to what is perhaps one of the most serious problems of the present day: the problem of bureaucracy and corruption. Some think that one solution of corruption is dictatorship. But even dictatorship is no solution of bureaucracy. To the contrary, we know that dictatorship breeds bureaucracy faster than other systems of government, and, in the bargain, makes it all-powerful.

Even as regards corruption, it is not generally realised that there is corruption on a gigantic scale in the dictatorships—only its form is changed. Instead of corruption in the sense of bribery and the like, there is grosser corruption in the form of lying, deceit, intrigue, terror, enslavement of the human mind, crucifixion of the dignity of man. All this corrupts human life far more than bribery and similar other things.

The only true solution of the problem both of bureaucracy and corruption is direct self-government of the people and direct and immediate supervision and control over the civil servants by the people and their elected organs. In the primary communities, as I have said above, there need be no paid civil servants. In the larger communities the civil servants would be directly under the control and supervision of the communal body concerned. Further, it would obviously be in the interest of the communities to keep the cost of the administration as low as possible. So there will be a natural check on proliferation of the bureaucracy. Thus as self-government develops, the civil servant becomes either unnecessary or subject to the immediate elected authority. . . .

The picture drawn here of the polity for India, and of social organisation in general, might perhaps appear to be idealistic. If so, I would not consider that to be a disqualification. An ideal cannot but be idealistic. The question is if the ideal is impractical, unscientific or otherwise ill-conceived. I have tried in the preceding pages to show that all relevant considerations lead irresistibly towards it.

The achievement of this ideal would, however, be a colossal task. Thousands, perhaps hundreds of thousands, of voluntary workers would be needed over a number of years to accomplish it.

The Government should lend its full support; but it is necessary to remember that the main burden of the task would have to be borne by voluntary political and social workers and institutions. The heart of the problem is to create the 'spirit of community', without which the whole body politic would be without life and soul. This is a task of moral regeneration to be brought about by example, service, sacrifice and love. Those who occupy high places in society—in politics, business, the professions—bear the heavy responsibility of leading the people by personal example.

The task also is one of social engineering, needing the help of the State; of scientists, experts, educationists, businessmen, experimenters; of men and women; of young and old.

It is a task of dedication; of creation; of self-discovery.

It is a task that defines India's destiny. It spells a challenge to India's sons and daughters. Will they accept the challenge?

NOTES

1. The words "socialist secular" were added by the forty-second amendment in 1976.
2. Tribes named in an official list or schedule.
3. Clause (f), regarding the right "to acquire, hold and dispose of property" was deleted by the forty-second amendment in 1976, but reinserted by the forty-fourth amendment of 1978 as Article 300-A: "No person shall be deprived of his property save by authority of law."
4. A legislative bill to reform Hindu family and social customs, finally enacted in several parts in 1955 and 1956.
5. Sir Charles Metcalfe (1785–1846). The passage quoted is from his 1830 Minute to the Board of Revenue.
6. Nehru, *Speeches, 1953–1957*, p. 12.
7. Michael Brecher, *Nehru: A Political Biography*, p. 235. (Italics added.)
8. Namboodiripad, *The Mahatma and the Ism*, p. vii.

9. *The Hindu* (Madras), July 8, 1969.

10. The resolution adopted by the Congress Party at Nehru's suggestion, containing the vaguer term "socialistic."

11. Ghosh, *Articles and Speeches*, p. 240.

12. For the ideas of Vinoba Bhave (1895–1984), see the first edition of this anthology, pp. 924–31.

13. The concept of cosmic order, which in the lives of human beings means the moral law or the path of duty.

Chapter 9

PAKISTAN: DEFINING AN
ISLAMIC STATE

Pakistan, emerging suddenly in 1947 as a nation, was immediately faced with fundamental questions affecting its basis as a state. What would be its relationship to the rest of the world, and especially to its neighbor India, from which it had been separated with great bitterness and bloodshed? How far should the government go toward assuming the responsibilities of a welfare state, or toward adopting the political institutions of the democratic West? And above all, what would be the status of the Islamic religion, which had been a crucial factor in the determination of Indian Muslims to found a separate state?

From the beginning of its existence, then, a central issue for the leaders of Pakistan was to define the relationship of the state and society to Islam. As the selections in chapter 14 of volume 1 indicate, this question of the role of Islam had been discussed throughout the long history of the Muslim presence in India.

During the nationalist period, as Indian leaders strove for an independent India, with representative political institutions based on Western models, Muslim spokesmen had insisted that the Western pattern of majority rule was not practical for India. Political representation should be based, they argued, not on a numerical counting of individuals, but on groups, so that the reality of the cultural, religious, and historical role of the Muslim community, comprising a quarter of the total population, would have its proper place. The selections in chapter 5 (this volume) show how Muslim leaders had enunciated the need for political arrangements that would permit Indian Muslims to develop, as Muhammad Iqbal put it, "on the lines of their own culture and traditions."[1] He and others had insisted that the future of Islam as a cultural force in India depended upon the existence of a Muslim homeland in the subcontinent. Muhammed Ali Jinnah had summed up this attitude in his famous speech at Lahore in March 1940 when he said that

Muslims "are a nation according to any definition . . . and they must have their homelands, their territory and their state" (see chapter 5). More dramatically, he told a gathering of Muslim students in 1945 that there was only one course open to them: "Fight for Pakistan, live for Pakistan, and, if necessary, die for the achievement of Pakistan, or else Muslims and Islam are doomed." Pakistan meant more than political independence; it meant above all, "the Muslim ideology, which has to be preserved."[2]

With the achievement of Pakistan, the preindependence visions of a separate homeland in the subcontinent for Muslims had to be translated into actual constitutional and administrative arrangements. There is nothing quite comparable to this task of basing a state on a religious ideology, except perhaps the creation of the state of Israel. Jinnah had shown remarkable political skills in negotiating the formation of the new state, but he did not live long enough to help in spelling out the meaning of Islamic imperatives in social, economic, and political realities. The difficulties in formulating the objectives and purposes of Pakistan are reflected in the controversies and tensions that produced four constitutions in thirty years, in 1956, 1962, 1973, and 1985.

In the writing of the constitutions, intense controversy centered on words and phrases that symbolized the aspirations and hopes of different groups in the country. There were a few non-Muslims, mainly Hindus who had remained in Pakistan, who advocated a secular state on the Indian model, in which no religion would have a constitutionally favored place, but few Muslims openly supported their position. Most people agreed that Islam should hold a place of special importance in the life of the nation, but there was much difference of opinion as to what its precise place should be. Some held that the principles of Islam should be applied in strict accordance with the Sharī̄a, the traditional basis of Islamic society. For this group, the models of a good society were to be found in the Islamic past, or at least in the texts that elaborated the details of an ideal society. The main exponents of this conservative point of view were the orthodox ulamā, or learned theologians, with Maulana Maududi as the best-known and most forceful representative. Opposing them were those, who, while accepting a special role for Islam, argued for an approach that would be flexible enough to adjust to the needs of contemporary society. This liberal group, often referred to as "modernists," included many of the best-known leaders in Pakistan, including, as the excerpt below suggests, Jinnah himself, the first governor-general, and Liaquat Ali Khan, the first prime minister. It is not clear from their speeches, however, that they were aware that even a moderate commitment to a religious orientation had an inner logic that impelled it toward a more rigorous definition.

It is important to keep in mind that the orthodox, conservative ulamā, who proposed giving Pakistan an Islamic constitution had, on the whole, opposed the creation of Pakistan. It was the liberal modernist Muslims, like Jinnah and Liaquat Ali Khan who had fought, as the leaders of the Muslim League, for a separate homeland for Muslims. The fact that the leading spokesmen of the League were westernized partly accounts for the opposition of the ulamā, but the ulamā also had theological reasons for their stand. They regarded nationalism, with its emphasis on the sovereignty of individual countries defined in territorial and cultural terms, as antithetic to the concept of a common brotherhood of all Muslims irrespective of race or culture. They also believed, with regard to the Indian subcontinent, that Islam would ultimately triumph, as it had in the past. Once Pakistan came into existence, however, many of the conservative ulamā migrated from their homes in India to Pakistan, as did their opponents, the leaders of the Muslim League. In Pakistan, the ulamā, like Maududi, became the bitter critics of the political leaders.

In July 1947, after the decision had been made that British India would be partitioned, elections were held for a Constituent Assembly to represent the areas to be included in Pakistan. (In the west, these included Sind, Baluchistan, the North-West Frontier Province and the western portion of Punjab; in the east, the eastern part of Bengal.) The assembly met in Karachi, and it was to this body, with Jinnah as governor-general, that power was transferred by the British on August 15, 1947. It was thus both a constitution-making body and a federal legislature.

Jinnah's death in September 1948, within a year of the founding of the nation, left the leadership of the country to Liaquat Ali Khan (1896–1951). Liaquat took a formal step in making a constitution when he moved the Objectives Resolution (given below) in March 1949. In subsequent months, the constitutional debates indicated the deep divisions that existed in the country. The leaders of the Islamic parties wanted a stronger assertion that Pakistan was an Islamic state, whereas others protested that Pakistan should be a modern, secular democracy. The representatives of East Bengal, in language foreshadowing the later secessionist movements, argued for more autonomy for the two wings of the country, East Pakistan and West Pakistan.

Liaquat's assassination in 1951 worsened the situation, especially because its motivation was unknown and many groups were suspected of being involved. In 1952 serious riots broke out in East Pakistan over the attempt to make Urdu the national language at the expense of Bengali, the language of the overwhelming majority of the people of the area. In West Pakistan, violent riots erupted against the Ahmadiyyas, a sect regarded as heretical by the orthodox ulamā. The Ahmadiyyas were followers of a nineteenth-century reformer, Mirza Ghulam of Qadiyan, who claimed in some sense to have been in the line of prophets. Because the orthodox regard Muhammad as the final figure in the prophetical line, Mirza Ghulam's claim was (and is) regarded as a peculiarly noxious heresy. The orthodox demanded that the government declare the Ahmadiyyas to be non-Muslims—a declaration finally made in 1984, when the Ahmadiyyas were forbidden, under severe penalties, to refer to themselves as Muslims.

Because of the near breakdown of law and order, the governor-general dissolved the Constituent Assembly in 1954. A commission was set up to inquire into the cause of the violence, and its findings, known as the *Munir Report,* after the judge who was commission chairman, analyzed in considerable detail the problems inherent in defining and establishing an Islamic state. An excerpt from the report is given below.

In 1956, a new Constituent Assembly finally enacted a constitution, in which Pakistan is described as an Islamic republic, under the sovereignty of Allah, where Muslims should be enabled to live their lives in accordance with "the Holy Qur'ān and the Sunnah." This constitution was abrogated in 1958, however, when general Ayub Khan (1907–1974) took over as military governor, declaring that the politicians were corrupt and incompetent. Ayub's takeover marked the beginning of the political dominance of the military forces in Pakistan. Although Ayub frequently criticized the ulamā for not understanding the nature of a modern state, the new constitution he promulgated in 1962 reiterated that Pakistan was an Islamic state, in which no law would be repugnant to Islamic teaching. In 1969, in the face of criticism from many quarters for his authoritarianism and the corruption of his family, Ayub fell from power.

There were, during these years, increased demands from East Pakistan for greater autonomy and for freedom from what was regarded as oppression by the central government. The two Pakistans were separated from each other not only by India but also by language, historical experience, and culture. It became increasingly clear that, despite the fact that the population of both sections was overwhelmingly Muslim, Islamic ideology was an insufficiently strong binding force. In 1970 a bitter civil war broke out, and in 1971 East Pakistan, assisted by India, seceded as the independent state of Bangladesh.

In the aftermath of the trauma of civil war and the secession of Bangladesh, Pakistan painfully reorganized itself. The military government led by General Yahya since 1969 was replaced in 1971 by a civilian administration under Zulfikar Bhutto. Bhutto sought to restore a sense of national identity and self-confidence to the shattered country and to this end formulated a new constitution in 1973. Like the previous constitutions, this one recognized God as sovereign and indicated that all legislation would be in accordance with the Sharīʿa. Such un-Islamic practices as usury, or the taking of interest, were forbidden. An important concession in the constitution was made to the conservative ulamā in that the president and commander-in-chief of the armed forces were to declare in their oath of office their belief in the finality of the revelation of the Prophet Muhammad. Friday, rather than Sunday, was declared the weekly holiday, and liquor stores were closed. On the whole, however, Bhutto's government did not press very vigorously for the Islamicization of Pakistan: this was the work of the military regime that, having overthrown Bhutto, came into power under General Zia-ul-Haq in 1977.

General Zia's commitment to make Pakistan a truly Islamic state can be understood in terms of personal religious zeal for Islam and of a military man's belief that an orderly society demands obedience by everyone to a common code of behavior, but it can also be seen as a search for political legitimacy for his regime. He was convinced that previous regimes had lacked such legitimacy because they had not given the people what they needed: a stable government and a just social order. These needs and aspirations were often summarized in Pakistan by the phrase "nizam-i-mustafa," meaning the system of life ordained by the Prophet Muhammad. It was this that Zia promised to the people. In Pakistan, Zia stressed, sovereignty did not belong to the people, as non-Muslims believed, but to "Almighty Allah and we are all his servants."[3] In accordance with this, Zia's regime sought to formulate precise laws that would embody Islamic principles. Punishments for crimes such as theft and adultery—for example, mutilation and stoning—were in accordance with Islamic law rather than Western codes.

But the great questions that had always been the subject of controversy in Islamic society remained: What is truly Islamic law in a changing world?

Who is the final authority among competing interpretations? And, finally, are the ulamā to control the administration?

Looking back over Pakistan's difficulties in defining an Islamic state, one can hazard the judgment that the ulamā have failed to provide a framework for the implementation of law in the present condition of Pakistan. On the other hand, their opponents, the Western-educated intellectuals, have been unable to formulate an ideology capable of binding the country together. It would seem that any attempt to provide Pakistan with such an ideology means coming to terms with a complex legacy consisting of the general Islamic tradition; the particular history of Islam in the Indian subcontinent; the structure inherited from the British; and Pakistan's relations in the modern world with both Islamic and non-Islamic countries.

The selections that follow seek to illustrate the dilemmas, frustrations, and solutions that have characterized Pakistan's political life as its leaders have tried to create a framework to accommodate the past and the future.

MUHAMMED ALI JINNAH: FOUNDER OF PAKISTAN (PART 2)

In chapters 3 through 7, the development of what may be thought of as alternative nationalisms in India was examined. One form was represented by the Indian National Congress, for which M. K. Gandhi and Jawaharlal Nehru were the most articulate spokesmen; the other was that of the Muslim League, with Muhammed Ali Jinnah as the driving force for the recognition that the Muslim community must have a defined and special place in any constitutional arrangement that would replace British rule.

During negotiations for Indian independence, Jinnah showed his extraordinary political skills as he opposed the demand of the members of the Indian National Congress that power be transferred to a Constituent Assembly in which they were the clear majority as shown by the elections that had been held. Selections from Jinnah's speeches and writings before 1947 are given in chapter 5.

A Vision of Pakistan

The following remarkable statement is from a speech Jinnah made on August 11, 1947 to the Constituent Assembly that had been created in preparation for the coming of independence. With its seemingly clear insistence that Pakistan would be a modern, democratic state, with equal freedom for all religions, it provides a striking prologue to the long debate on the place of Islam noted in the other selections. Jinnah died in 1948 before he had an opportunity to give constitutional form to his ideas.

[From Jinnah, *Speeches and Writings*, 2:399–404]

I cordially thank you, with the utmost sincerity, for the honour you have conferred upon me—the greatest honour that is possible for this Sovereign Assembly to confer—by electing me as your first President. I also thank those leaders who have spoken in appreciation of my services and their personal references to me. I sincerely hope that with your support and your co-operation we shall make this Constituent Assembly an example to the world. The Constituent Assembly has got two main functions to perform. The first is the very onerous and responsible task of framing our future Constitution of Pakistan and the second of functioning as a full and complete Sovereign body as the Federal Legislature of Pakistan. We have to do the best we can in adopting a provisional constitution for the Federal Legislature of Pakistan. You know really that not only we ourselves are wondering but, I think, the whole world is wondering at this unprecedented cyclonic revolution which has brought about the plan of creating and establishing two independent Sovereign Dominions in this sub-continent. As it is, it has been unprecedented; there is no parallel in the history of the world. This mighty sub-continent with all kinds of inhabitants has been brought under a plan which is titanic, unknown, unparalleled. And what is very important with regard to it is that we have achieved it peacefully and by means of an evolution of the greatest possible character.

Dealing with our first function in this Assembly, I cannot make any well-considered pronouncement at this moment, but I shall say a few things as they occur to me. The first and the foremost thing that I would like to emphasise is this—remember that you are now a Sovereign Legislative body and you have got all the powers. It, therefore, places on you the gravest responsibility as to how you should take your decisions. The first observation that I would like to make is this: You will no doubt agree with me that the first duty of a Government is to maintain law and order, so that the life, property and religious beliefs of its subjects are fully protected by the State. . . .

I know there are people who do not quite agree with the division of India and the partition of the Punjab and Bengal. Much has been said against it, but now that it has been accepted, it is the duty of everyone of us to loyally abide by it and honourably act according to the agreement which is now final and binding on all. But you must remember, as I have said, that this mighty revolution that has taken place is unprecedented. One can quite understand the feeling that exists between the two communities wherever one community is in majority and the other is in minority. But the question is, whether, it was possible or practicable to act otherwise than what has been done. A division had to take place. On both sides, in Hindustan and Pakistan, there are sections of people who may not agree with it, who may not like it, but in my judgment there was no other solution and I am sure future history will record its verdict in favour of it. And what is more it will be proved by actual experience as we go on that that was the only solution of India's constitutional problem. Any idea of a United India could never have worked and in my judgment it would have led us to terrific disaster. May be that view is correct; may be it is not; that remains to be seen. All the same, in this division it was impossible to avoid the question of minorities being in one Dominion or the other. Now that was unavoidable. There is no other solution. Now what shall we do? Now, if we want to make this great State of Pakistan happy and prosperous we should wholly and solely concentrate on the well-being of the people, and especially of the masses and the poor. If you will work in co-operation, forgetting the past, burying the hatchet you are bound to succeed. If you change your past and work together in a spirit that every one of you, no matter to what community he belongs, no matter what relations he had with you in the past, no matter what is his colour, caste or creed, is first, second, and last a citizen of this State with equal rights, privileges and obligations, there will be no end to the progress you will make.

I cannot emphasise it too much. We should begin to work in that spirit and in course of time all these angularities of the majority and minority communities, the Hindu community and the Muslim community—because even as regards Muslims you have Pathans, Punjabis, Shias, Sunnis and so on and among the Hindus you have Brahmans, Visahnavas, Khatris, also Bengalees, Madrasis, and so on—will vanish. Indeed if you ask me this has been the biggest hindrance in the way of India to attain the freedom and independence and but for this we would have been free peoples long long ago. No power can hold another nation, and specially a nation of 400 million souls in subjection; nobody could have conquered you, and even if it had happened, nobody could have continued its hold on you for any length of time but for this. Therefore, we must learn a lesson from this. You are free; you are free to go to your temples, you are free to go to your mosques or to any other places of worship in this State of Pakistan. You may belong to any religion or caste or creed—that has nothing to do with the business of the State. As you know, history shows that in England conditions, some time ago, were much worse than those prevailing in India today. The Roman Catholics and the Protestants persecuted each other. Even now there are some States in existence where there are discriminations made and bars imposed against a particular class. Thank God, we are not starting in those days. We are starting in the days when there is no discrimination, no distinction between one community and another, no discrimination between one caste or creed and another. We are starting with this fundamental principle that we are all citizens and equal citizens of one State. The people of England in course of time had to face the realities of the situation and had to discharge the responsibilities and burdens placed upon them by the government of their country and they went through that fire step by step. Today, you might say with justice that Roman Catholics and Protestants do not exist; what exists now is that every man is a citizen, an equal citizen of Great Britain and they are all members of the Nation.

Now, I think we should keep that in front of us as our ideal and you will find that in course of time Hindus would cease to be Hindus and Muslims would cease to be Muslims, not in the religious sense, because that is the personal faith of each individual, but in the political sense as citizens of the State.

Well, gentlemen, I do not wish to take up any more of your time and thank you again for the honour you have done to me. I shall always be guided by the principles of justice and fair-play without any, as is put in the political language, prejudice or ill-will, in other words, partiality or favouritism. My guiding principle will be justice and complete impartiality, and I am sure that with your support and co-operation, I can look forward to Pakistan becoming one of the greatest Nations of the world.

LIAQUAT ALI KHAN: THE FIRST PRIME MINISTER

On the death of Jinnah, Liaquat Ali Khan (1895–1951) had as prime minister the difficult task of organizing the government of the new state and of trying to write a constitution that would be acceptable to the various factions in the country. A representative of the Westernized, liberal group, he seemed to share Jinnah's vision of Pakistan as a modern nation state, where Muslims would be in a majority and would be able to create a society acceptable to Islamic teaching, with democratic political institutions, but he laid much more stress on religion as a belief system than did Jinnah.

The Objectives of the Constitution

The following selection is what is known as "The Objectives Resolution," adopted by the Constituent Assembly in March 1949. Although Liaquat stresses the democratic ideals of the Objectives, it should be noted that the constitution was not to be neutral toward all religions: Islam was to be the guiding principle. This permitted the possibility of wide disagreement over the application of Islamic precepts in the making of laws.

[From *The Constituent Assembly of Pakistan Debates*, 5(1):1–7]

I beg to move the following Objectives Resolution embodying the main principles on which the constitution of Pakistan is to be based:

"In the name of Allāh, the Beneficent, the Merciful;

WHEREAS sovereignty over the entire universe belongs to God Almighty alone and the authority which He has delegated to the State of Pakistan through its people for being exercised within the limits prescribed by Him is a sacred trust;

This Constituent Assembly representing the people of Pakistan resolves to frame a constitution for the sovereign independent State of Pakistan;

WHEREIN the State shall exercise its powers and authority through the chosen representatives of the people;

WHEREIN the principles of democracy, freedom, equality, tolerance, and social justice, as enunciated by Islam, shall be fully observed;

WHEREIN the Muslims shall be enabled to order their lives in the individual and collective spheres in accord with the teachings and requirements of Islam as set out in the Holy Qur'ān and the Sunna;[4]

WHEREIN adequate provision shall be made for the minorities freely to profess and practice their religions and develop their cultures;

WHEREBY the territories now included in or in accession with Pakistan and such other territories as may hereafter be included in or accede to Pakistan shall form a Federation wherein the units will be autonomous with such boundaries and limitations on their powers and authority as may be prescribed;

WHEREIN shall be guaranteed fundamental rights including equality of status, of opportunity, and before law, social, economic, and political justice and freedom of thought, expression, belief, faith, worship and association, subject to law and public morality;

WHEREIN adequate provision shall be made to safeguard the legitimate interests of minorities and backward and depressed classes;

WHEREIN the independence of the judiciary shall be fully secured;

WHEREIN the integrity of the territories of the Federation, its independence and all its rights including its sovereign rights on land, sea and air shall be safeguarded;

So that the people of Pakistan may prosper and attain their rightful and honored place amongst the nations of the world and make their full contribution towards international peace and progress and happiness of humanity."

I consider this to be a most important occasion in the life of this country, next in importance only to the achievement of independence, because by achieving independence we only won an opportunity of building up a country and its polity in accordance with our ideals. I would like to remind the House that the Father of the Nation, Qaid-i-azam, gave expression to his feelings on this matter on many an occasion, and his views were endorsed by the nation in unmistakable terms. Pakistan was founded because the Muslims of this subcontinent wanted to build up their lives in accordance with the teachings and traditions of Islam, because they wanted to demonstrate to the world that Islam provides a panacea to the many diseases which have crept into the life of humanity today. It is universally recognized that the source of these evils is that humanity has not been able to keep pace with its material development, that the Frankenstein monster which human genius has produced in the form of scientific inventions, now threatens to destroy not only the fabric of human society but its material environment as well, the very habitat in which it dwells. It is universally recognized that if man had not chosen to ignore the spiritual values of life and if his faith in God had not been weakened, this scientific development would not have endangered his very existence. It is God-consciousness alone which can save humanity, which means that all power that humanity possesses must be used in accordance with ethical standards which have been laid down by inspired teachers known to us as the great Prophets of different religions.

We, as Pakistanis, are not ashamed of the fact that we are overwhelmingly Muslims and we believe that it is by adhering to our faith and ideals that we can make a genuine contribution to the welfare of the world. Therefore, you would notice that the Preamble of the Resolution deals with a frank and unequivocal recognition of the fact that all authority must be subservient to God. It is quite true that this is in direct contradiction to the Machiavellian ideas regarding a polity where spiritual and ethical values should play no part in the governance of the people and, therefore, it is also perhaps a little out of fashion to remind ourselves of the fact that the State should be an instrument of beneficence and not of evil. But we, the people of Pakistan, have the courage to believe firmly that all authority should be exercised in accordance with the standards laid down by Islam so that it may not be misused. All authority is a sacred trust, entrusted to us by God for the purpose of being exercised in the service of man, so that it does not become an agency for tyranny or selfishness. I would, however, point out that this is not a resuscitation of the dead theory of divine right of kings or rulers, because, in accordance with the spirit of Islam, the Preamble fully recognizes the truth that authority has been delegated to the people, and to none else, and that it is for the people to decide who will exercise that authority.

For this reason it has been made clear in the Resolution that the State shall exercise all its powers and authority through the chosen representatives of the people. This is the very essence of democracy, because the people have been recognized as the recipients of all authority and it is in them that the power to wield it has been vested.

I just now said that the people are the real recipients of power. This naturally eliminates any danger of the establishment of a theocracy. It is true that in its literal sense, theocracy means the Government of God; in this sense, however, it is patent that the entire universe is a theocracy, for is there any corner in the entire creation where His authority does not exist? But in the technical sense, theocracy has come to mean a government by ordained priests, who wield authority as being specially appointed by those who claim to derive their rights from their sacerdotal position. I cannot overemphasize the fact that such an idea is absolutely foreign to Islam. Islam does not recognize either priesthood or any sacerdotal authority; and, therefore, the question of a theocracy simply does not arise in Islam. If there are any who still use the word theocracy in the same breath as the polity of Pakistan, they are either laboring under a grave misapprehension, or indulging in mischievous propaganda.

You would notice that the Objectives Resolution lays emphasis on the principles of democracy, freedom, equality, tolerance, and social justice, and further defines them by saying that these principles should be observed in the constitution as they have been enunciated by Islam. It has been necessary to qualify these terms because they are generally used in a loose sense. For instance, the Western Powers and Soviet Russia alike claim that their systems are based upon democracy, and, yet, it is common knowledge that their polities are inherently different. . . . When we use the word democracy in the Islamic sense, it pervades all aspects of our life; it relates to our system of government and to our society with equal validity, because one of the greatest contributions of Islam has been the idea of the equality of all men. Islam recognizes no distinctions based upon race, color, or birth. Even in the days of its decadence, Islamic society has been remarkably free from the prejudices which vitiated human relations in many other parts of the world. Similarly, we have a great record in tolerance, for under no system of government, even in the Middle Ages, have the minorities received the same consideration and freedom as they did in Muslim countries. When Christian dissentients and Muslims were being tortured and driven out of their homes, when they were being hunted as animals and burnt as criminals—even criminals have never been burnt in Islamic society—Islam provided a haven for all who were persecuted and who fled from tyranny. It is a well-known fact of history that, when anti-Semitism turned the Jews out of many a European country, it was the Ottoman empire which gave them shelter. The greatest proof of the tolerance of Muslim peoples lies in the fact that there is no Muslim country where strong minorities do not exist, and where they have not been able to preserve their religion and culture. Most of all, in this subcontinent of India, where the Muslims wielded unlimited authority, the rights of non-Muslims were cherished and protected. I may point out that it was under Muslim patronage that many an indigenous language developed in India. My friends from Bengal would remember that it was under the encouragement of Muslim rulers that the first translations of the Hindu scriptures were made from Sanskrit into Bengali. It is this tolerance which is envisaged by Islam, wherein a minority does not live on sufferance, but is respected and given every opportunity to develop its own thought and culture, so that it may contribute to the greater glory of the entire nation. In the matter of social justice as well, I would point out that Islam has a distinct contribution to make. Islam envisages a society in which social justice means neither charity nor regimentation. Islamic social justice is based upon fundamental laws and concepts which guarantee to man a life free from want and rich in freedom. It is for this reason that the principles of democracy, freedom, equality, tolerance, and social justice have been further defined by giving to them a meaning which, in our view, is deeper and wider than the usual connotation of these words.

The next clause of the Resolution lays down that Muslims shall be enabled to order their lives in the individual and collective spheres in accord with the teachings and requirements of Islam as set out in the Holy Qur'ān and the Sunna. It is quite obvious that no non-Muslim should have any objection if the Muslims are enabled to order their lives in accordance with the dictates of their religion. You would also notice that the State is not to play the part of a neutral observer, wherein the Muslims may be merely free to profess and practice their religion, because such an attitude on the part of the State would be the very negation of the ideals which prompted the demand of Pakistan, and it is these ideals which should be the cornerstone of the State which we want to build. The State will create such conditions as are conducive to the building up of a truly Islamic society, which means that the State will have to play a positive part in this effort. You would remember that the Qaid-i-azam and other leaders of the Muslim league always made unequivocal declarations that the Muslim demand for Pakistan was based upon the fact that the Muslims had a way of life and a code of conduct. They also reiterated the fact that Islam is not merely a relationship between the individual and his God, which should not, in any way, affect the working of the State. Indeed, Islam lays down specific directions for social behavior, and seeks to guide society in its attitude towards the problems which confront it from day to day. Islam is not just a matter of private beliefs and conduct. It expects its followers to build up a society for the purpose of good life—as the Greeks would have called it, with this difference, that Islamic "good life" is essentially based upon spiritual values. For the purpose of emphasizing these values and to give them validity, it will be necessary for the State to direct and guide the activities of the Muslims in such a manner as to bring about a new social order based upon the essential principles of Islam, including the principles of democracy, freedom, tolerance, and social justice. These I mention merely by way of illustration; because they do not exhaust the teachings of Islam as embodied in the Qu'rān and the Sunna. There can be no Muslim who does not believe that the word of God and the life of the Prophet are the basic sources of his inspiration. In these there is no difference of opinion amongst the Muslims and there is no sect in Islam which does not believe in their validity. Therefore, there should be no misconception in the mind of any sect which may be in a minority in Pakistan about the intentions of the State. The State will seek to create an Islamic society free from dissensions, but this does not mean that it would curb the freedom of any section of the Muslims in the matter of their beliefs. No sect, whether the majority or a minority, will be permitted to dictate to the others and, in their own internal matters and sectional beliefs, all sects shall be given the fullest possible latitude and freedom. Actually we hope that the various sects will act in accordance with the desire of the Prophet who said that the differences of opinion amongst his followers are a blessing. It is for us to make our differences a source of strength to Islam and Pakistan, not to exploit them for narrow interests which will weaken both Pakistan and Islam. Differences of opinion very often lead to cogent thinking and progress, but this happens only when they are not permitted to obscure our vision of the real goal, which is the service of Islam and the furtherance of its objects. It is, therefore, clear that this clause seeks to give the Muslims the opportunity that they have been seeking, throughout these long decades of decadence and subjection, of finding freedom to set up a polity, which may prove to be a laboratory for the purpose of demonstrating to the world that Islam is not only a progressive force in the world, but it also provides remedies for many of the ills from which humanity has been suffering.

MOHAMMAD MUNIR: THE CHIEF JUSTICE OF PAKISTAN

In 1953, riots broke out in Pakistan against the Ahmadiyya sect, on the grounds that they were heretical and non-Muslims. The riots were also aimed at the government's delay in meeting the demands of the most conservative elements for the establishment of a truly Islamic state.

Is There an Islamic State?

The commission set up under the chairmanship of Justice Munir to inquire into the causes of the riots issued a report that examined in detail the concept of an Islamic state. The conclusion that such a state is impossible in the modern world was rejected, of course, by orthodox groups, and the secularist position it seems to advocate would find few open supporters. The report is important, however, for emphasizing the problems inherent in having a religious ideology dominant in a modern state.

[From the *Munir Report*, pp. 201, 203, 210, 231–32]

It has been repeatedly said before us that implicit in the demand for Pakistan was the demand for an Islamic State. Some speeches of important leaders who were striving for Pakistan undoubtedly lend themselves to this construction. These leaders while referring to an Islamic State or to a State governed by Islamic laws perhaps had in their minds the pattern of a legal structure based on or mixed up with Islamic dogma, personal law, ethics and institutions. No one who has given serious thought to the introduction of a religious State in Pakistan has failed to notice the tremendous difficulties with which any such scheme must be confronted. The Quaid-i-Azam [M. A. Jinnah] said that the new State would be a modern democratic State, with sovereignty resting in the people and the members of the new nation having equal rights of citizenship regardless of their religion, caste or creed. When Pakistan formally appeared on the map, the Quaid-i-Azam in his memorable speech of 11th August 1947 to the Constituent Assembly of Pakistan, while stating the principle on which the new State was to be founded, said:

Every one of you, no matter to what community he belongs, no matter what relations he had with you in the past, no matter what is his colour, caste or creed, is first, second and last a citizen of this State with equal rights, privileges and obligations. . . . You are free; you are free to go to your temples, you are free to go to your mosques or to any other places of worship in this State of Pakistan. You may belong to any religion or caste or creed—that has nothing to do with the business of the State.

The Quaid-i-Azam was the founder of Pakistan and the occasion on which he thus spoke was the first landmark in the history of Pakistan. The speech was intended both for his own people, including non-Muslims, and the world, and its object was to define as clearly as possible the ideal to the attainment of which the new State was to devote all its energies. There are repeated references in this speech to the bitterness of the past and an appeal to forget and change the past and to bury the hatchet. The future subject of the State is to be a citizen with equal rights, privileges and obligations, irrespective of colour, caste, creed or community. The word 'nation' is used more than once and religion is stated to have nothing to do with the business of the State and to be merely a matter of personal faith for the individual.

We asked the *ulama* whether this conception of a State was acceptable to them and everyone of them replied in an unhesitating negative. . . . If Maulana Amin Ahsan Islahi's evidence correctly represents the view of Jama'at-i-Islami, a State based on this idea is the creature of the devil, and he is confirmed in this by several writings of his chief, Maulana Abul Ala Maudoodi, the founder of the *jama'at*. None of the *ulama* can tolerate a State which is based on nationalism and all that it implies: with them *millat*[5] and all that it connotes can alone be the determining factor in State activity.

The Quaid-i-Azam's conception of a modern national State, it is alleged, became obsolete with the passing of the Objectives Resolution on 12th March 1949; but it has been freely admitted that this Resolution, though grandiloquent in words, phrases and clauses, is nothing but a hoax and that not only does it not contain even a semblance of the embryo of an Islamic State but its provisions, particularly those relating to fundamental rights, are directly opposed to the principles of an Islamic State.

What is then the Islamic State of which everybody talks but nobody thinks? Before we seek to discover an answer to this question, we must have a clear conception of the scope and function of the State.

The *ulama* were divided in their opinions when they were asked to cite some precedent of an Islamic State in Muslim history. . . . Kifayat Husain, the Shia divine, held as his ideal the form of Government during the Holy Prophet's time, Maulana Daud Ghaznavi also included in his precedent the days of . . . Sultan Mahmud of Ghazni, Muhammad Tughlaq and Aurangzeb and the present regime in Saudi Arabia. Most of them, however, relied on the form of Government during the Islamic Republic from 632 to 661 A.D., a period of less than thirty years, though some of them also added the very short period of Umar bin Abdul Aziz.

Since the basis of Islamic law is the principle of inerrancy of revelation and of the Holy Prophet, the law to be found in the Qur'an and the *sunna* is above all man-made laws, and in case of conflict between the two, the latter, irrespective of its nature, must yield to the former. Thus, provided there be a rule in the Qur'an or the *sunna* on a matter which according to our conceptions falls within the region of Constitutional Law or International Law, the rule must be given effect to unless that rule itself permits a departure from it. Thus no distinction exists in Islamic law between Constitutional Law and other law, the whole law to be found in the Qur'an and the *sunna* being a part of the law of the land for Muslim subjects of the State. Similarly if there be a rule in the Qur'an or the *sunna* relating to the State's relations with other States or to the relations of Muslim subjects of the State with other States or the subjects of those States, the rule will have the same superiority of sanction as any other law to be found in the Qur'an or the *sunna*. . . . That the form of Government in Pakistan, if that form is to comply with the principles of Islam, will not be democratic is conceded by the *ulama*. We have already explained the doctrine of sovereignty of the Qur'an and the *sunna*. The Objectives Resolution rightly recognised this position when it recited that all sovereignty rests with God Almighty alone. But the authors of that Resolution misused the words 'sovereign' and 'democracy' when they recited that the Constitution to be framed was for a sovereign State in which principles of democracy as enunciated by Islam shall be fully observed. It may be that in the context in which they were used, these words could not be misunderstood by those who are well versed in Islamic principles, but both these words were borrowed from western political philosophy and in that sense they were both wrongly used in the Resolution. When it is said that a country is sovereign, the implication is that its people or any other group of persons in it are entitled to conduct the affairs of that country in any way they like and untrammelled by any considerations except those of expediency and policy. An Islamic State, however, cannot in this sense be sovereign, because it will not be competent to abrogate, repeal or do away with any law in the Qur'an or the *sunna*. Absolute restriction on the legislative power of a State is a restriction on the sovereignty of the people of that State and if the origin of this restriction lies elsewhere than in the will of the people, then to the extent of that restriction the sovereignty of the State and its people is necessarily taken away. In an Islamic State, sovereignty, in its essentially juristic sense, can only rest with Allah. In the same way, democracy means the rule of the *demos*, namely, the people, directly by them as in ancient Greece and Rome, or indirectly through chosen representatives as in modern democracies. If the power of the people in the framing of the Constitution or in the framing of the laws or in the sphere of executive action is subject to certain immutable rules, it cannot be said that they can pass any law that they like, or, in the exercise of executive functions, do whatever they like. Indeed if the legislature in an Islamic State is a sort of *ijmā*, the masses are expressly disqualified from taking part in it because *ijmā-i-ummat* in Islamic jurisprudence is restricted to *ulama* and *mujahids* of acknowledged status and does not at all extend, as in democracy, to the populace. . . .

We have dwelt at some length on the subject of Islamic State not because we intended to write a thesis against or in favour of such State but merely with a view to presenting a clear picture of the numerous possibilities that may in future arise if true causes of the ideological confusion which contributed to the spread and intensity of the disturbances are not precisely located. That such confusion did exist is obvious because otherwise Muslim Leaguers, whose own Government was in office, would not have risen against it; sense of loyalty and public duty would not have departed from public officials who went about like maniacs howling against their own Government and officers; respect for property and human life would not have disappeared in the common man who with no scruple or compunction began freely to indulge in loot, arson and murder; politicians would not have shirked facing the men who had installed them in their offices; and administrators would not have felt hesitant or diffident in performing what was their obvious duty. If there is one thing which has been conclusively demonstrated in this inquiry, it is that provided you can persuade the masses to believe that something they are asked to do is religiously right or enjoined by religion, you can set them to any course of action, regardless of all considerations of discipline, loyalty, decency, morality or civic sense.

Pakistan is being taken by the common man to be an Islamic State, though it is not. This belief has been encouraged by the ceaseless clamour for Islam and Islamic State that is being heard from all quarters since the establishment of Pakistan. The phantom of an Islamic State has haunted the Musalman throughout the ages and is a result of the memory of the glorious past when Islam, rising like a storm from the least expected quarter of the world—wilds of Arabia—instantly enveloped the world, pulling down from their high pedestal gods who had ruled over man since the creation, uprooting centuries-old institutions and superstitions and supplanting all civilisations that had been built on an enslaved humanity. What is 125 years in humanity history, nay in the history of a people, and yet during this brief period Islam spread from the Indus to the Atlantic and Spain, and from the borders of China to Egypt, and the sons of the desert installed themselves in all old centres of civilisation—in Ctesiphon, Damascus, Alexandria, India and all places associated with the names of the Sumerian and the Assyrian civilisations. Historians have often posed the question: what would have been the state of the world today if Muawiya's siege of Constantinople had succeeded or if the proverbial Arab instinct for plunder had not suddenly seized the *mujahids* of Abdur Rahman in their fight against Charles Martel on the plains of Tours in Southern France. May be Muslims would have discovered America long before Columbus did and the entire world would have been Moslemised; may be Islam itself would have been Europeanised. It is this brilliant achievement of the Arabian nomads, the like of which the world had never seen before, that makes the Musalman of today live in the past and yearn for the return of the glory that was Islam. He finds himself standing on the crossroads, wrapped in the mantle of the past and with the dead weight of centuries on his back, frustrated and be-wildered and hesitant to turn one corner or the other. The freshness and the simplicity of the faith, which gave determination to his mind and spring to his muscle, is now denied to him. He has neither the means nor the ability to conquer and there are no countries to conquer. Little does he understand that the forces, which are pitted against him, are entirely differ-ent from those against which early Islam had to fight, and that on the clues given by his own ancestors human mind has achieved results which he cannot understand. He therefore finds himself in a state of helplessness, waiting for some one to come and help him out of this morass of uncer-tainty and confusion. And he will go on waiting like this without anything happening. Nothing but a bold re-orientation of Islam to separate the vital from the lifeless can preserve it as a World Idea and convert the Musalman into a citizen of the present and the future world from the archaic incon-gruity that he is today.

It is this lack of bold and clear thinking, the inability to understand and take decisions which has brought about in Pakistan a confusion which will persist and repeatedly create situations of the kind we have been inquiring into until our leaders have a clear conception of the goal and of the means to reach it. It requires no imagination to realize that irreconcilables remain irreconcilable even if you believe or wish to the contrary. Opposing prin-ciples, if left to themselves, can only produce confusion and disorder, and the application of a neutralising agency to them can only produce a dead result. Unless, in case of conflict between two ideologies, our leaders have the desire and the ability to elect, uncertainty must continue. And as long as we rely on the hammer when a file is needed and press Islam into service to solve situations it was never intended to solve, frustration and disappointment must dog our steps. The sublime faith called Islam will live even if our leaders are not there to enforce it. It lives in the individual, in his soul and outlook, in all his relations with God and men, from the cradle to the grave, and our politicians should understand that if Divine commands cannot make or keep a man a Musalman, their statutes will not.

GENERAL AYUB KHAN: MARTIAL LAW ADMINISTRATOR

General Ayub Khan (1907–1974), who became the ruler of Pakistan when the army took over power from the civilian authorities in 1958, came into conflict with the conservative religious forces led by Maulana Maududi and his group, the Jama'at-i-Islami, when he promulgated family laws that were intended, among other things, to give greater protection to women in divorce and inheritance proceedings. These measures were attacked as un-Islamic.

The Revivalists Against National Unity

In the following excerpt from his autobiography, Ayub summed up what may be called the "modernist" view of the role of the religious authorities in national life.

[Ayub Khan, *Friends, Not Masters*, pp. 194–201]

My task, as I saw it, was to set up institutions which should enable the people of Pakistan to develop their material, moral and intellectual resources and capacities to the maximum extent. The essential prerequisite of this task was to analyse the national problems objectively. I could not convince myself that we had become a nation in the real sense of the word; the whole spectacle was one of disunity and disintegration. We were divided in two halves, each half dominated by a distinct linguistic and cultural pattern. The geographical distance between the two halves was in itself a divisive factor which could be exploited to create all kinds of doubts and suspicions among the people. We had inherited a deep antagonism which separated the people in the countryside from the urban classes. The latter represented a small minority in the total population, but it was a vocal minority and the people in the villages suffered from a sense of domination and exploitation by the elite of the towns. Then there were the regional identities, which often asserted themselves to the exclusion of the national identity. . . . But more than anything else it was the irreconcilable nature of the forces of science and reason and the forces of dogmatism and revivalism which was operating against the unification of the people. In more precise terms the essential conflict was between the *ulema* and the educated classes. All that was material, temporal and secular was identified with the educated and all that was religious and spiritual became the monopoly of the *ulema.* . . .

. . . How were these conflicts to be reconciled? Islam visualizes life as a unity and the Islamic code represents a complete cultural whole. . . . A man at home, at work, or at prayer is guided by the same code of behavior. . . . All this was true. But the picture of our society as I saw it, did not conform to this. In practice our life was broken up into two distinct spheres and in each sphere we followed a different set of principles. How were we to get out of this morass and adopt a unified approach to life? . . . We were fortunate to have a religion which could serve as a vehicle of progress. But superstition and ritualism had given us a fatalistic outlook which were completely contrary to the teachings and message of Islam. Muslim society could not move forward unless Islam was relieved of all the inhibiting and alien influences which had distorted its real character. . . .

. . . There was universal agreement that the country should have a democratic constitution and a constitution which should enable the Community to organize itself according to the essential principles of Islam and to develop and progress with the times. . . . The question arose as to how the Community should discern and define the principles of Islam. There was no ready answer to this. No precedent of an Islamic Constitution was available. The Holy Koran contained the principles of guidance but did not prescribe a detailed Constitution for running a country. . . . The conclusion was inescapable that Islam had not prescribed any particular pattern of government but had left it to the Community to evolve its own pattern to suit its circumstances provided that the principles of the Koran and the Sunnah were observed. . . . It was equally clear to me that this exercise must be conducted within the accepted democratic norms of which the most important is the participation of the people in the affairs of the State. The right of the people as a whole to organize and run their affairs could not be curtailed or compromised in any manner. . . . I knew that the ulema would not be satisfied with this arrangement. They claimed the exclusive right to interpret and decide matters pertaining to Islam. While they maintained the claim, they refrained from producing any detailed Constitutional document, knowing that such an attempt would only expose their internal differences.

The history of the ulema in this subcontinent has been one of perpetual conflict with the educated classes. The conflict came to a head during the struggle for Pakistan. . . . Now, I do not suggest that those among the ulema who opposed the creation of Pakistan were all men of easy conscience. Among them were people of ability and conviction, but there were also those who thought that Pakistan might mean the end of their authority. The best among them argued that the Indian freedom movement would be retarded if Hindus and Muslims did not act in union. Some also felt that Pakistan was essentially a territorial concept and thus alien to the philosophy of Islamic brotherhood, which was universal in character. Both these arguments were the result of confused thinking and revealed a lamentable ignorance of the problems which the Muslims of the subcontinent were facing. . . . [But] the opposition offered by some of the ulema was not wholly the result of confused thinking or lack of awareness of the problems of the Muslims. Behind it was the consciousness of power. . . . The ulema knew that the leadership of the Muslims in the subcontinent was gradually passing to the modern educated classes who had found an eloquent and powerful spokesman in the Quaid-e-Azam. . . . It was this new leadership that the ulema dreaded and against which they aligned themselves with the Indian National Congress. . . . Pakistan was the greatest defeat of the nationalist *ulema*. But they are a tenacious tribe and power is an irresistible drug. Soon after the establishment of Pakistan this type of ulema reorganised its forces. Now that Pakistan had been established, these people asked, who, indeed, except the ulema, could decide how the new Muslim state should be run. Some of the nationalist *ulema* decided to stay in India; others hastened to Pakistan to lend a helping hand. If they had not been able to save the Muslims from Pakistan, they must now save Pakistan from the Muslims. Among the migrants was Maulana Abul Aala Maudoodi, head of the Jama'at-e-Islami party who had been bitterly opposed to Pakistan. He sought refuge there and forthwith launched a campaign for the 'Muslimization' of the hapless people of Pakistan. This venerable gentleman was appalled by what he saw in Pakistan: an un-Islamic country, an un-Islamic government, and an un-Islamic people. How could any genuine Muslim owe allegiance to such a government? So he set about the task of convincing the people of their inadequacies, their failings, and their general un-worthiness.

All this was really a facade. The true intention was to re-establish the supremacy of the ulema and to reassert their right to lead the Community. . . . The political ulema had two courses open to them: either to re-examine their own position and to revise their attitudes so that the people might be able to gain from their knowledge in dealing with their problems; or to demolish the position of the educated classes in the eyes of the God-fearing but uneducated masses. Not unnaturally, they adopted the latter course. A society which had just emerged from a century of foreign domination and was faced with the practical problems of building a new country suffered from many defects and weaknesses. The ulema concentrated on these. . . . They succeeded in converting an optimistic and enthusiastic people into a cynical and frustrated community. The ulema claimed that they knew all the answers and could easily solve all the problems of the country but that they were helpless as the country was in the control of the modern educated classes who had disowned Islam and taken to Western ways. Since no leadership could provide an immediate solution to all the problems of the community, the ulema were able to build up a large following for their point of view. . . .

SYED ABUʾL-ALA-MAUDUDI: SPOKESMAN FOR ISLAMIC REVIVAL

Syed Abuʾl-ala-Maududi (1903–1979) was the most vigorous and persuasive spokesman for making Pakistan into an Islamic state. He made his reputation at an early age in India with the journal he started in 1933, *Tarjumān-uʾl-Qurʾān* (*Exegesis of the Qurʾān*), which deeply influenced Muslim thought. He opposed the pre-independence separatist movement for Pakistan on the grounds that the nationalism was based on Western, not Islamic, values. He went to Pakistan after partition, however, where his organization, the Jamaʾat-i-Islami (Islamic Association) campaigned for an Islamic constitution. He gained wide support among college students and government and factory workers. The selections given below illustrate the logic of his appeal for an Islamic society to be created in Pakistan with the assistance of the power of the state as well as the devotion of the people.

Islam and the Impact of the West

[From Maudoodi, *Islamic Law and Constitution*, p. 14 ff.]

Commencing with stagnation in the domains of knowledge and learning, research and discovery, and thought and culture, it [the degeneration of the Muslims] finally culminated in our political breakdown, making many a Muslim country the slave of non-Muslim imperialist powers. Political slavery gave birth to an inferiority complex and the resultant intellectual serfdom, which eventually swept the entire Muslim world off its feet, so much so that even those Muslim countries which were able to retain their political freedom could not escape its evil influences. The ultimate consequence of this evil situation was that when Muslims woke up again to the call of progress, they were incapable of looking at things except through the colored glasses of Western thought. Nothing which was not Western could inspire confidence in them. Indeed, the adoption of Western culture and civilization and aping the West even in the most personal things became their craze. Eventually, they succumbed totally to the slavery of the West.

This trend towards Westernism was also the result of the disappointment which came from the side of the Muslim religious leaders. Being themselves the victims of the widespread degeneration that had engulfed the entire Muslim world, they were incapable of initiating any constructive movement or taking any revolutionary step which could combat the evils afflicting Muslim society. Quite naturally, this disappointment turned the discontented Muslims towards that system of life which had the glamour of being successful in the modern world. Thus they adopted modern thought and the new culture of the West and blindly aped Western morals and manners. Slowly but surely the religious leaders were pushed into the background and were replaced, as regards power and control over the people, by men bereft of all knowledge of their religion and imbued only with the spirit of modern thought and Western ideals. That is why we find that many a Muslim country has, in the recent past, either completely abrogated the Islamic law or confined its operation to the domain of purely personal matters—a position conferred on the non-Muslims in a truly Islamic state.

In all Muslim countries suffering from foreign domination, the leadership of political and cultural movements fell into the hands of those who were shorn of all Islamic background. They adopted the creed of "Nationalism," directed their efforts towards the cause of *national* independence and pros-

Nationalism

perity along secular lines, and tried to copy step by step the advanced nations of our age. So, if these gentlemen are vexed with the demand for Islamic constitution and Islamic laws, it is just natural for them. It is also natural for them to sidetrack or suppress the issue, as they are ignorant even of the A B C of the Islamic Sharīʿa. Their education and intellectual development has alienated them so completely from the spirit and the structure of Islamic ideology that it is at least for the moment impossible for them to understand such demands.

As regards the Muslim religious leadership, it fares in no way better, because our religious institutions are tied up to the intellectual atmosphere of eight centuries ago, as a consequence of which they have not been able to produce such leaders of Islamic thought and action as could be capable of administering the affairs of a modern state in the light of Islamic principles. This is, indeed, a very real obstacle facing the Islamic countries in their march towards the goal of Islamic revolution.

This is the situation obtaining throughout the Muslim world and impeding the path of the establishment of Islamic constitution. The case of Pakistan is not, however, the same as that of other Muslim countries, certain similarities of situation notwithstanding. This is so because it has been achieved exclusively with the object of becoming the home land of Islam. For the last ten years, we have been ceaselessly fighting for the recognition of the fact that we are a separate nation by virtue of our adherence to Islam. We have been proclaiming from house-tops that we have a distinct culture of our own, and that we possess a world view, an outlook on life, and a code of living fundamentally different from those of non-Muslims. We have all along been demanding a separate homeland for the purpose of translating into practice the ideals envisaged by Islam, and, at last, after a long and arduous struggle, in which we sustained a heavy loss of life and property and suffered deep humiliation in respect of the honor and chastity of a large number of our womenfolk, we have succeeded in attaining our cherished goal—this country of Pakistan. If, now, after all these precious sacrifices, we fail to achieve the real and ultimate objective of making Islam a practical, constitutional reality which inspired us to fight for Pakistan, our entire struggle becomes futile and all our sacrifices meaningless.

Indeed, if a secular and Godless, instead of Islamic, constitution was to be introduced and if the British Criminal Procedure Code had to be enforced instead of the Islamic Sharīʿa what was the sense in all this struggle for a separate Muslim homeland? We could have had it without that. Sim-

ilarly, if we simply intended to implement any socialist program, we could
have achieved it in collaboration with the Communist and Socialist parties
of India without plunging the nation into this great blood-bath and mighty
ordeal.

The fact is that we are already committed before God and man and at
the altar of History about the promulgation of Islamic constitution and no
going back on our words is possible. Whatever the hurdles and however
great they are, we have to continue our march towards our goal of a full-
fledged Islamic state in Pakistan.

Islamic Law and Social Change

[From Maudoodi, *Islamic Law and Constitution*, p. 38 ff.]

The first objection that is raised is that because the Islamic laws were framed
thirteen centuries ago in the light of the requirements of a primitive society,
they cannot be of any use for a modern state of our days.

I doubt very much whether people who take this stand are conversant
even with the elementary knowledge of the Islamic law. In all probability,
they have heard from somewhere that the fundamentals of the Islamic law
were enunciated more than thirteen hundred years ago, and they have assumed that this law has remained static since then and has failed to respond
to the requirements of changing conditions of human life. On this misconception they have further assumed that the Islamic law will be unsuited to
the needs of the present-day society and will clog the wheels of progress.
These critics fail to realize, however, that the laws propounded thirteen and
a half centuries ago, did not remain in a vacuum; they formed part and
parcel of the life of Muslim society and brought into being a *state* which
was run in the light of these laws. This naturally provided an opportunity
of evolution to Islamic law from the earliest days, as it had to be applied to
day-to-day matters through the process of *Ta'wīl, Qiyās, Ijtihād,* and *Istihsān.*[6]

Very soon after its inception, Islam began to hold sway over nearly half
the civilized world stretching from the Pacific to the Atlantic and, during
the following twelve hundred years, the Islamic Law continued to administer the affairs of all Muslim states. This process of the evolution of Islamic
law, therefore, did not stop for a moment up to the beginning of the nineteenth century, because it had to meet the challenge of the ever-changing

circumstances and face countless problems confronting different countries in different stages of history. Even in our Indo-Pakistan subcontinent, the Islamic civil and penal codes were in vogue up to the beginning of the nineteenth century.

Thus, it is only for the last one hundred years that the Islamic law remained inoperative and suffered stagnation. But, firstly, this period does not form a big gap and we can easily make up for the loss with some amount of strenuous effort; secondly, we possess full records of the development of our jurisprudence, century by century, and there can be absolutely no ground for frustration or despondency, and our path of legal progress is thus already illumined.

Once we have grasped the fundamental principles and the basic facts concerning the evolution of the Islamic system of law, we cannot remain in doubt that this law shall be as responsive to the urges of a progressive society in the present and the future as it has been in the past. Only those who suffer from ignorance can fall a prey to such nonsense, while those who have a grasp of Islam and the Islamic law are aware of its potentialities of progress, and those who possess even a cursory knowledge of the history of its development can never suspect it of being an antiquated or stagnant system of life which cannot keep pace with the march of history.

Replacing Western Forms with Islamic Law

[From Maudoodi, *Islamic Law and Constitution*, p. 47 ff.]

If we really wish to see our Islamic ideals translated into reality, we should not overlook the natural law that all stable changes in the collective life of a people come about gradually. The more sudden a change, the more short-lived it is. For a permanent change it is necessary that it should be free from extremist bias and unbalanced approach.

The best example of this gradual change is the revolution brought about by the Holy Prophet (peace be on him) in Arabia. One who is acquainted even superficially with the history of the Prophet's achievements knows that he did not enforce the entire body of Islamic laws with one stroke. Instead, the society was prepared gradually for their enforcement. The Prophet (peace be on him) uprooted the practices of the "Age of Ignorance" one by one and substituted for them new, moderate principles of human conduct. He started his efforts for reformation by inculcating belief in the fundamentals of Islam, namely, the unity of God, the Life Hereafter and the Institution of Prophethood and by inducing the people to live a life of righteousness and piety. Those who accepted this message were trained by him to believe in and practice the Islamic Way of Life. When this was achieved to a considerable degree, the Prophet went a step further and established an Islamic State in Medina with the sole object of making the social life of the country conform to the Islamic pattern. . . .

Coming to our own times and our own country, Pakistan, if we wish to promulgate Islamic Law here, it would mean nothing less than the demolition of the entire structure built by your British masters and the erection of a new one in its place. It is obvious that this cannot be achieved by just an official proclamation or a parliamentary bill, because it is a stupendous task and demands a good deal of hard and systematic work on the basis of an all-embracing program. For instance, we need a thorough reorientation of our educational system. At present, we find two kinds of educational institutions running simultaneously in our country, namely, the old, religious "madrasahs" and the modern, secular universities and colleges. None of them can produce people needed to run a modern Islamic State. The old-fashioned schools are steeped in conservatism to such an extent that they have lost all touch with the modern world. Their education has been disconnected from the practical problems of life and has thus become barren and lifeless. It cannot, therefore, produce people who might be able to serve, for instance, as judges and magistrates of a progressive modern state. As for our modern, secular institutions, they produce people who are ignorant of even a rudimentary knowledge of Islam and its laws. Moreover, we can hardly find such persons among those whose mentality has not been affected by the poisonous content and the thoroughly materialistic bias of modern, secular education.

There is yet another difficulty. The Islamic law has not been in force for the last century or so. Consequently our legal code has become stagnant and has lagged behind the march of time, while our urgent need is to bring it abreast of the latest developments of the modern age. Obviously, this would require a considerable amount of hard work.

There is, however, an even bigger hurdle. Living as slaves of an alien power and deprived of the Islamic influence for a long time, the pattern of our moral, cultural, social, economic and political life has undergone a radical change, and is today far removed from Islamic ideals. Under such circumstances it cannot be fruitful, even if it were possible, to change the legal structure of the country all at once, because then the general pattern of life and the legal structure will be poles apart, and the legal change will have to suffer the fate of a sapling planted in an uncongenial soil and facing hostile weather. It is, therefore, inevitable that the required reform should be gradual and the changes in the laws should be effected in such a manner as to balance favorably the change in the moral, educational, social, cultural and political life of the nation.

Islamic Law Is Part of a Total Way of Life

[From Maudoodi, *Islamic Law and Constitution*, pp. 54 ff.]

Islam signifies the entire scheme of life and not any isolated part or parts thereof. Consequently, neither can it be appropriate to view the different parts of the *Shari'ah*, Islamic Law, in isolation from one another and without regard to the whole, nor will it be of any use to take any particular part and bracket it with any other "'ism". The *Shari'ah* can function smoothly and can demonstrate its efficacy only if the entire system of life is practised in accordance with it and not otherwise.

Many of the present-day misunderstandings about the *Shari'ah* owe themselves to this faulty attitude in judging its worth, namely, forming opinions about its different aspects separately. Some injunctions of it are isolated from the main body of Islamic Laws and then they are considered in the perspective of modern civilization, or they are viewed as if they were something completely self-contained. Thus, people take just one injunction of the *Shari'ah* at random, which becomes maimed after its removal from the context and then view it in the context of some modern legal system, and criticize it on the score of its incongruity with present-day conceptions. But they fail to realise that it was never meant to be isolated like that for it forms an organic part of a distinct and self-contained system of life.

There are some people who take a few provisions of the Islamic Penal Code out of their context and jeer at them. But they do not realize that those provisions are to be viewed with the background of the whole Islamic system of life covering the economic, social, political and educational spheres of activity. If all these departments are not working, then those isolated provisions of our Penal Code can certainly work no miracles.

For example, we all know that Islam imposes the penalty of amputating the hand for the commitment of theft. But this injunction is meant to be promulgated in a full-fledged Islamic society wherein the wealthy pay *Zakat* to the state and the state provides for the basic necessities of the needy and the destitute; wherein every township is enjoined to play host to visitors at its own expense for a minimum period of three days; wherein all citizens are provided with equal privileges and opportunities to seek economic live-lihood; wherein monopolistic tendencies are discouraged; wherein people are God-fearing and seek His pleasure with devotion; wherein the virtues of generosity, helping the poor, treating the sick, providing the needy are in the air to the extent that even a small boy is made to realize that he is not a true Musliim if he allows his neighbour to sleep hungry while he has taken his meal. In other words, it is not meant for the present-day society where you cannot get a single penny without having to pay interest; where in place of *Baitul Mal* there are implacable money-lenders and banks which, instead of providing relief and succour to the poor and the needy, treat them with callous disregard, heartless refusal and brutal contempt: where the guiding motto is: "Everybody for himself and devil takes the hindmost"; where there are great privileges for the privileged ones while others are deprived even of their legitimate rights; where the economic system, pro-pelled by greed and piloted by exploitation, only leads to the enrichment of the few at the cost of crushing poverty and intolerable misery of the many, and where the political system serves only to prop up injustice, class-privileges and distressing economic disparities. Under such conditions, it is doubtful if theft should be penalised at all, not to speak of cutting off the thief's hands! Because to do so would, as a matter of fact, amount to pro-tecting the ill-gotten wealth of a few blood-suckers rather than awarding adequate punishment to the guilty.

On the other hand, Islam aims at creating a society in which none is compelled by the force of circumstances to steal. For, in the Islamic social order, apart from the voluntary help provided by individuals, the state guar-antees the basic *necessities of life to all. But, after providing all that,* Islam enjoins a severe and exemplary punishment for those who commit theft, as their action shows that they are unfit to live in such a just, generous and healthy society and would cause greater harm to it, if left unchecked.

Similar is the case of the punishment for adultery and fornication. Islam prescribes a hundred stripes for the unmarried and stoning to death for the married partners in the crime. But, of course, it applies to a society wherein every trace of suggestiveness has been destroyed, where mixed gatherings of men and women have been prohibited, where public appearance of painted and pampered women is completely non-existent, where marriage has been made easy, where virtue, piety and charity are current coins and where the remembrance of God and the hereafter is kept ever fresh in men's minds and hearts. These punishments are not meant for that filthy society wherein sexual excitement is rampant, wherein nude pictures, obscene books and vulgar songs have become common recreations; wherein sexual perversions have taken hold of the cinema and all other places of amusement, wherein mixed, semi-nude parties are considered the acme of social progress and wherein economic conditions and social customs have made marriage extremely difficult.

From this discussion, I think, it has become fairly clear that what we, at present, technically call 'Islamic Law' is only a part of a complete scheme of life and does not have any independent existence in isolation from that scheme. It can neither be understood nor enforced separately. To enforce it separately would, in fact, be against the intention of the Law-Giver. What is required of us is to translate into practice the entire Islamic programme of life and not merely a fragment of it. Then and then alone can the legal aspects be properly implemented.

This scheme of the *Shari'ah* is, however, divided into many parts. There are aspects of it which do not need any external force for their enforcement; they are and can be enforced only by the ever-awake conscience kindled by his faith in a Muslim. There are other parts which are enforced by Islam's programme of education, training of man's character and the purification of his heart and his morals. To enforce certain other parts, Islam resorts to the use of the force of public opinion: the general will and pressure of the society. There are still other parts which have been sanctified by the traditions and the conventions of Muslim society. A very large part of the Islamic system of law, however, needs for its enforcement, in all its details, the coercive power and authority of the state. Political power is essential for protecting the Islamic system of life from deterioration and perversion, for the eradication of vice and the establishment of virtue and, finally, for the enforcement of all those laws that require the sanction of the state and the judiciary for their operation.

NOTES

1. Iqbal, *Speeches and Statements*, pp. 11–13.
2. Jinnah, *Speeches and Writings*, 2:174–75.

3. Quoted in *Dawn*, September 24, 1979.
4. The customs and sayings of the Prophet Muhammad.
5. Religious community.
6. *Ta'wīl* is the process of enlarging the applicability of a text by finding analogous situations; *qiyās* is to determine how one should act in the spirit of Islam, if there is no clear injunction available; *ijtihād* is the application of human reason in the interpretation of the meaning of a text; *istihsān* is to find the best procedure in the light of the teachings of Islam.

BIBLIOGRAPHY

Ali, Mohamed (or Muhammad). *My Life: A Fragment: An Autobiographical Sketch of Maulana Mohamed Ali*. Edited by Afzal Iqbal. Lahore: M. Ashraf, 1942.
—— *Select Writings and Speeches of Maulana Mohamed Ali*. Compiled and edited by Afzal Iqbal. Lahore: M. Ashraf, 1944.
Allana, G. *Quaid-e-azam Jinnah: The Story of a Nation*. Lahore: Ferozsons, 1967.
Ambedkar, D. R. *Mukti kon pathe? Asprishyaya ani darmantar*. Bombay: Bharat Bhusan, 1936.
—— *Thoughts on Pakistan*. Bombay: Thacker, 1941.
—— *What Gandhi and Congress Have Done to the Untouchables*. Bombay: Thacker, 1945.
—— Article in *Prabuddha Bhārat*. Bombay. October 27, 1956.
Ayub Khan, General Muhammad. *Friends, Not Masters: A Political Autobiography*. Lahore: Oxford University Press, 1967.
Azad, Maulana Abul Kalam. *India Wins Freedom: An Autobiographical Narrative*. Bombay: Orient Longman, 1959.
Baljon, J.M.S., Jr. *The Reforms and Religious Ideas of Sir Sayyid Ahmad Khan*. 2d rev. ed. Lahore: Orientalia, 1958.
Ball, Charles. *The History of the Indian Mutiny*. 2 vols. New York: S. D. Brain; London and New York, London Printing and Publishing, 1858–59.
Banerjea, Surendranath. *A Nation in Making: Being the Reminiscences of Fifty Years in Public Life*. London: Oxford University Press, 1925.
—— *The Speeches and Writings of Hon. Surendranath Banerjea*. Madras: Natesan, 1927(?).
Bolitho, Hector. *Jinnah, Creator of Pakistan*. London: John Murray, 1954.
Bose, Nirmal Kumar. *Selections from Gandhi*. 2d ed. Ahmedabad: Navajivan, 1957.
Bose, Subhas Chandra. *The Indian Struggle, 1920–1934*. London: Wishart, 1935.
—— *Netaji's Life and Writings, Part One, An Indian Pilgrim; Or, Autobiography of Subhas Chandra Bose, 1897–1920*. Calcutta: Thacker Spink, 1948.
—— *Netaji Speaks to the Nation*. Edited by Durlab Singh. Lahore: Hero Publications, 1946.
—— *On to Delhi; or, Speeches & Writings of Netaji Subhas Chandra Bose*. Edited by G. C. Jain. Delhi: Saraswati Pustak Mandir, 1946.
—— *Selected Speeches of Subhas Chandra Bose*. New Delhi: Publications Division, Government of India, 1962.

Brecher, Michael. *Nehru: A Political Biography.* London: Oxford University Press, 1959.

Chatterjee, Bankim Chandra. "Anandamath." Translated by T. W. Clark. Manuscript.

—— *The Abbey of Bliss: A Translation of Bankim Chandra Chatterjee's Anandamath.* Translated by Nares Chandra Sen-Gupta. Calcutta: P. M. Neogi, 1906.

—— "Letter from Bankim Chandra Chatterjee to Dr. Sambhu Chandra Mookerjee of March 14, 1872." In "The Secretary's Notes," *Bengal Past and Present* 8 (1914), Calcutta.

Chattopadhyaya, N. "Mahatma Gandhi at Rabindranath's Santiniketan," *Visva-Bharati Quarterly, Special Issue,* 1949.

Chintamani, C. Y., ed. *Indian Social Reform.* 4 parts. Madras: Thompson, 1901.

Constituent Assembly Debates, Official Reports. New Delhi: Lok Sabha Secretariat, n.d.

Constituent Assembly of Pakistan Debates.

The Constitution of India, As Amended up to the Constitution (Forty-fourth Amendment) Act, 1979. Lucknow: Eastern Book, 1979.

Dar, Bashir Ahmad. *Religious Thought of Sayyid Ahmad Khan.* Lahore: Institute of Islamic Culture, 1957.

Dayananda Saraswati, Swami. *Autobiography of Swami Dayanand Saraswati.* Edited by K. C. Yadav. New Delhi: Manohar, 1976.

—— *The Light of Truth. English Translation of Svami Dayananda's Satyartha prakasha.* Translated by Ganga Prasad Upadhyaya. Allahabad: Kala Press, 1960.

Desai, Mahadev H. *Day-to-day with Gandhi. Secretary's Diary.* Vol. 15. Edited by Narhari D. Parikh. Translated by Hemantkumar G. Nilkanth. Rajghat, Banaras: Sarva Seva Sangh, 1968, 1970.

Dutt, Romesh Chunder. *The Economic History of India Under Early British Rule.* London: Morrison and Gibb, 1901.

Fischer, Louis. *Gandhi, His Life and Message for the World.* New York: Harper, 1950.

Gandhi, Mohandas Karamchand. *An Autobiography, or the Story of my Experiments with Truth.* Translated by Mahadev Desai. Ahmedabad: Navajivan, 1927.

—— *The Collected Works of Mahatma Gandhi.* Vols. 1–72. New Delhi: Publications Division, Government of India, 1958–78.

—— *Communal Unity.* Ahmedabad: Navajivan, 1949.

—— *Hind Swaraj, or Home Rule.* Ahmedabad: Navajivan, 1946.

—— *The Nation's Voice.* 2d ed. Edited by C. Rajagopalachar and J. C. Kumarappa. Ahmedabad: Navajivan, 1947.

—— *Young India,* 1919–1922. New York: Huebsch, 1922.

Gandhi, Prabhudas. *Jīvanñu parodh.* Ahmedabad: Navajivan, 1948.

Ghose, Aurobindo. *Collected Poems and Plays.* 2 vols. Pondicherry: Sri Aurobindo Ashram, 1942.

—— *The Doctrine of Passive Resistance.* Calcutta: Arya, 1948.

—— *Speeches.* Calcutta: Arya, 1948.

—— *Sri Aurobindo Birth Centenary Library.* 30 vols. Pondicherry: Sri Aurobindo Ashram, 1970–76.

Ghose, Sankar, ed. *Congress Presidential Speeches.* Calcutta: West Bengal Pradesh Committee, 1972.

Ghosh, Ajoy Kumar. *Articles and Speeches.* Moscow: Publishing House for Oriental Literature, 1962.

Gokhale, G. K. *Speeches of the Honourable Mr. G. K. Gokhale.* Madras: Natesen, 1908.

Graham, G.F.I. *The Life and Work of Syed Ahmed Khan.* London: William Blackwood, 1885; reprint Karachi: Oxford University Press, 1974.

Guha, Nikiles. *The Complete Songs of Rammohun Roy.* Calcutta: Writers Workshop, 1973.

Gupta, J. N. *Life and Works of Romesh Chunder Dutt, C.I.E.* London: J. M. Dent, 1911.

Harijan. Ahmedabad: 1940, 1946–48.

Hindu. Madras, 1969.

Hindustan Times. New Delhi, 1945.

The Indian Quarterly Register. Calcutta: The Annual Register Office, 1928.

Iqbal, Muhammad. *Letters of Iqbal to Jinnah.* Lahore: M. Ashraf, n.d.

—— *The Mysteries of Selflessness.* Translated by Arthur J. Arberry. London: John Murray, 1953. (The Wisdom of the East Series)

—— *Poems from Iqbal.* Translated by V. G. Kiernan. London: John Murray, 1955. (The Wisdom of the East Series)

—— *The Reconstruction of Religious Thought in Islam.* Published by Javid Iqbal. Lahore: M. Ashraf, 1944.

—— *The Secrets of the Self.* Translated by R. A. Nicholson. Rev. ed. Lahore: M. Ashraf, 1944.

—— *Speeches and Statements of Iqbal.* 2d ed. Compiled by "Shamloo" [Latif Ahmad Sherwani]. Lahore: Al-Manar Academy, 1948.

Jinnah. *Some Recent Speeches and Writings of Mr. Jinnah.* Edited by Jamīl-ud-dīn Ahmad. 2 vols. Lahore: M. Ashraf, 1946–47.

—— *Speeches and Writings of Mr. Jinnah.* Compiled and edited by Jamīl-ud-dīn Ahmad. 2 vols. Lahore: M. Ashraf, 1942.

Jones, Marc E. *Gandhi Lives.* Philadelphia: D. McKay, 1948.

Keer, Dhananjay. *Savarkar and His Times.* Bombay: A. V. Keer, 1950.

Khan, Liaquat Ali. *Pakistan, the Heart of Asia.* Cambridge, Mass.: Harvard University Press, 1950.

—— *The Constituent Assembly of Pakistan Debates* 5 no. 1 (1949), pp. 1–7.

Khan, Sir Syed Ahmad. *Akhari Madamin.* Compiled by Muhammad Imām ud-dīn Gujerat and Maulvi Baba Makhdumi. 3d ed. Lahore: Malik Chunan ud-dīn, n.d.

—— *Sir Saiyyid Ahmad Khan's History of the Bijnor Rebellion.* Translated by Hafeez Malik and Morris Dembo. East Lansing: Michigan State University, 1972. (South Asia Series, Occasional paper no. 17)

—— "Letter to Mawlawi Tasadduq Husain," in *Sir Syed ke chand nadir khutut*. Compiled by Ahmad Husain Yaqubi. Meerut: Nandar, 1900.

—— *Writings and Speeches of Sir Syed Ahmed Khan*. Edited by Shan Muhammad. Bombay: Nachiketa, 1972.

Kripalani, Krishna. *Rabindranath Tagore, A Biography*. New York: Grove Press, 1962.

Lajpat Rai, Lala. *Writings and Speeches*. 2 vols. Edited by Vijaya Chandra Joshi. Delhi: University Publishers, 1966.

Macaulay, Thomas Babington. *Macaulay, Prose and Poetry*. Edited by G. M. Young. Cambridge, Mass.: Harvard University Press, 1952.

McLane, John R. (ed.) *The Political Awakening in India*. Englewood Cliffs, N.J.: Prentice-Hall, 1970.

Madhok, Balraj. *Indianisation*. Delhi: Hind Pocket Books, c.1969–70.

—— *Why Jana Sangh?* Bombay: Popular, n.d.

Maudoodī [Maudūdī], Syed Abū'l-Alā. *Islamic Law and Constitution*. Lahore: Pakistan Herald Press, 1955.

Mira [Muriel Slade]. *Gleanings Gathered at Bapu's Feet*. Ahmedabad: Navajivan, 1949.

Montagu, Edwin S. *An Indian Diary*. Edited by Venetia Montagu. London: William Heinemann, 1930.

Morison, Theodore. *The Economic Transition in India*. London: John Murray, 1911.

Morris-Jones, W. H. *Politics, Mainly Indian*. Bombay: Orient Longman, 1978.

Mozoomdar, P. C. *The Life and Teachings of Keshub Chunder Sen*. Calcutta: Thomas, 1887.

Müller, F. Max. *India: What Can It Teach Us?* London: Longmans, 1892.

Müller, F. Max, ed. *Ramakrishna, His Life and Sayings*. New York: Scribner's, 1899.

Munir Report. Report of the Court of Inquiry Constituted under Punjab Act II to Inquire into the Punjab Disturbances of 1953. Lahore: Government Printing Press, 1954.

Namboodiripad, E.M.S. *Economics and Politics of India's Socialist Pattern*. New Delhi: People's Publishing House, 1966.

—— *The Mahatma and the Ism*. 2d ed. New Delhi: People's Publishing House, 1959.

Naoroji, Dadabhai. *Essays, Speeches, Addresses, and Writings (on Indian Politics) of the Hon'ble Dadabhai Naoroji*. Edited by Chundlal Lallubhai Parekh. Bombay: Caxton, 1887.

Narayan, Jayaprakash. *Socialism, Sarvodaya and Democracy*. Edited by Bimla Prasad. New York: Asia Publishing House, 1964.

—— *Towards Struggle. Selected Manifestoes, Speeches & Writings*. Edited by Jusuf Meherally. Bombay: Padma, 1946.

Nehru, Jawaharlal. *An Autobiography*. London: John Lane, 1937.

—— *The Discovery of India*. New York: John Day, 1946.

—— *Independence and After. A Collection of the More Important Speeches of Jawaharlal Nehru from September 1946 to May 1949*. New Delhi: Government of India, 1949.

—— *Jawaharlal Nehru's Speeches, 1949–1964*. 5 vols. New Delhi: The Publications Division, Government of India, 1954–68.

—— *Recent Essays and Writings*. Allahabad: Kitabistan, 1934.

—— *Selected Works of Jawaharlal Nehru*. Vol. 7. New Delhi: Orient Longman, 1975.

—— *Soviet Russia, Some Random Sketches and Impressions.* Allahabad: Law Journal Press, 1928.

—— *Toward Freedom, The Autobiography of Jawaharlal Nehru.* New York: John Day, 1941.

Pirzada, S. S. *Evolution of Pakistan.* Lahore: The All-Pakistan Legal Decisions, 1963.

The Proceedings of the All Parties National Convention. Allahabad: Rafi Ahmed Kidwai, Secretary, All Parties National Convention, 1929.

Pyarelal. *Mahatma Gandhi—The Last Phase.* 2 vols. Ahmedabad: Navajivan, 1958.

Rajai Singam, S. Durai. *Gandhiji—The Ever Smiling Mahatma: An Anthology of Gandhian Humour.* 3 vols. Kuantan, Malaya, 1957.

Ramakrishna. *The Gospel of Ramakrishna.* New York: The Vedānta Society, 1907.

—— *Teachings of Sri Ramakrishna.* Almora: Advaita Ashrama, 1934.

Ranade, M. G. *Essays on Indian Economics.* Madras: Natesan, 1906.

Roy, M. N. *I Accuse.* New York: Roy Defense Committee of India, 1932.

—— *India's Message (Fragments of a Prisoner's Diary,* vol. 2). 2d rev. ed. Calcutta: Renaissance, 1950.

—— *New Humanism: A Manifesto.* Calcutta: Renaissance, 1947.

—— "Anti-Imperialist Struggle in India," *The Communist International,* no. 6, 1924.

Roy, Rammohun. *The Complete Songs of Rammohun Roy.* Translated by Nikiles Guha. Calcutta: Writers Workshop, 1973.

—— *The English Works of Rammohun Roy.* 6 parts. Edited by Kalidas Nag and Debajyoti Burman. Calcutta: Sadharan Brahmo Samaj, 1945–58.

—— *Rāmmohan granthābalī.* Calcutta: Bangīya-sāhitya-parishat, n.d.

—— "Tuḥfat al-muwaḥḥidīn," in *Tuḥfat'l-muwaḥḥidīn.* Translated by Moulavi Obaidullah el Obaide. Calcutta: Sadharan Brahmo Samaj, 1950.

Sarda, Har Bilas. *Life of Dayanand Saraswati.* Ajmer: Vedic Yantralaya, 1946.

Savarkar, Vinayak D. *Hindutva.* 4th ed. Poona: S. P. Gokhale, 1949.

Sayeed, Khalid bin. *Pakistan: The Formative Phase.* London: 1968.

Sen, Keshub Chunder. *Keshub Chunder Sen's Lectures in India.* London: Cassell, 1901.

Sengupta, Padmini. *Sarojini Naidu: A Biography.* New York: Asia Publishing House, 1966.

Singh, Anup. *Nehru, the Rising Star of India.* New York: John Day, 1939.

Sykes, Marjorie. *Rabindranath Tagore.* Calcutta: Longmans, Green, 1943.

Tagore, Debendranath. *The Autobiography of Maharshi Devendranath [sic] Tagore.* Calcutta: S. K. Lahiri, 1909.

Tagore, Rabindranath. *Boundless Sky.* Calcutta: Visva-Bharati, 1964.

—— "The Call of Truth," *Modern Review* 30 (1921), Calcutta.

—— *Collected Poems and Plays of Rabindranath Tagore.* London: Macmillan, 1961.

—— *Letters to a Friend.* Edited by C. F. Andrews. London: Allen and Unwin, 1928.

—— *Nationalism.* 2d ed. London: Macmillan, 1950.

—— *One Hundred and One Poems by Rabindranath Tagore.* Edited by Humayun Kabir. New York: Asia, 1966.

—— *Poems.* Edited by Krishna Kripalani. 2d ed. Calcutta: Visva-Bharati, 1943.

—— *Songs of Kabir.* Assisted by Evelyn Underhill. New York: Macmillan, 1917

—— *A Tagore Reader.* Edited by Amiya Chakravarty. New York: Macmillan, 1961.

—— *Talks in China.* Calcutta: Visva-Bharati, 1925.

Tendulkar, D. G. *Mahātmā. The Life of Mohandas Karamchand Gandhi.* 8 vols. Bombay: V. K. Jhaveri and D. G. Tendulkar, 1951–54.

Thompson, Edward J. *Rabindranath Tagore: His Life and Work.* London: Oxford University Press, 1921.

Tilak, Bal Gangadar. *Tilak: His Writings and Speeches.* 3d ed. Madras: Ganesh, 1922.

Toye, Hugh. *Subhash Chandra Bose: The Springing Tiger.* London: Cassell, 1959; Bombay: Jaico, 1959.

Vivekananda. *The Complete Works of the Swami Vivekananda.* 7 vols. Almora: Advaita Ashrama, 1924–32.

Washburne, Carleton. *Remakers of Mankind.* New York: John Day, 1932.

Wedderburn, William. *Allan Octavian Hume, C. B.* London: T. F. Unwin, 1913.

Yadav, K. C., ed. *Autobiography of Swami Dayanand Saraswati.* 2d rev. ed. New Delhi: Manohar, 1978.

Young India. Ahmedabad, 1925, 1927, 1931.

INDEX

OTHER WORKS IN THE COLUMBIA ASIAN STUDIES SERIES

INTRODUCTION TO ORIENTAL CIVILIZATIONS
Wm. Theodore de Bary, Editor

Sources of Japanese Tradition   1958   Paperback ed., 2 vols., 1964
Sources of Indian Tradition   1958   Paperback ed., 2 vols., 1964
Sources of Chinese Tradition   1960   Paperback ed., 2 vols., 1964

TRANSLATIONS FROM THE ORIENTAL CLASSICS

Major Plays of Chikamatsu, tr. Donald Keene   1961
Four Major Plays of Chikamatsu, tr. Donald Keene. Paperback text edition
                                                                      1961
Records of the Grand Historian of China, translated from the Shih chi of Ssu-ma
  Ch'ien, tr. Burton Watson, 2 vols.   1961
Instructions for Practical Living and Other Neo-Confucian Writings by Wang
  Yang-ming, tr. Wing-tsit Chan   1963
Chuang Tzu: Basic Writings, tr. Burton Watson, paperback ed. only   1964
The Mahābhārata, tr. Chakravarthi V. Narasimhan. Also in paperback ed.
                                                                      1965
The Manyōshū, Nippon Gakujutsu Shinkōkai edition   1965
Su Tung-p'o: Selections from a Sung Dynasty Poet, tr. Burton Watson. Also
  in paperback ed.   1965
Bhartrihari: Poems, tr. Barbara Stoler Miller. Also in paperback ed.   1967
Basic Writings of Mo Tzu, Hsün Tzu, and Han Fei Tzu, tr. Burton Watson.
  Also in separate paperback eds.   1967
The Awakening of Faith, Attributed to Aśvaghosha, tr. Yoshito S. Hakeda.
  Also in paperback ed.   1967
Reflections on Things at Hand: The Neo-Confucian Anthology, comp. Chu Hsi
  and Lü Tsu-ch'ien, tr. Wing-tsit Chan   1967
The Platform Sutra of the Sixth Patriarch, tr. Philip B. Yampolsky. Also in
  paperback ed.   1967

Essays in Idleness: The Tsurezuregusa of Kenkō, tr. Donald Keene. also in
paperback ed.   1967
The Pillow Book of Sei Shōnagon, tr. Ivan Morris, 2 vols.   1967
Two Plays of Ancient India: The Little Clay Cart and the Minister's Seal, tr.
J. A. B. van Buitenen   1968
The Complete Works of Chuang Tzu, tr. Burton Watson   1968
The Romance of the Western Chamber (Hsi Hsiang chi), tr. S. I. Hsiung. Also
in paperback ed.   1968
The Manyōshuū, Nippon Gakujutsu Shinkōkai edition. Paperback text
edition.   1969
Records of the Historian: Chapters from the Shih chi of Ssu-ma Ch'ien. Paper-
back text edition, tr. Burton Watson   1969
Cold Mountain: 100 Poems by the T'ang Poet Han-shan, tr. Burton Watson.
Also in paperback ed.   1970
Twenty Plays of the Nō Theatre, ed. Donald Keene. Also in paperback ed.
                                                                                 1970
Chushingura: The Treasury of Loyal Retainers, tr. Donald Keene. Also in
paperback ed.   1971
The Zen Master Hakuin: Selected Writings, tr. Philip B. Yampolsky   1971
*Chinese Rhyme-Prose: Poems in the Fu Form from the Han and Six Dynasties
Periods,* tr. Burton Watson. Also in paperback ed.   1971
Kūkai: Major Works, tr. Yoshito S. Hakeda. Also in paperback ed.   1972
*The Old Man Who Does as He Pleases: Selections from the Poetry and Prose of
Lu Yu,* tr. Burton Watson   1973
The Lion's Roar of Queen Śrīmālā, tr. Alex & Hideko Wayman   1974
*Courtier and Commoner in Ancient China: Selections from the History of the
Former Han by Pan Ku,* tr. Burton Watson. Also in paperback ed.   1974
Japanese Literature in Chinese, vol. 1: *Poetry and Prose in Chinese by Japanese
Writers of the Early Period,* tr. Burton Watson   1975
Japanese Literature in Chinese, vol. 2: *Poetry and Prose in Chinese by Japanese
Writers of the Later Period,* tr. Burton Watson   1976
Scripture of the Lotus Blossom of the Fine Dharma, tr. Leon Hurvitz. Also in
paperback ed.   1976
Love Song of the Dark Lord: Jayadeva's Gītagovinda, tr. Barbara Stoler Miller.
Also in paperback ed. Cloth ed. includes critical text of the Sanskrit.
                                                                                 1977
Ryōkan: Zen Monk-Poet of Japan, tr. Burton Watson   1977
*Calming the Mind and Discerning the Real: From the Lam rim chen mo of Tsonkha-
pa,* tr. Alex Wayman   1978
The Hermit and the Love-Thief: Sanskrit Poems of Bhartrihari and Bilhana, tr.
Barbara Stoler Miller   1978

The Lute: Kao Ming's p'i-p'a chi, tr. Jean Mulligan. Also in paperback ed.
1980
A Chronicle of Gods and Sovereigns: Jinnō Shōtōki of Kitabatake Chikafusa, tr. H. Paul Varley 1980
Among the Flowers: The Hua-chien chi, tr. Lois Fusek 1982
Grass Hill: Poems and Prose by the Japanese Monk Gensei, tr. Burton Watson 1983
Doctors, Diviners, and Magicians of Ancient China: Biographies of Fang-shih, tr. Kenneth J. DeWoskin. Also in paperback ed. 1983
Theater of Memory: The Plays of Kālidāsa, ed. Barbara Stoler Miller. Also in paperback ed. 1984
The Columbia Book of Chinese Poetry: From Early Times to the Thirteenth Century, ed. and tr. Burton Watson 1984
Poems of Love and War: From the Eight Anthologies and the Ten Songs of Classical Tamil, tr. A. K. Ramanujan. Also in paperback ed. 1985
The Colubmia Book of Later Chinese Poetry, ed. and tr. Jonathan Chaves 1986

COMPANIONS TO ASIAN STUDIES

Approaches to the Oriental Classics, ed. Wm. Theodore de Bary 1959
Early Chinese Literature, by Burton Watson. Also in paperback ed. 1962
Approaches to Asian Civilizations, ed. Wm. Theodore de Bray and Ainslie T. Embree 1964
The Classic Chinese Novel: A Critical Introduction, by C. T. Hsia. Also in paperback ed. 1968
Chinese Lyricism: Shih Poetry from the Second to the Twelfth Century, tr. Burton Watson. Also in paperback ed. 1971
A Syllabus of Indian Civilization, by Leonard A. Gordon and Barbara Stoler Miller 1971
Twentieth-Century Chinese Stories, ed. C. T. Hsia and Joseph S. M. Lau. Also in paperback ed. 1971
A Syllabus of Chinese Civilization, by J. Mason Gentzler, 2d ed. 1972
A Syllabus of Japanese Civiization, by H. Paul Varley, 2d ed. 1972
An Introduction to Chinese Civilization, ed. John Meskill, with the assistance of J. Mason Gentzler 1973
An Introduction to Japanese Civilization, ed. Arthur E. Tiedemann 1974
A Guide to Oriental Classics, ed. Wm. Theodore de Bary and Ainslie T. Embree, 2d ed. Also in paperback ed. 1975
Ukifune: Love in The Tale of Genji, ed. Andrew Pekarik 1982

MODERN ASIAN LITERATURE SERIES

Modern Japanese Drama: An Anthology, ed. and tr. Ted T. Takaya. Also in paperback ed.   1979

Mask and Sword: Two Plays for the Contemporary Japanese Theater, Yamazaki Masakazu, tr. J. Thomas Rimer   1980

Yokomitsu Riichi, Modernist, by Dennis Keene   1980

Nepali Visions, Nepali Dreams: The Poetry of Laxmiprasad Devkota, tr. David Rubin   1980

Literature of the Hundred Flowers, vol. 1: *Criticism and Polemics*, ed. Hauling Nieh   1981

Literature of the Hundred Flowers, vol. 2: *Poetry and Fiction*, ed. Hauling Nieh   1981

Modern Chinese Stories and Novellas, 1919–1949, ed. Joseph S. M. Lau, C. T. Hsia, and Leo Ou-fan Lee. Also in paperback ed.   1981

A View by the Sea, by Yasuoka Shōtarō, tr. Kären Wigen Lewis   1984

NEO-CONFUCIAN STUDIES

Instructions for Practical Living and Other Neo-Confucian Writings by Wang Yang-ming, tr. Wing-tsit Chan   1963

Reflections on Things at Hand: The Neo-Confucian Anthology, comp. Chu Hsi and Lü Tsu-ch'ien, tr. Wing-tsit Chan   1967

Self and Society in Ming Thought, by Wm. Theodore de Bary and the Conference on Ming Thought. Also in paperback ed.   1970

The Unfolding of Neo-Confucianism, by Wm. Theodore de Bary and the Conference on Seventeenth-Century Chinese Thought. Also in paperback ed.   1975

Principle and Practicality: Essays in Neo-Confucianism and Practical Learning, ed. Wm. Theodore de Bary and Irene Bloom. Also in paperback ed.   1979

The Syncretic Religion of Lin Chao-en, by Judith A. Berling   1980

The Renewal of Buddhism in China: Chu-hung and the Late Ming Synthesis, by Chün-fang Yü   1981

Neo-Confucian Orthodoxy and the Learning of the Mind-and-Heart, by Wm. Theodore de Bary   1981

Yüan Thought: Chinese Thought and Religion Under the Mongols, ed. Hok-lam Chan and Wm. Theodore de Bary   1982

The Liberal Tradition in China, by Wm. Theodore de Bary   1983

The Development and Decline of Chinese Cosmology, by John B.
Henderson   1984

STUDIES IN ORIENTAL CULTURE

FALL 08

FALL 05

FALL 2003

FALL 06

FALL 04

SPRING 09

SPRING 07

FALL 09

SPRING 10

FALL 10

RESERVE ITEM
RETURN TO
MILSTEIN LIBRARY
ROOM 208 BUTLER

FALL 11